Benjamin V. Cohen

Architect of the New Deal

Benjamin V. Cohen

Architect of the New Deal

William Lasser

A Century Foundation Book

Yale University Press   New Haven and London

Printed in the United States of America

A catalogue record for this book is available from the British Library.

The paper in this book meets the guidelines for permanence and durability of the Committee on Production Guidelines for Book Longevity of the Council on Library Resources.

10 9 8 7 6 5 4 3 2 1

Library of Congress Cataloging-in-Publication Data

Lasser, William.

Benjamin V. Cohen : architect of the New Deal / William Lasser.

p.   cm.

Includes bibliographical references and index.

ISBN 0-300-08879-5 (alk. paper)

1. Cohen, Benjamin V. 2. Statesmen— United States— Biography.   3. Intellectuals—United States—Biography.   4. Lawyers— United States—Biography.   5. New Deal, 1933–1939.   6. United States— Politics and government—1933–1953. 7. United States—Politics and government—1953–1961. 8. Liberalism—United States— History—20th century.   I. Title.

E748.C65 L37   2002

973.917′092—dc21

2001007151

To my father, Joseph Lasser,
in loving memory

The Century Foundation

The Century Foundation, formerly the Twentieth Century Fund, sponsors and supervises timely analyses of economic policy, foreign affairs, and domestic political issues. Not-for-profit and nonpartisan, it was founded in 1919 and endowed by Edward A. Filene.

Contents

Illustrations follow page 254

Foreword

In 1919, when Edward Filene founded the institution that would eventually become the Twentieth Century Fund and still later The Century Foundation, he was manifesting one of the principal beliefs of what we have come to call the Progressive Era: that systematic analysis and close examination of the facts could improve governance and extend progress. It is only fitting, therefore, that the trustees of The Century Foundation should have made an exception to their usual practice by agreeing to sponsor this work of biography.

Benjamin V. Cohen had a long relationship with the Twentieth Century Fund, serving as a trustee from 1948 to 1983. For a number of years, he was chairman of the finance committee and treasurer of the fund, but he is best remembered for his insights and recommendations relating to our policy research and writing agenda. In view of his public career and reputation, the record of Cohen's contributions to this organization is scarcely a surprise. That career, after all, was one of the century's outstanding examples of exactly what Filene had in mind. Cohen was, over the course of several decades, a leader and even a symbol of the often quite lonely struggle to insist on the importance of the application of intelligence to public questions.

A child of immigrants, Cohen became an outstanding lawyer and saw his first government service working for the Shipping Board during World War I. More than a decade later, Cohen was fortunate to connect with President Franklin D. Roosevelt at a time when there was a rare confluence of fresh ideas and political purpose. As Arthur M. Schlesinger, Jr., writes in the preface that follows, Cohen's ability and thoroughness stood out even among the extraordinary group that gathered around the presidency of Roosevelt and the New Deal.

A major figure in Roosevelt's "Brain Trust," Ben Cohen may be best known for his work in drafting the Securities Act and other legislation that remade the regulation of markets in the United States—and became a model for many other nations. He later played a critical role in the events that led to the development of the Lend-Lease Act, which proved so essential to the defense of Britain during the uncertain early years of World War II. He served his nation after the war by representing it on several United Nations bodies.

Whatever titles Benjamin Cohen held, however, it was his judgment that presidents and elected officials really treasured. And, even relatively late in life, Cohen's judgment often proved superior to that of the bulk of those attempting to shape policy. Cohen, for example, was among the early critics of American involvement in the Vietnam War.

William Lasser, Alumni Distinguished Professor of Political Science at Clemson University, has pulled together the threads of Cohen's career in a way that not only illuminates one extraordinary individual but also sheds light on a tumultuous century for America and the world. There is much in this book that will add to the knowledge of those who have studied America closely during the period beginning with the Great Depression and extending through the years of the Vietnam War. For those with only spotty knowledge of this complex era, Lasser, looking through the lens of Cohen's life, provides an important account of several major public policy struggles, and of the development of American liberalism at its most critical juncture.

On behalf of the trustees of The Century Foundation, I express our gratitude to Bill Lasser for this serious and extensive study of the life of someone we are proud to recognize as one of the builders of this institution and one of the architects of some of the nation's most valuable solutions to the challenges of the twentieth century.

Richard C. Leone
President, The Century Foundation

Preface

In 1932, at the bottom of the most calamitous depression in modern history, Governor Franklin D. Roosevelt of New York pledged himself to "a new deal" for the American people. The phrase, soon capitalized, was quickly applied to the torrent of initiatives loosed by FDR as president in the cause of relief, recovery, and reform — initiatives that in the end remolded the social landscape of American life.

The spirit of the New Deal was a belief in public action on behalf of the ill-housed, ill-clad, ill-nourished, the generally ill-privileged, in American life. As FDR said in his second inaugural, "The test of our progress is not whether we add more to the abundance of those who have much; it is whether we provide enough for those who have too little." This was the New Deal creed.

The New Deal was not the work of a single man. Benjamin V. Cohen, the subject of this admirable biography, once observed that FDR mobilized "the energy, experience and knowledge" of the nation. Young men and women flocked to Washington to join the assault on economic depression and social humiliation. As Rexford G. Tugwell of FDR's brain trust put it in the exuberant rhetoric of the time, the New Dealers were rolling up their sleeves and making America over.

Among the New Dealers, Ben Cohen was perhaps the most quietly influential. He was a remarkable man — gentle, proud, sensitive, ascetic, determined, with acute ideas and insights uttered in a wavering, quavering, singsong voice. First of all, he was a superb lawyer. In drafting New Deal legislation, he wrote every clause with fastidious respect for technical precision, precedent, and continuity. When statutes were challenged in court, he was a master in the selection of test cases, the preparation of briefs, and the strategy of argument.

Legal craftsmanship is an exercise in process. Ben was equally committed on questions of substance. He subscribed wholeheartedly to FDR's "test of our progress." Some historians have too easily classified Cohen as a disciple of Justice Louis D. Brandeis and therefore hostile on principle to what Brandeis called "the evils of bigness" in the economy and the polity. But Cohen and his New Deal partner Thomas G. Corcoran, as Professor Lasser demonstrates, lacked the Brandeisian faith in smallness and localism. They believed that national problems demanded national remedies, and their aim was to use the national government to make capitalism work as efficiently as possible in an economy that would be technologically advanced as well as socially humane. Their mission was, in effect, to rescue capitalism from the capitalists.

I first met Ben Cohen in 1946. He was fifty-two (I was twenty-nine), and although he retained his concern for civil rights and civil liberties, the war had shifted his primary interest from domestic to foreign policy. His small apartment on Massachusetts Avenue, cluttered with books and papers, became an intellectual arsenal in the 1950s for the liberals of Americans for Democratic Action and for liberal legislators on the Hill. In writing about the age of Roosevelt and in assessing the ups and downs of the Cold War, I found myself drawing copiously on Ben's wisdom and experience.

By the time John F. Kennedy arrived in the White House in 1961, Ben was the established sage to whom New Frontiersmen regularly repaired for wisdom and consolation. If only we had listened more carefully to what he told us! He was the first person I knew to warn about the perils of involvement in Vietnam. I will never forget a long luncheon in 1961 when he said to me with quiet intensity that we were embarked on a dangerous course. I thought he was unduly agitated. Five years later I understood how prescient he was.

A school of thought arose in the 1960s dedicated to the proposition that intellectuals should have nothing to do with power except to oppose it. This was not Ben Cohen's view. In Max Weber's distinction, he believed in the ethic of responsibility rather than in the ethic of ultimate ends. He liked to quote words that I suspect he himself had contributed to FDR's last State of the Union address: "Perfectionism, no less than isolationism or imperialism or power politics, may obstruct the paths to international peace."

His example shows that it is quite possible to deal with realities without yielding convictions, quite possible to accept the compromises in program and action often required by the democratic process without compromising ideas and values. Forever generous of time and of heart, incorruptible and wise, a great public servant and a truly noble man, Ben Cohen remains as a model of the intellectual who spends a life in public affairs without betraying his conscience or violating his ideals.

Arthur M. Schlesinger, Jr.

Acknowledgments

I am deeply grateful to The Century Foundation (formerly the Twentieth Century Fund) for its very generous support for this project, and particularly to Beverly Goldberg, who provided invaluable guidance and unwavering encouragement throughout the long process of turning a proposal into a book. I trust that the foundation finds this book a fitting tribute to Ben Cohen and to its own work.

I also received financial support from a number of other sources. I am thankful to the National Endowment for the Humanities, which provided me with a Constitutional Fellowship; the Franklin and Eleanor Roosevelt Institute, the Harry S Truman Foundation, and the American Philosophical Society, which provided grants for travel and research; and Clemson University, which provided a generous sabbatical leave and a number of grants.

Many scholars have shared with me their suggestions, criticisms, and advice, and allowed me to benefit from their wisdom and expertise. Above all I would like to thank Arthur M. Schlesinger, Jr., who was a source of inspiration to me even before I met him, and who has become a mentor and, I dare say, a friend. His description of Ben Cohen as a "model of the intellectual who spends a life in public affairs without betraying his conscience or violating his ideals" could just as easily be said of him.

Others who read all or part of the manuscript and whose assistance I very much appreciate include Alan Brinkley, Richard Polenberg, R. Shep Melnick, John W. Johnson, Leonard Greenspoon, Timothy O'Rourke, and Richard C. Leone. I would also like to thank my colleagues at Clemson—particularly Marty Slann and Dave Woodard—for their encouragement and support.

Ben Cohen's friends and family have been extremely supportive of this project, and have been very kind to me in many ways. Cohen's nephew, the late Bernard Freund, and Bernard's late wife, Ruth, talked with me on many occasions about their uncle, entertained me graciously when I visited Muncie, and combed through boxes of memorabilia to supply me with letters and photographs. I have also appreciated the support of Cohen's niece, Selma Jeanne Cohen, and Cohen's great-nephew Daniel Freund, and have benefited greatly from the kindness and assistance of several friends of Cohen and the Cohen family in Muncie, including Warren Vander Hill of Ball State University and Martin D. Schwartz.

Many of Cohen's friends and associates graciously shared with me their memories of Cohen and of the New Deal. David Ginsburg, who serves as Cohen's executor and who was his close friend, has been especially generous. Several of those who helped me are, sadly, not here to see the completion of the project. These include Joe Rauh, Abba Schwartz, and Sir Isaiah Berlin. Others who allowed me to interview them for the book or who provided other assistance include Tim Corcoran and Carol Lubin.

Many others provided various types of assistance. I am thankful to the many archivists and librarians who patiently helped me on many occasions, especially to David Wigdor and the staff at the manuscript division of the Library of Congress and to the archivists and librarians at the National Archives, the Franklin D. Roosevelt Library, Harvard University, the Harry S. Truman Library, the Dwight D. Eisenhower Library, the Public Record Office in Kew, the University of Minnesota, and the University of Virginia. The research librarians and staff at Clemson University have also been extremely helpful. I appreciate also the assistance of Dr. John Hare of the Joslin Clinic in Boston for advice on Cohen's medical history, to Ms. Ruth Slann of Clemson, S.C., for her help in translating documents from Hebrew; and to John L. Keiser and Isaac Harris for providing me with photographs, letters, and other materials regarding Jane Harris. It has also been a pleasure to work with the editors and staff at Yale University Press.

Of course, I thank my friends and family for their love, patience, and support. I know they have heard much more about Ben Cohen than they wanted to. My uncle, Sherman Davis, provided me with the benefit of his historical expertise on many occasions and always provided a sounding board when I needed one. My mother-in-law, the late Florence D. Shroder, housed and fed me on my many trips to Washington, and listened carefully and patiently as I tried to sort out my thoughts after a day of research. I wish she had been able to see the publication of the book. My wife, Susan J. S. Lasser, continues to serve as my editor and confidante, and my best friend. My children, Max Hoffman and Adina Rose, provide a continual reminder that there are more important things in life than meeting deadlines and writing books. Finally, I would like to thank my parents, Joseph and Shirley H. Lasser. My father did not live to see this book, but he was profoundly responsible for its existence, and it is with great love and not a little sadness that I dedicate it to him.

1

Introduction

Without Ben Cohen's contributions and mind, there would have been
no Lend-Lease, no destroyer bases deal, no successful fight against
inflation, no effective securities legislation, no attack upon great
public utility holding companies, to name only a few.

—*Edward F. Pritchard*

It was a scene symbolic of the New Deal itself. On one side sat the
representatives of the nation's largest and most powerful public utility
companies, the embodiment (or so the New Dealers would have it)
of corporate greed and excess. Led by Wendell Willkie, head of the
Commonwealth & Southern Corporation and soon-to-be candidate for
president of the United States, they had employed the leading lights of
the private bar to argue their case. On the other side were clustered the
finest legal minds the federal government could muster, led by Assistant
Attorney General Robert Jackson and supported by a host of admirers
and well-wishers. In the front of the courtroom sat the justices of the
Supreme Court of the United States; behind and around the combat-
ants crowded the interested and the curious of New Deal Washington.

At stake on that early spring day in February 1938 was the constitutionality of the Public Utility Holding Company Act of 1935, the last
in a triad of statutes designed to save the nation from the unregulated
financial manipulations that had led to the crash of 1929 and the disastrous Depression. The utility companies had failed to stop Congress
from imposing strict controls on their financial operations and prac-

tices; now, they had one last chance to prove that the New Deal did not apply to them.

Underscoring the importance of the case, the Supreme Court allotted six full hours for oral arguments. But the excitement surrounding *Securities and Exchange Commission* v. *Electric Bond & Share* did not keep the Court from sticking to its strict time schedule. Two other cases had to be disposed of first, and it was 4:20 in the afternoon before the case was called. A less punctilious institution than the Supreme Court might have held the case over for the next day, but Chief Justice Charles Evans Hughes pushed ahead, calling on the utilities companies to begin their case. Fully aware of the scheduled adjournment time, former Solicitor General Thomas D. Thacher rose from his seat and spoke for ten minutes, uttering his last word at precisely 4:30, just as the chief justice leaned across the bench and nodded in announcement of the end of the session.[1]

The defendants resumed their argument at noon the next day, calling on the Court to invalidate the Holding Company Act as an illegal extension of Congress's power to regulate interstate commerce and as a violation of the Fifth, Sixth, Eighth, and Tenth Amendments to the Constitution. At 1:40 in the afternoon they yielded to Assistant Attorney General Jackson, who was responsible for introducing the government's response. Jackson, whose presentation straddled the Court's lunch break, did not conclude until after 4:15. He had done a professional job of introducing the government's case, but the more important task of convincing the justices that Congress had not overreached itself was left to his co-counsel, who after twenty-four hours of waiting at last had his chance to speak.

Awkward and unaccustomed to the public stage, Benjamin V. Cohen rose to address the Court. In deference to tradition, he wore formal striped trousers, though he chose a conventional double-breasted suit jacket in place of a cutaway coat. His nervous manner, quavering voice, and trembling hands marked him as a neophyte before the Supreme Court, in striking contrast to the seasoned veterans who had argued the utility company's case earlier in the day. Stooping slightly and peering up at the justices from behind wire-rimmed spectacles, Cohen looked more like a professor than a high-level government attorney. Certainly a different lawyer would have cut a more dashing figure, but no one could have begrudged Cohen the opportunity to present the government's argument. Though scores of lawyers had worked together on the pleadings and ten had signed the brief, everyone knew that *Electric*

Bond & Share was Ben Cohen's case. "Every page of every brief" carries his imprimatur, wrote David Ginsburg, then a junior co-counsel. "His strategy and his intelligence characterizes every argument."[2]

Despite the late hour and counsel's deficiencies as a courtroom lawyer, Cohen's words ran like electricity through the Supreme Court chamber. The justices, no less than the audience, were riveted. Wrote Ginsburg: "The Justice [Brandeis] relaxed with an almost beatific smile on his face; [Hugo] Black perched himself on the edge of his chair, cupped his face in his hands and didn't move.... [Owen] Roberts simply glowered and looked away; [Harlan Fiske] Stone leaned back, put his head on his chair and stared at the ceiling . . . the Chief's eyes began to sparkle and he sat rigidly erect."

So mesmerizing were Cohen's arguments that the justices scarcely noticed as he spoke for seventeen minutes, holding the Court a remarkable five minutes past its scheduled closing time.[3]

At forty-three, Benjamin Victor Cohen still enjoyed a reputation as one of the "bright young men" who had come to Washington to serve Franklin Roosevelt. His legal ability, developed at the University of Chicago and honed at Harvard, stood out as remarkable even in the talented circles of the New Deal. Already he had amassed considerable experience in finance, government, and foreign affairs, and had collected a broad range of friends and associates stretching from New York to Cambridge to London. Among his many accomplishments, he could list major roles in drafting the landmark financial legislation of the New Deal—the Securities Act of 1933, the Securities Exchange Act of 1934, and the Public Utility Holding Company Act of 1935.

Yet exactly what Ben Cohen did, and how he did it, remained a mystery even to many Washington insiders. His official title was general counsel to the National Power Policy Committee, a minor interagency board housed in the Interior Department. Unofficially he served as a kind of presidential adviser at large, consulting frequently with Harvard law professor Felix Frankfurter and often taking his cues from Roosevelt himself. On rare occasions, as in the *Electric Bond & Share* hearing or during the congressional debate over the utilities bill, Cohen could be seen in broad daylight, but generally he played his role in almost total darkness, leaving the public appearances to his friend and alter ego, Tommy Corcoran. While others played "palace politics," observed *Newsweek* magazine, Cohen "enveloped himself cuttlefish-fashion in a murky camouflage of protective privacy. He wrote no articles, made no speeches, didn't gallop in and out of the White House daily—in fact, didn't even have his name stenciled on his office door."[4]

The clandestine nature of Cohen's activities made it easy for friends and critics alike to exaggerate his influence. He and Corcoran were easy targets for congressional opponents and the unfriendly press, who depicted them as "mysterious Johnnies—only here they are Tommies and Bennies—pulling strings, dropping whispered words in cloak rooms and back rooms and over telephones from headquarters." Cohen and Corcoran "was precisely the firm name for which the anti–New Deal politicians had been looking," explained the journalist Heywood Broun, since it could be used to attack Roosevelt's policies while at the same time stirring up both anti-Semitism and anti-Catholicism. New Deal critics depicted Cohen both as a "bumptious plotter who swaggers around the halls of Congress and puts pressure upon the President to do his will and bidding," and as "a sort of Conan Doyle villain named Prof. Moriarity [sic], who used to plot vast schemes in a subterranean den piped for lethal gas which could be administered to the unwary."[5]

Even friendly reporters could not resist inflating Cohen's influence, if only for the sake of a good story. "In Washington it is known that the President does not take a step without" Cohen and Corcoran, beamed the *Jewish Daily Forward* in 1937. "The 36 year old Irishman and the 42 year old Jew are the two pillars upon which the present democratic regime rests." The following year, the Cohen and Corcoran story so gripped the Washington press corps that the two men were featured on the cover of *Time* magazine, above the caption "They call themselves catalysts." Eventually, even the normally staid *New York Times* got carried away. Reporting on Cohen's return from a visit to London, the *Times* called him "one of the two young lawyers said to wield more influence with President Roosevelt than any other American" and described the arrangements for meeting Cohen's ship at the Port of New York as "a system of secrecy and protection more elaborate than any remembered in the port by customs men and others who have met ships for the last generation."[6]

Cohen's lifelong friends were also given to sweeping statements about his New Deal and wartime contributions, especially in their later years. Corcoran, perhaps, was the worst offender. "Ben was in substance our economic administration during the war," he recalled in 1969. "The whole structure of wage and price controls was his work. He built the SEC [Securities and Exchange Commission]. Even now, no man understands these forces as he does. Lend-Lease was his. He kept the civilian economy on a noninflation basis all through the war." "Without Ben Cohen's contributions and mind," echoed Edward F. Prichard, who worked with Cohen during the war, "there would have been no Lend-Lease, no destroyer bases deal, no successful fight against inflation, no effective securities legislation, no attack upon great public utility holding companies, to name only a few."[7]

Historians have taken a far more sober approach to Cohen's accomplishments and influence. In accounts of the New Deal, Cohen is rarely if ever allowed to assume center stage; standard histories of the period typically do little more than acknowledge his presence in the wings, at best allotting him a supporting role in a minor subplot. Monographs on specific subjects are kinder, and more accurate, but by their nature such accounts emphasize only individual aspects of Cohen's multifaceted life and career.

In part, at least, Cohen's lack of historical standing is his own fault. He kept no diary, saved few letters, and gave interviews with great reluctance—and, even then, he minimized his own contributions. He rarely kept extensive notes of his activities, and was careful to handle sensitive issues in person, rather than in writing, whenever possible. Unlike many of his colleagues and contemporaries, Cohen left no published account of his life and made no effort to ensure that his life's work would be properly recognized or commemorated.

But the lack of recognition accorded to Cohen transcends his personality and style, deriving in large measure from the nature of his activities. For most of his professional life, Cohen was doing other people's work. He wrote speeches for others to deliver or expressed his views in memoranda for others to incorporate into their own proposals and arguments. He rarely worked alone, making it difficult if not impossible for a biographer to sort out his specific contributions to any final product. He was passionately involved in the world of ideas, yet left no systematic account of his political principles or political philosophy.

Accurately and authentically reconstructing Ben Cohen's life, therefore, is no easy task. The record of his accomplishments must be built up from bits and pieces of fragmentary evidence, much of which has survived only by chance, and most of which is deeply encrusted in legend and mythology. His public philosophy must be distilled from a vast array of statutes, memoranda, legal opinions, and letters, and from a handful of formal writings, speeches, and interviews. Ultimately, understanding Ben Cohen requires probing deeply into an intellect and personality that resisted such intrusions even from those who knew him well.

Yet the effort is worthwhile, not only to preserve Cohen's memory but also to extend our understanding of the Roosevelt era and to appreciate its implications for our own time. Cohen was with the Roosevelt administration from the First One Hundred Days until the very end, and stayed on to serve Harry Truman for seven more years. His activities spanned the full range of both domestic and foreign policy, beginning with the financial crisis of 1933 and continuing through the war and the nuclear era. Before and after the New Deal, Cohen was deeply involved in the economic and political development of Palestine and in the creation of the State of Israel. He was a chief architect of the modern regulatory state, a model for future generations of presidential assistants, and a primary exponent of the philosophy of American liberalism.

Above all, Ben Cohen provides an extraordinary window into the intellectual heart of a critical and formative period of modern American history. Ben Cohen's life was the life of a mind, and his story is the story of the creation of modern America.

2

Origins

He was born in Muncie, Indiana—the "Middletown" of the Lynd's
famous sociological study of a representative American community.
. . . Perhaps this mid-western small-town-background was of
influence in shaping his attitudes.
—*Jerome Frank, "Ben Cohen," 1945*

Exactly what brought Ben Cohen's father to Muncie, Indiana, in
1881 remains a mystery. Certainly it was not the Jewish community,
which consisted of a handful of German immigrants in the clothing
business; there was not even an organized Jewish congregation. Nor,
on the surface, was there an obvious economic motive. Muncie in the
early 1880s was a "placid county-seat of some 6,000 souls," set in the
midst of Midwestern farm country, according to an early account. "On
the streets . . . on fair days lawyers, doctors, the officials of the county
courts, and the merchants walked about in their shirt sleeves. . . . The
house painter went along with his ladder on his shoulder. In the still-
ness there could be heard the hammers of the carpenters building a new
house for the son of a merchant who had married the daughter of a
blacksmith."[1]

A man in his early twenties, Moses Cohen came to Muncie from
Indianapolis, where he had lived for seven years since emigrating from
Graievo, Poland. With him was his wife, Sarah Ringolsky Cohen, barely
seventeen. According to local historians, Cohen and his wife were the
first Eastern European Jews to arrive in Muncie. In 1882 the couple was

joined by Sarah's parents, also Polish immigrants. Moses and his father-in-law, Harris Ringolsky, soon went into business together.

Both the marriage and the business partnership prospered. "M. Cohen & Co." began as a typical frontier-town trading post: "dealers in hides, furs, pelts, tallow, grease, feathers, beeswax, junk, etc.," as the 1889 Muncie city directory put it. But the subsequent discovery of natural gas reserves near Muncie created an economic boom, and Moses Cohen and Harris Ringolsky rode the rising tide of industrial development. By the early 1890s they had moved to new quarters and were now dealing in "scrap iron and metals, rags, rubber and bones." By the turn of the century they had moved once again and had turned their exclusive attention to wholesale scrap iron, steel, and metals. Business flourished, and the two partners became respectable members of Muncie's growing business community.[2]

Moses and Sarah Cohen's family grew as quickly as the business, and eventually it came to number five children—three boys and two girls. The youngest, born September 23, 1894, was named Benjamin Victor.

In later years much would be made of Benjamin Cohen's Hoosier origins. Muncie, of course, was "Middletown," made famous as the subject of a comprehensive sociological study by Robert S. and Helen Merrell Lynd in the late 1920s. It was a city, as the Lynds put it, "as representative as possible of contemporary American life." Cohen's roots in this most middle of middle American cities would eventually provide a kind of Lincolnian undercurrent to his otherwise cosmopolitan existence. Typical is an account by Jerome Frank, written in 1945 in an effort to strengthen Cohen's candidacy for a job in the State Department. In Muncie, wrote Frank, "young Ben went to the public schools and lived the life of the average boy of a middle-class family. Perhaps this mid-western small-town-background was of influence in shaping his attitudes. At any rate, he has a thoroughly home-spun American outlook, an innate loyalty to American democratic ideals, [and] a keen sensitivity to American economic and political moods."[3]

In many ways, the Cohens' life in Muncie was that of a typical upper-middle-class family. Ben Cohen grew up in a handsome and substantial house; his mother had a live-in servant to help with household chores. He attended the public schools, and he often ate dinners at the home of his grandparents, who lived next door. Documentary evidence of Cohen's early years is sketchy, but there is little to contradict the small-town-America image of his upbringing.

Except, of course, that the Cohens were Jewish. Although the Jews of Muncie were tolerated well enough, especially early on, they were not quite accepted into the mainstream community. In the 1920s, wrote the Lynds, "Jewish merchants mingle freely with other business men in the smaller civic clubs, but there are no Jews in Rotary; Jews are accepted with just enough qualification to make them aware that they do not entirely 'belong.'" Anti-Semitism was "less felt in the days before the Jews had come so largely to dominate the retail life of the city and before the latest incarnation of the Klan," the Lynds concluded, but it was doubtless present at least in some form in earlier years. Still, by the time the Klan became a major presence, Cohen was long gone. He had only good memories of Muncie. The only incident he could recall that had even remote overtones of anti-Semitism was when he was denied a part in a school play. At the time, he blamed it on his manner of speech. "Only later did it occur to him that it may have been anti-Semitism."[4]

Like Jewish communities everywhere, Muncie's was culturally and religiously diverse. It was also highly transitory, marked by "extreme restlessness, a moving from community to community." Cohen's family reflected both tendencies. His mother's parents kept a kosher home, and his father at one time found work as a Hebrew school teacher in Indianapolis. Yet his mother did not keep kosher, and later turned to Christian Science, though without rejecting her Jewish identity. In the late 1930s the rabbi of the Muncie temple described the "two Christian Scientists in the Middletown Jewish community" (one of whom was most certainly Sarah Cohen): "The motives which seem to have prompted their acceptance of Christian Science are the desire for social acceptance by the Christian community, and, more particularly in one case, the desire for more intensive religious expression than is manifest in the Jewish synagogue in Middletown. However, these Christian Scientist members of the Jewish community suffer no particular isolation from the Jewish community, and are still, in the main, regarded as Jews. From time to time they attend the services at the synagogue and retain a loose affiliation with the Jewish group. The general attitude toward them on the part of the Jews of the community is that they may be Christian Scientists by choice, but are still Jews at heart."[5]

From this melange, Cohen seems to have picked up a smattering of Hebrew and a passing acquaintance with Jewish holidays and customs. He more strongly identified with being an American, and came to believe that "the only thing that distinguished him and his family" from their neighbors was religion.[6] In later years, his circumstances and the social prejudices of others encouraged close relationships with many Jews, including Felix Frankfurter, Julian Mack, and Max Lowenthal, but Cohen was also comfortable with non-Jews who accepted him. He was equally comfortable attending a Passover seder or a secularized Christmas dinner.

The casual eclecticism of Cohen's religious background gave him little guidance or support in finding the answers to the deep and troubling questions that all human beings must face. "If the quest for the spirit, the essence brings you peace and calm," Cohen wrote to his friend and confidante Jane Harris at the age of thirty-six, "far be it from me to deprive you of that solace. If Christianity in general and Catholicism in particular by holding forth the prospect of great bliss in the hereafter, has made the unbearable burdens of the world bearable for masses of suffering humanity, perhaps it should be extolled as the faith of the faiths and the truth of truths. But if others find solace in anthroposophy or in Christian science [sic] or in Marxian socialism or even in Freudianism, perhaps a philosophy of pluralism may admit them all as the divine truth. But I wonder whether much of this devotion to faith is more than a flight from reality—comforting, maybe; but solving nothing." "Truth and life after all is something you cannot put your hand on," Cohen concluded. "As the great historian Renan said, 'La verité est dans les nuances' [the truth is in the nuances]. But one cannot catch or dissect a 'nuance,' and I should not try."[7]

Like many of their fellow Jews, the Cohen family's ties to Muncie were shallow and fleeting. For Cohen himself, however, the connection was much deeper. As he told a reporter years later, "I was very fond and proud of Muncie when I was a boy and bragged quite a bit about it." When his parents took him with them to Chicago in 1910 (Cohen's brothers had gone to the big city a few years earlier), Cohen—like many teenagers before and since—was devastated. "I cried like a baby," he recalled. "I thought it was tragic that my name would not be inscribed on the honor role [sic] at the high school because I was not to finish there."[8] Eventually Cohen's sister Bessie married and moved to California, leaving only his sister Pearl Freund and her family in the old hometown. In later years Cohen would return to Muncie on an occasional basis, usually for a family event or reunion. In the 1930s Cohen would write that his apartment in New York was "the only home I have," but deep down Muncie remained an anchor. In his will he remembered Ball State University along with Harvard, and he was buried, at his own request, in the Freund family plot in Muncie's Jewish cemetery.

Cohen completed the last year of his secondary education at University High School, which is located next to the University of Chicago's Hyde Park campus. He was, by all accounts, an exceptional student. "At the early age of four," runs a description in the University High yearbook, "Ben Victor Cohen was discovered by his parents munching an algebra. They at once enrolled him in U. High, where he has continued to devour books becoming a prize student and a delight unto his teachers." The student editors of the University High yearbook expressed their own judgment: "We like Ben even if he does study," they wrote. " 'It takes all kinds of people to make a school' so Ben is in the right place."[9] Cohen himself admitted to having been "a studious and retrospective youngster" who "did well at my studies, but not much else." A classmate remembered him as "very quiet and good-looking too," adding, "he must have had some inferiority complex." Despite his shyness, Cohen participated in the Clay Club, which sponsored debates, mock trials, and public readings. "Because of his high-pitched voice," concluded Joseph Lash, Cohen was not the star of the club, but what Ben was unable to achieve there, not to mention the dance floor and the sports field, he more than made up for in the classroom." Some of Cohen's awkwardness in social matters, and especially with women, can be attributed to his age—only sixteen upon graduation in 1911.[10]

From University High the University of Chicago was a logical step. Cohen majored in political science and political economy, but after two years he was accepted into the law program and was taking most of his classes there. In 1914 he received a Ph.B. with honors in law and in political science and political economy, followed a year and a summer later by a J. D. Among his academic honors were Phi Beta Kappa (1913), the Order of the Coif (1915), and election as a university marshal.

Cohen's grade point average was 5 1/2—between an A and an A minus in the system in use at the time. Years later, Cohen recalled that his record was "all A's" except for public speaking, since "I had trouble with breathing so I couldn't speak well." In fact he did receive a B minus in public speaking, and also received B's in English composition and comparative government, a B plus in municipal problems, and more than half a dozen A minuses. In law school his grades were more spectacular, supposedly the highest ever awarded by the University of Chicago. Out of thirty-three law school classes—compressed into less than two years—Cohen received thirty-two A's and a single A minus, in a course on equity.[11]

Cohen rarely spoke of his college and law school experiences, and

it is difficult to draw clear connections between his educational background and his later approach to political life. His undergraduate
courses gave him as much of a background in economics as in politics,
and included statistics, corporation finance, accounting, trade union-
ism, population and standard of living, and research in labor problems.
Throughout his life Cohen remained conversant in economic theory
and practice, and was comfortable with accounting practices and high
finance.

The most famous professor he encountered at Chicago was Charles
Merriam, who was both a noted scholar and a leading progressive politician. (Cohen himself organized the Progressive Club for the Bull Moos-
ers in 1912.) Cohen identified Merriam as one of his personal heroes,
and took his course on municipal problems. On the law faculty were
such eminences as Ernst Freund, Roscoe Pound (visiting from Harvard), and James Parker Hall, who served as dean. Also on the law faculty was Julian W. Mack, then a federal judge, and later one of Cohen's
mentors. Mack's judicial duties kept him out of the classroom during
Cohen's tenure at the law school, and there is no evidence that they knew
each other at the time. Cohen took Hall for torts and constitutional law,
later listing both Hall and Pound as professional references.

One other Chicago professor is worth mentioning because Cohen
himself noted his influence. He was Harold G. Moulton, Cohen's fresh-
man economics instructor and later a widely renowned professor and
head of the Brookings Institution. Moulton, a specialist in what he
called "the financial organization of society," wrote an important text-
book on the subject a few years after Cohen was graduated. His arguments were considered "cogent and convincing, his views moderate and
fair-minded." Precisely tracking Moulton's influence on Cohen is impossible, of course, but the gist of Cohen's New Deal work on stock
exchange and public utility regulation is entirely compatible with Moulton's approach.[12]

No letters of recommendation from Cohen's college days are ex-
tant, although there is little question as to what such letters must have
said. A letter of reference written three years later by Edward B. Burling,
chief counsel of the U.S. Shipping Board (and later a founder of the
well-known Washington law firm of Covington and Burling), is probably typical. "Mr. Cohen is a man of remarkable natural legal capacity,"
Burling wrote. "His industry is prodigious. He has an amazingly keen
mind and is fertile in resource. . . . You will not find many men of keener
intelligence or better character."[13]

Cohen's law school classmates summed up their legal education this way: "We find in our self-analysis that after three years of plodding we are still but upon the threshold of 'the storehouse of legal learning,' and that our somewhat inflated confidence as to the future has subsided, though alongside of it has grown up a feeling of security in our past and a reliance upon our equipment. . . . Our ideas of right and wrong are materially modified and for the former clinching arguments of 'Natural Justice' we substitute 'Smith v. Jones,' 'the constitution,' or 'the statute.' . . . In short, we may not know much law, but we feel we are somewhat more nearly the analytical machine that they tell us the legal mind should be."[14]

With his outstanding record and with the support of the Chicago faculty, Cohen won an Ames fellowship for a year of study at Harvard Law School, leading to the s.j.d. degree in June 1916. It seems likely that Cohen's decision to apply to Harvard, as well as the school's decision to accept him, was influenced by Roscoe Pound, although Ernst Freund's influence might also have been considerable. At Harvard, Cohen took courses in equity, bankruptcy, municipal corporations, jurisprudence, and Roman law. He also took a course in public utilities from Felix Frankfurter, then a second-year professor of law. As at Chicago, Cohen's academic work was exemplary. His lowest grade was a 75 in Roman law (75 and higher being an A); his highest was an 81 from Frankfurter.

Frankfurter was a dozen years older than Cohen, and the future justice was just beginning a career that would take him to the heights of academic and political life. Born in Vienna, he had arrived in the United States a month before Cohen was born. After a series of fits and starts, Frankfurter decided to attend Harvard Law School, enrolling in 1903. "There was a dominating atmosphere, first, of professionalism and what I think is an indispensable quality of true professionalism, the democratic spirit," he recalled of Harvard. "What mattered was excellence in your profession to which your father or your face was equally irrelevant. And so rich man, poor man were just irrelevant titles to the equation of human relations. The thing that mattered was what you did professionally."[15] When Frankfurter had the chance to return to Harvard in 1914 as a member of the faculty, he jumped at it.

Although Frankfurter also taught criminal law, at least at first, the public utilities course became his trademark. Despite the narrow-sounding title, the course was apparently rather disorganized, with the professor routinely indulging himself and his students in storytelling and name-dropping. "We were not learning law," one student recalled. "That was not our business. We were gaining some measure of understanding of law that both reflected and shaped a nation's growth—some understanding of its method and some appreciation of its content." Another student put it more succinctly, and in verse:

You learn no law in Public U
That is its fascination
But Felix gives a point of view
And pleasant conversation.

Frankfurter enjoyed the class as much as his students did. "I'm having a happy time of it here," he wrote in November of his first semester. "These youngsters are an inspirational lot."[16]

As a professor, Frankfurter considered it his goal to make his students understand the connection between the law and the larger society of which it is a part. "We fail in our important office if they do not feel that society has breathed into law the breath of life and made it a living, serving soul," he told the American Bar Association in 1915. "We must show them the law as an instrument and not an end of organized humanity. We make of them clever pleaders but not lawyers if they fail to catch the glorious vision of the law, not as a harsh Procrustean bed into which all persons and all societies must inexorably be fitted, but as a vital agency for human betterment."[17]

Frankfurter's course in public utilities was not Cohen's first exposure to "sociological jurisprudence," as this new approach to law was known. He had heard it in Chicago from Roscoe Pound, who is considered the founder of the movement. Whatever its source, the idea that law is molded by outside forces and must be harnessed to the needs of society was strongly imprinted on the young law student. Frankfurter's lecture notes on public utilities are virtually a blueprint for the later struggles of the New Deal.

"The underlying principle of this Course," Frankfurter told his students,

is that there is on the part of the community a dependance [*sic*] on certain businesses, on certain enterprises, in the management of which it is not wise, nor safe to leave the individual to unregulated action. In the early days of the 14th, 15th, and 16th centuries, such businesses were primitive, and the miller, the stage-coach diver and the innkeeper were the only kinds of callings that the courts felt called upon to deal with. . . . This state continued until the beginning of the 19ᵗʰ century; and then that great series of events, which has been called the Industrial Revolution, took place. This undoubtedly changed the aspect of the law, because it changed the aspect of life. New principles came into existance [*sic*] because new circumstances had risen. . . .

We are all getting to realize that legal institutions are relative and depend upon time and place and circumstances. . . .

[I]n the immediate decades ahead, during your time and mine, there will be a continued extension of government activity and governmental supervision of business. . . . All must feel the pressure of economic and social problems, that certain evils demand answer, that there is much room for improvement, and that government is one of the most important agencies in answering these demands and in the furtherance of these improvements. . . . There is an increased sense of collective or social responsibility in regard to the problems that modern industrial civilisation raises. . . . Therefore, I think that the law which deals with these problems is one of the most important branches of the law; and one that requires the most painstaking consideration and the exactest kind of thinking. . . .

[T]here are still many unsolved problems and new problems consistently arise. Their correct solution devolves upon you and your contemporaries as those problems will come to you, as practisioners [*sic*], as legislators, as judges and administrators.[18]

The charismatic young professor quickly attracted the very best students, who clung to him as disciples. "Frankfurter's attitude toward his students was paternal," wrote one commentator years later. "In addition to trying to inspire them, he all but adopted his favorite pupils. . . . He became absorbed in their private lives and their ambitions. . . . Having a warm, bubbling, aggressive personality, he tended unconsciously to dominate many of his pupils. At the same time, he enjoyed the companionship of students who fought with him in class." The very best students were invited to Frankfurter's home on Brattle Street for Sunday evening salons.[19]

In the young Ben Cohen, Frankfurter found not only an intellect worth cultivating, but a personality he could dominate and direct. For

years after Cohen left Harvard, Frankfurter contributed guidance, offered advice, and opened up opportunities. In return, the professor imposed upon his former student for help on a range of projects. "FF
liked to arrange things—mainly good things," Cohen recalled. Frankfurter was wholly or partially responsible for finding Cohen his judicial clerkship and his first legal job in New York; for bringing Cohen to
Washington in the early New Deal and convincing him to stay; and for
introducing Cohen to Zionism.[20] Unquestionably there was something
of a father-son relationship between Frankfurter and Cohen, including, eventually, a strong degree of tension as Cohen began to break free
from Frankfurter's influence.

The two men were also drawn to each other by their common roots
in Judaism. Frankfurter was not a practicing Jew; he married a non-Jew
and was a self-described agnostic. For much of his early life, he explicitly rejected Judaism and regarded it only as a barrier to be overcome.
After graduating from Harvard, for example, Frankfurter set his sights
on the prestigious law firm of Hornblower, Byrne, Miller and Potter.
"Lots of Harvard people were in there. I'd heard that they had never
taken a Jew and wouldn't take a Jew. I decided that that was the office
I wanted to get into not for any reason of truculence, but I was very
early infused with, had inculcated in me, a very profoundly wise attitude toward the whole fact that I was a Jew, the essence of which is that
you should be a biped and walk on the two legs that man has. . . . You
should take that ultimate fact that you were born of some parents instead of these other parents as much for granted as the fact that you've
got green-brown eyes instead of blue eyes."[21]

Frankfurter took a similar line in explaining his outrage over the
controversy surrounding the nomination of Louis Brandeis to the Supreme Court in 1916. His "deep conviction of cruel wrong to Brandeis,"
he wrote, was no mere expression of "racial particularity," she explained.
"I feel even more strongly against Jewish self-seekers . . . than their
Gentile analogues. I feel deeply about the Brandeis matter because it
raises deep moral issues."[22]

Still, Frankfurter was not completely cut off from his cultural heritage. In fact it may have been the controversy over Brandeis—in the
spring of 1916, during Cohen's year at the law school—that first heightened his sense of Jewish identity. Added to the Brandeis nomination
fight were two very personal issues that underscored Frankfurter's Judaism—the death of his father, and his growing involvement with Marion
Denman, the Congregationalist minister's daughter who would become

his wife. As H. N. Hirsch observes, "Frankfurter, who had so recently moved in fashionable Washington circles and had been appointed to the Harvard faculty, was jarred back to the very real ambiguity and fragility of his status and position. His religion and his culture . . . which he had once come to regard as little more than accidents, suddenly loomed once again as powerful forces in his life." [23]

Doubtless some of these concerns rubbed off onto Cohen, who for the first time was forced to deal with the same set of issues. Employment opportunities for Jewish law students were sharply limited, often arbitrarily so. Many firms simply refused to hire Jews; others would hire them but treat them as second-class citizens. The federal government had no official policy regarding Jews, but—as the Brandeis nomination fight demonstrated—there were many places in which Jews were not welcome. Like Frankfurter, Cohen would have to learn the hard way that his Jewish identity was not purely a function of reality or of self-image, but of how he was regarded by others.

One man who well understood the difficulties facing even the best Jewish law students was Julian W. Mack. Born in San Francisco in 1866, Mack spent most of his early life in Cincinnati, where Jews enjoyed full acceptance in the social, economic, and political life of the community. From Cincinnati Mack went directly to Harvard Law, where he flourished under the tutelage of James Barr Ames, the leading law professor of his day. (A few years later, Mack founded the Ames fellowship, which funded Ben Cohen's year at Harvard.) Harvard in the 1880s was largely free from overt anti-Semitism, which was considered "ungentlemanly, un-American and assuredly un-Bostonian." Mack spent three years studying in Berlin and Leipzig, then returned to the United States and settled in Chicago, where he became a practicing attorney, law professor, and local judge. In 1902 he accepted an offer to become one of the original members of the law faculty at the University of Chicago, a position he retained (though usually in absentia) for nearly forty years.[24]

Mack fit easily into secular society, but his increasing concern over the plight of Jewish immigrants brought him closer and closer to a leadership role in the Jewish community. As Cohen himself put it, "Mack identified with his fellow Jews, whether Russian, Polish or German; they were his people, so he *had* to work with them and for them."[25] He became the head of the Jewish charities in Chicago, a founder of the American Jewish Committee, president of the Immigrants' Protective

League, and eventually president of the American Jewish Congress and the Zionist Organization of America.

In 1911, President William Howard Taft appointed Mack to the new United States Commerce Court, based in Washington, as a circuit judge. Within three years the commerce court was abolished, however, and Mack, along with the other judges of appellate rank, became an "additional" circuit court judge, to be assigned to crowded dockets at the discretion of the chief justice. For the most part, he divided his time between the New York and Chicago circuits.

Almost immediately upon ascending to the bench, Mack began a tradition of choosing his law clerks from among the top Harvard graduates, as recommended to him first by Roscoe Pound and then by Felix Frankfurter. Mack, Pound, and Frankfurter were especially interested in placing Jewish students, who otherwise had few federal clerkship opportunities. One of Mack's first clerks was Max Lowenthal, who eventually married Mack's niece Eleanor. Another was Cohen, whose close relationships with Pound and Frankfurter—not to mention his connection with the University of Chicago—made him an obvious choice. Cohen worked with Mack from 1916 to 1917, largely in Chicago. For the most part Mack heard cases on appeal from the federal district courts in the Seventh Circuit, which comprised Illinois and surrounding states. In addition to the routine tasks performed by judicial law clerks, Cohen probably played a substantial role in helping Mack write his opinions, a chore the judge never found to his liking.

Mack's reported opinions from 1916–17 deal mostly with an array of dry and technical subjects: land claims, patent disputes, supervision of railroad receiverships, and contract disputes. They are, as a rule, tightly argued and heavily reliant on precedent; there is little to reveal Mack's approach to the law or his views on public policy. An exception involved an otherwise uninteresting contractual dispute between a coal company and a shipping concern. Struggling to interpret the meaning of the contract, Mack indulged in a rare expression of legal philosophy: "Precedent can throw but little light on the sound interpretation of such contracts [as are involved in this case], especially as to implying unexpressed obligations: each has its own individuality, its own background and surrounding circumstances. Words are only symbols, and at times, even in the most formal agreement, but elliptical expressions of the mutual understanding; the underlying mutual intent, sought by both parties to be clothed in the language used, must be ascertained; text, context, and extrinsic circumstances, including prior negotiations and relations, may be considered to enable the court to view the matter from the standpoint of the parties at the time of making the contract." After analyzing both parties' expectations and interests, Mack concluded that if the contract "be reasonably susceptible of a construction in accordance with their mutually expressed aim," the court was bound to so construe it.[26]

Cohen's year with Mack provided him with an opportunity to hone his legal skills, particularly in the drafting of precise arguments on highly complex topics. More important was Mack's personal friendship and influence and his sense of compassion and concern for others. The two men became very close, and would remain so for years; there is no record of even a hint of disagreement or tension between the two. Cohen's surviving letters to Mack, when not dealing with purely professional subjects, reveal a level of candor generally absent in his letters to Frankfurter or anyone else, with the exception of his friend and confidante Jane Harris. Mack's replies, in turn, could be sensitive and understanding in a way that Frankfurter's are not.

As his clerkship year drew to a close, the twenty-two-year-old Cohen faced the difficult question of his next career move. His association with Pound, Frankfurter, and Mack strengthened his decision to pursue "a public career in matters relating to the law." Exactly how to proceed, however, was unclear. One possibility was to follow Pound and Frankfurter into the academy; another was to work directly for the government. Still another was to postpone the decision and get some practical legal experience.

Pound, for one, urged the last course. "I think on the whole you probably have to go into the office for a few years if only [because] the University Presidents and Trustees are inclined to demand what they are pleased to call 'practical experience,'" he wrote Cohen in March 1917. Besides, Pound advised, "what you need is a little of the self-confidence which comes from experience, and enables one to use his latent punch effectively." Cohen, however, was resistant to Pound's suggestion. As he explained later, "I never thought of going into private law practice."[27]

While Cohen hesitated, world events made his next career move clear; within weeks, the United States declared war against Germany. Cohen's first inclination, like that of millions of his fellow countrymen, was to enlist. Though his poor eyesight disqualified him from general military service, he was able to qualify for "special or limited military service" as an attorney, until a 1918 examination for appointment to the Army's Central Officers Training School found further problems: a "slight fine involuntary tremor," protruding eyes (proptosis), and a slightly enlarged thyroid. On the basis of these symptoms, the examining physician diagnosed hyperthyroidism; that, along with "very defective vision," made Cohen unfit for active military duty.[28]

Cohen would show signs of thyroid disease at various points throughout his life. The course of thyroid disease is not entirely predictable, however, and tracking the progression of the disease in Cohen's particular case is difficult, both for a lack of specific medical documentation and because the treatment of the disease in the pre-modern era was unscientific and imprecise. In later years, Cohen developed an enlarged thyroid gland (goiter), which was surgically removed; the removal of the gland instantly cured him of *hyper*thyroidism but made him immediately susceptible to *hypo*thyroidism, a condition marked by the underproduction or nonproduction of thyroid hormones. Today, hypothyroid patients are routinely treated with synthetic hormone replacement therapy; their hormone levels can be precisely monitored through blood testing and their medication adjusted accordingly. In Cohen's day, however, the best the doctors could do was to prescribe medicines derived from animal thyroid glands, at dosages that were largely a matter of guesswork. Thus even if Cohen did receive hormone replacement therapy, it is likely that his thyroid levels fluctuated and that he suffered, at times at least, from hypothyroidism.

Besides causing physical symptoms, high or low thyroid hormone levels can also affect behavior and can even be associated with moderate or severe mood disorders. Hyperthyroidism leads to anxiety, nervousness, restlessness, and irritability; sufferers may need less sleep, have extraordinary amounts of energy, have difficulty controlling their emotions, and even display symptoms of mania. Hypothyroidism, by contrast, slows the body's metabolism and can cause fatigue, weakness, lack of energy, and depression. Depression can also result, less commonly, from hyperthyroidism.

Some of the symptoms Cohen displayed in later life may have been associated with thyroid disease. His ability to subsist on little or no sleep, for example, was legendary, and he could do extraordinary amounts of work over short periods. Yet he was often anxious and irritable, could show a fierce temper, and sometimes overreacted emotionally to stress or loss. In later life, especially, his mood was frequently melancholic, and at times he lapsed into depression. But these symptoms do not necessarily point to thyroid disease, and may have been manifestations of an underlying mood disorder.

In any event, there is little evidence that Cohen's thyroid condition

caused him any significant problems in 1917, and despite the army doctor's verdict it was not difficult for him to find a civilian role in the war
effort. Once again, Frankfurter was inclined to arrange things and was
well positioned to help; the Harvard professor started the war as an assistant to the secretary of war, then moved on to become secretary and
counsel to the President's Mediation Commission, and finally chairman
of the War Labor Policies Board. Along the way he built up a network of
young men in key positions across the government—precursors to the
"Happy Hot Dogs" who populated Washington during the New Deal.
Cohen was one of Frankfurter's earliest "boys" in Washington, taking
a job with the United States Shipping Board in August 1917.

The Shipping Board was established in 1916 for the purpose of
"encouraging, developing, and creating a naval auxiliary and naval reserve and a merchant marine to meet the requirements of the commerce of the United States." With the outbreak of war, its functions
became enmeshed with the larger war effort, and particularly with war
mobilization issues. Cohen performed various duties, mostly of a technical nature. "I have had considerable experience in the drafting of
requisition charters and operating agreements and handling questions
of interpretation arising thereunder," he explained. Cohen also created a new schedule of compensation for refrigerated vessels, which the
Board adopted. Unquestionably the board was pleased with his work,
and Cohen received a particularly warm endorsement from its chairman, Edward B. Burling. "His chief characteristic, I should say, is an
entire and complete devotion to whatever duty is placed upon him,"
Burling wrote. "If there were any supreme authority capable of assigning to each man the work for which he is best fitted, I believe Mr. Cohen,
in view of his particular fitness for his work here, would be ordered to
continue his present task." But Cohen wanted to be closer to the war
effort, and Burling dutifully recommended him to the army and the
State Department. No offers were forthcoming.[29]

One of Cohen's duties for the Shipping Board was to draft a bill
"to provide workmen's compensation for seamen and their dependents."
The bill, written in the summer of 1918, was never enacted; Congress
opted instead for a rather lame expansion of the seaman's right to re-
cover damages for death or injury. Still, Cohen's bill is of some interest,
not least because it is the first bill known to be written by a man who
two decades later would be the leading legislative draftsman of the New
Deal. The proposed act was modeled after a number of state and federal laws passed after 1908. Such acts had a dual purpose. On the sur-

face, they were designed to provide a simple and standardized mechanism whereby workers (as well as their survivors and dependents) could be compensated for injuries sustained on the job. More broadly, such acts aimed to create a clear financial incentive for employers to promote worker safety and health. All the early workmen's compensation statutes either permitted or required employers to pool their risks through a public or private insurance program.

Cohen's statute, for example, provided that the widow of a seaman covered by the act was entitled to a weekly stipend of 35 percent of her husband's weekly pay, plus an additional 10 percent of the weekly pay for each dependent child, up to a total of 65 percent.[30] Workers who became totally disabled were entitled to 60 percent of their regular weekly pay, for the duration of the disability. (Over the course of many pages, the bill laid out a variety of other detailed compensation schedules.) Employers were required to "secure compensation to seamen employed by them by insuring and keeping insured the payment of such compensation with any state or federal insurance fund or bureau," or with a private insurance company authorized by the secretary of commerce to provide such insurance.

The bill, and the way Cohen went about preparing it, foreshadow the legislative methods he used during the New Deal. First, as he explained to Felix Frankfurter in 1920, he conferred with interested parties on all sides of the issue. These included "a prominent Marine Insurance man"; the director of insurance of the Shipping Board; the managers of the American Steamship Owners' Mutual Protective and Indemnity Association; and a New York admiralty lawyer who had been responsible for "having the New York state compensation act declared unconstitutional in so far as it conflicted with admiralty jurisdiction." Second, Cohen displayed a keen sense of pragmatism, writing a bill that was not perfect but that stood at least some chance of success. "Were I drawing an ideal Act, I think I should provide that all vessels must be insured in one fund which should be run by the owners of the vessels insured on the mutual or co-operative principle," he wrote Frankfurter. "But I feared that it would be difficult enough to get the Bill enacted without encountering the opposition that such a provision might arouse." Finally, he opted for an administrative arrangement that stressed "flexibility and simplicity," choosing to enlarge the powers of the federal district courts of admiralty and their appointed commissioners rather than creating a separate federal commission. Again, he relied on the views of those with practical experience: "I found satisfaction expressed with the procedural provisions of the Act," he wrote, "from nearly everyone who was familiar with admiralty practice and seamen's cases."[31]

Cohen's position at the Shipping Board had given him valuable practical experience, but the difficult decision of what to do next—postponed by the war emergency—still loomed. Now twenty-four, Cohen had excellent credentials, a growing reputation for loyalty and competence, and outstanding connections to those in power. Though obviously a progressive in the tradition of his mentors—especially Pound, Mack, and Frankfurter—his political philosophy was still evolving. If he was motivated by a desire to serve the public, it was not to implement any particular social, political, or personal agenda, and except for his dislike of private practice he does not seem to have had strong feelings about what professional course to pursue.

On a personal level, he remained lonely and isolated, especially from his peers. In many ways he resembled an awkward schoolboy whose intellect was developed far beyond his years but whose social skills and personal life were severely lacking. He stood an inch and a half under six feet but weighed a mere 146 pounds. Except for a more youthful hairline, Cohen's overall appearance as a young man was probably not far removed from Jerome Frank's description, written when Cohen was nearing fifty:

> Of more than average height, he stoops slightly and slouches when he sits. He is owl-eyed, for his large be-spectacled vision is a bit myopic [a deliberate understatement; his uncorrected vision in both eyes was 20–200]. His ivory-skinned face is unusually broad; a naturally high forehead has become extended, as his wispy dry hair has receded. When he talks, usually with a sort of casual drawl but with an occasional quiver, his low-toned voice being often full of humorous inflections, he has a way of bringing his round chin forward and upward in a slow circular motion so that he peers at you in a kindly fashion from beneath half-closed eyes. His gestures are ungainly, but slow, calm, unimpassioned, and not unpleasing. He smiles much, but in a shy, engaging, wistful way, his countenance at times reflecting a quizzical sadness."[32]

As events turned out, Cohen had little time to decide on his future path or to dwell on his frustrations or disappointments. In June 1918, Julian Mack was elected to the presidency of the Zionist Organization of America; a few months later, he became the president of the first

American Jewish Congress. When the congress decided to send a delegation of American Jews to the Paris Peace Conference to work toward
the creation of a Jewish state in Palestine, Mack, along with Louis Marshall of the American Jewish Committee, was selected to lead it. When
the judge left for Paris in March 1919, Cohen went with him.

3

Zionist Attorney

Through . . . Zionism he also came to know the European and world
scene, the importance of understanding history, the meaning of
power and diplomacy, the role of moral force, the art of negotiation,
the need for tenacity and optimism.

—*David Ginsburg, 1983*

Given Cohen's connections to Julian Mack and Felix Frankfurter,
some involvement with Zionism was probably inevitable, for by 1917
both Mack and Frankfurter were deeply committed to the Zionist cause.
Cohen's association with Mack and Frankfurter also drew him inexorably into the orbit of Louis Dembitz Brandeis, who, in addition to
serving as an associate justice of the United States Supreme Court, was
also the leading American Zionist of his day.

In his seventh decade of life at the end of World War I, Louis
Brandeis could count enough achievements for two or three careers.
He had been a phenomenally successful lawyer who managed to pursue the public interest while amassing a considerable fortune. He had
served as an adviser to presidents and would-be presidents, earning an
appointment as the first Jewish justice on the Supreme Court. And he
had emerged as the dominant Jewish figure of his day, assuming the
leadership of the splintered and disorganized American Zionist movement. Though philosophically he leaned toward Jefferson, physically he
resembled another president: "more like Lincoln above . . . less broadly
and commonly Lincoln below, in the mouth and chin," as one contem-

porary put it. His "large head . . . stubborn black hair streaked with iron gray . . . striking, dark face, [and] . . . sensitive hands" created "singularly an impression of originality and power."[1] Brandeis's physical appearance as well as in his zeal for justice led Franklin Roosevelt to nickname him "Isaiah"; his younger colleagues simply called him "the Justice."

Brandeis's relationship to Felix Frankfurter was close and of long standing, dating back to 1905, when Frankfurter was a student at Harvard Law School and Brandeis a practicing attorney. "It was almost inevitable for Frankfurter to be attracted to Brandeis," writes the Frankfurter biographer H. N. Hirsch. "He was the 'people's attorney,' he was Jewish, he was interested in the political issues Frankfurter himself was coming to examine." Brandeis was a generation older than Frankfurter, and soon became a mentor to his younger colleague. He provided Frankfurter with advice, information, and, not least of all, money. The latter was designed to "defray the disbursements of our joint adventure," as Brandeis put it, and allowed Frankfurter to carry out his extensive public service activities. In time, Brandeis came to regard Frankfurter almost as a son. "You know how much Felix has been to us," Brandeis wrote to Frankfurter's wife-to-be in 1919; "half son, half brother; a bringer of joy, an enricher of life."[2]

The connection between Mack and Brandeis was of more recent vintage. Though the two men had known each other for some time, their active association began only in 1915, when Brandeis persuaded Mack to join an "advisory council" of the Provisional Executive Committee for General Zionist Affairs. The only other member of the committee was Frankfurter. The Brandeis-Mack friendship grew slowly. "They addressed each other for some time with an almost curious formality," writes Harry Barnard—"'Mr. Brandeis' and 'Judge Mack,' or, after a while, 'Dear Brandeis' and 'Dear Mack.' It was a long time before they relaxed into the comradely 'L.D.B.' and 'J.W.M.' It took still longer before their correspondence included personal references and, finally, messages of affection." Still, from 1915 on, Mack and Brandeis worked closely together on Zionist affairs, and when Mack was selected to head the Zionist Organization of America, he was widely regarded as Brandeis's "Prime Minister."[3]

Ben Cohen, barely twenty-four years old when he left for Paris, had only the most formal association with Justice Brandeis in these early years. Their relationship was limited to businesslike correspondence, largely reports on "political matters" sent by Cohen in Europe to Brandeis in Washington. Even so, Cohen's connection to American

Zionism clearly marked him as a member of the Brandeisian circle, an orbit inhabited not only by Frankfurter and Mack but also by a host of lesser-known figures with whom Cohen would develop close personal and political friendships. Cohen's connection to Brandeis led both contemporaries and historians to assume—incorrectly, as it turns out—that the two men were always in agreement on their approach to politics and social policy.

Brandeis's economic and political philosophy was rooted in a profound distrust of "bigness." Like many progressives, Brandeis regarded the industrial revolution of the late nineteenth century with deep suspicion. Modern economic and political structures—large corporations, trusts, even big government—not only were inefficient but constituted a threat to both democracy and the human spirit. "Half a century ago," wrote Brandeis of the days of his youth, "nearly every American boy could look forward to becoming independent as a farmer or mechanic, in business or professional life; and nearly every American girl might expect to become the wife of such a man. Today most American boys have reason to believe that throughout life they will work in some capacity as employees of others, either in private or public business; and a large percentage of women occupy like positions." The resulting transformations "in the lives of the workers, of the owners and of the general public, are so fundamental and far-reaching," he wrote on another occasion, "as to lead . . . scholars to compare the evolving 'corporate system' with the feudal system; and to lead other men of insight and experience to assert that this 'master institution of civilized life' is committing it to the rule of a plutocracy."[4]

Brandeis applied this essential philosophy to his every endeavor. Early on, for example, he undertook a major overhaul of the American life insurance industry, wresting control from three huge corporations and giving it to savings banks, which were "modest" institutions run by "faithful treasurers" and "obscure but conscientious citizens." In 1910, Brandeis successfully settled a bitter strike by New York garment workers, negotiating a settlement that reduced the power of *both* the union and the management in favor of a system he called industrial self-government. Always, for Brandeis, the emphasis was on the individual: "Our objective is the making of men and women who shall be free—self-respecting members of a democracy—and who shall be worthy of respect."[5]

Brandeis's economic and political ideas found full expression in the

"New Freedom" program of Woodrow Wilson, which Brandeis helped develop and steer through Congress. In essence, the Wilson-Brandeis program aimed to create "regulated competition," specifically by breaking the extraordinary power of corporate trusts. Thus, the Clayton Act of 1914 strengthened and clarified existing antitrust law, while the Federal Trade Commission was created and given broad power to investigate "Big Business" and to enforce compliance with the anti-monopoly regime. But the FTC was also given the power to permit trade agreements when appropriate; the problem for Brandeis was not collusion per se but the use of trade agreements to squeeze out competition.[6]

Never a religious Jew, Brandeis converted to the Zionist cause late in life. "In mediating a settlement of the garment workers' strike in New York City in 1910," wrote Ben Cohen in summarizing the justice's life, "he became conscious of the fact that he was dealing with an immigrant industry consisting mostly of Jews and that he himself was a Jew. . . . A few years later he became deeply interested in and an outstanding champion of the Zionist cause."[7] But there were other forces at work in pushing Brandeis toward Zionism. The future justice's ties to Judaism, though buried under decades of devotion to pure rationalism, were strong. As a child, Brandeis revered and respected his uncle Lewis Dembitz, a lawyer, scholar, and political activist who was also an orthodox Jew (among his many accomplishments, Dembitz was one of the three men who nominated Abraham Lincoln for the presidency in 1860). Brandeis himself attributed his interest in Zionism to a 1910 meeting with the newspaper editor Jacob de Haas, who first made Brandeis aware of his uncle's interest in Zionism.[8]

Whatever the roots of Brandeis's interest in Zionism, however, much of its appeal was purely intellectual. The effort to create a Jewish state in Palestine provided a perfect opportunity for Brandeis to test his theories of political economy and put them into practice. Palestine, as Brandeis conceived it, was to become a new Athens, built on a human scale and dedicated to justice and democracy. That Palestine would be a Jewish state, of course, was hardly irrelevant. "I find Jews possessed of those very qualities which we of the twentieth century seek to develop in our struggle," he told a 1914 Zionist conference: "a deep moral feeling which makes them capable of noble acts; a deep sense of the brotherhood of man; and a high intelligence, the fruit of three thousand years of civilization." The new Palestine was to be a model of economic efficiency, premised on the rejection of bigness—a glorious attempt to re-create the Jeffersonian world of individual craftsmen and farmers that America had long since abandoned.[9]

Yet Brandeis was no Luddite. His approach to reforming society depended on an intimate understanding of the workings of the modern world, and he was more than willing to use modern technology and techniques to achieve his goals. His most lasting contribution to the development of American law was probably the "Brandeis brief," in which he marshaled evidence from economics, sociology, medicine, and other relevant disciplines on behalf of his legal arguments. On and off the Supreme Court he championed social experimentation and innovation. His objection to modernity was not to progress itself, but to a social, economic, and political system that made progress impossible. Nevertheless, his principled opposition to bigness put Brandeis at odds with the dominant trend of nineteenth- and twentieth-century American life.

Ben Cohen, by contrast, did not share Brandeis's fear of bigness or the desire to return to a simpler past, whether real or imagined. Although he occasionally turned to Muncie as a place of refuge and to reconnect with his family, his life was firmly anchored in the excitement of big cities—Chicago, Boston, New York, Washington, Paris, and London. His education at the University of Chicago and at Harvard placed him at the center of modern thinking, and he accepted the integrated nature of modern society as a matter of course. Cohen was not entirely happy with modern American society, and spent the first half of his life working to reform it. But he did not object to bigness in and of itself and in no way sought a return to the past. There was, in other words, not the slightest hint of Jefferson in Ben Cohen's outlook.

Cohen's trip to Paris marked the beginning of two years of intense activity on behalf of Zionism. "In January, 1919, at the request of Justice Brandeis and Judge Julian W. Mack," he wrote years later in an introduction to a book by his friend Julius Simon, "I, then a young lawyer and a novice in the Zionist movement, embarked for London and Paris to help the Zionist leaders present their case at the [Paris] Peace Conference and at the conferences to follow, concerning the Palestine mandate. I was also to serve as a sort of liaison officer between the American and European Zionists."[10] Cohen served faithfully, staying on at the Zionist Office in London after the peace conferences for nearly two years and remaining an active player in Zionist affairs for much of the rest of his life. But in contrast to the experiences of Brandeis, Mack, and Frankfurter, Cohen's involvement with Zionism did not reawaken ancient ties to Judaism, nor did it result from a sense of evolving Jewish identity. Zionism, for Cohen, was less a cause than an assignment, and while he pursued that assignment with characteristic effort and energy, his involvement was more often in the service of other people's dreams than of his own.

In London, Cohen was immediately engaged in the negotiations over the language of the proposed Palestine mandate—an international agreement that authorized Great Britain to administer the territory of Palestine on behalf of the League of Nations. That the peace conference would result in the adoption of such an arrangement was not a matter of absolute certainty, but nearly so. The British position had been articulated in the 1917 Balfour Declaration, which stated that "His Majesty's Government views with favor the establishment in Palestine of a national home for the Jewish people, and will use its best endeavors to facilitate the achievement of this object." In August 1918 President Woodrow Wilson publicly announced his "deep and sincere interest in the reconstructive work [of the Zionists Commission] in Palestine at the instance of the British Government." In September British forces completed their occupation of Palestine, strengthening their claim to act as the mandatory power; and in December President Georges Clemenceau of France privately acceded to the arrangement. The main work of the Zionist delegation in Paris thus revolved around the need to formalize the mandate and to work out its many details.[11]

At least two drafts of the proposed mandate had been prepared before the American delegation arrived on the scene. The first was written by Herbert Samuel, a leading British Zionist and later the first high commissioner of Palestine; a second, based on the Samuel draft, was produced by Julius Simon and others in December 1918. The Simon draft specified that "the High Commissioner should always be a Jew and the principal administrative positions in the Palestinian government [should] be held by Jews." Unfortunately for the Zionists, it soon became apparent that this formulation would not be acceptable to the British government, and that in any event the British were not prepared to discuss the details of the mandate for some time; as Simon put it, such discussions were "a long way off." Thus the Zionists, meeting in January 1919 in London, decided to present to the peace conference not a draft mandate, but merely a brief statement of their cause. This comprised two short paragraphs, both of which were later incorporated with minor changes into the final mandate. The first declared that "the Allied Powers recognize the historical connection of the Jewish people with Palestine and the grounds for reconstructing their National Home in that country." The second asserted that "Palestine shall be placed under such political, administrative and economic conditions as will secure the establishment of the Jewish National Home in Palestine."[12]

Their proposal finalized, the Zionist delegation moved on to Paris, where they were invited to present their case before the Council of Ten, which represented the Allied powers. This was a moment of great symbolic importance, for it gave the Zionist movement a degree of legitimacy never before conferred upon it. In form, the proceedings constituted a request by the Zionist representatives for the inclusion of the Balfour Declaration—or, at least, its essence—into the final peace agreement. Five men spoke, including Chaim Weizmann (but not Cohen, of course, who was merely a junior member of the delegation). The American representative to the council, Secretary of State Robert Lansing, followed with a few questions designed to make it clear that the establishment of a "Jewish National Home" did not equate to an "autonomous Jewish Government," and the Zionists left. There was no formal resolution of the Palestine question, but two days later André Tardieu, the French ambassador to the United States, announced that the major powers had decided in favor of Great Britain as the mandatory power for Palestine.

Although Weizmann described the Zionists' appearance before the council as "a marvelous moment . . . the most triumphant of my life," the proceedings underscored the sharp divisions within the Jewish community over Palestine, as well as continuing tensions between the governments of Great Britain and France on the Palestine question. Sylvain Lévi, who appeared before the council as the representative of France's non-Zionist Alliance Israélite Universelle (and whose views reflected the position of the French government), sounded a discordant note. To the dismay of Weizmann and the other Zionists, Lévi warned of the myriad practical problems attached to the Zionist program for Palestine. But he stopped short of objecting to a British mandate, arguing instead that the Zionists' goals should be scaled back to more reasonable and realistic proportions. Weizmann and his Zionist colleagues were predictably incensed by Lévi's performance, but the speech, like the others presented that day, had little practical effect. Lévi's words merely reflected the French government's grudging acceptance of the British mandate for Palestine.

In these early stages of the peace conference, Cohen was greatly overshadowed by his more well-known colleagues. His role became somewhat more prominent, however, when the conference met a year later in San Remo, Italy, to work out the details of the arrangement for Palestine. Julius Simon gave Cohen high praise for his work: "When the time came to draft the Mandate in earnest," he recalled, "Cohen took over. He worked almost daily with the representatives of the [British] Foreign Office delegated to this task. In spite of his youth, he brought a mature judgment to a difficult problem, firmness in matters of substance, and a conciliatory attitude in form—the capacity to distinguish between the essential and the non-essential." Cohen's specific accomplishments, according to Simon, were many:

> [He] worked hard on the final wording of the Mandate and succeeded in embodying in it . . . the recognition of the Zionist Organization as the "Jewish Agency," for the purpose of advising and cooperating with the Administration in Palestine in . . . "matters as may affect the establishment of the Jewish national home." He also secured in the body of the Mandate the inclusion of the provision that "The administration of Palestine . . . shall facilitate Jewish immigration . . . and shall encourage . . . close settlement by Jews on the land, including state lands and wastelands," and that the administration shall promote "close settlement and intensive cultivation of the land," and "arrange, with the Jewish Agency . . . to construct or operate . . . any public works, services and utilities and develop any of the natural resources of the country." [13]

Cohen did participate in drafting the language of the mandate, but his role in the process—indeed, the role of the Zionists as a whole—can be easily overstated, and it seems likely that Simon's assessment exaggerated Cohen's influence. The Zionists at San Remo functioned essentially as adjuncts of the British Foreign Office; their mutual antagonist was the French government, which (as Lévi's speech in Paris foreshadowed) was willing to allow a British mandate but wanted the Zionist program kept to a modest scale. In this larger game, Cohen and his colleagues mainly watched, worried, and waited.

Cohen's long series of descriptive reports sent home to Justice Brandeis are a virtual catalog of enforced passivity. Even the timing of the decision-making process was out of their hands. "We have been in Paris patiently awaiting the discussions on the boundaries of Palestine," he wrote in January 1920. Both for information on what was happening and as pathway for indirect influence, the Zionists were almost wholly dependent on the British delegation. "Mr. Forbes Adam [of the British Foreign Office] is so kind as to tell us many things in confidence, which we might not otherwise know," Cohen wrote in March. "I shall try to sum up the situation here," he reported from San Remo a few weeks later, "although it is not easy in the present state of uncertainty to distinguish reasonable appraisal from idle speculation." The nature of the Zionists' role at San Remo is neatly captured by Cohen's comment to Brandeis as the conference reached its end. "I have seen," he informed Brandeis on April 25, "but have not as yet been able to secure a copy of what was agreed to."[14]

Because the Zionists had won their victory in principle in 1919, the negotiations leading up to and during the San Remo Conference were less a matter of excitement at what might be gained than a matter of concern as to what might be lost. The French—despite their agreement to a British mandate—now begrudged their ostensible allies the fruits of their victory. "You really can hardly imagine the bitterness of the feeling of the French against the British just now," Cohen wrote Brandeis in February 1920; "it bustles out at all points; it almost seems to be a recrudescence of the repressed memories of their hereditary hostility." The tensions between the French and the British seemed most pronounced in disputes over the boundary line to be drawn between British-controlled Palestine to the south and French-controlled Syria to the north. "The most that the French have been willing to concede on the North is a line starting south of Tyre and running north around Metullah and Baniss," Cohen informed Brandeis in late March. "And the French have not been very generous in their negotiations with the British experts on their bases."[15] The protracted territorial dispute reflected the French government's continued resentment at the overthrow of the 1916 Anglo-French (or Sykes-Picot) Agreement, which regarded Palestine as a part of Syria and placed it under French control.

In late March and early April 1920, on the eve of the San Remo agreement, Cohen and his colleagues were beset by a separate crisis, this one arising out of riots and disturbances by Palestinian Arabs, who constituted the vast majority of the population of the territory. "Foreign Office apparently considerably disturbed [by] reports [of] happenings in Palestine," Cohen cabled on April 1, "and Syria has officially sounded Sokolow as to [the] attitude [of the] Zionists to [the] proposal to substitute for [the] Mandate an agreement between [Emir] Feisal[,]

Zionists and British regarding Zionist rights in Palestine which would involve Feisals suzerainty." Feisal, who had just become king of Syria, had earlier made clear his willingness to exclude Palestine, "in consequence of its universal character," from his call for Arab independence. The main advocate of this alternative to the mandate was the influential Lord Curzon, who four years earlier had expressed strong concerns even about the Balfour Declaration. Curzon, Cohen reported on information from friends in the Foreign Office, "is so oppressed with the difficulties of the Zionist programme that he is unwilling frankly to adopt a Zionist policy for the Empire, satisfying himself with merely an adherence to the Balfour Declaration without particular regard to what may be required for its substantive fulfillment." [16]

Despite Curzon's renewed opposition, the Zionists knew they retained the strong support of Prime Minister Lloyd George, whose opinion mattered the most. "Whatever ideas Mr George may be flirting with," Cohen observed, "his real desire and intentions are, I believe, that the Declaration be faithfully carried out." In any event, "wherever in the past there has been serious conflict between George and Curzon, we are told that George prevails." Still, this new complication was "disheartening," particularly with victory so close at hand. "Although Lord Curzon had never given his formal consent to the Mandate," Cohen observed, "we all thought that it would be acceptable to him, particularly if certain provisions safeguarding alleged Arab rights were inserted out of consideration to Arab feeling." Weizmann, just returning from Palestine, was "greatly over-wrought": "his entire confidence and faith in Great Britain for the time being gone." [17]

As Cohen's friends in the Foreign Office had predicted, Curzon's last-minute attack on the mandate proved to be of little consequence. By May 2, with the Palestine treaty at last in hand, Cohen could report on Curzon with more detachment. "I perhaps should also add that some of my remarks about Lord Curzon written in the excitement of the moment now seem to be rather unfair," he wrote. "He fought honestly and loyally for us in the Supreme Council, and while his matter-of-fact mind may find difficulty in grasping the true purpose of Zionism, I think we shall always find him quite honest and candid in his dealings with us." In the triumphant mood of the moment, Cohen could even be generous to the French. "Further thought as well as further knowledge makes me believe that my report from San Remo as to the attitude of the French was unjust," he wrote in the same letter. "What apparently they were principally concerned with was their protectorate over the

Christian people in Palestine, they feigned official ignorance of the Balfour Declaration not so much out of a desire to oppose at this late date its principle, as out of a desire to have the principle worded in language which would plainly preserve their traditional rights in Palestine."[18]

Cohen's brief assignment in Paris placed him in what the contemporary observer E. J. Dillon called the "temporary capital of the world." To be there during the peace conference, Dillon wrote, was "to occupy a comfortable box in the vastest theater the mind of men has ever conceived." The eclectic mix of delegates and dignitaries from around the world—winners and losers, rich and poor, hopeful and hopeless—created a unique panorama. "Festive banquets, sinful suppers, long-spun-out lunches" were commonplace; the "outer, coarser attributes of luxury abounded in palatial restaurants, hotels, and private mansions." Yet beneath this superficial festivity was a deep sense of weariness. "The people of the armistice were weary and apprehensive," wrote Dillon—"weary of the war, weary of politics, weary of the worn-out framework of existence, and filled with a vague, nameless apprehension of the unknown."[19]

The Zionist delegates in Paris were luckier than most, since from the beginning they could be reasonably confident of a successful outcome. And unlike their Central and Eastern European brethren, the American and English Zionists were relatively unencumbered by the far more uncertain issues surrounding the status of the Jews of Europe. For Ben Cohen, Paris (along with London, to which he returned frequently) was an exciting new world filled with powerful and exotic people and challenging professional experiences. The peace conference was his first exposure to high-level politics and diplomacy, and from the little that is known of his days in Paris, Cohen appears to have enjoyed every minute. "The tone of your letters is so cheerful, the work you are doing so tremendously important," wrote Judge Mack to Cohen in October 1919, "these, with the absence of Felix and the others make it all the more desirable for you to remain on the job. I'm sure you are enjoying it."[20]

Cohen even found time for an active social life. Although he lived "abstemiously," patronizing "economic" eating places, there was much to do, and Cohen developed friendships not only with his Zionist colleagues but also with several members of the American and English delegations. Above all, he found himself in the frequent company of two young women, both at work and after hours. One was the twenty-two-year-old Margery Abrahams, who served as Cohen's secretary in

London and who accompanied him to Paris. The other was the slightly younger, and far more vivacious, Ella Winter, who had just been graduated from the London School of Economics and who served in Paris as secretary to Felix Frankfurter.

That Cohen sought Winter's company is not surprising. She undoubtedly caught the eyes of many men in Paris, including the fifty-three-year-old journalist Lincoln Steffens, whom she later married. "As she went dancing about among the delegates, lobbyists, and correspondents," wrote Steffens, "it seemed to me that she was one of the happiest things I had ever seen." Steffens's description of Winter is not an objective portrait, of course, but she must have made a similar impression on Cohen, whose infatuation was similarly instantaneous and total. "This girl danced," Steffens reported. "Her eyes danced, her mind, her hands, her feet danced as she ran—she literally trotted about on her errands." Steffens's portrait was seconded in more sober terms by Abrahams, who, at least where Cohen was concerned, was her rival: she was "very attractive," Abrahams recalled, "with a fresh pink complexion, though not really beautiful, but she had a ready wit."[21]

Winter met Cohen immediately upon her arrival at the peace conference. It was not an auspicious beginning to their relationship. "In Paris I hastened to Felix's headquarters and found myself talking to Ben Cohen, a tall, slender, trembling young American whose clothes hung insecurely on a diffident frame," she recalled in her autobiography. "His fingers were long and skinny, and his hands didn't know what to do. He had a long nose, straight brown hair brushed slantwise from a broad white forehead above rimless glasses, and a shaking frightened voice. His quivering irresolution was due to a painful shyness." Winter's description of Frankfurter, whom she first saw in Paris three days later, underscores her dismissive view of Cohen. "And now the door opened and Felix rushed in, looked at me a puzzled second, and then held out a warmly welcoming hand. He was as gay and charming as last year, still a coiled spring of energy, ready to bound to the next subject; but for the moment he was concerned with me, giving me his full attention." That attention included Frankfurter's "dazzling smile" and "strong small white teeth"; and "he sat on my desk, like a bird on a telegraph pole, ready to hop away."[22]

Despite this unpromising start, Cohen and Winter spent a considerable amount of time together, enough to give Cohen hope for the future of the relationship. They continued to see each other in London, where Cohen worked for the Zionist Organization of America and

Winter worked at the American embassy. "I saw Ben Cohen often," Winter recalled. "He had become increasingly devoted, but inside myself I was marking time." Whatever relationship Cohen and Winter had ended a short time later, when Steffens returned to London. Winter's rejection of him "hit Cohen hard," according to Felix Frankfurter's sister Stella, who was there. Winter, Frankfurter suggested, had set her mind on "greatness," an ambition fulfilled shortly thereafter when she married the flamboyant Steffens.[23]

Cohen, although twenty-four when he arrived in Paris, was far younger in terms of emotional development, and his brief fling with Winter—however much of it was in his own mind—was by all accounts his first romantic encounter. As such, its impact was undoubtedly magnified. His intellectual talents had catapulted him into the world of the wealthy, famous, and powerful, but, as the Winter episode suggests, he was not one of them. To Stella Frankfurter, and perhaps to Winter as well, "Ben was not made for marriage. . . . His rising inflection kept women off . . . I couldn't imagine anyone being in love with him."[24]

Cohen's infatuation with Winter blinded him to the charms of Abrahams, with whom he would maintain a lifelong, though apparently celibate, friendship. Abrahams had come to the Zionist Office in London directly from Oxford, where she had studied history, and, as she admitted years later, fell in love with Cohen. "It was quite natural when you meet a young man of that caliber, but he had no emotional interest in me." Yet Cohen and Abrahams maintained a long-distance friendship over the years, and Cohen would see her frequently when he traveled to England. Even then, the possibility of a relationship beyond friendship was not entirely unthinkable. The relationship between Cohen and Abrahams, as her daughter recalled it, always retained something of the awkwardness and shyness—and yet the sexual possibilities—of an adolescent friendship.[25]

In 1919 and 1920, in any event, Margery Abrahams's friendship was little consolation for Cohen's unrequited love for Ella Winter. The failure of his first real foray into the world of romance weighed heavily on Cohen during his two years in London and Paris, and contributed to his growing unhappiness—an unhappiness made far more acute by the increasing tensions within the Zionist movement, particularly between Weizmann and Brandeis. By 1921, Cohen was more than happy to return to New York.

What, then, of Mack's reference in October 1919 to the "cheerful" tone of Cohen's letters? One can only speculate, but there is at least cir-

cumstantial evidence to suggest that Cohen's change of mood was related to his relationship with Ella Winter. For it was in the fall of 1919
that Winter's brief acquaintance with Lincoln Steffens blossomed into
love. She "saw much of him" in London, wrote Winter and Granville
Hicks in their co-edited volume of Steffens's letters, "and helped him
to meet the persons he was interested in." When Steffens returned to
Paris in December, "he wrote Ella Winter daily, often two and three
times a day," and she reciprocated. Steffens, who despite his infatuation
with Winter at first professed only friendship—she was "not for me of
course. Too young"—described his letters as forcing "me to clear my
own mind while I was clearing hers, not only on politics, but on how to
choose a husband from among her several suitors in England." Eventually Steffens returned to England, "disapproved of all the other candidates for husband and recommended myself, with reasons, for a while."
Cohen, with all her other suitors, was out of luck.[26]

Cohen's personal misfortune coincided also with his increasing
frustrations at work. His role as "liaison officer" between the American and European Zionists became increasingly delicate as 1920 turned
to 1921. The two groups were united in their general goal of a Jewish
homeland in Palestine under a British mandate. But they disagreed on a
variety of specific policy matters and had very different conceptions of
their Jewish identities and of how Palestine fit into the larger framework
of Jewish culture and life.

The potential for a rift between the Europeans and the Americans
became painfully clear as early as the summer of 1919, when Louis Brandeis came to London to make a report to the Greater Actions Committee of the Zionist Organization. "To the amazement of his listeners,"
reported Julius Simon, Brandeis "urged that immigration [into Pales-
tine] be discouraged until malaria was stamped out and that all available
funds be devoted to this purpose." He also urged the appointment of
Robert Szold (a member of the Brandeis circle, and a relative unknown
outside the United States) as political agent of the Zionist executive in
Palestine. Neither suggestion was outrageous in its own right, but each
pointed toward the fundamental and eventually irreconcilable differences between the Americans and the Europeans.[27]

Brandeis's insistence on the control of malaria reflected his general
view that the Balfour Declaration, once incorporated into the formal
peace treaty in the form of the mandate, marked the end of political Zionism. From that point forward, the key to the development of

Palestine was "decentralisation and the introduction of modern business methods." According to Brandeis, the implementation of the Zionist plan had to be organized by a small and efficient operation based in Palestine, which should be led by the Americans, who had far more experience in both public and business administration. Brandeis also opposed any suggestion of "diaspora nationalism," firmly objecting to the idea that his nationality was anything but American. Both the malaria proposal and the appointment of Szold reflected Brandeis's interest in ordered and measured economic development.

For the Europeans, however, the mandate marked not the end but the beginning of political Zionism. For them, the creation of a Jewish homeland provided the first opportunity in over two thousand years to create a genuine sense of Jewish nationhood. The Jews of Europe, so long dispersed among hostile or at best indifferent nations but never a part of any of them, could become a people once more. Weizmann and his colleagues denounced the Americans as advocating "Zionism without Zion," and called for a "central national effort" to colonize Palestine. The European position is nicely summed up by the advice given by Max Nordau, a Hungarian Jew living in London, to Julius Simon, who was about to embark on a trip to America. "You are going to America and will meet Jacob Schiff," said Nordau. "Try to win him over . . . try to have him and other rich American Jews provide the funds to bring one million Jews to Palestine quickly and to settle them on both sides of the Jordan. One-third may die, one-third may re-emigrate, but we shall have the country."[28]

Brandeis's heavy-handed tactics in 1919 hardly helped matters. At the same meeting at which he appeared before the Actions Committee, the group took up the question of the makeup of the "Jewish Agency," which, under the mandate, would be responsible for working with the British authorities in the administration of Palestine. Brandeis, predictably, wanted to keep control entirely with the Zionist Organization, in which the Americans had and would likely continue to have considerable influence. Weizmann, seeking to use the Jewish Agency as a catalyst for the reaffirmation of Jewish national identity throughout the world, argued for opening the agency to "such other organizations as were willing to participate in building up Palestine," including the Jewish Minority Councils in Eastern Europe.[29] Brandeis, presiding over the Actions Committee meeting, called the question on a motion adopting his position; the vote turned out to be four to four, with numerous abstentions. Brandeis looked around and ordered his associates to find Jacob de Haas, who was not in the room. De Haas arrived, voted in favor, and Brandeis declared the motion carried.

The final break between Brandeis and Weizmann came at the London Zionist Conference of 1920, just months after the formal approval of the mandate at San Remo. Before and during the conference, Brandeis worked with Lord Reading—a prominent British Jew who had served as viceroy of India and was then chief justice of England—to develop a plan for the development of Palestine. The Reading Plan, as it became known, called for the suspension of Zionist congresses for three or four years, and for the establishment of a small executive, comprising seven members, to carry forward the work of the movement. Brandeis kept Weizmann informed of these discussions and, according to Simon, was "under the impression that Weizmann approved of the plan." At the last moment, however, Weizmann called on the other British members of the proposed executive and undermined Brandeis's efforts. Simon, Frankfurter, and Cohen tried to repair the damage, but Brandeis was implacable: "Dr. Weizmann, you are not a man with whom I can work," he announced.[30] The conference ultimately established a small executive consisting of only three members, including Julius Simon, but Brandeis—now repudiating the entire proceeding—refused to agree to the appointment of an American. Relations between the Americans and the Europeans became even worse a few days later, when Brandeis learned that the Zionist Commission in Jerusalem had been forced to use the trust funds of the Joint Distribution Committee to cover a financial imbalance. The justice was outraged, informing Simon that he would no longer send funds to Hadassah through the Zionist Commission or the Zionist Executive, but only directly to the Hadassah office in Jerusalem.

The simmering tensions and then outright hostility between the Americans and the Europeans put Ben Cohen in an impossible position. He was deeply devoted to Mack, who was in turn fiercely loyal to Brandeis, and he fully embraced Brandeis's conception of the future of political Zionism. Cohen's remarks to a reporter at the conclusion of the San Remo conference, for example, might have come from Brandeis himself: "Zionism as a political movement has ended," he remarked. "With the creation of a Jewish national home, its work now is the development of Palestine and the bringing there of Jewish immigrants from Eastern Europe. The development will be largely agricultural. Palestine now has a population of 700,000. In the time of David it had 2,000,000. It can readily support two or three times 700,000."[31]

Yet Cohen was also deeply attached to many of the European Zionists, and especially Weizmann. "He was not only the head of the Zionist Organization but the confidant of Balfour and his government," Cohen recalled. Weizmann's experiments with alcohol were "so advanced, they're only beginning to show effect now—his ideas that power and energy could be used to create food and his dreams of the way to multiply crops in the tropical zone." Weizmann, for his part, took to Cohen as well. As Margery Abrahams recalled, he "relied on Ben and said proudly he [Cohen] was of East European origin."[32] Moreover, Cohen, like many young Americans before and since, quickly developed something of an affinity for Great Britain (even his letters home occasionally incorporated British spellings and mannerisms). Because he was living in London and working with the European Zionists every day, it was also natural for him to develop strong friendships and a deep sympathy with his colleagues there.

When the Brandeis-Weizmann clash turned personal, therefore, Cohen was torn. His political loyalties were to Brandeis, but his personal sympathy was toward Weizmann, who, he believed, had been treated shabbily. "Weizmann was eager to secure and retain the cooperation of American Jewry under Brandeis' leadership," he recalled in his later years. "He probably shared more of Brandeis' ideas than most of his Eastern European colleagues and probably did give Brandeis the impression he was going along with his plan. But if Brandeis had not been so deeply absorbed in his own plan, he might have been more conscious of the inner conflict within Weizmann in sponsoring a plan that would have called upon his old comrades in arms from Eastern Europe to turn over the increasingly important management of the organization to a small group of Western Jews loosely affiliated with, or newcomers to, the Zionist movement."[33]

Cohen, along with Julius Simon and Nehemia de Lieme, sought vainly to bridge the gap between the American and European Zionists. "No one has worked harder the last year to bind forces and feelings together than I have," he wrote Mack in August 1920. But the stress and strain of trying to hold together so fragile a coalition as the Zionist Organization soon began to take their toll, and the difficulty of Cohen's position soon became apparent to others. "I am profoundly anxious about Ben Cohen," wrote Bernard Flexner to Judge Mack in October.

"I came away from London and so did my sister with the very deep conviction that Cohen should be brought home and that a failure to do so might result disastrously. When I urged Cohen, while L.D.B. was still in London, to remain I had no idea how unhappy in mind he was. Otherwise I should have urged that he return either with L.D.B. or with me. . . . As you know, every letter that has come from him either to me, Felix or Szold has confirmed the above impression." Brandeis saw the note and urged Mack to bring Cohen home. "He must be protected from nervous prostration and should not be allowed to delay a day unnecessarily."[34]

Mack agreed, and urged Cohen to return to help in preparations for the upcoming convention of the Zionist Organization of America. But Cohen, unable to choose between his desire to come home and his loyalty to Simon and de Lieme, demurred. "I do not see that I could be of any use at the Convention and I doubt whether I ought to leave here before the Mandate and boundary questions are definitely out of the way." Mack, in turn, did not press the point. "All of us feel that you yourself must decide what you want to do and what you ought to do. The purpose of my original cable was to make you feel that we will welcome any decision that you make. Personally, if you feel that you can do it, I agree with you that you would do better to stay on until the great questions are decided rather than to come here for the convention, and especially for the reasons that you yourself give. But I want you to know if you come to the other conclusion, we should not feel that you are shirking."[35]

Cohen stayed in London throughout the winter and spring. His efforts and sympathies now shifted to Simon and de Lieme, who had accepted positions in the new, smaller executive and who hoped to use those positions, as Simon put it, "to create conditions which would have enabled the Brandeis-Mack group to return to the fold."[36] In January 1921, however, yet another internal dispute — arising, this time, from Weizmann's refusal to support their recommendations on the reorganization of the Zionist efforts in Palestine — led Simon and de Lieme to resign from the executive.

Cohen detailed his views on the growing crisis in a long letter to Judge Mack on January 1, 1921. The villain of the piece was now Weizmann, who had "failed either through weakness or desire to support" Simon and de Lieme "wholeheartedly in their work." The tone of Cohen's rhetoric reveals the depth of his feelings of betrayal by Weizmann. "A house divided against itself cannot stand," he wrote. "It was quite clear to me from the time the agreement was made with the Keren Hayesod group that it could not be regarded as a settlement but was in fact only a manoeuvre in their struggle for control. And they must control or be controlled. There is no half-way course: no compromise short of disaster is possible." On January 7, Cohen continued his narrative: "The situation is grave, very grave. . . . It would in all the circumstances be immoral for Mr. Simon and Mr. De Lieme, to remain upon the Executive under present conditions. Their authority is not respected and is constantly being undermined in one way or another. . . . But in any event it is clear that the issues must be drawn. If Dr. Weizmann and Mr. Sokolow cannot see their way clear to give unqualified support to the standards of Mr. Simon and Mr. De Lieme, then they must choose colleagues with whom they can work without friction. . . . But whatever happens, it is essential that there be an end of checkmating and compromising."[37]

With the Actions Committee preparing to meet in London, Cohen feared the possibility of "a compromise in our internal affairs on the basis of assigning special fields of activity to various members of the Executive or Cabinet. But in one form or another it would be the perpetuation of the old system. . . . It is clear that there can be no compromise on the issue of a small homogeneous Executive."[38]

Completely reversing his position of the previous summer, Cohen now urged Mack to come to London to support Simon and de Lieme and to prevent the negotiation of such a compromise. But Mack urged caution, particularly in view of Weizmann's upcoming visit to North America, and made it clear in any event that practical considerations made it impossible for either he or Brandeis to travel to London in time for the Actions Committee meeting. "Although greatly desirous to confer [I] regret [that] our adequate attendance [at the] February meeting [is] impossible," Mack wrote in a telegram sent on January 16. "[I am] Strongly of [the] opinion [that the] present situation [of the] movement [is] critical and [that the] future [of] Palestine demands immediate composition [of our] differences and agreement upon [a] course enabling immediate raising [of] funds and beginning harmonious work rebuilding Palestine." He concluded by urging Cohen to persuade Simon and de Lieme to withdraw their resignations from the executive.[39]

Given Cohen's agitated state of mind, it is not surprising that he took Mack's telegram as a personal rebuke. Mack had, in effect, rejected all three of Cohen's suggestions—declining to come to London, favoring continued efforts at compromise with Weizmann and his colleagues, and urging the withdrawal of the Simon and de Lieme resignations. Cohen reacted immediately and impulsively. "Tender forthwith my resignation [as] member [of] national executive," he cabled to Mack the following day. "[It is] Impossible for me [to] represent American Executive [any] longer. Your decision in my judgment [is a] grave blow [to the] effective regeneration [of the] movement and a repudiation of all for which we struggled. Fear you have been misled [by] those having no real understanding. . . . [Y]ou may rest assured [that] Simon [and] Delieme [*sic*] will not reconsider resignation. Having repudiated their standards it is now [the] duty [of the] American Executive [to] elect their successors so that there may be no delusion as to what American Zionism stands for."[40]

Mack replied the same day. "Amazed [by] your misunderstanding," he telegraphed. Mack and Brandeis's telegram urging Simon and de Lieme to withdraw their resignations was intended not to undermine their position but to strengthen it; if the leaders of the movement might meet in the United States, a solution might still be worked out. The "time for all resignations," wrote Mack, "is after such hopes [are] defeated." But Cohen was not to be mollified. A withdrawal of the resignations was "inconceivable," he cabled on January 19. It was time for "the views, standards and feelings of American Zionism" to be "authoritatively and unequivocally set forth. And as there has been so much talk over here about division in our ranks, I think our spokesman should come with full power and authority to speak on behalf" of the organization. "I cannot refrain from saying," Cohen concluded, "that I think it was wrong, from your own standpoint, to have urged the withdrawal of the resignations of Mr. Simon and Mr. de Lieme without consulting me."[41]

Cohen had legitimate points of contention with Mack and Brandeis, but the tone of his letters and his deep sense of personal injury seemed, to Mack, disproportionate. "Frankly, I confess I do not understand your misunderstanding about our views and position here or what could have led you to believe that we disagree with you and therefore to tender your resignation," he wrote on February 1. "I further cannot understand your feeling of hurt as indicated by your letter of January 21 just received, at our asking Simon and deL[ieme] directly and not through you, to withhold their resignations."[42]

Cohen had now alienated himself from the Weizmann group and stood in danger of alienating himself from Mack and Brandeis as well. "I had expected from America [a] vigorous stand against political activity [of] irresponsible groups which had made constructive work impossible," he cabled on January 31, "but frankly fear now [that it is] necessary [to] work out arrangements with these groups as [the] attitude of America seems too negative and uninformed to assist actively [in the] constructive movement in international organization against them." But Cohen's personal ties to Mack were too strong, and by the end of February his tone—if not the substance of his position—had lost some of its edge. Moreover, his American friends were aware of his temperament and his talents, and were willing to give him the benefit of the doubt. "My affectionate welcome, Dear Ben," wrote Frankfurter upon Cohen's return to the United States in April. "I *am* glad you are here. Soon you will see your labors in their true perspective. Even now you must know the deep gratitude we all feel."[43]

Cohen's tour of duty in Europe was over. Three months after his return, Brandeis and Mack were ousted from their leadership positions in the Zionist Organization of America by a group more sympathetic to Weizmann; Cohen, along with Frankfurter, Stephen S. Wise, and several others, resigned from the American executive. Three months after that, at the Zionist Congress in Carlsbad, Simon made a last, unsuccessful attempt to steer the movement back in the direction that Mack and Brandeis had advocated. The Mack-Brandeis group then turned its attention to an independent effort to sponsor economic development in Palestine, first through the Palestine Development Council and then through the Palestine Economic Corporation.

Cohen's own assessment of his two years in Europe, which must be pieced together from the responses of his correspondents, was harsh. Brandeis praised Cohen's "service worthy of the cause," and noted Cohen's "entire forgetfulness of self—indeed a constant underevaluation of your own achievement which has been important." Cohen must have expressed a similar sense of self-deprecation to de Lieme, whose response is telling. "I think it is an over-appreciation of yourself to think that I would see your disintegration before your leaving Europe. It is only that you came to a complete and fuller knowledge of your own self. You make discoveries and think that with these discoveries begins your disintegration. You are hopelessly immodest. What you think a new process was always so."[44]

Cohen's last months in London marked a time of personal and professional crisis. For the first time in the documented record, Cohen showed signs of the emotional instability that would eventually develop into a full-fledged state of depression; his agitation and irritability stand out, for the first time, as affecting his professional performance.

But Cohen's self-assessment was not entirely inaccurate. He had succeeded in helping to hammer out the terms of the Palestine mandate,
though precisely what his specific contributions were, no one—not even
Cohen—could know. In his role as liaison between the American and
the European Zionists, however, he could claim nothing but failure.

4

Lawyer and Investor

And so I cannot help thinking that if the materialist is blind to the
beauty and meaning of life, the seeker of the spirit, essence, or
quintessence is apt to find a world empty and bereft of beauty and
of meaning.

—*Cohen to Jane Harris, August 1931*

Cohen returned from London in the spring of 1921 with his personal and professional future once more in doubt. He had no job, no
license to practice law, not even a place to call home. His first step was to
decide whether to return to Chicago, move to New York City, or settle
somewhere else—perhaps Boston or Washington. Ultimately this decision was not difficult; although his family was in Chicago, his friends
and professional associates (with the exception of Felix Frankfurter)
were all in Manhattan. New York would be home—"the only home I
have"—even years later, when he lived and worked in Washington.[1]

With his proven legal talent and unmatched connections, Cohen
had little difficulty finding work. Immediately upon reaching New York,
he was hired by Max Lowenthal to assist in the management of a major
bankruptcy case involving E. F. Drew & Co. Cohen's appointment came
indirectly from Mack, who had named Lowenthal as receiver in the case
in October 1920. His salary also came from Mack, at least in a sense,
since the judge had to approve the fees paid to Lowenthal for his services and expenses. Mack provided for his protégés nicely, approving
some $70,000 in allowances to be paid to Lowenthal for salary and ex-

penses over a period of eighteen months. Cohen received some part of that $70,000 (which was worth ten or more times that amount in today's dollars), although just how much cannot be known.

Despite the financial rewards of the receivership arrangement, its routine work provided little intellectual challenge, and Cohen occupied himself by reprising his earlier role of helping Mack write his judicial opinions, this time "informally and without compensation." Since he was not the lawyer of record in the Drew & Co. case there was still no need for Cohen to take the bar exam, and he put off that chore until 1923—some eight years after graduating from law school. When he was finally admitted to the bar, his professional options expanded greatly. Frankfurter, still indulging his habit of "arranging things," spelled out the alternatives. "I've been thinking much over your next professional step," he wrote. "What kind of thing do you want to do? A 'big office' connection, or business (!) or—what? My own sense of your especial field calls for some connection that would leave you with a little free time for the writing of a book . . . Subject?—any of a dozen."[2]

Cohen, however, chose none of these options, instead taking over the Drew & Co. receivership from Lowenthal, who earlier in the year had married Judge Mack's niece and was thus obliged to give up the job. Cohen was an obvious choice to inherit the position, and with it its generous allowances; there is no reason to think that Mack would have approved less for Cohen than he had for Lowenthal. In any event, it was enough, as Cohen put it later, to allow him "to make some investments," and Cohen became an active player in the booming stock market of the mid-1920s.[3]

In later life Ben Cohen rarely discussed his days on Wall Street, and when he did he routinely played down their significance. The impression he wanted to leave was that his investment activities were merely "marking time between public work." As he told the author Joseph Lash, after the receivership "I became interested in the Securities Market," obtaining "the education necessary to deal with" the stock exchange legislation he would frame during the New Deal. Wall Street, in other words, was merely an interlude. "Embarked on private practice in New York City, Cohen soon became known as an able lawyers' lawyer," wrote Jerome Frank in 1945. "After but eleven years . . . having acquired a competence sufficient to support himself modestly for the rest of his life, Cohen, at the age of thirty-nine, returned to Washington." Cohen himself admitted to being "moderately" successful in the market, although Lash does note that Cohen "invested lucratively in Chrysler Corporation stock, among others, and when a Chrysler automobile came down the street in those years he gave a proprietary chuckle."[4]

Cohen's reluctance to talk about his Wall Street experience stemmed from both personal and political considerations. He was naturally reticent, to be sure, but added to this was the need to protect his reputation as a New Deal reformer; it would hardly have done for the man who was taking on Wall Street to be revealed as a big-time trader himself. But there is an even simpler explanation. The man who in later life was appropriately known as a prudent and savvy investor— who shared his expertise with friends and relatives and who helped manage the portfolio of the Twentieth Century Fund—had been a brash, inexperienced, and overconfident speculator in the 1920s, and he had paid a heavy price.

Cohen's story was hardly unique. The bull market of the 1920s was unprecedented in American history; investors large and small began to assume that all investments were bound to make money, and that the downside risks were all but nonexistent. By 1929 some 1.5 million Americans were investing in stocks and bonds; of these, perhaps half were buying "on the margin"—putting down as little as $10 cash for the purchase of $100 worth of securities. The amount of money owed to brokers for such margin accounts climbed from $1 billion in 1920 to $8.5 billion in early October 1929.

As the bull market hit its stride in 1927 and 1928, investors could watch their fortunes grow steadily, almost literally day by day. Not surprisingly, they continued to pour their savings and whatever part of their income they could afford into the market—often into one or a handful of favored stocks. Cohen, for example, began buying Chrysler on a grand scale in 1926, less than a year after its shares were first listed on the New York exchange. His initial investment of just over $4,000 grew steadily throughout 1927 and 1928 and, at its peak, was worth over $13,000. But Cohen's initial investment was only the beginning: he bought steadily—400 shares in March of 1926, 200 in April, 500 in May and June—at prices that averaged $30 to $40 a share. By the end of the year he owned some 4,300 shares, worth over $180,000. And he kept buying, adding more than 100 shares a week throughout 1927. By the fall of 1927 Cohen had accumulated 8,500 shares, and the price per share had nearly doubled; his portfolio was now worth over half a million dollars. When Chrysler peaked at 140 1/2 in 1928, Cohen owned 11,000 shares, worth more than $1.5 million—a true fortune in the currency of the day. With share prices so high, Cohen could afford his proprietary chuckle when a Chrysler came down the street. He could also afford to live off his investments alone—in 1929, he earned no wage or salary income at all.[5]

But Cohen's wealth, like that of his fellow investors, existed only on paper. His portfolio was dangerously concentrated in one company, and he was heavily in debt, for he too had played the margin, using his Chrysler shares as collateral. Some idea of Cohen's indebtedness can be gathered from his 1929 tax return, on which he reported over $37,000 in interest payments. Using average loan rates for the period, his total indebtedness might have been between $500,000 and $600,000. As long as Chrysler kept increasing in value—or at least did not drop—Cohen's debt was easily manageable (his shares of Chrysler paid dividends of over $33,000 in 1929). When Chrysler began to fall, however, Cohen, like millions of others, faced dreaded and repeated margin calls.

Cohen's troubles began well before the stock market crash of October 1929. Automobile stocks in general, and Chrysler in particular, peaked in 1928 and fell steadily throughout 1929. Cohen began selling on September 24, 1929, presumably to meet margin calls; the share price by then had dropped by more than half, to under $63. By October 15—two weeks before the crash—Chrysler had fallen below $55 a share—about the average price Cohen had paid for his shares. Two weeks later, on the day after the crash, the price was down to $31.81, and Cohen's sell-off began in earnest; he dumped 2,000 shares on October 30 and 31 alone. When Cohen sold his last Chrysler shares on November 6, the price had recovered slightly to $35.06 a share, but he was wiped out. All told, between September 24 and November 6 he sold his entire holding of 11,100 shares, at an average price of $48.01 a share. He thus recovered some $533,000—just about enough to repay his brokers' loans. His entire $1.5 million in Chrysler stock had been reduced to nothing.

The crash left Cohen almost, but not completely, bankrupt. None of his financial records from 1930 or 1931 remain, but his 1932 income tax return suggests modest holdings in stocks, more or less canceled out by still-unpaid broker's loans. By that year, the stock market had fallen to a depth that would have been unimaginable in the glory years of the 1920s. The Dow Jones Industrial Average, which had peaked at 386.10 on September 3, 1929, fell to 41.22 on July 8, 1932—a drop of almost 90 percent (most of that loss came not in 1929, but in 1930 and 1931). Cohen's reported dividends of $2,015.37 in 1932 suggest holdings (at average dividend yields) of around $30,000; his reported interest payments of $690.29 suggest outstanding loans of approximately the same amount. That he was allowed to continue holding stocks on a nearly 100 percent margin suggests the dire conditions for Wall Street brokers in the early Depression. With stock values so low, many were content to allow their customers to carry debt loads that would not have been permitted in the late 1920s. In any event, with interest rates around 2 percent and average dividends over 6 percent, such debts could be easily handled.

Although Cohen remained solvent, he could no longer subsist without a paycheck. The bulk of his income for 1932 came in the form of a $2,217 fee as special master, a temporary judicial post, which more than likely derived from a case before Judge Mack. He also received nearly $700 as an "executor's fee." Even so, money was tight, at least in comparison to the heady days of the mid-1920s. After moving to Washington in 1933, for example, Cohen more than once complained about the difficulty of continuing to maintain his New York apartment; and at one point he put his financial concerns directly to Frankfurter. "I should like to come back home and help the Judge [Mack], who really needs help," Cohen wrote on January 1, 1934. "I also think it would give me more economic security for the future."[6]

Cohen's finances, like those of the rest of the country, improved substantially after 1932. His association with the Roosevelt and Truman administrations provided steady employment for the next twenty years, at an income more than sufficient for a man without family or other obligations. His modest stock holdings, meanwhile, appreciated steadily. The Dow Jones average rebounded substantially after its July 1932 low, more than doubling by the end of May 1933 and tripling by July 1935. By then Cohen was actively investing again, and in time would be able to fall back on the security of a well-padded portfolio.

By the 1950s, Cohen could at last live up to Jerome Frank's description of a man with "a competence sufficient to support himself modestly for the rest of his life." His stock holdings continued to accumulate, and by the end of his life were worth over $3 million. But he never lived extravagantly; money was to be invested, or perhaps given away, but never carelessly spent on himself. How much of this financial caution is attributable to Cohen's brush with financial disaster in the late 1920s and early 1930s is impossible to know, since we know so little of his attitude toward money before 1929. But there is no doubt that Cohen's Wall Street experiences left their mark. When he came to write the major financial legislation of the New Deal, Cohen did not have to look far to understand both the potential and perils of Wall Street.

Cohen's career as a Wall Street trader did not keep him from taking on a variety of public service projects throughout the 1920s. Even when he was not practicing law for remuneration, he busied himself with a variety of work on behalf of progressive causes. Cohen's public service work centered around the activities of his colleague Max Lowenthal and his mentor, Felix Frankfurter.

The details of Cohen's work for Lowenthal remain obscure. It is known that Cohen worked closely with Lowenthal in the late 1920s on behalf of the Amalgamated Bank of New York, which, like many other banks, had been hard-hit by the Depression. The bank had been founded in 1923 by Sidney Hillman, leader of the Amalgamated Clothing Workers of America. The first labor bank in New York State, its purpose was to ensure that "the fullest protection will be afforded the workers in their savings." Sitting on the first board of directors, among others, were Hillman, Fiorello LaGuardia, and Lowenthal. Lowenthal and Hillman had known each other since at least 1920, when Lowenthal assisted Frankfurter with the defense of Hillman in a case arising out of a labor dispute in Rochester, New York. Later, Hillman played an active role in the New Deal and served as co-chair of the wartime Office of Production Management.[7]

The Amalgamated Bank had always adopted a conservative approach in banking matters, placing the safety of the workers' deposits at the top of its list of priorities. With that principle in mind, Lowenthal insisted shortly after the 1929 crash that the bank begin to sell its securities for cash. The conversion of securities put great pressure on the bank's surplus fund, but Lowenthal argued that the surplus was "there solely to protect the depositors' holdings" and should be used for that purpose. Thus the bank survived the Depression; even at the worst point in the national banking crisis it held 99 percent of its assets in cash or its equivalent, and it never delayed payments to depositors. It was "the advice of Max Lowenthal," Hillman said later, "that helped more than anything else to keep our banks open during the Hoover banking collapse."[8]

Working in the background through all this was Ben Cohen. "You know of the devotion, the study, the endless days and nights Mr. Cohen and others gave to the Amalgamated Bank of New York during the last several years of crisis in the banking world," Lowenthal wrote Hillman in 1934, "and the brilliant success that has attended on such efforts—how the Amalgamated Bank has come through sound and secure, despite the fact that it was without those contacts with the great world of finance that the larger institutions had."[9] Exactly what Cohen did is unclear, but even allowing for the exaggerations of a friend, his work must have been significant and substantial.

Cohen's work for Frankfurter is easier to track. By the mid-1920s, Frankfurter had established himself as the nation's foremost advocate of progressive causes, taking over the role played by Louis Brandeis in the days before his elevation to the Supreme Court. Brandeis himself regarded Frankfurter as very much a surrogate, generously providing his protégé with both advice and money. "You have had considerable expense for traveling, telephoning and similar expenses in public matters undertaken at my request or following up on my suggestions & will have more in the future no doubt," Brandeis wrote Frankfurter in 1916. "These expenses should, of course, be borne by me."[10]

Following in Brandeis's footsteps and under his general direction, Frankfurter took on a broad array of progressive causes. He continued Brandeis's work on behalf of laws regulating the conditions of labor, including efforts to establish minimum wage, maximum hours, and child labor laws. He took on the cause of organized labor, fighting against the courts' use of the labor injunction to frustrate collective bargaining. He worked closely with the staff of the *New Republic* to enunciate progressive principles and to expand on progressive arguments. Frankfurter also worked hard, both publicly and behind the scenes, to convince the American people that Nicola Sacco and Bartolomeo Vanzetti—who had been convicted on charges of murder and robbery by the Commonwealth of Massachusetts in 1921—had not received a fair trial. Frankfurter failed—Sacco and Vanzetti were executed in 1927—but his role in the case contributed to his fame and, in retrospect, to the advancement of progressivism.[11]

Until 1923, Cohen's work with Frankfurter was limited mainly to Zionist activities. In that year, however, Frankfurter asked Cohen to assist the National Consumers' League in its efforts to write a minimum wage statute for women that might survive constitutional review by the courts. Frankfurter's motivation in deciding to hand off this assignment to Cohen was at least partly self-serving: he could not abandon the NCL entirely—Brandeis had long supported its efforts, and the justice's sister-in-law was an active member—but he was anxious at the time to avoid direct personal involvement in the league's activities.

It was not that Frankfurter disagreed with the NCL's goals or purposes. Founded in 1892 as "an educational movement . . . to awaken consumers' interest in their responsibility for conditions under which

goods are made and distributed," the league had been effective in lobbying the government for legislation to improve the lives and working
conditions of women, eliminate child labor, and, generally, to ameliorate the suffering of working people.[12] It had had less success in the
courts, which had invalidated a number of progressive laws on constitutional grounds. Frankfurter shared the league's ideals, but he had
difficulty working with its leadership, which included a number of talented and independent women, including Florence Kelley, Molly Dewson, and Josephine Goldmark (Justice Brandeis's sister-in-law). "Frankfurter's attitude toward women in general was quite condescending,"
concludes his biographer H. N. Hirsch. He spoke disparagingly of professional women on more than one occasion, and was particularly dismissive of "the Ladies," as he called Kelley and her colleagues.[13]

The 1923 clash between Kelley and Frankfurter stemmed from the
Supreme Court's decision that year in *Adkins* v. *Children's Hospital*—a
case that was sponsored by the NCL and that Frankfurter himself had
argued before the Court. Speaking for a bare majority of his colleagues,
Justice George Sutherland struck down a District of Columbia statute
establishing a minimum wage for women. Freedom of contract is "the
general rule and restraint the exception," Sutherland proclaimed; the
minimum wage statute was "a naked, arbitrary exercise" of legislative
power, in violation of the due process clause of the Fifth Amendment.
By extension, the due process clause of the Fourteenth Amendment appeared to ban similar legislative efforts by the states.[14]

Adkins left the progressive reformers with two choices: they could
continue to work within the constraints set by the Court, trying somehow to devise a bill that would pass constitutional muster, or they could
abandon the legislative effort altogether and press for a constitutional
amendment. Frankfurter, disappointed with his own failure before the
Court, leaned toward the latter approach. "We have had fifty years
of experiment with the Fourteenth Amendment," he wrote in an unsigned editorial in *The New Republic*, "and the centralizing authority
lodged within the Supreme Court over the domestic affairs of forty-
eight widely different States is an authority which it simply cannot discharge with safety either to itself or the States."[15]

Kelley shared Frankfurter's view that a constitutional amendment
was the only alternative. Frankfurter, however, felt that the league
should confine itself to the less glamorous task of devising a minimum
wage law that would satisfy the courts. "Of course we shall have to deal

somehow or other—whether by constitutional amendment or by reversal of attitude on the part of the Court itself—with the present interpretation placed by the Court upon the due process clauses," he confided to Cohen in June 1923, "but that is a wholly impractical campaign for the Consumers' League to enter upon. My whole tactics [*sic*] has been to get them to concentrate upon things that are within their purview and, still more, within their resources." Left unsaid was the simple fact that Frankfurter did not want to deal with the leadership of the league, and especially Kelley, and he was happy to delegate the task to Cohen. "Thank you a thousand times for all your help in this as always when I call upon you. It is to me an endless satisfaction to work things out with you."[16]

Cohen's assignment from Frankfurter was to draft a statute that would survive a constitutional challenge even under the *Adkins* precedent. From early on, his focal point was an apparent loophole in Justice Sutherland's otherwise hostile opinion. Referring to the District of Columbia statute at issue in that case, Sutherland had written:

> The law takes account of the necessities of only one party to the contract. . . . It compels [the employer] . . . to pay at least the sum fixed in any event, because the employee needs it, but requires *no service of equivalent value* from the employee. It therefore undertakes to solve but one-half of the problem. The other half is the establishment of a corresponding standard of efficiency. . . . To the extent that the sum fixed exceeds the *fair value of the service rendered*, it amounts to a compulsory exaction from the employer for the support of a partially indigent person, for whose condition there rests upon him no peculiar responsibility, and therefore, in effect, arbitrarily shifts to his shoulders a burden which, if it belongs to anybody, belongs to society as a whole.

Sutherland concluded, "A statute requiring an employer to pay in money, to pay the value of the services rendered, even to pay with fair relation to the extent of the benefit obtained from the service, would be understandable. . . . But a statute which prescribes payment without regard to any of these things" is simply "the product of a naked, arbitrary exercise of power."[17]

Cohen thus shifted his attention from the concept of a minimum wage based on the cost of living to a "fair" wage based upon the facts and circumstances of each particular industry. Modeling his draft bill on the standard minimum wage act drawn up by the National Consumers' League and on an existing Massachusetts statute, Cohen proposed

1. Retaining the fact-finding and standard-determining machinery of minimum wage legislation.

2. Substituting a fair wage for a cost-of-living wage, providing, however, that fair wage standards could be established only where existing wages were found to be insufficient to provide the necessary cost of living. It was thought that the fair wage standard might meet the objections of the *Adkins* case to the cost-of-living standard.

3. Providing for enforcement both by publicity and by penalties, but saving the publicity feature in case the penalties were held void.

The basic assumption of the Cohen bill, as Molly Dewson described a later draft, was that "the departments of labor are equipped to do fact finding, and are doing so now, and certainly their statistical departments could analyze employer reports on wages." Armed with these statistical data, the states would be in a position to defend minimum wage statutes as "fair and reasonable." [18]

In choosing this approach, Cohen was following directly in the legal footsteps of Brandeis, who in 1908 had convinced the Court to uphold an Oregon statute setting maximum work for women. Brandeis, too, had begun from an apparently adverse Supreme Court decision—in his case, the 1905 case of *Lochner* v. *New York*, which invalidated a state law limiting bakers to no more than ten hours of work a day or sixty hours a week. Likewise, Brandeis had built on the Court's concession that similar laws might be constitutional if they were demonstrably related to legitimate governmental concerns. Yet while the future justice's famous "Brandeis brief" backed up his legal argument with social science statistics, Cohen went a step further, requiring the state departments of labor to compile statistics that were, in effect, individual and ongoing "Brandeis briefs" for each industry in advance of litigation—indeed, even before they imposed minimum wages in the first place.

The NCL leadership met in June to decide whether to pursue a constitutional amendment or a new statute. Florence Kelley remained staunchly opposed to "further tinkering with legislation," which, ironically, had been Frankfurter's view. But Frankfurter by now had warmed to Cohen's approach, and in any event was still opposed to the League's involvement with a constitutional amendment. Convincing Kelley to support the Cohen bill was now the key task, but it would not be easy. "Mrs. Kelley is a very hard customer, as those of us who have been working with her for years well know," Frankfurter wrote. "The thing to bear in mind is that she has given her life to causes before you and I were born, which at the end of her whole life are largely dust and ashes. Of course, that doesn't mean we should allow her to run away with her own ideas and subscribe to them if we don't believe them. But it does mean that we should patiently keep at it." Frankfurter urged Cohen to arrange a meeting between Kelley and those "most persuasive people with her"—a group that included Julian Mack and Robert Szold. He also suggested that Cohen line up the support of Clara Mortonson Beyer, who served on the District of Columbia wage board. "If she agrees that in practice your present formula will not work differently than the old law did, we will have a powerful recruit for our point of view." [19]

For various reasons, nothing much came of Cohen's first minimum wage bill. The NCL turned its attention instead to the Child Labor Amendment, ratified by Congress in 1924 and designed to reverse the Supreme Court decisions striking down two different federal child labor statutes. As in the case of the minimum wage, Frankfurter and Cohen argued for a statute that would work within the limits set by the Court, but Kelley still "wanted a Constitutional amendment." The proposed amendment was highly controversial, drawing the opposition of numerous powerful interests. Frankfurter and Cohen correctly predicted that the amendment route "would take much time and could not be obtained," and indeed the proposal fell well short of approval by the required three-fourths of the states. [20]

Frankfurter and Cohen were thrust into the controversy over minimum wages yet again in 1928, when the NCL sponsored a new bill—known as the Brereton bill, in honor of its sponsor—in the New York State legislature. Cohen and Frankfurter, who apparently had nothing to do with the bill, immediately opposed it. In broad outline, the bill was similar to Cohen's 1923 draft; it authorized the commissioner of labor to investigate the wages of women and minors in various industries, and, upon finding "a substantial number . . . of women and minors employed in any industry . . . who are not paid a fair equivalent for services rendered," to appoint a committee "to determine, after due hearing, what is a fair wage for experienced and inexperienced women and minors." However, the Brereton bill was fatally flawed, as Cohen and Frankfurter saw it, in providing no penalties beyond the publication of the names of employers who were found to pay substandard wages.[21]

Cohen objected to the Brereton bill for two additional reasons as well. First, as Frankfurter summarized Cohen's views, "appropriate provision ought to be made to limit the bill to those who are exploited below the margin of a fair existence." The problem, as Frankfurter put it to Molly Dewson of the NCL, was that Sutherland's *Adkins* opinion

> didn't mean that any law which provides for the regulation of "fair" compensation would be sustained. . . . One can only hope that legislation assuring "a fair equivalent for services" would be sanctioned by the Supreme Court in those situations where "liberty of contract" would be deemed insufficient to secure a fair equivalent. The purpose of adding some such qualification as "wages insufficient to supply the cost of living, etc." is to indicate that the requirement of public regulation of fairness is made only in cases of workers who are not able to take care of themselves, and as to whom "an unfair wage" is disabling for the attainment of the rudimentary needs of life. I know this sounds awfully meagre to you. . . . But please have in mind not you and me and other wise and good guys, but the gentlemen who are on the Supreme Court of the United States—or at least five of them.[22]

Cohen also objected to the Brereton bill's provision of mere notification, but no hearing, for an employer found to be paying substandard wages. He drafted yet another minimum wage proposal addressing these concerns, but once more no action was taken.

The minimum wage issue at last came to a head in 1932 and 1933, when the National Consumers' League again put the matter at the top of its agenda in several states. By now, clear battle lines had been drawn. On the one side were the lawyers, principally Cohen and Frankfurter, who continued to press for a narrow, carefully drawn statute designed to survive the scrutiny of even a hostile Supreme Court. (Frankfurter, by now, had long abandoned the idea of a constitutional amendment covering this or any other progressive legislation.) On the other were Dewson, Kelley, Goldmark, and Elizabeth Brandeis Raushenbush (the justice's daughter), who were impatient after decades of inaction and who preferred a bolder, more aggressive approach.

In addition to their very real differences in substance, the two groups were divided by temperament. Cohen found "Miss Dewson" in particular to be "extremely difficult to work with," and complained to Frankfurter repeatedly. Frankfurter, now safely removed from the front lines, urged Cohen to look beyond his differences with Dewson. "Of course Josephine Goldmark is a very different story from Molly Dewson, as I realized when I had to take on Dewson as research secretary," he advised Cohen in January 1933. "But after a while you will also appreciate Molly Dewson's qualities. She is really a grand girl and completely devoted and disinterested, has given herself to good works for a good many decades and likes to see results and is naturally at times impatient of what appears the foolishness of people like Sutherland. So please put up with her and don't mind abruptness. She really has a kind and a big heart." A week later, Frankfurter had to repeat himself: "Please have patience with the ladies, trying though they may be," he wrote. "After all, their objectives are your objectives and their disinterestedness is complete. The rest ought to be ironed out through patience and skill in making them see things or in rephrasing." Judging by the surviving correspondence, Cohen was not completely unjustified in accusing Dewson of impatience and abruptness. "Where is your statement as to why the Minimum Wage Bill would be held constitutional?" she demanded on one occasion. "Every day that passes without an answer to this question, is weakening the enthusiasm in Connecticut." But she could also be appreciative. "Thank Heavens you are so angelic," she once wrote, "and are pursuing your drafting with such dispatch."[23]

Matters were at an impasse. "[Frances] Perkins, Dewson . . . and even Goldmark have got it into their heads that the educational processes of the wage boards work too slowly," Cohen complained to Frankfurter. "They therefore want to limit their [the boards'] functions to the establishment of one basic time rate for experienced adult women workers and to leave the rates for minors, learners and apprentices and piece rates entirely to the labor commissioner." Cohen believed "that it is extremely important that the act should be so drawn that it appears to afford the machinery for the self-government of the industry and not the imposition of even just and careful fiats of the labor department." Another point of difference was over whether the act should be "based on the emergency and limited to the period of the emergency," an idea suggested by Elizabeth Brandeis's husband, Paul Raushenbush. "Even this I cannot agree to as I do not believe any very effective results can be obtained until some economic stability has been achieved," Cohen wrote. There were continuing differences over the definition of a "fair" wage, with Cohen putting the emphasis on the value of the services rendered and the others, especially Elizabeth Brandeis Raushenbush, preferring a standard based on the prevailing wage for work of a similar character. "In providing that wages shall be fixed so as to protect the workers from oppressive and unreasonable wages as you define them," Cohen cautioned her, "you require the department to fix a wage that as a matter of law must be a living wage. That I think requires the court squarely to overrule Sutherland's decision." Finally, Cohen and the NCL clashed over whether the bill should include penalties beyond merely the publication of the names of offending employers, and over various administrative provisions in the competing drafts.[24]

Frankfurter sided with Cohen on all the major points, including the "fair wage" standard and the question of allowing the wage boards to set rates for minors, apprentices, learners, and pieceworkers. On January 10, 1933, he so advised Josephine Goldmark. A week later, however, he indicated to Elizabeth Brandeis Raushenbush his willingness to compromise on the rate-setting question. "If your technical experts tell me that adding different minimum fair rates for 'different employments within an occupation' is really an impractical standard and administratively self-defeating," he wrote, "I should join in your judgement and not insist upon it."[25]

Cohen was frustrated and unhappy over the whole affair, which had dragged on for far too long. But he had gained sufficient confidence to stand up to Frankfurter, perhaps for the first time. "You seem to be committed to yielding to . . . [Goldmark and Brandeis's] judgment on taking from the wage boards the power to classify employments within an industry," he wrote.

> It is difficult to be put in the position of "enfant terrible" and stubbornly hang out against the whole gang of you. But that is just my position. . . . If we are trying to frame a "fair value of the service" law to meet with an [*sic*] degree of plausibility Sutherland's view and are not merely betting on the Supreme Court reversing itself, prudence if not necessity dictates drafting the act so as to impress the court that a genuine effort is being made to have regard to the value of the service rendered. . . . Some of the ladies, particular [*sic*] Elizabeth do not believe in the fair wage theory and naturally everything that one tries to put in the act to make it plausible to the court meets with their ob-

jections. . . . Let the ladies decide whether they prefer their law with the sanction of publicity only or our law with the sanction of penalties. I do not think they have a fair chance to get both.

Cohen made the same point to Josephine Goldmark. "If you want a mandatory law you have got to consider the scruples and prejudices of the judicial mind," he wrote. "If you are content with a publicity law, it is a different matter. In that case you can proceed frankly on the cost of living principle, which is what Elizabeth really wants. But if this is too apparent to the court, it will throw out the mandatory clause unless it is prepared expressly to overrule the Adkins decision."[26]

In the end, Elizabeth Brandeis Raushenbush agreed to accept the Cohen-Frankfurter bill and to have it introduced in Pennsylvania. In New York, however, the legislature was persuaded to pass two minimum wage laws, letting Governor Franklin D. Roosevelt decide which one to sign and which one to veto. The two bills were identical except for three points. The first bill—Molly Dewson's—was specifically designed for the emergency, was applied to men as well as women and minors, and provided for enforcement only through the sanction of publicity. The other—Cohen's bill—avoided any reference to the economic emergency, was limited to women and minors, and provided for the sanction of penalties. Governor Roosevelt, undoubtedly guided by Frankfurter, signed Cohen's version. Three years later, Roosevelt—now president of the United States—would see the Supreme Court declare Cohen's law unconstitutional, part of its overall assault on the New Deal.[27]

As the 1920s turned into the 1930s, the Depression began to close in with gathering force. Wall Street, shaken by the 1929 crash, turned from bad to worse. By one index, the stock market reached a peak of 237 in September 1929, fell to 160 by mid-November, struggled back to 190 by April 1930, then collapsed entirely, reaching a low of 46 in March 1933. Banks failed in record numbers—nearly 2,300 in 1930 alone. Unemployment, which stood at only 4 percent in 1929, rose to 9 percent in 1930, 16 percent in 1931, and 25 percent in 1933. Numbers alone cannot tell the whole story; America, so recently riding a crest of unprecedented prosperity, seemed all of a sudden to be crashing down upon itself.

For Ben Cohen, too, a decade that had started out with such promise and that had taken him so far was ending with disappointment. His associations with Mack and Frankfurter had led him to the center of world events, but since his return to the United States in 1921 he had been relegated to little more than a bit part in public affairs, and even that role had brought him mostly frustration and disappointment. He had accumulated a portfolio of considerable size, only to see most of it evaporate overnight. He had no interest in joining a corporate law office or in pursuing a private legal career of any sort and, whether by design or inaction, had forsaken academic employment.

Nor did Cohen express much interest in a job in Washington. Late in 1929, Frankfurter and others suggested Cohen's name to Lewis Meriam of the Interior Department, who was looking for an adviser on Indian problems and legislation. "That he knows nothing, I assume, about Indian affairs or Indian law, is immaterial," Frankfurter wrote in a glowing letter. Cohen resisted the offer, but Frankfurter did not give up. "Despite Cohen's withdrawal suggest you insist on his continuance by giving him a free hand in the selection of his assistant," Frankfurter wired Meriam. Meriam hastened to reassure Cohen on this point, but to no avail. A similar effort by Frankfurter to place Cohen with the Re-construction Finance Corporation—Herbert Hoover's principal anti-Depression agency—also failed. "Cohen doesn't seem interested in the kind of work we are doing," reported Eugene Meyer, who worked at the agency. "He is more interested in the big legal principles than in a great administrative grind."[28]

Cohen's personal life was equally directionless. He remained close to Mack, Lowenthal, Szold, and Frankfurter, although tensions in his relationship with Frankfurter had begun to creep in. Still, all these men were older than he was, and he remained a junior associate. His relation-ship with his family had grown more distant: his father was dead, his mother, brothers, and sisters scattered. He had relatively little contact with his family, save an occasional visit to Muncie.

There was only one person in whom Cohen could confide, and with whom he could claim friendship on an equal basis. Her name was Jane Krohn. Nine years younger than Cohen, Krohn arrived in New York in the early 1920s to study the violin at the Juilliard School of Music. The Macks and the Krohns had known each other in Cincinnati, and it was at Judge Mack's that Cohen and Krohn met. Jane had a sweet face, wavy dark hair, and deeply expressive eyes, and Cohen was immedi-ately taken with her. But Cohen's feelings were not reciprocated, and in 1924 she married Cohen's roommate, Louis Harris, instead. (Har-ris too had studied with Frankfurter, but after the war he had forsaken a legal career and had returned to New York to salvage his family's raincoat-manufacturing business). The new couple took a two-month honeymoon in Palestine, leaving Cohen, once again, to deal with his disappointment. "I think Ben really wanted to be closer to people but just didn't know how," observed Jean Pennypacker, who had known both Cohen and Krohn in the 1920s. "He treated women as equals, never talked down to them. He sent them books."[29]

That she was now Jane Harris did not mean that her relationship with Cohen was over. On the contrary, Cohen and Harris developed a deep emotional bond; Cohen was a frequent guest at the Harris home, and he remained close friends with Lou. After Cohen moved to Washington, he returned to New York frequently, often every weekend, mainly to see Jane and Lou. Jane also traveled frequently to Washington to be with him. They shared an interest in tennis and a passion for books; he longed to share her love of music. He was extremely fond of the Harris children, and especially of Anne, who was chronically ill for much of her life. After Lou's death in 1953, Cohen took on a protective role, both financially and personally, for Jane and the children.

However close his relationship with Jane and her family, though, it was not what Cohen wanted, and as the roaring twenties turned into the Great Depression Cohen's mood sank like the national economy. He had lost his fortune, and his professional accomplishments lagged far behind his promise and potential. Fast approaching his fortieth birthday, Cohen—and the nation—faced, at best, an uncertain future. "This great country of ours surely has hit on evil days," he wrote Frankfurter two weeks before Franklin D. Roosevelt was sworn in as the thirty-second president of the United States. "If one could only do something constructive about it. . . . But it seems that Paul must pay for Peter's sins. I still believe in the efficiency of human effort despite my mistrust in man."[30]

Even in February 1933, Cohen had no plans to go to Washington. He had already rejected at least two efforts to place him in the nation's capital, and he was not yet convinced about the desirability of national solutions to the country's problems. "I am not pleading against the working out of any carefully formulated plan of national action, if such can be worked out," he wrote. "I am pleading against discarding small and useful experimentation in the states. I am pleading for shoes for our soldiers in place of a beautiful and expensive banner. . . . Constitutional difficulties apart, the surrender of all labor legislation and control to the government in Washington might lead to difficulties almost as great as those attending prohibition."[31]

As at other key moments in Cohen's life, however, the decision on what to do next would not rest entirely in his own hands. Frankfurter, for his part, was still intent on "arranging things." And more important, perhaps, Julian Mack was also making discreet inquiries about where to place Cohen in the new administration. The pull of his two mentors, in the end, would prove too strong to resist.

5

Newcomer to Washington
The Securities Act of 1933

I have been working hard. I don't like it. And what's the use.

—*Cohen to Jane Harris, September 7, 1933*

Ben Cohen's role in the New Deal began on December 19, 1932, less than six weeks after the November elections and nearly three months before Franklin Roosevelt became the thirty-second president of the United States. Three days earlier Felix Frankfurter had received a letter from Joseph Eastman, a member of the Interstate Commerce Commission (icc) and a onetime protégé of Louis Brandeis. "I am in need of help on a very important question," wrote Eastman. "Senator Hastings has introduced a bill . . . which amends the bankruptcy act in order to provide a better system for the voluntary reorganization of corporations, including railroad corporations. . . . If you have the time available, I should greatly appreciate it if you would let me know what you think of the Hastings bill, and if you do not approve it what scheme of legislation with respect to receiverships and reorganizations you think ought to be substituted. I find it a very difficult question because there is a great deal of law involved upon which I am very imperfectly informed up to the present time." Frankfurter immediately forwarded Eastman's letter to Cohen, along with a copy of the Hastings bill. "Of course we ought to do a bang-up job for him," Frankfurter wrote. "Of course Max [Lowenthal] is the fellow to do it, and also of course Max is by the laws of nature such a one-case man that certainly at this distance I will not be able to wean him from his present work. So I turn to you and charge you with the public duty of putting your ideas on paper for me and also extracting what help you can from Max."[1]

Lowenthal's expertise on railroad reorganization was widely recognized; his "present work," in fact, was the completion of a book called *The Investor Pays*, a history of the Chicago, Milwaukee & St. Paul bankruptcy proceedings and a general indictment of existing receivership practices in the railroad industry. (Lowenthal did not point out that he himself had been a financial beneficiary of the receivership system in other industries in the early 1920s.) Indeed, Frankfurter's approach to Cohen may have been little more than an indirect approach to Lowenthal, who despite his book deadlines did take an active role in analyzing the Hastings bill. By late January, Frankfurter's letters on railroad reorganization were addressed to "Ben and Max," and Cohen's role was reduced to commenting on and elaborating Lowenthal's points.[2]

Cohen's views on railroad reorganization were not completely his own, therefore, and reflected Lowenthal's strong influence. Still, the Lowenthal-Cohen critique of the Hastings bill (which Frankfurter later adopted as his own) is worth a brief examination. Many of the concerns that emerged during the discussion of railroad reorganization would re-emerge a few months later, when Cohen applied himself to the question of securities reform.

The necessity of saving the nation's railroad system from financial ruin was one point on which the outgoing Hoover administration and the incoming Roosevelt administration agreed. The industry's problems, evident even before the Depression, had deepened into a full-blown crisis by late 1932. As a group, the railroads were heavily in debt, had high labor costs (the result of heavy unionization), and faced mounting competition from the trucking industry and from oil pipelines. Passenger traffic had been unprofitable for years, and government regulation made it difficult for the industry to respond to changing circumstances. Ironically, the depressed state of the railroad industry throughout the 1920s had discouraged speculation in railroad securities, so that railroad stocks were among the least hard-hit by the crash. But the railroads were almost completely dependent for revenue on other businesses, and as the economy declined the industry suffered accordingly. By 1932, revenues were at barely half their 1929 levels, and thirteen railroads entered receivership. Bond and stock prices tumbled, and even the healthiest companies were in serious danger of bankruptcy.

To Roosevelt's preinauguration "brain trust"—led by Columbia professors Raymond Moley and Rexford Tugwell and New York lawyer

Adolph A. Berle—the plight of the railroads was a microcosm of the problems facing American industry as a whole. Put simply, they viewed the railroads as the victims of unbridled competition; the solution to the industry's problem, therefore, was efficient and effective government planning. "It is necessary that each rail service should fit into and be coordinated with other rail services and with other forms of transportation," Roosevelt told a 1932 campaign audience in a speech prepared by Moley and Berle. "We might well . . . survey all of our national transportation needs, determine the most efficient, the most economical means of distribution and substitute a national policy for national lack of planning, and encourage that growth and expansion which are most healthful to the general welfare." As Tugwell put it in a more general context, "competition in most of its forms is wasteful and costly. . . . Unrestricted individual competition is the death, not the life, of trade."[3]

In specific terms Roosevelt recommended that the "consolidation of railroads which are lawful and in the public interest be pressed to a conclusion," and urged that the Interstate Commerce Commission be relieved of its duty to require competition on lines where traffic was insufficient to support more than one carrier. He also called for a restructuring of the laws concerning railroad receiverships, in order to protect holders of securities against "irresponsible or self-interested managers."[4]

But the railroad receivership problem was but one part of the larger problem of corporate reorganizations. The original Hastings bill, introduced in June 1932, was a broad but mild attempt to reform corporate reorganization procedures. Congress took no immediate action on the measure, but after the election Hastings capitalized on a growing sense of concern about the railroads and offered a narrower bill aimed specifically at that industry. His main concern was to streamline and expedite railroad reorganizations, "chiefly by decreasing the opportunities of dissenting security-holders to obstruct" the proceedings. This approach was heartily endorsed by the railroads and their bankers, as it would have made it easy for them to take control of their own reorganizations.[5]

To Cohen and Lowenthal, the ability of the railroads to manage their own bankruptcy proceedings was the main vice of the existing system, a point laid out exhaustively in Lowenthal's soon-to-be-published book. Focusing on the Chicago, Milwaukee, & St. Paul case, Lowenthal detailed the methods used by the railroads to achieve their objectives. The first step was to select a judge "who is most likely to appoint as re-

ceivers the men proposed by the bankers." Then "the bankers' lawyers
. . . find a creditor of the railway to bring a lawsuit against it and ask
as part of that lawsuit that the railway property be taken over by court
receivers. Finding such a "friendly creditor" was not difficult; one of
the railroad attorneys in the Chicago, Milwaukee, & St. Paul case did
so by approaching the leaders of the Binkley Coal Company at his club.
"I went over and saw them both," the lawyer reported, "told them what
I had been asked to ask them, asked them if they would be willing to
act. They wanted to be quite sure that this was what the railroad wanted
done, it was a friendly thing, and not in any way unfriendly. . . . They
said all right, if that was what was wanted, they would be willing to act."[6]

The next step was the creation of bondholder and stockholder protection committees, ostensibly to represent the interests of those who
owned the railroad's securities. But the railroad made sure that representation on these committees was not open to everyone; instead,
"protective committees were formed by certain of the preferred stockholders, and bondholders." In fact, as the Interstate Commerce Commission concluded after an investigation of the Chicago, Milwaukee, &
St. Paul reorganization, "the bankers . . . framed up the committees
favorably to themselves, put themselves on the bondholders' protective
committee and constituted themselves reorganization managers." They
selected the members of the stockholders' committee "for their adver-
tising value in attracting the stockholders to the bankers' program. . . .
They were selected with the idea that the prestige of their names and
positions would insure the success of the committees in securing deposits of stock."[7]

Now the whole incestuous circle was complete. The company,
"forced" into bankruptcy by a friendly creditor controlled by its own
lawyers and bankers, was confronted in court by bondholder and share-
holder committees beholden to the same interest. To make matters
worse, the bankers and lawyers typically arranged things so that all receivership fees would come out of the pockets of the security holders.
Using their extraordinary leverage, the bankers in the Chicago, Milwaukee, & St. Paul case proposed a reorganization plan under which
they would buy up the outstanding securities for 48 cents on the dollar. Security holders who did not agree to this plan would receive nothing. The bankers' plan easily won the approval of the courts and of the
Interstate Commerce Commission . The ICC expressed some concerns
that "we have a situation which is fundamentally unsatisfactory and requires reform," but it yielded to the bankers' concerns about the dan-

ger of delay. Eventually even the United States Supreme Court agreed, although Justices Stone, Brandeis, and Holmes dissented.[8]

Lowenthal and Cohen argued persuasively that the Hastings bill did nothing to change the fundamental dynamics of this system. "Reorganizers under the pressure of economic facts have been obliged to assume very large powers," Lowenthal wrote in a memorandum to Frankfurter. "But with such powers must come rigid safeguards and effective public supervision and control of reorganizations. Controlling groups cannot regard reorganizations as a matter of their own private concern." Lowenthal suggested three main amendments to the Hastings bill, all designed to "make more effective and to increase the powers of the reorganizers and at the same time to impose rigid safeguards to insure their fair exercise." In the main, these recommendations closely tracked Lowenthal's scathing indictment of the Chicago, Milwaukee, & St. Paul proceeding.

First, "the trustees, certainly in the case of railroads, should be permanent public officials, whose appointment does not lie with a particular judge before whom the petition happens to be brought." A special division of the Interstate Commerce Commission created especially for the purpose was best, since, as Cohen put it, "I am afraid of the pulling of strings even in the ICC in the appointment of trustees and even more so in the appointment of counsel." Second, the trustees should be given broad authority. "Reorganization committees today are largely self-constituted," Lowenthal wrote. "But they may often articulate the views of a strong minority rather than the real interests of the creditors as a whole." The trustees would be "guardians of the rights of the great body of creditors"; they would be "authorized to constitute a reorganization committee representing the various classes of interests involved, with one of the trustees as chairman," and would have power to propose a reorganization plan for consideration by the court. Finally, with these guidelines in place there was no reason to follow the approach of the Hastings bill and allow individual creditors to opt out of the reorganization plan. "Such a provision would seem to take away in large measure the advantages hoped from the bill in respect to railroad reorganizations, where liens and mortgages of all kinds abound." Instead, once two-thirds of the creditors had signed onto a plan that was openly and fairly arrived at with the participation of all interested parties, that supermajority would be able to force the minority to participate.[9]

Of these three suggestions, only the last was included in the final version of what became the Railroad Reorganization Act of 1933, also known as Section 77 of the Federal Bankruptcy Act. Even more disappointing, as Lowenthal explained in a November 1933 *Harvard Law Review* article, "Section 77 does not abolish the old procedure. In consequence, if directors, bankers, or lawyers advising or having influence over a railroad board prefer the old procedure, they may arrange for an equity receivership of the old type. Whether they will succeed depends upon the judge to whom they apply"—and the railroads could still go "shopping" for the friendliest judge. The new law did expand the powers of the ICC beyond what Hastings had proposed, but it did not go nearly as far as Cohen and Lowenthal would have liked.[10]

Lowenthal saw little of value in the Railroad Reorganization Act and called for a "thorough-going reform." Cohen, writing to Frankfurter as Congress was putting the finishing touches on the bill, viewed the controversy as the initial skirmish in a much broader struggle for a general reform of corporate reorganizations. "True the initial memorandum that I prepared . . . emphasized the need and possibility of public control primarily in the case of the railroads where the machinery in large measure was actually at hand," he wrote. "This was in a measure tactics in order that our kindling might catch fire. But I did not wish to stop with the kindling. I thought the memorandum on corporate reorganization would start with the provisions for control in the railroad section, indicate . . . that these did not go far enough, and point out that the corporate provisions should contain these provisions in reinforced form."[11]

Cohen's supporting role in the analysis of the Railroad Reorganization Act hardly put him at the center of the emerging Roosevelt administration, but it did draw him inexorably closer to Washington. Once FDR took office on March 4, new legislation was proposed and enacted at such a dizzying pace that his further involvement was all but inevitable.

Roosevelt's inauguration seemed to coincide with the lowest point of the Depression. On his second day in office, the president declared a national banking holiday, a desperate move designed to cope with the near-total collapse of the national banking system (earlier, Roosevelt had spurned an offer by outgoing president Herbert Hoover to act jointly on the problem while Hoover was still in office). Roosevelt then called Congress into special session to pass legislation expanding his authority to deal with the crisis. The new Congress reconvened on March 9 at 12:00 noon; by 8:30 that night the Emergency Banking Act was on the president's desk and ready for his signature.

The banking act marked the beginning of the "First One Hundred Days," a breakneck period of legislative activity designed to deal with the most pressing aspects of the economic crisis. The Economy Act (March 20) slashed the federal budget deficit, at least for the moment; the Civilian Conservation Corps (March 31), Federal Emergency Relief Act (May 12), and National Industrial Recovery Act (June 16) addressed the nation's massive unemployment problem; and the Agricultural Adjustment Act (May 12), Emergency Farm Mortgage Act (May 12), and Farm Credit Act (June 16) tried to deal with the disaster that had struck American agriculture. Finally, the Securities Act of 1933, enacted in June, made an initial stab at reforming the nation's securities markets.

Reform of the securities markets could not have been described as urgent, especially in comparison to the nation's other problems. In symbolic terms, however, securities reform claimed a high priority. Modern economists downplay the link between the crash of 1929 and the broader economic downturn that followed, but to millions of Americans the crash was the precipitating and defining moment of the Great Depression. The evils and excesses of bankers and brokers came to represent the abdication by American business of its fundamental responsibility to serve, rather than exploit, the American people. "There can be only one great principle to guide our course in the coming years," Roosevelt had said in closing his 1932 campaign. "We have learned the lesson that extravagant advantage for the few ultimately depresses the many. . . . We must put behind us the idea that an uncontrolled, unbalanced economy, creating paper profits for a relatively small group, means or ever can mean prosperity." The president put the lesson even more simply in his inaugural address: "The money changers have fled from their high seats in the temple of our civilization." [12]

Because the enactment of securities reform during the First One Hundred Days was driven more by politics than by economics, the administration's first efforts at stock market regulation offered mostly the appearance of action rather than fundamental reform. The president's March 29 message to Congress on stock market regulation, for example, did little more than endorse the principles of honesty and disclosure and proclaim, "Let the seller also beware!" [13] Such ideas were hardly controversial, but they were also of little pressing importance. As one newspaper commented, "For immediate purposes these provisions are of less value than they would have been several years ago." [14]

Ideas for regulating the stock markets had nonetheless been kicking around the fledgling administration since long before Inauguration

Day. The key player during the transition was Sam Untermyer, an old progressive who had been fighting for stock market regulation since the Wilson administration. By January 18, Untermyer had sent a draft bill to Raymond Moley, who played an active part in the early New Deal and who would serve briefly as an assistant secretary of agriculture. The Untermyer proposal was essentially a revised version of his 1914 idea to place regulatory authority over the stock markets in the Post Office Department, and its failure to adapt to the changing realities of Wall Street over two decades made the proposal clearly unacceptable. Thus Roosevelt, without repudiating Untermyer, turned for new ideas to Attorney General Homer Cummings and Secretary of Commerce Daniel C. Roper. They in turn asked Huston Thompson of the Federal Trade Commission to dress up a draft bill that had been prepared earlier within the Commerce Department.[15]

By mid-March, therefore, there were two administration proposals on securities reform. In typical fashion, Roosevelt tried to finesse his way around the problem by suggesting that the two bills dealt with different subjects—Thompson's with the securities themselves and Untermyer's with the securities exchanges—and thus were complementary. Yet despite this rhetoric, Roosevelt was clearly moving away from Untermyer's approach and toward Thompson's, and it was the latter bill that he sent to Congress in late March.

The Thompson bill, however, seemed to please no one. It was, as one historian has written, "a jerry-built structure . . . [which] reflected the confusion that had bedeviled securities legislation since the progressive period."[16] Among those who turned against the bill was Sam Rayburn, chairman of the House Interstate Commerce Committee and one of its original sponsors. Rayburn held hearings in early April and became convinced that Thompson's approach was unworkable. Recognizing the importance of passing some sort of securities regulation early on, Rayburn called on Moley, who in turn went to Felix Frankfurter.

Frankfurter enlisted three lawyers, all with Harvard connections, to draft a new bill: James M. Landis of Harvard Law School; Thomas G. Corcoran, a lawyer then working at the Reconstruction Finance Corporation in Washington; and Cohen, who was an obvious choice to help with the proposed securities legislation. He was well-versed in the field of securities law, both in theory and practice, agreed at least superficially with Frankfurter's political views, and had long ago proved his loyalty and usefulness to his former professor. Cohen, in fact, had been following the progress of the various securities reform proposals even before Frankfurter asked him to get directly involved, apparently preparing a critique of the administration bill in early April for Frankfurter to use "if you should find it possible to appear before the committee or to communicate with the committee, or some of its members."[17] Cohen, however, still had no intention of actually going to work in Washington.

Jim Landis, the second member of Frankfurter's team, was Harvard Law School's first professor of litigation. "I asked Mr. Landis to go with me," Frankfurter explained later, "partly because I knew I needed help on details, partly because I thought it would be very valuable experience for our professor of Litigation." Landis, then thirty-three years old, had spent much of his time and energy since joining the Harvard faculty exploring "the nature and variety of the sanctions available to government to bring about conformance with its statutory mandates and in dealing with the nature of standards capable of reasonable enforcement." A good case study for both issues was state securities regulations, and Landis and his seminar students spent many hours examining their intricacies. A man with "sharp features" and "bright, scowling eyes," Landis was cool, intense, and analytical, but he could also be testy and tactless.[18]

The third man in the troika was Thomas G. Corcoran—"Tommy the Cork," as Roosevelt would call him. Corcoran, too, was a former Frankfurter student, having been graduated from Harvard Law School in 1925. He combined considerable intellectual ability with a gregarious, expansive manner and a knack for winning friends and admirers. Later in the New Deal, Corcoran's wit and charm—as well as his talent for singing Irish songs at the piano—made him a White House favorite. Still later, the same range of talents made him the consummate Washington lobbyist and power broker.

Corcoran stayed at Harvard for an additional year after graduation to study with Frankfurter, then took a yearlong clerkship with Justice Oliver Wendell Holmes. In 1927 he took a position with Cotton & Franklin, one of the most prestigious law firms in New York. At first he was infatuated with the world of Wall Street, working long days but thrilled with the prospect of "messing other peoples' business," as he put it, and with the possibility of winning a fortune for himself. But the crash turned his job to drudgery, and the hard work, long hours, and low compensation began to take their toll. "An epidemic of sickness and furloughs hit the office about the middle of November," he reported in 1931, "and I have been working all night as well as day for what seems an eternity." At last, in 1932, he gave up Wall Street to take advantage of a job offer in Washington. (The final blow from Cotton & Franklin might have been a pay cut, but Corcoran's brief flirtation with Wall Street was pretty much over anyway.) "I am, of course, very happy that you have escaped from the house of bondage," Frankfurter wrote on hearing the news. "I know you will have a very good time and you will be doing very useful work. But just remember that you are an incorrigible romantic—thank God—and that before many months the bloom will have been brushed off the rose and the gold from the butterflies [*sic*] wings. In other words, don't be too disappointed if at the end of a few months you will again find fallible and finite human beings fallible and finite."[19]

Corcoran's new job was with the Reconstruction Finance Corporation (RFC), which was the Hoover administration's front-line agency in the battle to revive the failing economy. Modeled on the old War Finance Corporation, the RFC's mandate was to provide low interest loans to troubled banks, other financial institutions, and railroads (Corcoran called it the "Resurrection" Finance Corporation). By July 1932 the agency had loaned out over $1 billion, but with little apparent effect. An expansion of its powers that summer gave it the authority to make loans for relief, public works, and agricultural credit, but political controversy and economic ineffectiveness continued to take their toll. Though the RFC would eventually play an important role in the New Deal, under Hoover it became a symbol of the administration's willingness to favor large corporations over the ordinary citizen, and of the government's helplessness in the wake of the economic catastrophe. The collapse of the banking system in the final days of the Hoover presidency only underscored the RFC's—and Hoover's—failure.[20]

For Corcoran, however, the RFC opened up a new world of opportunity. He spent his time, as he put it, "untangling the labyrinth of investments that had strangled American bankers after the stock market crash," dealing with "the tough cases that were financially complicated." He enjoyed the Washington atmosphere and was delighted to be back in closer contact with Justice Holmes, whom he continued to see regularly. He was also becoming increasingly useful to Frankfurter, who now had a reliable source of information in the capital. In January 1933, for example, Corcoran provided Frankfurter with a detailed memorandum proposing changes to RFC operations, some of which were incorporated into the Emergency Banking Act of 1933.[21]

Yet despite his connections to Frankfurter, Corcoran at first was not wildly enthusiastic about either Roosevelt or the New Deal. Even so, his practical expertise in the technicalities of legal finance and his growing reputation as one of the best-connected men in Washington made his recruitment by Frankfurter almost automatic. And there was one additional factor that might have influenced Frankfurter to bring Corcoran onto the team: Corcoran's new boss at the RFC was Jesse Jones, a powerful Texan with close ties to the Texas congressional delegation, and especially to Sam Rayburn—who was, of course, the chairman of the House committee that would decide the fate of the securities bill.

The motivating principle of both the Thompson bill and the bill that Cohen, Corcoran, and Landis would write was the same: truth in securities. Both bills required the seller of any security (with specific exceptions) to disclose certain information to prospective buyers, typically through a document known as a prospectus. In this respect both bills echoed the British Companies Act and numerous state "blue sky" laws (so called, it is said, because "one Midwestern legislator . . . declared that if securities legislation were not passed, financial pirates would sell citizens in his state everything *but* the blue sky).[22] In terms of the way this principle was implemented, however, the Thompson bill and the Cohen-Corcoran-Landis bill were as different as night and day.

The British Companies Act, revised in 1929, required only that the seller of securities deposit a copy of the prospectus for any such sale with the registrar of companies on or before the date of the publication of the prospectus. The only duty of the registrar in connection with the prospectus was "to assure himself that it is dated and signed as required. He has no authority to refuse to accept the prospectus because it does not contain the disclosures required by the act." The Thompson bill went further, authorizing the Federal Trade Commission to *revoke* registration if there were defects in the prospectus or if the stock offering was unsound. To Landis and Cohen, such an approach not only amounted to "lock[ing] the barn door after the horse had been stolen," but also "held an incalculable threat over the sellers of securities, so dire and yet so unpredictable that it is doubtful whether responsible investment bankers would have willingly chosen to subject themselves to the possibility of its exercise."[23]

What Cohen, Corcoran, and Landis wanted was a truth in securities law that protected investors yet did not place an undue burden on the issuers of securities. Their bill—like the British Companies Act and in line with Roosevelt's original message—gave no government body the authority to pass on the investment quality of securities, but it did give the FTC the power to suspend registration of any security "if inade-

quate compliance with the stated requirements for disclosure or misrepresentations of fact were found to exist in its registration statement."
The key to the enforcement of the act was that the FTC had to act within
thirty days of being notified of the pending sale of a new security, and
that the security in question could not be sold until the end of that
thirty-day period. Thus the bill in effect required not the registration
of securities put up for sale but rather the "registration of *offerings of
securities*" whose sale was pending. The bill thereby struck a compromise by adding teeth to the British Companies Act without giving the
government the power to rule on the soundness of stock offerings and
without placing the sellers of securities in a kind of legal limbo during
which they could sell securities that might later be found in violation of
disclosure requirements.[24]

There were other differences between the Thompson and the
Cohen-Corcoran-Landis drafts. Thompson's bill placed liability on any
seller of securities who knew of any falsehood in the prospectus, and
on "the persons signing such statement." Such an arrangement pre-
sumed a simple relationship between seller and buyer, with the middle-
man subject to liabilities only if he was aware of falsehoods in the prospectus. As Cohen, Corcoran, and Landis knew well, however, life on
Wall Street was far more complicated. Wall Street was a byzantine and
ever-changing world of underwriters, specialists, distribution syndi-
cates, and noncontrolling holders. Federal controls had to include not
only the formal buyer and seller but also the array of accountants, lawyers, appraisers, and other professionals who were involved in the issuance of securities. Cohen, Corcoran, and Landis were "particularly anxious through the imposition of adequate civil liabilities to assure the
performance by corporate directors and officers of their fiduciary obligations and to impress upon accountants the necessity for independence and a thorough professional approach." "It is right that the directors be held to very rigid standards of responsibility," wrote Elizabeth
Sanford Epstein, who assisted Cohen in early work on the securities bill,
"but if the signer [of the prospectus] exercised the utmost diligence and
had reason for his belief in the truth of the statements, an absolute . . .
liability is scarcely justified." Thus the bill exempted from liability a corporate officer who "had reasonable ground to believe and did believe
that the statements therein were true and that there was no omission to
state a material fact."[25]

Epstein, apparently with Cohen's approval, laid out a variety of
other objections to the Thompson approach. She criticized the bill, for

example, because it did not "clearly and specifically . . . provide that
the income statements and the balance sheets should be prepared in accordance with rules and regulations formulated from time to time by
the administrative authorities"; for failing to require income statements
for more than one year ("Obviously one year's record may be entirely
misleading. . . . Without the proper safeguards such statements can be
meaningless as a source of information"); and for requiring that the
prospectus indicate only the purpose of the issue. ("This is entirely in-
adequate in view of the practice of stating one or two minor purposes
with the general carry-all 'other corporate purposes.' . . . The bill should
require the specific purposes to be stated in so far as known at the time.
Only such a provision will pre[v]ent the abuse of operating utilities
borrowing for the benefit of holding companies without saying so.")[26]
These and other arguments by the Cohen, Corcoran, and Landis team
illustrate their deep appreciation of the realities of life on Wall Street—
an appreciation gained, at least in the case of Cohen and Corcoran, from
firsthand experience.

To complete the process of writing their draft of the securities
bill, Cohen and Landis took a room at the Carlton Hotel, an elegant
establishment a block or so from the White House. The hotel was
popular with visiting businessmen, and Cohen and Landis found themselves sharing the same lodgings as the financier J. P. Morgan, who
had been called to testify before the Senate committee investigating
the financial industry. With Corcoran joining Cohen and Landis in the
evenings, they immediately began working on the securities bill. By
Saturday evening April 8 they had their draft of the bill "in reasonable shape." On Monday, just before Rayburn's committee met to consider the bill, Cohen, Landis, and Frankfurter breakfasted with Huston
Thompson and assured him that the new draft merely provided "per-
fecting" amendments to his original version. To Landis, it appeared that
Thompson "obviously knew his draft was unsatisfactory," but Thompson told FDR's secretary, Marvin McIntyre, that "the 'brain trust crowd'
. . . had ruined my Bill."[27]

Landis and Cohen accompanied Frankfurter to the Rayburn committee hearing on April 10, after which Frankfurter and Rayburn conferred privately. Rayburn then asked Landis and Cohen to continue to
refine the bill with the assistance of Middleton Beaman, the chief legislative draftsman for the House of Representatives, and his assistant,
Allan Perley. This process took ten painstaking days, largely because
the "very persnickety" Beaman, as Frankfurter described him, insisted

on a line-by-line review of the bill before redrafting could even begin.[28] Meanwhile, despite the efforts of Frankfurter and others to delay or scuttle it, the Thompson bill continued to wend its way through the Senate.

The ten-day redrafting process brought Cohen and Landis into open conflict. In part, their disagreements were substantive, centering on how specific the statute should be in detailing what information would be required in the securities registration statement. Cohen advocated a very specific schedule contained in the bill itself; Landis wanted to leave much of this out and trust to the discretion of the Federal Trade Commission. The friction between the two men ran deeper, however. As Frankfurter explained it later, "Jim has again been awkward in handling Ben's sensitiveness. . . . He doesn't seem to take into account the inevitable difficulties in having him, a very much younger man, ask Ben to take a subordinate status." Landis, moreover, thought of himself as the academic expert, and bristled at Cohen's attempt to provide the voice of experience. "Jim's psychology on such matters," wrote Corcoran on a slightly different occasion, "is adamantine resistance lest showing any open-mindedness towards the dictates of experience appear as weakness." Whatever the cause, Cohen disliked such conflicts and sought to escape back to New York. "Teamwork," he wrote Frankfurter, "is impossible."[29] Frankfurter talked Cohen into staying, and left it to Corcoran to smooth relations between his two partners. The strategy worked, at least in the short term, and by April 17 Frankfurter could report to Corcoran that "you must have done—as I assumed you did—a marvelous job with Jim and Ben. For Ben writes me, 'things were a little trying for a while, but I guess we will pull through all right. Tom is a prince and someday will be a king.' "[30]

Cohen and Corcoran forged an instantaneous friendship. Unlike Landis, Corcoran made no attempt to compete with Cohen on an intellectual level—even though (as his Harvard record suggests) he was quite capable of doing so. Instead, he concentrated on lobbying behind the scenes to overcome opposition to the bill in the Treasury Department and elsewhere.[31] But there was undoubtedly a deep, personal attraction between the two men, who became lifelong friends despite later disagreements on political philosophy and principles. It is perhaps worth noting too that Corcoran, unlike all of Cohen's other friends at the time, was younger than Cohen.

Cohen won his substantive argument with Landis, and a specific schedule of disclosure requirements was included in an appendix to the bill, rather than in the main text. This was intended partly as a compromise between Landis and Cohen, but it also reflected Beaman's belief that "it would probably be glossed over by the committee after it had exhausted its patience on the bill itself." Beaman was right; although the House committee and an ad hoc subcommittee insisted on several changes to the original draft, the schedule of required disclosures was never touched. After a five-hour debate, the bill was approved by the House of Representatives on May 5. "Everything moved on schedule," Cohen reported to Landis, who had returned to Cambridge to meet his classes. "The debate was rather dry and much of it off the point, but the votes were there. When it was all over, Rayburn remarked he did not know whether the bill passed so readily because it was so damned good or so damned incomprehensible."[32]

The Thompson bill was approved by the Senate with amendments three days later, and the bills were sent to a conference committee, which met over the next two weeks.[33] The House delegation was led by Rayburn, the Senate delegation by Duncan Fletcher (D-Fla.). Cohen and Landis were there, along with Beaman and Perley. (Corcoran, as usual, was busy during the day at the RFC and could work on the securities bill only at night.) Also present were Ollie Butler and Walter Miller, who had been involved with the preparation of the original Thompson draft. It was immediately apparent that the conference committee would not be able to compromise between the House and Senate bills, but would have to make a choice between them.

From the beginning Rayburn gave the House an enormous advantage. Towering above the other House delegates in power and prestige, Rayburn had been invited by Senator Fletcher to chair the first meeting of the committee. He immediately took charge, asking Fletcher to make a motion as to whether the House or Senate version of the bill should be made the committee's working draft. Fletcher, of course, moved that the Senate bill should be used; Rayburn took a vote, announced that the outcome was a tie (the House voting nay, the Senate aye), and that Fletcher's motion was thereby defeated. Since the committee had rejected the idea of using the Senate bill, Rayburn concluded, the House version would become the working draft. Rayburn's success at manipulating the committee in this fashion reflected not only his own power, but the dynamics of the committee itself. The Senate delegation was divided and distracted with other business; Fletcher was content to leave the leadership of the committee to Rayburn; at least one influential member of the Senate delegation, Hiram Johnson of California, was more concerned with preserving Title II of the Senate bill (which dealt with foreign securities) than with the details of the main section; and another, Carter Glass of Virginia, left the meetings never to return once he realized that the House bill did not conflict with his own banking bill.[34]

Cohen and Landis provided technical assistance to the House negotiators, making several adjustments in the details of the final bill, but the conference was clearly dominated by Rayburn. In the end the conference adopted several changes, the most important of which were the shortening of the waiting period following registration of securities from thirty days to twenty and the elimination of a provision, contained in both the House and Senate versions, "making it a federal crime to sell securities in a state if the sale, apart from its protection under the interstate commerce clause, would be in violation of state law." The conference also watered down Senator Johnson's Title II, which called for the creation of a government body to regulate foreign securities held by Americans. Under a "compromise" fashioned by Landis, Title II was approved with the condition that its provisions would not go into effect until the president determined that they were in the public interest. As a result, American holders of foreign securities were left unprotected by the act until 1939.[35]

"I am afraid it is a little unfortunate for us that the Act passed so nearly as we drafted it," wrote Cohen to Landis when it was all over. "That gives us too much of a parental interest in the darned thing. The rules and regulations and the decisions of the courts have as much chance of satisfying us as the clothes that strangers might choose for our babies." Ironically, Landis himself would soon be appointed as a federal trade commissioner, with responsibilities for the securities industry, and so would be principally responsible for writing those very rules and regulations.[36]

In other respects, however, Cohen was justified in his concern that the act passed too easily. Most important, the skirmish over the Securities Act provided little real experience for Cohen or Corcoran in the ways of Washington politics. The bill was relatively uncontroversial: its central principle had the endorsement of both the president and overwhelming majorities of the House and Senate (all the Republicans on the House delegation signed the conference report, and the Senate Republicans, while not signing, did not publicly object). The business community put up a small struggle but recognized that the Cohen-Corcoran-Landis bill was milder than the Senate version, and their attacks were mild. In any event, whether the Wall Street lobbyists recognized it or not, the House drafters were strongly sympathetic to their interests. When Rayburn, Cohen, and Landis met with representatives of the business community during consideration of the bill, for example, they endured a dressing-down by New York lawyer (and later secretary of state) John Foster Dulles. Then they settled down to listen to his companion's criticism of "certain technical features" of the bill, much of which, Landis admitted, "had merit." As a result of the meeting, Landis and Cohen made "a number of technical changes primarily in the schedules to the bill that had not had a thorough going over by the subcommittee." The extent to which business considered its defeat of the Senate bill to be a substantial victory is reflected in the comments of t.r.b., the liberal political columnist for *The New Republic*. "The bankers and brokers who came down were able to shoot it to pieces," he wrote of the Senate bill. "The administration . . . covered up this instance of ineptitude by asserting that the only feature in which Mr. Roosevelt was really concerned was the publicity feature. To that there was no real opposition. For the rest, the bankers rewrote the bill."[37]

On the House floor, the predominant criticism of the bill was that it did not go far enough, and was in effect too friendly toward business. Several congressmen echoed the views of Ollie Butler, who during committee hearings suggested that the differences between the original Thompson bill and the new Cohen-Corcoran-Landis draft were "clear cut. All arguments in support of the original draft must necessarily favor the investor. All those in support of the new draft must necessarily be to the advantage of the director." One congressman pointed out that the new draft placed enforcement power not in the Treasury Department but in the Federal Trade Commission, "easily one of the most futile of the bureaucratic agencies in Washington."[38]

Besides facing relatively little serious opposition, Cohen and Corcoran had other advantages in 1933 that they would not enjoy in later years. They remained almost completely in the background, where they could function quietly and effectively. They benefited from the leadership of Frankfurter, who wielded considerable influence in the inner circles of the White House. And above all they could rely on Sam Rayburn, who steered their bill masterfully through his House subcommittee and full committee, on the House floor, and in what could have been a difficult conference. Life in Washington would not always be so easy.

All this aside, Cohen had emerged as an indispensable asset both to

Frankfurter and to the New Deal effort to regulate the securities industry. In this sense he was a victim of his own success, for he was not happy in Washington and wanted desperately to return to New York. Part of the problem was that he missed his friends, particularly Jane Harris. "All the way from Washington I travelled to see you," he wrote her in June, "and not a word you send to me. Is that right? And now you go away from New York—far, far away. Is that right?" In October, he complained again. "It is tough to have to be away from New York. How I long to be back—free from all toil and trouble."[39] When Harris, for medical reasons, was ordered to spend some time in quiet solitude, Cohen, for obvious reasons, was sympathetic. "I know it is damnably hard when one is far away from those persons and things one most wants to be near," he wrote, "but one with your wonderful qualities of mind and heart can maintain that spirit of equanimity and serenity which will enable you to regain your strength and your health even through the trying isolation that you are subject to for a period, which I hope will be very brief."[40]

Though his letters to Jane Harris display a broader malaise, for the most part Cohen's complaints had to do with the nature of his work. Frankfurter, through his network, found Cohen two jobs: as a "temporary expert" with the new securities division of the Federal Trade Commission—"to help the Commission get going," as Tommy Corcoran put it, and as general solicitor of the Public Works Administration. (Despite his two positions, Cohen drew but one salary, earning $3000 for roughly half a year at Public Works.) Neither job was particularly suited to Cohen's tastes; his work on the FTC kept him too close to Landis, while at Public Works, as he complained to Frankfurter, "I am as you know without real influence on fundamental policies and I have no hankering for the general run of administrative work." At about the same time, he complained to Harris, "I am not particularly happy with my work in Washington, altho [sic] it keeps me quite busy. I try to handle both Public Works and Securities at the same time and accomplish nothing at either."[41] Despite this self-assessment, Cohen was thought "absolutely invaluable" at the PWA, at least according to Corcoran, and it seems that Cohen found that job preferable to working with Landis at the trade commission.[42]

Part of Cohen's problem at Public Works stemmed from disagreements over how the agency should deal with the massive unemployment problem. Cohen watched with annoyance as key members of the administration debated the agency's long-range goals: on the one side were those who valued public works projects mainly as jobs creation programs; on the other were those who insisted that all such projects provide "lasting work of genuine and permanent value to the country." Cohen, sympathizing with both positions, took a pragmatic approach. In the short term—meaning over the winter—he argued that the compelling need for jobs demanded an immediate make-work program. In the intermediate term (beginning in the spring), the Public Works Administration could afford to be more choosy. Not that the winter work would be completely unproductive; "Useful work during the winter, I am convinced, could be done in very large volume on the railroads for maintenance and equipment and also for much needed grade eliminations." In addition, the PWA could get a head start on long-term housing projects by ordering certain materials immediately, "thus providing work for the winter, although work on the ground could not start before spring."[43]

Roosevelt's answer to the Public Works question was to split off all make-work programs into a new agency, to be headed by Harry Hopkins. Meanwhile, the PWA would focus on more substantial projects. The creation of the new agency made political sense, since it allowed both sides to claim a sort of victory. But the compromise displeased Cohen. "While I am all for doing in a special way and quickly work that can get out this winter," he wrote Frankfurter, "I view with considerable concern the possibility of a large fund . . . being administered through the politic ridden state relief boards upon uneconomic make work schemes." Instead, he proposed again "my pet scheme of grade crossing eliminations," which would create jobs right away while at the same time stimulating trade and industry."[44]

Through all of this Cohen stayed in Washington, urged on by Frankfurter and drawn, for some reason, to Corcoran, who seemed to inspire a respect bordering on awe. Yet Cohen might still have succumbed to the urge to return to New York had it not been for Peggy Dowd, the U.S. Treasury typing-pool secretary who was assigned to Corcoran and who worked late hours with the Cohen-Landis-Corcoran team. Seeing beyond Cohen's political and professional complaints, she recognized his deep loneliness and persuaded Corcoran to find a larger apartment and take in Cohen as a roommate. In late October (or early November), Cohen moved with Corcoran and five other lawyers into an old house in Georgetown.[45] "I think Ben will be a lot happier with us," Corcoran reported, and he took out further insurance against Cohen's departure by "carefully working Elizabeth Sanford"—who had worked closely with Cohen in New York—"into other work in the Treasury so she'll remain here to help keep him." The final ingredient in the recipe was a nudge from Justice Brandeis, and Cohen was persuaded to stay in the capital through the fall and early winter. By year's end, Cohen was still complaining to Frankfurter, though Corcoran believed, or wanted to believe, that Ben was "happier than he writes."[46]

The house where Cohen and Corcoran lived for the next three years was the famous (or infamous) "Little Red House." The house was an antebellum mansion built in 1858; its most famous prior occupant was Gen. Ulysses S. Grant, who had lived there during the Civil War. The living room held an ornate grand piano, which Corcoran put to good and frequent use. Cohen and Corcoran's roommates included a number of young lawyers, including Frank Watson, Merrit Willits, Dick Gugenhime, Ed Burke, and Richard Quay. Each of these men held down regular government jobs during the day but worked nights and weekends on various New Deal projects. Their acknowledged leader was Corcoran, who called them his "little chicks." They shared expenses, which were enormous; "[t]he telephone bills alone," writes Katie Louchheim, "ran to $500.00."[47] (The epithet "Little Red House" was coined in 1934 by Rep. Fred A. Britten [R-Ill.], a staunch conservative and unremitting critic of Roosevelt and the New Deal. The nickname was meant to evoke the image of left-wing radicalism, of course, but it also recalled "The Little Green House" of ill-repute in the Harding Administration. But when reporter Max Stern of the Washington *Times-Herald* paid a call, he found a "group of well-tailored, well-behaved young men harmonizing" at the piano. "He felt let down," writes Louchheim, "to be asked to sing second bass, not to the '*Internationale*' but to 'Git Along Little Doggie.'"[48])

Despite all this, Cohen, on the very first day of 1934, seemed to have made up his mind to jump at the chance of returning to New York for good. His opportunity was a standing offer from Julian Mack to provide assistance on matters concerning the interborough railroad reorganization. "I have been quite concerned that the Judge [Mack] does not seem to regain his usual zeal and alertness," Cohen had written Frankfurter in November. "I don't know that there is anything that can be done or that one should worry about, but still that has been one of the reasons that has made me feel that it might be just as well if I could be in New York to be near him." By New Year's Day, Cohen had added other arguments to his brief. He was concerned about money, his assets having been reduced to a nearly negligible amount. Returning to New York, he wrote

Frankfurter, "would give me more economic security for the future. In Interborough nearly all phases of the economic problem are involved and so I probably could do as much or more from the long range point of view. It is hard to keep up two residences. In Washington I live with Tom and six others. It is pleasant in a way, but Georgetown is too far out when one works every night."[49]

Yet, in the end, Cohen stayed on. Perhaps what kept him in Washington was the looming fight over an extension of the Securities Act to regulate not merely the issuance of new securities but the stock exchanges themselves. "I wish that I could find time to do work on the stock exchange bill," he told Frankfurter in his January 1 letter, "and also to keep more in touch with the work of the [Federal Trade] Commission on the securities act and also to begin the fight for proxy control— which I think lies at the very root of our corporate problem."[50]

More likely, the main reasons Cohen did not leave Washington were his growing friendship with Corcoran and his inability to say no to his mentor, Frankfurter. In any event, Cohen's decision to stay on was only temporary, and he would continue to struggle with his future plans all through 1934. Meanwhile, there was much to be done.

6

Into the Maelstrom
The Securities Exchange Act of 1934

In working on the Truth in Securities Bill and other New Deal
legislation, Tommy Corcoran and Ben Cohen, taken together, made
the brightest man I ever saw.

—*Sam Rayburn*

The Securities Act of 1933 was a quintessential product of the First
One Hundred Days. Far from attempting a fundamental reform of
stock exchange practices, it took only a tentative first step toward federal
regulation. Introduced and passed along with so much other New Deal
legislation, the bill faced only scattered and disorganized opposition,
both inside and outside Congress. Above all, it was cautious in the extreme, going out of its way to avoid a clash with business on fundamental issues. "I get the impression that the better educated offices in New
York are becoming reconciled to the Act," Cohen reported in June 1933.
"I was told today that the head of National City Company even went
so far as to express the opinion privately that the Act was workable."[1]

As 1933 turned into 1934, pressures for a more fundamental reform
increased. The focal point for reform sentiment was a long and involved Senate investigation of abuses on Wall Street, an inquiry that
piled up evidence of corporate greed, recklessness, and impropriety.
Led by a former prosecutor named Ferdinand Pecora, the investigation
created plenty of opportunities for reformers to point out the weak-
nesses and shortcomings of the Securities Act, and to call for a more

thorough treatment. It did not help the Wall Street interests that the Pecora investigation coincided with a stall in the markets' modest recovery from their 1932 low; radical critics of the stock markets were now joined by many businessmen, who feared for their livelihoods. As historian Michael Parrish has written, these businessmen "shared with other Americans a hunger for economic stability, and . . . viewed the exchanges as disruptive, unpredictable organizations which constantly threatened that stability."[2] Even so, the major players on Wall Street remained staunchly opposed to additional federal action.

Although some sort of new legislation was clearly on the way, the Roosevelt administration was deeply divided over how to proceed. The Securities Act of 1933 had ducked several difficult questions—most important, the appropriate level of governmental involvement in regulating the stock exchanges and the relationship between the securities markets and the banking and credit systems. Deciding these questions risked encroaching on the territory of many powerful players, including the leaders of the New York Stock Exchange, the various regional exchanges, key members of Congress, and the Federal Reserve Board. The Securities Act provided little or no guidance on how to deal with these issues, and in fact proved something of a hindrance by creating yet another interested party—namely, the newly empowered Federal Trade Commission.

Wall Street, which had responded only weakly during the debate over the Securities Act of 1933, was far better prepared for this new fight. Led by New York Stock Exchange chairman Richard Whitney, the antiregulation lobby attacked not only the prospect of further regulation, but also the mild reforms already enacted in the Securities Act. When President Roosevelt asked Secretary of Commerce Daniel C. Roper to convene a special committee to examine the 1933 act and propose additional legislation, Whitney jumped at the opportunity to participate, though only to frustrate meaningful change. The Roper committee was unable to reach agreement on the big issues, and in the end produced only a minority report proposing self-regulation by the exchanges under the supervision of a weak and friendly government board.

Wall Street's mounting assault on the Securities Act deeply disturbed Cohen, especially because the financial interests had earlier seemed willing to accept the new regime. "The bankers try by hook and crook to bring [our] securities Act into disrepute," he wrote Jane Harris in September. "And that is the reward for one's effort. It is better to bask in the sun, while the birds sings [sic]." A few weeks later, he told Harris that he would meet with some of her "banking friends," but only "if they are genuinely interested in the workings of the Securities [Act]." "If they only wish to complain about the iniquities of the Act," he warned, "then it would be a waste of their time as well as mine."[3]

While the Roper committee deliberated and Wall Street marshaled its forces, Frankfurter's team went back into action. This time, the initiative came from Ferdinand Pecora and Max Lowenthal, both of whom were now working for Senator Fletcher's Banking Committee. In December 1933, they asked Cohen to draft a new securities bill. The White House, through Raymond Moley, signaled encouragement, although Cohen was apparently unaware that Roosevelt had done so. Cohen asked two younger colleagues to prepare a first draft, then sat down with Corcoran and Landis to finish the job. By the time Congress returned for its 1934 session, the bill was ready.

The Cohen-Corcoran-Landis bill, which formed the basis of the Securities Exchange Act of 1934, had four major purposes. First, it extended the reach of federal law by requiring the registration of *all* listed securities, old as well as new, unless specifically exempted. Second, it sought to reduce or eliminate any "insider advantage," whether based on superior information or on deliberate fraud and deceit. Third, it aimed to rationalize the activities of the stock exchanges by clearly separating basic functions among different players—prohibiting brokers, for example, from serving as dealers or underwriters. Finally, it sought to reduce the degree of speculation in the markets, largely by imposing strict controls on credit. The "broad hope," as Arthur Schlesinger has written, "was that the stock exchanges, properly regulated, would serve thereafter as a place of investment rather than of speculation and gambling."[4]

By far the most important aspect of the bill was the effort to limit speculation, and in fact this concern pervaded all aspects of the bill. Contemporary economists defined speculation as the very opposite of investment (the term "securities" suggests the distinction). Speculation comprised all transactions in low-grade securities, which were securities "of such a nature that the risk of loss to the investor is acknowledged to be relatively large." Speculation-grade securities thus included those issued fraudulently, those issued by new and untested companies, those issued by companies involved in new or untested industries, and those issued by companies in inherently risky industries, such as gold mining or oil drilling. Speculation also included all forms of stock and bond transactions in which the investor's profit (or loss) came not from the underlying value of the security but from gains or losses resulting from short-term factors, such as market frenzies or panics.[5]

Speculation covered a broad range of activities, from the harmful to the beneficial. Investments in new companies and new industries, of course, were generally benign. "We should not go so far as to prevent entirely the marketing of speculative issues," wrote H. G. Moulton, formerly Cohen's economics professor, in 1921. "On the contrary, we must permit the ready financing of new enterprise or become industrially stagnant."[6] At the other extreme were forms of speculation that were actually harmful, the most obvious being examples of outright fraud and deception, direct market manipulation, and sophisticated short-term strategies, of which "selling short" (borrowing securities in the hope of making a profit when the price fell) was the most infamous.

The challenge facing the drafters of the Securities and Exchange Act was to separate legitimate from illegitimate forms of speculation, regulating the former and banning the latter, all the while ensuring that productive economic activities were not stultified. The solution, as Moulton argued in 1921 and undoubtedly in his classes as well, was "to shift risks of starting and financing new enterprises to the classes which can best afford to bear the risks; namely, the larger private investors and capitalists, rather than the rank and file of small investors," and to make the business of *promoting* securities unprofitable. "It should be made impossible for men to float new schemes, take their profits out of the promotion process, and then sell out, leaving the enterprise to work out its own salvation, as best it may."[7]

The various provisions and purposes of the Securities Act of 1934—requiring disclosure, regulating insider trading, separating the functions of underwriting and promotion to the public, and imposing strict controls on credit—were all related to the fundamental goal of eliminating, reducing, or channeling speculation. In part, the drafters of the bill were motivated by a desire to protect the unsophisticated investing public. But reducing speculation was also designed to promote economic stability for the nation as a whole. Excessive speculation in the stock market caused major upheavals in the nation's credit system, weakened the banking system, and destabilized the money supply and the nation's credit. True stock market reform therefore required not only the regulation of the securities markets, but also a more fundamental restructuring of the credit system.

The authors of the bill were explicit about these concerns. Laying the foundation for national regulation under the commerce clause of the Constitution (which gives the federal government control over interstate, rather than local, commerce), they linked the problems of the stock markets to the broader national interest.

> Frequently the prices of securities on such exchanges and markets are susceptible to manipulation and control, and the dissemination of such prices gives rise to excessive speculation, resulting in sudden and unreasonable fluctuations in the prices of securities which (a) cause alternately unreasonable expansions and unreasonable contractions of the volume of credit available for trade, transportation, and industry in interstate commerce, (b) hinder the proper appraisal of securities . . . , and (c) prevent the fair valuation of collateral for bank loans and/or obstruct the effective operation of the national banking system and Federal Reserve System. . . .
>
> National emergencies, which produce widespread unemployment and the dislocation of trade, transportation, and industry, and which burden interstate commerce and adversely affect the general welfare, are precipitated, intensified, and prolonged by manipulation and sudden and unreasonable fluctuations of securities prices and by excessive speculation on such exchanges and markets, and to meet such emergencies the federal government is put to such great expense as to burden the national credit.[8]

The link between the stock exchanges and the national credit system made regulating the exchanges a matter of national concern. In turn, the federal government's central role in policing the credit system (through the Federal Reserve System) provided the key instrument of national control.

The reason for the close connection between the stock markets and the credit system was simple. At virtually every level from investment bank to individual investor, the securities industry was greatly dependent on bank credit. Investors—including Cohen in the 1920s—borrowed heavily from brokers via margin accounts. Brokers, in turn, borrowed money from banks. Investment banks borrowed to provide the funds needed to underwrite new offerings, allowing them to provide their clients with working capital even before all the securities were sold. Without massive amounts of bank credit, the securities industry would have been unable to meet industrial demand for working capital.

The problem with the system was that all of this borrowing was secured only by the value of the securities themselves, which was of course determined by stock market prices. Rising prices allowed for more borrowing and for the sale (and purchase) of new securities. In a boom cycle, stock prices would rise far higher than any true valuation of the underlying assets could justify, allowing all parties to carry an even greater credit load, and further feeding the bull market. All of this was highly remunerative to all concerned, from individual investors to brokers and banks.

Once prices peaked and began to turn down, of course, there was trouble. The first to feel the pinch were individual investors, who, like Cohen in 1929, were forced to cover their margin accounts with additional capital. Investors facing margin calls typically met those demands by selling shares, which further depressed stock prices and led to additional margin calls. Investors who got out quickly lost relatively little. Those who waited too long—until the market crashed—could lose even more than they had originally invested.

The problem was even more serious, albeit less immediate, for the commercial banking system. A drop in stock market prices set off a chain reaction that severely damaged the national economy and, with it, the banks. The banks' first problem was that some debtors—including individual investors, brokers, and even investment banks—were forced to default on their obligations. Worse yet, banks might eventually face a run on deposits, as investors drew down their cash deposits to meet their credit obligations. And a general decline in industrial activity would further damage the banks, which in the end could turn only to the Federal Reserve System and the federal government.

The solution, at least as far as Cohen and his co-authors were concerned, was to limit the credit available to the securities markets and thus force Wall Street and the banks to focus less on speculation and more on solid, conservative investments. Without the fuel provided by easy credit, stock prices would more closely reflect the real assets of the nation instead of rising and falling on the hopes and fears of speculative investors.

The Securities Exchange Act was not inspired by a Brandeisian opposition to "bigness." In fact, the Cohen-Corcoran-Landis approach had the effect of concentrating, rather than decentralizing, corporate power. As margin requirements were tightened, it would become increasingly difficult for small investors to compete effectively; as the market became less volatile, unsophisticated investors would find it a less tempting place to put their money. And although Cohen's original bill required a strict separation of functions among brokers, floor traders, underwriters, and specialists—requirements that might appear to follow the Brandeisian ideal of decentralization—in practice these restrictions made it more difficult for the smaller regional stock markets to compete with their big city counterparts. Cohen and his colleagues were well aware of the centralizing tendencies of the bill, and publicly endorsed them. "As I understand your argument," a member of the House Interstate Commerce Committee asked Tommy Corcoran, "we should tell the little fellow to keep out of the market." "Right," answered Corcoran. "He is not wanted in the market?" the congressman persisted. "Yes, that is right," Corcoran repeated.[9]

Cohen, Corcoran, and Landis incorporated these ideas into their bill with the help of several other Washington lawyers. The initial draft had been prepared by two young lawyers, I. N. P. Stokes and Telford Taylor. This first draft was then read and revised by a range of key figures, including Landis, Corcoran, John Flynn (who worked for Senator Fletcher) and Winfield Riefler (of the Federal Reserve Board). Cohen received the revised draft on February 1, 1934, and worked over the next ten days to put the bill in its final form. Sam Rayburn and Duncan Fletcher introduced the bill in the House and Senate respectively on February 10.

The central provisions of the bill were in place before Cohen began his work. The proposed statute placed administrative control of the securities exchanges in the Federal Trade Commission, which was given broad regulatory authority. In particular, the FTC was required to set minimum requirements for margin accounts and to establish limitations on short sales. All traded securities were subjected to disclosure requirements that paralleled the schedules enacted in the Securities Act of 1933, and exchange members and specialists were limited to trading only on their own accounts or on accounts for which they acted as brokers. The bill also banned various methods of manipulating stock prices, including such arcane devices as pools, wash sales, and matched orders.[10]

Cohen strengthened all these provisions and added more. He spelled out the FTC's broad regulatory powers in greater detail, giving the commission the authority to require financial information on companies whose securities were publicly traded; to prescribe procedures to be followed in the preparation of all accounts and in the valuation of all assets and liabilities; to establish rules governing membership in the exchanges (including the classification of members, uniform rates of commissions, minimum units of trading, and the expulsion and disciplining of members); and to suspend trading in any registered security for up to ninety days. Cohen also gave the commission authority over unregistered (or "over the counter") stocks, and over proxy solicitations.

Even as he increased the FTC's authority in all these areas, Cohen limited the commission's discretion by setting out several key rules directly in the statute. Most important, Sections 6 and 7 of the bill created strict requirements governing credit, for individual traders as well as for brokers. Margin credit was to be available only for trading in listed securities, and only to "which ever is the higher of (1) 80 per centum of the lowest price at which such security has sold during the previous three years; or (2) 40 per centum of the current market price." The FTC could make stricter rules, but it could not relax these requirements. In addition, brokers were required to borrow all funds from a Federal Reserve System member bank and could not accumulate liabilities in excess of ten times their assets. Cohen's bill prohibited all trading for the purpose of "pegging, fixing, or stabilizing the price" of any security without the approval of the FTC, and banned all trading "for the purpose of raising or depressing the price of . . . securities or for the purpose of creating . . . a false or misleading appearance of active trading."[11]

Cohen's draft also went further than its predecessors in restricting the activities of brokers, dealers, underwriters, and specialists. Brokers were banned from functioning as dealers or underwriters. Specialists were prohibited from dealing on their own accounts, and could deal only in fixed price orders. The net result was that exchange membership was limited by definition "to commission brokers who executed orders for the public." (In adding these provisions, Cohen was apparently deferring to the views of his co-drafters, especially Flynn. His own view was that these provisions were "too radical to withstand congressional scrutiny.") In addition, directors, officers, and owners of more than 5 percent of the securities of any company were required to disclose their holdings and issue monthly reports of their trading activities, and they could not make profits on the securities of their own companies if they were held for less than six months.[12]

All these provisions were carefully designed to limit speculation, in all its forms, and thus to tie investment profits more directly to the real value of the companies traded. Detailed disclosure requirements, restrictions on exchange members and underwriters, and the prohibition of various forms of price manipulation would eliminate the unfair advantage held by stock exchange "insiders," who had previously profited from inflated stock prices at the expense of the trading public. At the same time, however, the bill greatly restricted the activities of small traders, who had largely played the market with money borrowed from banks and brokers. The power taken away from inside players was thus transferred not so much to the general public as to those with sufficient amounts of capital, and sufficient long-term resolve, to compete rationally and effectively in the securities markets.

Wall Street lost no time in reacting to the proposed stock exchange legislation, mounting a multipronged assault. Its message was loud and clear: the proposed measure was bad for the stock markets, bad for business, and bad for the country. "[The] National Securities Act is a matter of grave concern to every owner of real estate or securities, to all officials of corporations and banks," ran Richard Whitney's message to brokers. "It is no exaggeration to say that very few of your friends or clients can afford to disregard this new menace to national recovery." In a letter to the heads of corporations whose stock was traded on the New York exchange, Whitney outlined the government's new powers under the bill and concluded, "These powers are so extensive that the Federal Trade Commission might dominate and actually control the management of each listed corporation." What Whitney really wanted to do, according to *Time* magazine, was

> to sit down and have a heart-to-heart with every small businessman in the land. The Stock Exchange president was sure that he had a case which could win countless little fellows over to his side—the man with the small tool factory in Indianapolis, the owner of a little cannery in California, the proprietor of Grand Rapids' biggest department store. Each of these little corporations had stock which was unlisted on any exchange. The Exchange bill, as Mr. Whitney wanted to tell each small businessman, made this stock ineligible as collateral for loans either at banks or brokerage offices. The local corporation might get it[self] listed on some registered exchange but, if so, the corporation officers would be brought directly under the power of the

Federal Trade Commission and would incur all the contingent liabilities provided for in the proposed law.[13]

Arguments like these, which included some justifiable criticisms mixed up with overly pessimistic interpretations of the statutory language and a number of outright misrepresentations, eventually began to take their toll. The opponents of reform succeeded in characterizing the bill as a "very extreme" measure whose ultimate purpose was to ensure that "security markets will cease to exist." As part of their effort to depict the bill as a radical measure, the Wall Street lobby turned their guns on the men who wrote it, including Cohen, Landis, and Corcoran. The bill "is a typical product of the liberal legalities of the New Deal," opined *Time* magazine:

> It was drafted largely by bright young men who know how to get from A to B by glittering legal steps, regardless of the economic consequences. . . . Most of the actual drafting was done by shy Benjamin Victor Cohen of PWA's railway division and Thomas Corcoran, RFC counsel. Lawyer Corcoran used to work in the Manhattan legal firm of Cotton, Franklin, Wright & Gordon. Lawyer Cohen is a protégé of Felix Frankfurter. Both are young, brilliant, determined. Both live with a half-dozen other New Dealers in "Bachelor Hall," a large, comfortable house in Georgetown. . . . Lawyers Cohen and Corcoran are typical of the host of radical young lawyers in Washington who keep well in the background while they fabricate the advanced measures Congress is supposed to pass without reading.[14]

As the attacks continued, the authors of the securities bill were treated as exhibit number one in what became, in its most extreme form, a general campaign to link the New Deal to a "communistic plot" to bring about "a social and economic revolution in America." In the midst of the House hearings, opponents of the bill produced a book, written by a school superintendent from Indiana named William Wirt, that purported to provide evidence of just such a plot, led by unnamed "brain trusters." A special investigation ensued, and the conspiracy theory collapsed. But the idea that the New Deal was the product of radical thinking was slow to die out. This was the point at which "Bachelor Hall" became the "Little Red House in Georgetown," while Cohen and Corcoran themselves became "the scarlet fever boys." Cohen, as a Jew, was particularly vulnerable; as the campaign against the measure faltered, for example, Whitney declared that the authors of the bill were "a bunch of Jews out to get [J. P.] Morgan."[15]

These charges of radicalism seemed to puzzle Cohen. "It has been a strange fight for me to be mixed up in," he confided to Frankfurter in May. "[L]ike a man being chased from behind with a pitch fork[,] I have had to keep on." Cohen was particularly distressed by the vitriol heaped on Tommy Corcoran. "Poor Tom has had to bear much more than his fair share of the battle," he wrote in the same letter to Frankfurter. "Because of his sheer ability as well as his brilliant fluency and superb advocacy, I have left him to bear the brunt of the attack. And because of his strength he has been the more feared by far of the two [of] us. The result is that attempts are made to poison people's minds against him. The most hostile members of the house committee, for example, talk against him, pretend to dislike him in particular and at times even to express relative confidence in me—a doubtful compliment indeed." Then Cohen turned to words that perhaps reflected as much his own feelings as Corcoran's: "Of course, Tom understands it all, but still he is a very tender and sensitive soul, much more so than his usual cheerful mien would lead one to believe. And he has been dreadfully alone in the battle. Because of his strength, few people realize that even he may be a bit disheartened and discouraged at times."[16]

Not all Cohen and Corcoran's newfound publicity was negative, of course. Corcoran testified before both the House and Senate committees, putting on an impressive show while lavishing praise on Cohen, who sat silently beside him. "I do not pretend to know as much about [the stock exchange bill] as Mr. Cohen," said Corcoran at one point, "who took charge of the actual drafts of drawing up the measure." Much positive publicity came from liberals who regarded Cohen and Corcoran as their new champions. The most vocal spokesman for this group was Flynn, who besides his job on the Senate Banking Committee staff was the financial columnist for *The New Republic* magazine and a freelance writer on economic matters. In a long article in *Harper's*, published after the Securities Exchange Act was finally adopted, Flynn proclaimed that "the marines . . . have landed in Wall Street" to do "battle in a fifty-years war" against an enemy that is "powerful, rich, vigilant, unscrupulous, and plays for vast stakes." Of the marines, Flynn singled out Cohen for doing "the actual writing" of the first version, which he called "a tremendously effective measure," and for rescuing the final bill from those who had tried to weaken it beyond recognition. "An abler example of legislative writing has never made its way into the statute books," he concluded. Cohen basked in the publicity of Flynn's article, even if it did overstate his radical tendencies. "Flynn," he wrote to Jane Harris, "pays me some very high, if undeserved, compliments."[17]

Cohen and Corcoran's unaccustomed high profile discomfited Felix Frankfurter, causing the first open strains in the relationship between the younger men and their mentor. Part of the problem was that Frankfurter was away in Oxford for academic year 1933–34 and had begun to realize that much could be, and indeed was being, accomplished in his absence. His consolation had been the knowledge that the Cohen-Corcoran-Landis "unit" was keeping him fully informed and was operating under his personal generalship, with Corcoran as field commander. But the frenzy of the stock market fight, the rapidly shifting battle lines, and the growing sophistication of the troops in Washington made this arrangement little more than wishful thinking by the spring of 1934. "Much has gone over the dam since you went away and affairs have proceeded pretty far toward concrete forks in the road," wrote Cohen and Corcoran in June. "You'll need, we should think, considerable detailed knowledge of what has gone on just to listen understandingly."[18]

Even as Cohen and Corcoran reassured Frankfurter of how badly they needed him, the subtle reversal of roles could not be missed: now it was Cohen and Corcoran who were dispensing the advice and Frankfurter who was taking it. "Tom has placed the situation regarding your return very fairly," wrote Cohen in May. "It is difficult to urge you too strongly knowing your desire to grasp the opportunity of your European contacts—an opportunity that does not come every year or even every ten, particularly when one cannot underwrite what can be accomplished by your return, but there is no question of the need of real direction, real understanding, and some real personal force over here. The men attached to you are working hard, but their spirits are a little low and their consciousness of any coherent program is somewhat dulled." When Frankfurter sent along his congratulations on the final passage of the stock exchange bill, Cohen and Corcoran's response took on a slight air of condescension. "Your Stock Exchange congratulations are premature," they wrote. "Wait until we see the makeup of the Commission."[19]

Cohen and Corcoran's growing self-confidence fueled in Frankfurter a fierce resentment, which he expressed in repeated put-downs of Cohen and Corcoran and constant reminders that he was the master and they the disciples. "I'm pleased that B.V.C. is again staying," he wrote after Cohen threatened once more to leave Washington. "Dear, dear, dear—what children." In May, Frankfurter addressed a letter to his "Dear Little Boys," prompted, it seems, by a presidential invitation to Corcoran to come to the White House to entertain on the piano:

> Of course you have been having a good time, but it has been so good that even the newspapers write about it, and I am glad to learn that it is not a one-sided good time, that you don't overdo the brain but realize the importance of letting the mind rest and working your fingers, even if it's only the exercise that comes from tickling the piano. Do I infer that you have been giving public concerts and that you have been letting anybody listen to you, even silly men who don't know that young as you are, so very very young, you have somehow or other managed to snatch wisdom that the old haven't got. And those must be marvelous revels by night in a little red house they tell me about, and I am particularly excited by your strange ways of sleeping in that little red house every night. That's awfully funny, for I suppose when men get to be old and wise they don't sleep every night, or at least not every night in the same bed. And what darling children you must be to have wormed your way not only into the heart but even into the mind and will of the President of the United States, so that he says what you tell him to say and he does what you tell him to do. That must be very wonderful, to get a wonderful man like that to have so much confidence in you, little children that you are, that he lets you think for him and even act for him. . . .
>
> Well, . . . I am so glad that you are having such a good time. For while I know it's usually bad for little children, whether they are piano players or draftsmen, to get too much public attention when they are very, very young, I know that you're such hard-headed little youngsters that there isn't the slightest danger of all this public acclaim of your juvenile games and performances either spoiling you or making life as it gets duller when you grow up seem too dull when compared with your gay childhood. I only wish I were a little boy or at least young enough to share a little bit in all your games.
>
> Your old friend,
> FF[20]

Frankfurter, as he wrote these words, had attained the ripe old age of fifty-two. As for his little boys, Corcoran was now thirty-three, while Cohen was only four months shy of his fortieth birthday.

While Frankfurter fumed in Oxford, Cohen, Corcoran, and Landis tried to cope with Wall Street's increasingly successful attempt to portray the proposed stock exchange legislation and its authors as dangerously radical. Eventually they were forced to make changes in the bill, and, after eight days of negotiation in March with representatives from the Treasury and the Federal Reserve Board, they produced a revised version. The new bill divided the responsibility for administering the act between the FTC and the Federal Reserve Board, giving both agencies far more discretion and flexibility. Margin requirements were eased to allow brokers to lend up to 100 percent of the lowest price of the security over the preceding thirty-six months, but not more than 75 percent of the current market price. The Federal Reserve Board was given the power to ease these requirements, but only in "extraordinary circumstances" and when "vitally essential to the accommodation of commerce and industry." Moreover, the FTC was given the authority to permit exchange members to trade on their own account when it was "not in the public interest to deny access to the trading premises" for such purposes. Other specific provisions of the first bill were similarly revised to allow for a more flexible administration.[21]

Predictably, these revisions did not satisfy Richard Whitney, who with his Wall Street colleagues continued to fight against the bill. The new bill still aimed at a restriction of credit, after all, and made no effort to move toward allowing the exchanges to regulate themselves. "I do not believe that the use of credit in connection with forward commitments, whether in the purchase of securities, of commodities or of homes, or in the sowing of crops in the expectation of harvest can be otherwise than beneficial when wisely and reasonably employed," Whitney told the Senate Banking Committee in April. "I am not in accord with the provisions of this bill which seem designed to punish stock exchanges for imaginary offenses, nor am I in accord with those provisions which would throttle industry, contract credit, diminish the liquidity of securities and postpone the return of prosperity." But even those who disliked the revised bill seemed to be moving toward acceptance of the need for some sort of stock exchange legislation, especially after Roosevelt himself reiterated the need for legislation "which has teeth in it." Still, as *The New Republic's* T.R.B. remarked, the president "by no means wants the complete dental equipment with which it [the bill] was born."[22]

The need for further concessions to Wall Street led Sam Rayburn to call for additional revisions to the bill in late March. As a result, the bill was weakened still further, with the FTC and the Federal Reserve Board being given even wider latitude. When the House Interstate Commerce Committee continued to object, Rayburn appointed a subcommittee to complete further revisions. The subcommittee returned in mid-April with a bill containing yet weaker margin requirements, with almost complete discretion accorded to the Federal Reserve Board; greatly reduced reporting requirements; and the elimination of all statutory rules governing the solicitation of proxies.[23]

At the same time, the bill also ran into opposition in the Senate. The reformers' chief antagonist was Sen. Carter Glass (D-Va.), who viewed the nation's banking system as something of a personal fiefdom. Glass seemed not to recognize the intimate if indirect connection between the securities market and the credit system, and wanted "to prevent the Federal Reserve Board from being mixed up with stock gambling." His proposed solution was the elimination of all broker's loans. He also proposed the creation of a brand new, specialized commission to regulate the markets, an idea that found favor with many businessmen.[24]

Glass's proposed credit restrictions would have been a disaster for Wall Street, and also for the Federal Reserve, which was by now committed to playing some sort of role in securities regulation. But his suggestion of a new commission—which eventually came to be known as the Securities and Exchange Commission (SEC)—soon found favor. In the end the Senate accepted an awkward compromise that divided credit control between the Federal Reserve Board and the new commission, with the Fed exercising control over credit issued by banks to brokers and the SEC supervising loans from brokers to customers. With that, the Senate agreed to the bill.

There were still several differences between the House and Senate versions of the proposed law, necessitating the appointment of a conference committee in mid-May. Three major issues were left to be resolved. First, the conference had to decide between vesting regulatory authority in the FTC (as in the House bill) or in a new securities commission (as in the Senate version). Second, the House bill still contained specific (though weakened) margin requirements, while the Senate bill left all such issues to administrative discretion. Finally, the House bill placed all control over credit matters with the Federal Reserve Board, while the Senate bill offered the Banking Committee's awkward compromise arrangement.

Once again the president entered the picture, although this time he managed mainly to add to the confusion. First, Roosevelt told Senator Glass that he favored the Senate version of the bill. Then, after considerable lobbying by Landis, he turned back to the House version. A week later, Roosevelt switched course again, accepting a Raymond Moley–orchestrated compromise that split the difference between the House and Senate bills. Glass and the Senate were given their separate commission, while the House conferees insisted on specified margin ratios and on giving control over credit to the Federal Reserve Board. With these issues resolved, it was easy to settle a variety of smaller differences, and the bill was agreed to. The president signed the Securities Exchange Act of 1934 into law on June 6.

There is some question about Cohen's role and attitude during these protracted negotiations, and, more generally, about how well he had learned to navigate in the treacherous waters of Washington politics. Michael Parrish, in his careful account of the origins of the Securities Exchange Act, depicts Cohen as a hard-liner, opposing all attempts to weaken the act. Parrish suggests, for example, that Cohen "had opposed the administrative shift" in the bill that came about during the late-March negotiations between the drafting team and representatives from the Federal Reserve, the Treasury, and the New York brokerage houses. According to Parrish, Cohen regarded the Federal Reserve Board as "a captive of current financial folklore, and too respectful of Wall Street sentiment. . . . He favored unified administration under the Federal Trade Commission and hoped to limit all margin revisions to 'a finding of grave national emergency.' " Parrish adds that Cohen wanted to limit exchange membership "to brokers and to prevent members from trading on their own accounts except in the case of odd-lot dealers and specialists." John Flynn cast Cohen in a similar role, as did Raymond Moley, who recalled that Cohen and Corcoran "grumbled darkly about the 'denaturing' of their bill" in the final compromise, although Moley added that Cohen and Corcoran "obeyed orders loyally enough, and there was no show of rebelliousness" until after the bill was approved and the new securities commissioners appointed.[25]

Cohen himself remembered his role differently. His initial purpose in writing the Securities Exchange Act, he told Joseph Lash, was to strike a balance "that showed we weren't turning things over to" the stock exchanges but which recognized that "we shouldn't tear them up." Cohen agreed with Flynn generally, "but thought he exaggerated and he did all the more when he felt the Stock Exchange wanted to continue the old ways while Flynn thought they ought to be determined by Congress." Instead, Cohen believed he could work with the more reasonable representatives from Wall Street "to get them to ameliorate their positions." Thus Cohen participated in a series of discussions with Wall Street men, beginning as early as March, and perhaps earlier. "Flynn [was] always respectful of me," Cohen recalled, "and if he had known of some of my work in conferences with the Exchanges he would have disapproved. . . . Roosevelt . . . was concerned that we should not rock the boat when the country was in panic conditions. There was considerable discussion that Tom & I might rock the boat." Cohen's real antagonists in the complex negotiations in late March were not the Wall Street interests, but the Federal Reserve Board. "The Federal Reserve Board came in with the purpose of trying to stop us," he explained to Lash. "Instead we showed we knew what we were doing. We got some people on the private side to side with us, but they had to move carefully."[26] Cohen's insistence on unified administration of the act, at least in his view, was less the result of an unwillingness to compromise than of a deliberate negotiating strategy.

There is little if any hard evidence to contradict Cohen's own recollections. The only real evidence of his rigidity comes from various drafts of the bill prepared by Cohen and from the testimony of Flynn and Moley. Unquestionably Cohen did present hard-line positions at key points in the negotiations, but he may have done so merely as a tactic. Flynn not only had his own reasons for depicting Cohen as a hero of the anti–Wall Street left, but also had been deliberately misled— or at least misinformed— by Cohen. Moley, for his part, did not single Cohen out but merely reported the "grumbling" of Cohen *and* Corcoran, though he admitted that their objections did not amount to real rebelliousness until after the new SEC commissioners were appointed. Cohen's attitude at that point resulted not from dissatisfaction with the act itself, but from personal disappointment at not being offered one of those positions.[27]

One contemporary source explicitly confirms Cohen's version of the story. In a letter to Sen. Edward P. Costigan (D-Col.) urging the appointment of Cohen to the Securities and Exchange Commission, Max Lowenthal summed up Cohen's role in the process of negotiating and refining the initial draft. "The public will probably never know how he [Cohen] prepared the bill under great pressure," Lowenthal wrote, *"how he resisted proposals to make it more drastic,* with what modesty and resourcefulness he won to his view the entire group that went over his draft, *and how he was the first of all to urge changes in the initial draft* when there was a brief interval for reflection."[28] It is possible, of course, that Lowenthal overstated his case, especially since these words were part of an active campaign for Cohen's appointment to the new commission. However, it seems unlikely that he would distort Cohen's approach and attitude completely.

If anyone was taking a hard line, then, it was not Cohen but Corcoran. As the public spokesman for the drafters of the bill, Corcoran was forced to defend the original bill in public testimony, a task he took on and accomplished with great zeal and for which he endured merciless attacks. Having staked out this extreme position, Corcoran then found that almost all his colleagues were actively giving ground in search of compromise. (Corcoran eventually reveled in the role of "anti-business" reformer. In a conversation with Raymond Moley after Joseph P. Kennedy was appointed the first chairman of the Securities and Exchange Commission, Corcoran remarked, "Oh well, we've got four out of five anyhow." When pressed, Corcoran explained, "What I mean is that four are for us and one is for business." Moley objected to this vision of the social order as being "divided between business" and "some mythical 'us,'" and Corcoran backed down and apologized, but a year later he remarked, "Fighting with a businessman is like fighting with a Polack. You can give no quarter.")[29]

If it is wrong to suggest that Cohen was uncompromising, it is equally wrong to give him credit, at this point, for exhibiting great political savvy. It is difficult to justify Lash's conclusion that, at this early stage, Cohen and Corcoran "were magnificently attuned to what was politically possible and always realized that whatever power they had emanated from Fletcher and Rayburn and above all the President, who gave them their marching orders."[30] In fact, Cohen and Corcoran were still neophytes and learning painful lessons. Their connections to the White House were embryonic, their personal relationship with Roosevelt essentially nonexistent. They certainly took orders from Rayburn and to a lesser extent Fletcher, but the stakes were much higher than they had been in 1933, and these men, however powerful, did not dominate the field. Although the final version of the Securities Exchange Act was in great part identical to Cohen's initial draft, the political compromises that led to its passage were made at a level to which they had not yet been admitted.

Nor was Cohen ready or willing at this point to move closer to the center of power. The ultimate success of the securities bill did not erase his overwhelming unhappiness with his life and work in Washington. The events of the summer only reinforced his feeling, as he had written Jane Harris in the spring, that "I want to come home, really I do."[31] The focal point of Cohen's discontent, at least professionally, was the on-again, off-again rumors that he would soon be named as one of the first SEC commissioners. That he might not have accepted the position did not make it any easier for Cohen when the offer never came.

Cohen's name was widely mentioned as a possible appointee to the commission, which was to consist of three Democrats and two Republicans. On June 22, the *New York Times* listed Cohen and Corcoran among eleven possible nominees, describing them merely as "lawyers who aided in the preparation of the Stock Exchange bill." (Two of the five eventual nominees, Landis and George C. Matthews, were already dealing with securities matters as members of the Federal Trade Commission, and were considered virtually automatic appointments.) Cohen was also on a more important list of nine that Raymond Moley sent to Roosevelt in early June. "He is as able as Landis and more experienced," Moley advised the president. "He has participated to a greater extent than anyone else in the drafting of both [the] Securities and Stock Exchange Acts. His personality would gain friends as people grew to know him. Enormously well thought of by Judge Mack, Frankfurter, etc."[32]

At Frankfurter's suggestion, Corcoran began an active campaign for what Cohen called his "lost candidate." The operation included enthusiastic letters of recommendation from Judge Mack, Ben Flexner, Max Lowenthal, and others. Frankfurter wrote a general letter but stopped short of an endorsement of Cohen. He might have felt that a personal endorsement would have been awkward or even counterproductive, given that "the leading Jewish bankers and leading Jewish Wall Street lawyers feel about Ben Cohen's influence and the myths of my own influence in the administration precisely as their non-Jewish colleagues in finance and at the bar," as he explained to Corcoran. But it is also possible that Frankfurter had his own reasons for preferring that Cohen not be appointed, or that he chose not to risk overextending himself on so delicate an appointment.[33]

By June 26, Cohen was convinced that "it does not look as I would be named to the commission—too much politics even among the New

Dealers." Roosevelt's decision, announced on July 1, was to appoint financier Joseph P. Kennedy, who had been a major contributor to the 1932 campaign; Landis and Matthews of the FTC; Ferdinand Pecora; and Robert T. Healy, an expert in public utilities who had served as general counsel to the FTC since 1934. Roosevelt made it clear that he wanted Kennedy as chairman, although officially the members of the commission elected their own leader. Over the next several weeks, Cohen considered the possibility of becoming general counsel to the commission, a position that the *New York Times* described as "fully as arduous as that of a commissioner," at least for the first year. In June, Cohen believed "I could have the General Counselorship if I wanted it," but after the election of Kennedy as chair the appointment became problematic. For one thing, Kennedy had his own man in mind, a Massachusetts judge named John Burns. Perhaps more important, the appointment of the "radical" Cohen would have sent precisely the wrong signal to Wall Street. As Thomas K. McCraw has suggested, the appointment of Joe Kennedy was largely motivated by politics: "With new investment at a standstill and the financial community now furious at the New Deal, Kennedy was exactly the kind of person who could help break the 'strike of capitalism' that obstructed national recovery. The Securities Act of 1933 . . . had done nothing to prime the pump of renewed investment. Many financiers began to blame the continuing drought on the New Deal in general and the Securities Act in particular. . . . Roosevelt knew that something had to be done, and in his mind the Kennedy appointment was not so much a sop to enemies in the Street as a clear signal that the American president wanted action in the securities markets."[34]

Some months later, the reporters Drew Pearson and Robert S. Allen advanced the claim that Cohen's exclusion from the SEC had been partly due to anti-Semitism. They attributed his failure to win the general counsel post, by contrast, to Landis's opposition. In Pearson and Allen's version of events, Landis had particularly objected to Cohen's demand that he "must have a salary equal to that of a commissioner and must have a certain amount of independent latitude." Landis countered that "Ben must understand . . . that he will be an employee of the commission and will take his orders from me." Much later, Landis acknowledged that Cohen wanted the position but felt that "the chairman was entitled to have his own counsel."[35]

Cohen was upset about the whole experience. In his bitterness, he tried to convince Harris—and himself—that the final decision on the job was his own. "I could have had that [position] if I wanted it," he wrote, "but the plots and counterplots were disgusting to me. I made conditions so that there would be no mistaking my position, and my friend Landis who I always knew was a snake in the grass, showed his fangs. And so I think I am lucky to be out of it."[36]

Angry and humiliated, Cohen withdrew, taking advantage of an opportunity to travel to Europe. "I am going to London professedly on Palestinian matters," he wrote from aboard ship, "but the real reason is that I want to get away." His decision to leave Washington was now firmer than ever. "Felix in his usual compromising way is trying to hold me in the picture," he wrote in the same letter, "but my mind is made up. J'ai finis. . . . I shall have to return to Washington for a few weeks, but I am coming back to New York. I am not sure what I shall do, but shall probably practice some sort of law, even though I won't like it. I'm through being a brain-truster."[37]

Frankfurter, in fact, did have other ideas. Despite the flaring of tensions between the two men, the Harvard professor still wanted Cohen in a position to work indirectly for him. The first possibility was to place Cohen as general counsel to the Committee on Economic Security, a cabinet-level group led by Frances Perkins that was developing the legislation that became the Social Security Act. With Cohen due back from England on August 8, Frankfurter sought to move preemptively; as Tommy Corcoran noted, "Felix suggests that Ben being the kind of blushing violet he is it would be very wise to try to have the appointment go through before Ben comes back on the ground and has an opportunity to be shy about it." Cohen, of course, was less shy than simply resolved to go home, and he cannot have appreciated Frankfurter's attempt at manipulation. In any event Frankfurter had little real power with Perkins or her people, and Cohen was passed over.[38]

Cohen returned from England to find Washington "as bad as ever," and he reported again that he expected "to come home" soon. But still he hesitated. ("So it always goes with me," he had written to Harris in another context in June. "I linger and tarry until it is too late.") Once more he withdrew from the situation, this time taking a trip to Muncie, his hometown. By the time he returned to Washington, Cohen had resigned himself to staying on. "Felix is trying to shanghai me into the power situation and trying to hold me over the winter," he wrote Harris. "I don't want to stay, but he puts it on personal [grounds]. . . . I am afraid I will have to do it anyway. I don't know what to do about the apartment [in New York], but I hate to give it up. It is the only home I have."[39]

Still unable to resist the demands of Frankfurter, and drawn by his growing friendship with Corcoran, Cohen decided to stay in Washington, this time for good—he would never return to New York on a permanent basis. Late in the year he was appointed by Harold Ickes as general counsel to the National Power Policy Committee, a post he would hold until 1940. His first task at Power Policy was to deal with the complex problem of public utility holding companies. It was a problem that would occupy his attention off and on for the next six years.

7

The Public Utility
Holding Company Act

Tom and I will be branded as dangerous radicals again . . . although

we are in fact about the only real conservatives in Washington.

—*Ben Cohen to Jane Harris, January 12, 1935*

The year 1935 began with great promise for the New Deal. The 1934 midterm elections had been an unqualified triumph for Roosevelt and the Democrats, with the president's party actually gaining ground in both houses for the first time in history. The Democrats now controlled nearly three-quarters of each house, and it was generally assumed "that Congress will pass nearly every bill the President wants and kill nearly every bill he does not want." Although here and there Congress would show its independence, on the whole the president's program was expected to pass without difficulty.[1]

Even big business now seemed to resign itself to the political realities of the moment. In November 1934, the United States Chamber of Commerce followed the lead of the American Bankers' Association and pledged its cooperation with the New Deal's recovery program. Amazingly, even Richard Whitney of the New York Stock Exchange moved to the president's side. In an interview with the *New York Times* after a month of operating under the Securities Exchange Act, Whitney praised the law as offering "a new safeguard to the investor which should stimulate rather than hamper the volume of legitimate trading."[2]

Characteristically, Roosevelt took advantage of his new ascendancy to move in two directions at once. To business, he stressed the overriding need to promote the economic recovery. "Our first task," he told the Advisory Council of the Committee on Economic Security in December, "is to get the economic system to function so that there will be a greater general security." Underscoring the new spirit of cooperation, the administration took small but significant steps to reassure the business community. Thus the Home Owners Loan Corporation announced that it would soon cease operations in anticipation of the resumption of normal lending activity by private institutions, while the head of the Reconstruction Finance Corporation urged his staff to be more sympathetic to corporate loan applicants.[3]

These feints to the right were accompanied by strong hints of new action extending and expanding the New Deal. In his speech to the Committee on Economic Security, for example, Roosevelt outlined a broad new program of social insurance. In a letter to the mayors of ninety-four cities, likewise, the president promised "that the coming session of Congress will give further attention to proposals involving unemployment relief, public works, unemployment insurance, old-age pensions, and housing." Elsewhere, Roosevelt talked about the regulation of public utilities, the extension of the National Industrial Recovery Act, and the preparation of legislation to "take the profit out of war."[4]

The president's annual message, delivered in person on the first full day of the new congressional session, emphasized the administration's progressive agenda. "The outlines of the new economic order, rising from the disintegration of the old, are apparent," he told Congress. "We test what we have done as our measures take root in the living texture of life. We see where we have built wisely and where we can do still better." Roosevelt pledged new and expanded programs in work relief, social security, and affordable housing. And while he did not dwell on the theme, Roosevelt warned that "Americans must forswear that conception of the acquisition of wealth which, through excessive profits, creates undue private power over private affairs, and, to our misfortune, over public affairs as well." Finally, the president called for "the restoration of sound conditions in the public utilities field through the abolition of the evil of holding companies," though in doing so he apparently misquoted his own prepared text, which called only for the "abolition of the evil features of holding companies."[5] Roosevelt's comment—whether Freudian slip or deliberate policy shift—presaged the next major battle of the New Deal.

Relations between the Roosevelt administration and the public utility industry had never been cordial. Early on, tensions centered on the Tennessee Valley Authority (TVA) Act, enacted in May 1933. At the center of the TVA was the belief that electric power should be cheap, abundant, and available to everyone. As FDR put it, "power development . . . leads logically to national planning for a complete river watershed involving many States and the future lives and welfare of millions. It touches and gives life to all forms of human concern." To Roosevelt, the TVA embodied the transformative possibilities of modern government; as Arthur Schlesinger has noted, perhaps no other creation of the early New Deal "expressed more passionately a central presidential concern."[6]

To the public utility companies, however, the TVA Act represented not the hope of future prosperity but the loss of future profits. The problem was simple: government production and distribution of cheap power threatened to undercut private production, eventually forcing lower prices and lower profits. "To take our market," said Commonwealth & Southern President Wendell Willkie in congressional testimony, "is to take our property."[7]

The TVA, as Willkie well knew, was only the beginning. Down the road, Roosevelt had in mind a much broader program of rural electrification and, most important, legislation for the reform of holding companies. After unsuccessfully opposing the TVA Act, the Willkie-led power companies tried to cut their losses by working with the administration, negotiating an agreement under which the power distribution network was divided geographically between the TVA and the private sector. For the moment, at least, cooperation seemed possible.

In mid-1934, however, Roosevelt threw down the gauntlet. On July 9, he signed an executive order creating the National Power Policy Committee (NPPC), chaired by Secretary of the Interior Harold Ickes and housed within the Public Works Administration (PWA). Roosevelt charged the NPPC with developing "a plan for the closer cooperation of the several factors in our electrical power supply—both public and private—whereby national policy in power matters may be unified and electricity may be made more broadly available at cheaper rates to industry, to domestic and, particularly, to agricultural consumers." As if this direct attack on utility profits were not enough, the president reminded the committee that "there undoubtedly will be legislation on the subject of holding companies and for the regulation of electric current in interstate commerce," and directed that "this Committee should consider what lines should be followed in shaping this legislation."[8]

The NPPC was the brainchild of Morris Cooke, who served as head of the Mississippi Valley Committee in the Department of the Interior. As early as February 1934, Cooke had suggested the need for a national power policy based on the widest distribution of electric power at the cheapest rates. Such a policy, he argued, required federal legislation to regulate holding companies. Cooke transmitted these suggestions to Secretary Ickes in April, and Ickes sent them along to the president. Ickes was at least partially motivated by his desire to concentrate federal power policy within the Interior Department.[9]

Thus at the very moment Roosevelt was mending fences with the business community in general, relations between the administration and the public utility industry were quickly deteriorating. In September, preferred stockholders of the Alabama Power Company moved to challenge the TVA Act in court, filing a case that would eventually reach the Supreme Court. Prominent attorneys opined that the bill was unconstitutional, and a federal judge in Birmingham expressed the view that the federal government could not make and sell electric power as a business, but only as an incidental by-product of its legitimate operations, such as navigation control or flood protection.[10]

As fall turned to early winter, Roosevelt continued to make conciliatory speeches to business while simultaneously pressing forward on the power question. On a trip through the Tennessee Valley in early December, Roosevelt praised community-based power cooperatives and attacked the private companies, at least indirectly. Noting that power production was up and prices down since the creation of the TVA, Roosevelt told a crowd at Tupelo, Mississippi, that he would no longer tolerate "the kind of rugged individualism that allows an individual to do this, that or the other thing that will hurt his neighbors." In Birmingham, the president blasted "these obstructionists, few in number" who "are leaving no stone unturned to block, to harass and to delay this great national program."[11]

Meanwhile, in late summer, the National Power Policy Committee began to get down to its business. At the committee's second meeting, on August 29, 1934, Robert Healy of the Federal Trade Commission requested the appointment of Benjamin Cohen as legal counsel. Healy, a Vermont Republican and former judge, had served as solicitor general of the FTC since 1928, and in that capacity had led a long investigation into the conduct and operations of utility holding companies. Accordingly, the committee selected Healy to head up its efforts to write new holding company legislation. Healy was attracted to Cohen by his reputation for legislative draftsmanship and by his experience with the securities legislation of 1933 and 1934. "I have great respect for the ability of Ben Cohen drafting bills that will stand the test," he told the committee. When Morris Cooke indicated that he had already made approaches to Cohen, Healy interjected: "Don't let Cohen get away from you. There may be other plans for him, I know, but I think he will be more intrigued by this than anything."[12] Felix Frankfurter urged Cohen to take on the assignment, and eventually Cohen capitulated.

Cohen prepared for the drafting of the Public Utility Holding Company Act, as always, by gathering information. Beginning in early October, he and Healy spoke with a wide range of interested parties, including industry executives, state power officials, and, later, bankers and academics. As Healy wrote, "I desire to avail myself of the advice of those whose experience in the particular field of public utility holding companies should make their suggestions useful."[13]

Cohen's approach, at least at first, was to try to break "the deadlock of distrust that threatened the healthy growth of the utility industry." He quickly discovered, however, that achieving that goal would be difficult. Some of the utility executives he spoke with were unhelpful; the chairman of the board of the Electric Bond and Share Company, for example, "tended to discuss problems that I presented and kept his own suggestions, if he had any, pretty much to himself." But not all the utility officials were hostile. Some recognized the need for at least a minimal federal role, and others actually welcomed government intervention.[14]

This confusion within the ranks of the public utility industry reflected a combination of factors. While the industry displayed hostility toward federal regulation in general and to New Deal reform proposals in particular, opposition to regulation was mitigated by a growing recognition of the industry's problems and by the fear of even more drastic consequences if regulation were not implemented in the near future. Industry opinion was also influenced by Wall Street's surprising acceptance of the Securities Exchange Act, by the general rise in business conditions, and by the improvement of relations between the administration and business. At the time of Cohen's discussions with utility executives—the fall of 1934—Roosevelt's rhetorical attacks on the public utilities had not yet fully taken hold.

Whatever chance there was of resolving the utility holding company question in a friendly and cooperative way was swept aside once the president ramped up his assault against the power companies. In addition to his vague but generally unfriendly comments in public speeches, Roosevelt moved against the power companies privately—though hardly secretly. At a meeting with members of the NPPC on the evening of November 23 at Warm Springs, Georgia (Cohen, along with Healy and Ickes, was absent), the president strongly attacked the holding company system. As reported by TVA chairman David Lilienthal, Roosevelt declared that "a holding company which exists for the control of operating companies was against the public interest and, since it couldn't be regulated, should be abolished. To this end, he wanted legislation drawn. The question was what method should be used to effect this result, and he dropped the suggestion of taxation as a means of eliminating holding companies of this kind." Earlier in the day, Roosevelt had taken pains to brief the White House press corps on the evils of holding companies—though the conversation was off the record and only hinted at the possibility of new legislation.[15]

By late November it was clear to those who followed such matters that the president's nascent utility crusade posed a serious threat to the broader possibility of government-business cooperation. "President Roosevelt's recent speeches indorsing [*sic*] public ownership and operation of power-plants were disconcerting, to say the least," wrote the financial columnist Robert Winsmore in early December. "Equities, as well as earnings, are being constantly threatened by increasing clamor for reduced rates to consumers, higher taxes and new publicly-financed competition. Obviously, the public-utility units of the country are being pilloried and cudgeled as once the railroads were."[16]

It was in this atmosphere—indeed, on the very day that Roosevelt spoke to the NPPC members in Warm Springs—that Cohen forwarded to Judge Healy a draft bill "for the regulation of holding companies and affiliated interests." The original draft has been lost, but Cohen's long and descriptive cover letter has survived. Cohen's summary of the original draft is an extremely important document, since it was prepared before the president began his heightened rhetorical campaign against the public utilities industry, and before the president's decision—hinted at in November and announced in January—to try to abolish, rather than merely regulate, the holding companies. The summary thus provides a glimpse into Cohen's approach to holding companies before the matter was clouded by presidential intervention.

Cohen began by "recognizing, not merely that the holding-company form has been shamefully abused, but there are certain difficulties springing from the absence of arms-length bargaining among controlled affiliated interests, and these difficulties by their very nature, require some regulation if the holding company form is to be allowed to stand." He immediately made it clear, however, that abolition of holding companies would be both unwise and impractical. "Although the abuses connected with the holding company have been great," he wrote, "it has been represented that the use of this form has induced economy and efficiency in operations where small and territorially related units have been coordinated. Whether the increased economy and efficiency which may possibly have been obtained in some instances through the use of the holding company form could have been secured in other ways is a question as to which men may differ. But not only is the holding company a very real actuality today but the huge amounts of capital tied up in holding companies cannot readily be untied." Rather than eliminate holding companies, therefore, Cohen's proposal sought to regulate and restrict "the use of the holding company form" and to provide "a mechanism through which, over a period of time, existing holding company structures may be simplified, and their fields restricted to a sphere where their economic advantages may be demonstrable."[17]

Cohen's recognition of the economies of scale that stem from at least some holding company arrangements marks his political philosophy as sharply different from that of the Brandeisian liberals, who opposed bigness as a matter of principle. "Through size," Brandeis had written in a 1933 Supreme Court opinion, "corporations, once merely an efficient tool employed by individuals in the conduct of private business, have become an institution—an institution which has brought such concentration of economic power that so-called private corporations are sometimes able to dominate the state." In the modern corporation, Brandeis continued, "Ownership has been separated from control; and this separation has removed many of the checks which formerly operated to curb the misuse of wealth and power. And, as ownership of shares is becoming continually more dispersed, the power which formerly accompanied ownership is becoming increasingly concentrated in the hands of the few." "The limit of efficiency in business is reached at a fairly early stage," Brandeis wrote elsewhere, and "the disadvantages of size outweigh in many respects the advantages of size." The only exception Brandeis admitted was in the gathering of information, which required the resources of great enterprises, though Brandeis sought to blunt even that advantage by giving the government a major role in the dissemination of knowledge to large and small concerns alike.[18]

Cohen's views on holding companies, like his approach to the regulation of the securities exchanges, reflected less the Brandeisian discomfort with bigness and more the pragmatism of his old instructor, H. G. Moulton, who by then was head of the prestigious Brookings Institution. In his 1921 book on the banking system, for example, Moulton noted that "the phenomenal consolidation movement in the fields of transportation, manufacturing, and commerce in the last quarter of the nineteenth century was necessarily paralleled in the fields of both commercial and investment banking. Indeed, the two movements have developed hand in hand, each having been necessary to the continuance of the other; the growth of huge banking institutions made possible the assembling of the capital required by corporate consolidations; and, conversely, the development of giant-scale corporate industry required and made profitable the development of financial institutions of commensurate resources." The growth of holding companies simply reflected a continuation of this trend, despite the restrictions imposed by the Clayton Act of 1914 (in the passage of which Brandeis, as an adviser to Woodrow Wilson, played a major part). There were potential dangers in large-scale integration, of course, and Moulton concluded that the consolidation movement had "proceeded quite far enough." But still he accepted the highly integrated financial system as an inescapable fact of modern life.[19]

For Cohen, then, limiting the abuses of the holding company presented a technical problem rather than a philosophical one. Put simply, holding companies were a cause of concern when they were used to provide an additional layer of organization which unscrupulous utilities and brokerage firms could use to confuse the proverbial widows and orphans who entrusted their savings to Wall Street. As Roosevelt himself put it,

> A certain friend of mine . . . finds that the fifteen or twenty thousand dollars he put in is invested, about two-thirds, in bonds of utilities, not stocks, but bonds. What kind of utilities? Holding companies, all of them holding companies, none of them operating companies. . . . Those bonds have printed on them that behind them is so much stock. Let us call the first company the A Company, and their bonds state that they have

so much stock of B Company, C Company, D Company, in the
treasury of the A company, as security of those bonds. Then
you analyze and ask, what is the common stock of B, C, and
D Companies? You will find that they are holding companies.
And you will also find that they have outstanding certain bonds
which are backed by the common stocks of E, F, G, H, and I
Companies. And then you will come down to those companies
and perhaps they are operating companies or perhaps they are
holding companies too. Sometimes you get the pyramid of the
holding company principle up to the fourth dimension.

While his friend lost more than 60 percent of his original investment,
Roosevelt concluded, others got rich. "There is one man who put in a
thousand dollars into one of these little electric light companies about
1900, and today his thousand dollars is twenty thousand dollars, although he has never done a damn thing to make it worth twenty thousand dollars."[20]

To combat such schemes, Cohen's draft bill imposed federal registration on all holding companies "which use the channels of interstate
commerce" or "which have during the past seven years made a public
offering of any of their securities in interstate commerce." Registered
companies would then be required to file registration statement information "comparable with, but somewhat more comprehensive than, the
information required from companies whose securities are registered
on national securities exchanges." Registered companies were obliged
to obtain permission from the Securities and Exchange Commission for
the sale or issuance of new securities, and for the "acquisition of capital
assets and securities of other companies."[21]

In addition, Cohen's proposal aimed to streamline the utilities industry and break up both vertical and horizontal conglomerates when
such forms of organization were not justified by economic efficiency. In
Cohen's words,

The ownership by registered holding companies of properties
and securities not strictly related to the utility business is rigidly
limited. Electric holding companies are not permitted to have
any interest in interstate gas pipe lines. Service and construction contracts with operating companies are forbidden unless
they are put more upon a mutual or cooperative basis, and such
mutual or cooperative companies are subject to rigid regulation
by the Commission. . . . Upstream loans are forbidden as well

as commissions on inter-corporate security transactions. . . .
The Commission is further given power to compel the simpli-
fication of holding company structures where they are unnecessarily complicated and to require the divestment by holding
companies of subsidiaries having no economic relation to the
other companies in the system.

Although the SEC would be "endowed with adequate powers to meet attempts at evasion," the bill also provided what Cohen described as "the
mechanism through which the Commission may afford the necessary
incentives to induce the holding companies voluntarily to adjust their
activities to the long-range interest of their own security holders who
ultimately can profit only from the useful economic functions which
these companies may perform."[22]

Jim Landis and Tommy Corcoran helped Cohen to refine his draft
of the holding companies bill, and a revised version was ready by late
December. Cohen's draft was circulated among the NPPC members, but
Cohen objected to sending an early version of the bill to Roosevelt, preferring to "have the benefit of the committee's criticism without in any
way having the committee approve the bill, so that if any changes are desired later, it would not appear to be going contrary to the committee's
wishes."[23] Comments from the various members of the NPPC came back
to Cohen in early January with some suggestions for minor changes.
The committee discussed the bill on January 17 and decided to send it
to the president, with a report to follow.

Although Cohen's approach to holding company regulation had not
changed since he began working on the draft bill in November, the
political situation was evolving rapidly. Roosevelt's State of the Union
message, with its slip-of-the-tongue calling for the abolition of holding
companies, was delivered on January 4. Lawyers at the Federal Power
Commission (FPC) had in fact been working on a bill to abolish holding companies since Commissioner Frank McNinch's return from the
November 23 meeting at Warm Springs; their scheme involved the use
of taxation to make holding companies an unattractive form of corporate organization. Lawyers at the Justice Department were taking a
similar approach. Roosevelt again endorsed the idea of radical change
at a meeting of the National Emergency Council on December 11, indicating that he would permit holding companies to exist if "they are
paid for the service of management only; and provided they do not hold
stock in any of the companies which they manage," and only if invest-

ment trusts were kept out of the management of companies in which they held securities.[24]

From this point on, pressure against the holding companies built relentlessly. Critics included officials of the Federal Trade Commission and the Federal Power Commission, David Lilienthal of the TVA, and Rep. Sam Rayburn, chairman of the powerful Interstate Commerce Committee. On January 13, Rayburn took to the House floor to demand the abolition of all holding companies, although the next day he backed away, calling holding companies a "temporary necessary evil." Other congressional leaders went even further, demanding the abolition of holding companies as a first step toward public ownership.[25]

A week later, the president moved to clean up the disarray, calling several advisers to the White House; Corcoran attended the meeting, but apparently Cohen did not. The central question at the meeting, held on January 21, was whether to take the regulation route advocated by Cohen or the taxation approach endorsed by the Treasury, the FPC, and, at one point, the president himself. A larger meeting was held on February 5, with Cohen and Corcoran both in attendance.

As in the 1934 negotiations on the Securities Exchange Act, Cohen and Corcoran were virtually alone at the February 5 meeting in arguing for moderation. The only real advantage they had in this confrontation was that the Cohen bill, and not one of the competing drafts, had provoked the meeting. It was clear that Roosevelt himself preferred the elimination of the holding companies, however, and that in any event he wanted the bill to send a strong message to the utilities industry. In the end, the conferees decided to accept Cohen's overall approach but to add language condemning holding company abuses and to include a provision allowing the Securities and Exchange Commission to compel the dissolution of holding companies unless it could be shown that a particular operating company "cannot be operated as an independent system without the loss of substantial economies which can be secured by the retention of control by such holding company."[26]

This "death penalty provision" soon came to dominate the debate over the public utility holding company bill, not only at the time but in later accounts as well. Because Cohen accepted the death penalty provision without public complaint, he was often assumed to have been its creator, although in fact he had privately argued against it. The moderate regulator thus became the radical reformer, an image that fit perfectly with the reputation Cohen had inherited from the securities battle a year before. Moreover, the debate over public utility regulation cemented Cohen's reputation as a Brandeisian liberal, since the death penalty provision seemed to fit so tightly with Brandeis's philosophical opposition to bigness. Corcoran was tarred with the same brush, making his post–New Deal conservatism seem a complete betrayal of principle. Cohen, at least, was aware of the irony at the time. "Tom and I will be branded as dangerous radicals again," he wrote Jane Harris a week before his meeting with Roosevelt, "although we are in fact about the only real conservatives in Washington."[27]

Cohen's now-amended bill faced difficulties from inside the administration even after the White House conference seemed to have settled matters. The crux of the problem was Cohen's decision to place responsibility for administering the law with the Securities Exchange Commission rather than the Federal Power Commission. From Cohen's point of view, this allocation of responsibilities made good sense, since the most serious problems in the power industry had less to do with matters of power production and transmission than with problems of corporate and financial organization and structure. Jealously guarding their turf, however, FPC officials called for the predominant role, and also demanded that amendments to the Federal Water Power Act be linked to passage of the holding company bill. Another White House meeting was held, and FDR handed down his verdict, which split the difference. Cohen was given more or less explicit instructions to increase the role of the Federal Power Commission, but not nearly to the extent that the FPC had wanted. Roosevelt also ordered Cohen to include the water act amendments as section II of the holding company bill. The FPC was not happy with Cohen's redraft, but the squabbling was forced to an end in early February, when both Rayburn and Sen. Burton K. Wheeler demanded a bill they could introduce immediately. After a final revision by the Justice Department, the bill—now known officially as the Public Utility Holding Company Act of 1935 and informally as the Wheeler-Rayburn bill—was introduced into both houses of Congress.

Now that the bill was made public, the internal administration disputes faded into the mists, to be replaced by an all-out war between the utilities industry and the would-be regulators. The power industry lobbyists were led by Wendell Willkie, chairman of the Commonwealth & Southern Electric Company and, six years later, the Republican nominee for president of the United States. Two years older than Cohen, Willkie was born in Elwood, Indiana, less than twenty-five miles from Muncie. Like Cohen, Willkie did not stay in Indiana; after graduating from law school and serving in the army during World War I, he moved to Akron, Ohio, where he quickly established himself as a successful attorney. He received an introduction to the electric power industry as the legal representative of the Northern Ohio Traction and Light (later Power and Light) Company, built up a substantial reputation as a speaker and debater, and became active in Ohio Democratic politics; he was close to Newton D. Baker, President Wilson's secretary of war and a prominent internationalist. In 1929, Willkie took a job with the Commonwealth & Southern in New York, and by 1933 he was named its president.

Willkie's status as the chief representative of the public utility industry was odd at best. He had achieved the role, as his biographer points out, largely because "among utility executives he was one of the least vulnerable to the criticisms commonly made of utility practices." Commonwealth & Southern was the closest thing to a model of the modern utility company that one could find in 1935. Its output was high, its prices low, and its corporate organization efficient. Even Senator Wheeler remarked to Willkie that "if there had not been any more abuses in some companies than there have been in yours . . . you probably would not have been faced with some of the provisions that you are faced with at the present time."[28]

Willkie had clashed with the New Deal over the TVA in 1933, but even so he had approached the public utilities regulation issue with the hope of a mutually satisfactory resolution through negotiation and compromise. But the president's hard-hitting speeches led Willkie to respond in kind, and anything less than a full-scale war between the administration and the utility industry now seemed remote. In a debate against David Lilienthal in New York on January 21, Willkie returned the administration's now hostile rhetoric in kind, letting loose a series of scathing personal and political attacks against the New Dealers. He denounced those who favored "socialism" in the form of public ownership of utilities, who were "enamored with European economic and social concepts" that were held with "religious phrenzy . . . against which no amount of argument or factual presentation will prevail." "Those who oppose the utility organization," he concluded, "assume an attitude of superior virtue and patriotism. They seek to paint us who represent private enterprise in the utility business as anti-social, unpatriotic and the despoilers of men."[29] When Willkie and two other utility executives came to the White House to meet with Roosevelt, Lilienthal, and McNinch, the result was foreordained. The meeting went nowhere, ending with what Lilienthal called "a real argument," led by Willkie. At the end Willkie asked, "Do I understand then that any further efforts to avoid the breaking up of utility holding companies are futile?" The president said simply, "It is futile."[30]

After January 1935, Willkie became the leading contender for the position of New Deal enemy number one. His leadership in the utilities fight would catapult him to the top of the Republican ticket in 1940, just as his fire-eating remarks in 1929 and 1930 had brought him to the top of Commonwealth & Southern. With Cohen now cast in the role of radical reformer, these two men from Indiana came to represent the two poles in the bitter fight over utilities regulation, and of the New Deal itself. Both men played their roles well. But as with professional actors playing antagonists on the stage, there was no personal animosity between them, and they grew to respect each other and to form a warm relationship. Behind the scenes, moreover, the substantive differences between the apparent radical and the apparent reactionary were surprisingly small.

The holding company bill was now before Congress, where it was referred to the House and Senate Commerce committees, led by Representative Rayburn and Senator Wheeler. The Rayburn committee was first to take up the measure, holding hearings beginning in mid-February. The utility company witnesses were forceful and effective, arguing that the bill would have a "disastrous effect" on the value of utility investments, whether in holding companies or operating companies. They quickly put the administration's witnesses on the defensive, picked up key allies on Rayburn's committee, and seemed to be winning the battle for public opinion. By mid-March, with the Senate yet to act, the holding company bill was in serious trouble.

The utility companies' early success in opposing the holding company bill can be attributed to their impressive organization and their ability, in the face of adversity, to present a united front. Yet while the industry pulled together, the White House fell victim to disorganization, hesitancy, and fragmentation. It quickly became apparent that the administration's internal disputes had been swept under the carpet rather than settled, and they soon found their way back to daylight. In testimony before the Rayburn committee on March 1, for example, Judge Healy weighed in against the death penalty provision, arguing that the complete dismantling of the holding company system was unnecessary. Healy then made matters worse by announcing that he would propose amendments designed to protect investors in holding company securities, principally by giving the Securities and Exchange Commission "some discretion" in enforcing the death penalty provision.

It did not help the administration that the Rayburn hearings began just days after the Supreme Court's decision in the *Gold Clause* cases, which presented a constitutional challenge to the administration's 1933 decision, authorized by Congress, to abrogate all promises to pay public or private debts in gold. The Court sided with the administration but subjected Roosevelt to a stern lecture in the process. In language presaging the Court's full-scale attack on the New Deal in May, Chief Justice Hughes declared that Congress's decision to renege on its own promise to pay debts in gold was unconstitutional and could be upheld only because the United States government could not be sued without its consent. The *Gold Clause* cases greatly emboldened Roosevelt's critics, who could now argue with some conviction that the entire New Deal was unconstitutional. The Rayburn hearings on the Public Utility Holding Company Act presented the first opportunity for conservatives to weigh in with their newly invigorated rhetoric.

Despite his strong anti-utilities rhetoric in December and January, the president remained aloof and removed throughout February and early March, clinging to the fiction that the dispute was a congressional matter and even pretending that he had not seen a copy of the Wheeler-Rayburn bill before its introduction in Congress. Not until mid-March did the president answer the bill's critics. Roosevelt's response came in the form of his transmission to Congress of the National Power Policy Committee's report on public utilities, which was accompanied by a strong written endorsement. "I have been watching with great interest the fight being waged against public-utility holding company legislation," he wrote on March 12. "I have seen much of the propaganda prepared against such legislation. . . . I have seen enough to be as unimpressed by it as I was by the similar effort to stir up the country against the Securities Exchange bill last spring." [31]

The NPPC report itself was written largely by Cohen, and had been in preparation since the fall. Cohen worked on the final version of the report throughout February, trying to find language that would satisfy both the White House and Judge Healy. "Judge Healy is not quite prepared to recommend the abolition of the holding company," Cohen wrote Ickes on February 8, not mentioning that he shared Healy's view. "I hope that during the next few days I may be able to work out language satisfactory to Judge Healy which will not be patently inconsistent with the President's desire to eliminate the holding company."[32]

Ultimately, the NPPC report did manage to steer a middle course between the radical approach demanded by the White House and the more moderate tack favored by Healy and Cohen. For Roosevelt's sake, Cohen filled the report with unjudicious language condemning holding companies, and provided an explicit endorsement of the death penalty provision. Thus the report denounced "the holding company excrescence" as "a form of private socialism inimical to the functioning of democratic institutions and the welfare of a free people"; exposed the schemes and devices "by which a few clever men have woven the amazing network of control and influence" to "bring about a concentration of control in fewer and fewer hands"; and decried the growth of holding companies as frequently motivated "by promoters' dreams of far-flung power and bankers' schemes for security profits."[33] But the report, in its details at least, left room for moderation. While it frequently pointed toward the elimination of holding companies, for example, the language of the report always provided a loophole or qualification delaying or preventing the actual imposition of the death penalty. The report called for the *"practical elimination within a reasonable time of the holding company where it serves no demonstrably useful and necessary purpose."* The holding company was not to be wiped out at one stroke, but subjected to a "continual process of whittling down complicated capital structures and of disassociating operating properties not related to each other geographically or economically." The goal—consistent with Cohen and Healy's approach all along—was to shrink down the holding company structure "without undue dislocation of investment and the loss of operating economies which flow from economically and geographically integrated public-utility systems."[34]

Writing to Healy, Cohen admitted a discrepancy between the moderate language of the report and the death penalty provision of the bill itself. However, he expressed the hope that the discrepancy "might disappear in any event with a more liberal interpretation of the Bill" by the SEC and the courts—an interpretation that, one suspects, the NPPC report was itself designed to help bring about. Cohen's effort to induce the courts to give back what Roosevelt was trying to take away is evident in a letter to Willkie dated March 21. "Speaking frankly and not for the record," he wrote, "I really wish you would free yourself from the emotional concomitants of the immediate struggle. I wish that you could free yourself from the idea that our words are 'pregnant.' I wish you could dispassionately try to understand what we are really trying to do. If you could do this, I think you would find yourself much more sympathetic with our efforts to simplify corporately and territorially the utility structures and to root out a lot of unnecessary intercompany transactions than with the efforts of those who regard the present utility structures [as] sacrosanct." As for protecting the rights of security holders, Cohen again stressed his expectation of flexible and reasonable enforcement: "When we first considered the question of simplifying the utility structure, I was very much troubled as to the rights of the different security-holders. But as I have studied the question and the way the courts have dealt with similar problems, I have become convinced that under the bill the courts of equity will have adequate power to adjust liens and priorities to the extent necessary without impairing the essential equities of the different parties." "If we want to avoid the sort of regulation which we both abhor," Cohen added, "we have simply got to simplify the rules of the game. I for one am not interested in regulation which absorbs the energy of the industry in debating the rules of the game. We need that energy in playing the game, in operating and developing the industry."[35]

By this point, however, the congressional debate was rapidly spinning out of control, and the NPPC report had little impact. (Healy's testimony, which effectively undercut the report which he himself had signed, did not help.) Rayburn's committee was in revolt, with only two members besides the chairman fully behind the administration bill. For the moment, but only for the moment, the Senate was in calmer seas, with Wheeler's committee voting out a bill on May 13 that made only minor changes to the administration's proposal.

Rayburn, meanwhile, tried to regain control of his committee by negotiating a "compromise" that represented, in effect, a capitulation to the utility interests. The new language would have allowed a holding company to control four regional systems, and would have excluded even the very large holding companies from its most important provisions. Cohen and Corcoran were not included in these negotiations, but word eventually leaked out, and Roosevelt ordered Rayburn to cut off negotiations and return to the administration bill.

Judging by later accounts, Cohen was deeply stung by his exclusion from the Rayburn negotiations. The subject arose a year later when Frankfurter asked Cohen for advice in responding to a letter he had received on the subject. Cohen advised Frankfurter to ask his correspondent "what would he have thought if the Government representatives in undertaking such negotiations had insisted that Mr. Willkie be excluded from the conferences and should be kept from any knowledge of the course of developments until an agreement had been reached?" Unwilling to blame Rayburn himself or Walter Splawn of the House committee staff, Cohen advised Frankfurter to "tread delicately here because of the embarrassing and equivocal position into which Sam and Walter were maneuvered by the utilities."[36]

The long delay in the House enabled the Senate to take the lead on the utilities issue. The full Senate, after an acrimonious debate, passed the Wheeler bill by a thin margin on June 11; two attempts to pass amendments gutting the death penalty provision were turned aside by one and two votes. Though a few minor changes were made, the bill that went to the House substantially embodied the principles and language of the original Wheeler-Rayburn draft.

Despite some talk of sending the Senate bill directly to the House floor, it was instead sent to Rayburn's committee, which was now overtly hostile to the president's position. On June 22, the committee approved a much-weakened form of the original bill; the death sentence was replaced by a provision giving the SEC discretionary power to dissolve holding companies, and the Senate's requirement that public utility systems be "geographically and economically integrated" was watered down to a vague requirement that such systems be "physically interconnected or capable of physical interconnection and which under normal conditions may be operated as a single interconnected and coordinated system confined in its operations to a single area or region, in one or more States." Roosevelt immediately denounced the Rayburn committee bill and called again for the death sentence, but the House passed the new version anyway, on July 1.[37]

The House's rejection of the Senate bill set up a bitter conference committee debate that stretched out over two months. Eventually, both houses accepted a compromise crafted by Frankfurter and Sen. Alben Barkley (D-Ky.) that allowed the SEC to "permit a registered holding company to control one or more additional integrated public-utility systems" if three conditions were met:

(A) Each of such additional systems cannot be operated as an independent system without the loss of substantial economies which can be secured by the retention of control by such holding company of such system;

(B) All of the additional systems are located in one State, or in adjoining States, or in a contiguous foreign country; and

(C) The continued combination of such systems under the control of such holding company is not so large (considering the state of the art and the area or region affected) as to impair the advantages of localized management, efficient operation, or the effectiveness of regulation.

Roosevelt accepted the arrangement in a letter prepared by Wheeler, Rayburn, and Corcoran. "From my point of view [the proposal] . . . represents a greater concession from the Senate bill than I should like to see made," he wrote. "But I understand the urgent desire of many members of both Houses to have a bill worked out at this Session, and to that end I hope the House will find this proposal of the Senate conferees acceptable."[38]

The bill, in the end, was not too different from what Cohen had supported before FDR's intervened to insist on the death penalty provision. As finally signed into law on August 26, the Public Utility Holding Company Act of 1935 gave substantial administrative discretion to the SEC to eliminate holding companies that were economically harmful or useless, while preserving those that conferred a clear economic benefit.

The battle over the Public Utilities Holding Company Act brought Cohen and Corcoran a great deal of public attention, most of which was unflattering and unhelpful. They had been subjected to negative press reports before, of course, particularly during the 1934 fight over the Securities Exchange Act; but the protracted struggle over the public utilities bill exacted a much higher toll. Most disturbing to Cohen and Corcoran was an intense but bitter scandal that erupted in early July 1935—just before the House voted down the death penalty provision in the holding company bill.

The controversy began when Rep. Ralph Owen Brewster (R-Maine) rose in the House in opposition to the death penalty provision. "During the consideration of the death-sentence clause in the holding company bill," he declared, "Thomas G. Corcoran, Esq., coauthor with Benjamin V. Cohen, Esq., of the bill, came to me in the lobby of this Capitol and stated to me, with what he himself called 'brutal frankness,' that if I should vote against the death sentence for public utility holding companies he would find it necessary to stop construction on the Passamaquoddy Dam in my district."[39] Brewster's charges immediately became a lightning rod for the anger and emotion of those on both sides of the death sentence issue. The House lost no time in authorizing a Rules Committee investigation of both the specific charge against Corcoran and the administration's lobbying practices in general. The Senate, taking the opposite tack, authorized a parallel inquiry two days later, to be chaired by Senator Hugo Black and to be focused on alleged abuses by the utilities lobby.

Within a week the president requested a formal statement from Corcoran "of all your dealings" with Brewster; Corcoran complied on July 6, then appeared before the Rules Committee on July 9. Corcoran's version of events—corroborated by Ernest Greuning, a former editor of *The Nation* and a personal friend of Brewster—exonerated himself and exposed the congressman's duplicity. The Passamaquoddy project had already been approved and the money appropriated before their conversation; Brewster had previously agreed to use his influence in Maine to secure passage of supporting legislation in the state legislature. In any event, Brewster had been a consistent supporter of the administration's position on the death penalty. Only at the very last minute—on the afternoon of July 1—did Brewster inform Corcoran that his "difficult political position in Maine" made it impossible for him to speak in favor of the bill. Explained Corcoran, "I therefore said to Mr. Brewster in effect, 'If your peculiar political position is so delicate as you say, I want to make it clear that I am not accusing you of running out, but that it is best that you and I be brutally frank now to avoid personal misunderstandings as to our relations on "Quoddy" in the future. If as you say you are not a free man politically and must take power company support into your calculations, then you'll understand perfectly that from now on you can't expect me to trust you to protect "Quoddy" or trust your assurances that we'll get that Maine Power Authority out of the Maine Legislature.' "[40]

It was only after this conversation that Brewster informed Corcoran not only that he would refuse to speak in favor of the death penalty provision, but also that he would actually vote against it. First, Brewster told Corcoran that he was going to absent himself from the vote; later, that he would vote against the death penalty. Corcoran's statement at the Rules Committee hearing that Brewster had offered to "go back to my hotel and not be present at all during the voting" caused the congressman to shout, "You are a liar!" Corcoran replied, "We'll see if I'm a liar," and declared that Gruening would testify in his defense.[41]

All agreed that Corcoran had handled himself masterfully in the

Rules Committee. Ferdinand Pecora, who sat beside Corcoran through-out the hearing, called the performance "marvelous," and Brewster emerged as wholly discredited. After the hearing, Corcoran himself wrote Roosevelt, "I do feel that I may have convinced the Committee this morning that, however few effective guns I carry I'm a man o' war flying one flag—and that Mr. Brewster is a just a shady privateer with forged letters of marque from both sides!"[42]

Corcoran's victory was sweet, but it was damaging in the long run. The bad feelings created by the incident spilled over into the Senate's counterinvestigation of the utility lobby, led by the crusading and mer-ciless Black, and then into the House-Senate conference on the hold-ing company bill. Most important, the administration's effort to use the Black committee to pressure the conference committee into accepting the death penalty failed completely, and the final bill was hardly a com-plete victory for the administration. The Brewster-Corcoran fight also left a trail of hostility to Corcoran, the first in a long series of conflicts and confrontations that would ultimately lead to his downfall.

Given the close relationship between Cohen and Corcoran and their already established reputation as a de facto partnership, it was in-evitable that some of the publicity over the Brewster affair (and thus some of the hard feelings) would spill over from Corcoran to Cohen. Three days before Corcoran's appearance before the Rules Commit-tee, for example, the *Washington Herald* featured a photograph of both men (taken from one of the public drafting sessions) under the caption " 'Death Sentence' Author Faces Lobby Grill." The *Washington Times*, likewise, speculated on July 5 (incorrectly, as it turned out) that the House committee would call both Corcoran and Cohen to testify, along with others. The aftershocks of the Corcoran-Brewster affair also con-tributed to Cohen's exclusion from the final conference negotiations in August.[43]

The Brewster affair taught Cohen and Corcoran a bitter lesson—that excessive publicity, whether positive or negative, could compro-mise their ability to function in their evolving roles as presidential go-betweens and troubleshooters. From that point on they made every effort to avoid the public spotlight. "Since the long Summer battle over the utility holding company abolition clause," commented Arthur Krock of the *New York Times* at the beginning of Roosevelt's second term, "Messrs. Corcoran and Cohen have been permitted to fade into that potent background where they prefer to dwell." The *Literary Digest* put it more colorfully: "Zoologists say some land tortoises live 200 years because they don't stick out their necks when in danger. Perhaps similar discretion has something to do with the prolonged political life of the singular team of Corcoran & Cohen."[44] Their low profile helped Cohen and Corcoran to function more effectively in their roles as presidential advisers and intermediaries. But their new modus operandi would have unfortunate consequences: Cohen and Corcoran would be forever relegated to the shadows of the Roosevelt administration, never to gain high public office or to have the opportunity to receive the public acclaim and recognition they both desired.

8

At the Center of Power

The role of chief adviser is undoubtedly held at present by Thomas
Corcoran, "Tommy the Cork." . . . It might be more accurate to say
that it is jointly held by Tom and his even more anonymous associate
Ben Cohen.

—*Stanley High, 1937*

By the middle of 1935, Cohen and Corcoran had moved from the
periphery of the Roosevelt administration to its very center. Corcoran
especially was becoming a fixture at White House social functions,
delighting the president with melodious Irish ballads, sung to the ac-
companiment of the piano or accordion. Cohen typically stayed away
from these affairs, both because he was less comfortable than Corcoran in such settings and because Roosevelt did not welcome his serious and melancholic personality. But Cohen, as much as Corcoran,
was quickly threading his way toward the White House inner circle.
Little by little, and without apparent conscious effort, Cohen and Corcoran were becoming loyal and indispensable staff officers at New Deal
headquarters.

Felix Frankfurter, true to form, gave Corcoran and Cohen a behind-
the-scenes push toward the Oval Office. On March 19, 1935, in the midst
of the legislative battle over the Public Utility Holding Company Act,
Frankfurter wrote to Roosevelt and urged the president to appoint what
later presidents would call a chief of staff. "In a word," Frankfurter
explained, "there isn't a lawyer in New York, with a sizable practice,

who has not more dependable facilities and more systematic help in the preparation of the materials for his own action than has the President of the United States, in finding his way through the maze of materials on the basis of which he is called upon to act." Frankfurter continued: "Really, I have been shocked at the way in which fat reports are submitted to you without any precis, without any intellectual traffic directions. Equally intolerable is it that you should not have at your disposal the kind of preliminary sifting of legislative proposals and bills that you had when you were Governor of New York. I know your generosity, your readiness to carry the burdens of all sorts of people; I also know your incredible resources of strength and spirit. The country needs them all as never before, but you ought not be made to do the work of understudies." [1]

Roosevelt took no action on this suggestion. But Frankfurter's letter did point to a real problem, and a year later the problem of presidential staff assistance became part of the agenda of a committee, headed by Louis Brownlow, that was appointed to study executive reorganization. In 1937, the Brownlow committee would report back with its brief but dramatic conclusion: "The president needs help." Brownlow and his colleagues would recommend the appointment of six presidential assistants who would be young, bright, and "directly accessible to the President," and who "would not attempt to exercise power on their own account." They would have, in the committee's famous phrase, "a passion for anonymity." [2]

Frankfurter's advice was expressed in terms almost identical to those of the Brownlow committee report:

> Of course the person that you need calls for an unusual combination of qualities. He must be strictly anonymous, outside the current of publicity and politics, be very discreet, capable quickly and reliably of going to the heart of a complicated governmental problem, sure to have mastered all the relevant considerations, and possessed of the power of effective and accurate speech both orally and on paper. He should have wide knowledge of the various governmental agencies, be a shrewd judge of personalities, care passionately about your purposes but be very calm and self-possessed in the pursuit of the means for realizing them. Since so much of our legislation implicates legal and constitutional problems, I think it is indispensable that he should not merely be a lawyer, but a very good lawyer up to all

the tricks of the best law offices in New York, as well as familiar
with the mysteries of the judicial process.

"You will say that I am giving the specifications for a paragon," Frankfurter concluded. "Well, I am, but there is one such, strangely enough,
ready to hand." Frankfurter's recommendation for this sensitive and
critical position might have been Ben Cohen, but it was not. Instead,
Frankfurter's nominee was Tommy Corcoran.[3]

The choice of Corcoran over Cohen was shrewdly and unemotion-
ally calculated. The factors that tipped the balance involved neither
intelligence nor experience, but personality. "Very, very rarely do you
get in one man such technical equipment, resourcefulness, powerful
and persuasive style, unstinted devotion, wide contacts and ric[h] experience in legal, financial and governmental affairs," wrote Frankfurter
of Corcoran. Cohen could match his friend in legal talent and could
draw on a greater range of experience. But he could never compete with
Corcoran's wit and charisma, nor with his "silver smile . . . engaging
manner . . . infectious enthusiasm . . . and . . . Irish charm." As journalist Alva Johnston explained, "Tommy's talents as a minstrel and an
entertainer have given him an enormous advantage over the old Brain
Trusters, not one of whom was a riot at a house party. In addition to
being a statesman, Tommy is a card. The President readily joins in singing when Tommy strikes up a tune. Tommy is not only a great number on the accordion, but an all-round jester after the President's own
heart." Corcoran's magical effect on Washington's secretarial corps was
legendary, and he quickly became a favorite of Roosevelt's personal secretary, Missy LeHand. "She sensed that Corcoran's charm, storytelling, and singing would be welcome diversion for FDR," writes Patrick
Anderson, "and she added his name to the select list of people she invited to the small parties she sometimes gave for Roosevelt at the White
House."[4]

In any event, Frankfurter knew that once Tommy Corcoran had
established himself at the center of power Ben Cohen would be right
behind him. By 1935, the two men were nearly inseparable; they moved
and acted as one, and it becomes increasingly difficult to separate out
their individual activities. They played off each other, and the press,
public, and Washington insiders alike blended the reality of their separate personas into the single entity of "Cohen and Corcoran," or, for
those who preferred it, "Corcoran and Cohen." In time, their complex
individual identities gave way to caricature. There is much truth, but

also some exaggeration, in Arthur Schlesinger's description of the two men, which follows the typical pattern: "Corcoran's brashness supplemented Cohen's shyness, as his perpetual high spirits offset Cohen's occasional moodiness. In the same way Cohen's wisdom balanced Corcoran's impetuosity, and Cohen's rectitude, Corcoran's opportunism. Cohen was the man of ideas and reflection; Corcoran, though he had plenty of ideas, was preeminently the salesman and promoter."[5] Corcoran and Cohen themselves contributed to their stereotyped images— Corcoran as the "White House court jester" and Cohen as the "dreamy intellectual," Corcoran as the outgoing Irishman, Cohen as the scholarly Jew—above all because these roles were useful in their political work. But Corcoran, as Schlesinger suggests, was Cohen's intellectual equal, contributing greatly to their joint work product; while Cohen, in his own way, was an adept salesman.

In the end, however, both men would suffer for their distorted images. By the end of the decade, Corcoran's enthusiastic and cutthroat lobbying on behalf of controversial presidential policies would earn him a reputation as a political "hatchet man." Having suppressed his intellectual prowess for so long, few would remember that he had graduated first from his class at Brown or that he had been selected by Frankfurter as law clerk to Justice Holmes. "Tom has changed a great deal since the last time I talked to him at any length—several years ago," wrote David Lilienthal in his journal. "There is something hard and tough in his appearance and manner now, and it all came back to me—the resemblance to the hard-bitten cynical tough-guy ward leaders, in Chicago." Cohen, similarly, was now saddled with the image of the self-effacing, unambitious scholar, an image forever captured by the Brownlow committee's famous tag line. True or not, Ben Cohen would forever be seen as having a "passion for anonymity."[6]

By 1934, Cohen and Corcoran had begun to help with speechwriting, a role they would play with particular gusto in the 1936 campaign. Early on, they worked with Raymond Moley, then on their own, and finally they became full members of the president's speechwriting team.

Moley's influence was already on the wane when Cohen and Corcoran began working with him on speechwriting. An early member of the brain trust, Moley was a strong advocate of national planning and of business-government cooperation. Early on, Moley's views did not conflict openly with Roosevelt's, but by 1933 and 1934 the president became increasingly irritated with business opposition to his programs and policies, and by the time Cohen and Corcoran came on board, Moley and the president were on very different wavelengths. Even as Roosevelt pushed his rhetorical campaign against the utility industry, for example, Moley was arranging a series of dinners aimed at easing tensions between the administration and business leaders.[7]

Corcoran began working with Moley on presidential speeches in 1935. "Late in September," recalled Moley, "I had begun to let him [Corcoran] assist me by gathering preliminary information for the President's use. Once or twice I had even brought him with me to the White House when Roosevelt and I had made plans for speeches, and, with Roosevelt's knowledge, had let him try his hand at speech drafting."[8] Corcoran attacked his information-gathering duties with gusto, employing a growing group of young assistants. A memorandum of instructions dated November 5, 1935, suggests the thorough and systematic approach Corcoran expected of his staff:

1. *Bibliography*

A. Before starting a new line of research, look through the bibliography for relevant titles. Working from comprehensive books on the subject is more economical of time than wading immediately into magazine or newspaper files.

B. After reading or looking at a book, write a sentence or two, indicating briefly its contents, its quality, its point of view, the personality of the author, and any other important facts. Then see if the title is contained on a card in the bibliography. If it is, have your comments typed on the card. If there are already comments on the card, add your own and initial them. If there is no card for the book, prepare one. Classify it under one of the heads of the bibliography. *Do this with every book you read or skim through, even though it is worthless for our purposes.* It will save others a lot of time.

C. If there are any books you have already read, but have not prepared cards and/or comments on, do so as soon as possible.

D. If you run across particularly suggestive titles, note them down. . . .

2. *Disposal of typed notes*

A. Two carbons and the original for everything you have typed.

B. Keep one copy in your file.

C. Leave the rest clipped together—marked "For File" where Miss Thomas can get them. Do this at the end of every day. If you have not done so, go through your own file, separate the copies, keep one, and see that Miss Thomas gets the rest. This is vitally important.

3. *Biography*

A. If you run across any personalities in your research, about whose background it would be well to be somewhat informed, jot down their names, positions, etc., with a brief note of their relevance to your research. Give these names and notes to Miss Thomas.[9]

Corcoran's men "would spend the night digging up law, statistics and literary quotations for him," wrote Alva Johnston. "The men who work for Corcoran know no hours. He won't have anybody about him who grumbles at being kept up till three or four A.M. On that account Tommy developed an aversion to husbands. The benedicts want to see their wives. They want to go home for dinner and play bridge, and that sort of thing. He regards it as a calamity to the public service when one of his hitherto trustworthy young lieutenants gets married."[10]

By every indication, Corcoran worked well with Moley, with Cohen helping out in the background. Moley's assessment of Corcoran in early 1936 is instructive, although the story was recounted several years later, after much hostility had passed between the two men. "While Tom was still no great shakes as a stylist, he had picked up a [great] deal of what he needed to know by watching what had happened to his drafts. He had learned quickly. He showed promise of being able to absorb much more. This wasn't to suggest that his judgments on policy were sound, or that he didn't have to be watched for efforts to grind the Wilson-Brandeis little-business ax. But when that had been said, the fact remained that he could be exceedingly useful."[11]

Moley's pique at the "Wilson-Brandeis little-business ax" is more a reflection of later developments than an accurate picture of Corcoran's attitudes in late 1934 and early 1935. That Moley brought Corcoran onto the speechwriting team itself suggests that the two men (and, by extension, Cohen) were not entirely at odds on policy matters. Over the next two years, Roosevelt moved to the left, while Moley, if anything, moved the other way, becoming a champion of business against what he saw as government hostility to private enterprise. Cohen and Corcoran, meanwhile, followed their chief, at least to all public appearances. But at the earlier stages of their relationship Moley, Cohen, and Corcoran were on similar ideological planes, supportive of business in general, but also favoring government regulation of business excesses.

Roosevelt's fireside chat of September 30, 1934, is an example. Delivered just five weeks before the midterm elections, the speech was a carefully reasoned defense of the New Deal's regulation of business. At the same time, it avoided the kind of inflammatory rhetoric that marked the president's contemporaneous speeches on the public utility industry. Exactly what words were contributed by each man is for the most part impossible to say, but in many ways the speech precisely embodies the ideas that Cohen and Corcoran had put into action in the Securities Act and Securities Exchange Act, and which would soon guide their approach to holding companies. "Men may differ as to the particular form of government activity with respect to industry and business," Roosevelt began, "but nearly all are agreed that private enterprise in times such as these cannot be left without assistance and without reasonable safeguards lest it destroy not only itself but also our processes of civilization." An obvious example was the regulation of securities. "In this we have had assistance from many bankers and businessmen, most of whom recognize the past evils in the banking system, evils in the sale of securities, evils in the deliberate encouragement of stock gambling, evils in the sale of unsound mortgages, evils in many other ways in which the public lost literally millions of dollars." [12]

Roosevelt then turned to a long discussion of the National Recovery Agency, whose planning function made it a favorite of Moley, then turned to another of Cohen's favorite issues, public works. Here Cohen and Corcoran had specific advice from Frankfurter, who—with an eye on the Irish Corcoran and Jewish Cohen—suggested that "the tone of the whole speech should be that of impressive English restraint rather than Celtic ardor or Oriental exuberance." Cohen and Corcoran complied with Frankfurter's suggestion; after defending public works programs on moral grounds, Roosevelt praised the English example: "England has her peculiarities and we have ours, but I do not believe any intelligent observer can accuse England of undue orthodoxy in the present emergency." [13]

Roosevelt's concluding words, like much of the speech, nicely summarize the pragmatism of the early New Deal. The language, again, reflects Cohen and Corcoran's influence:

In our efforts for recovery we have avoided, on the one hand, the theory that business should and must be taken over into an all-embracing government. We have avoided, on the other hand, the equally untenable theory that it is an interference with liberty to offer reasonable help when private enterprise is in need of help. The course we have followed fits the American practice of government, a practice of taking action step by step, of regulating only to meet concrete needs, a practice of courageous recognition of change.

"More than other Fireside Chats," write the historians Russell D. Buhite and David W. Levy, "this one had a single and concentrated focus: the relations between capital, labor, and the government in a free society. And more than other Fireside Chats, this one frankly revealed a thoughtful philosophy about how those relations should be conducted." [14]

Corcoran's reaction to Moley's series of business dinners in late 1934 is also telling. While others in the administration were openly hostile to Moley for being disloyal to liberalism and to Roosevelt, Corcoran was apologetic, at least as Moley told the story:

> Tom Corcoran called in alarm from Washington. He understood what I was doing, he said. Why, one of Felix's best friends was the conservative Lord Eustace Percy! But his "kids," his hundred and fifty "kids" in Washington who looked upon me as a guide and mentor (which, of course, was nonsense), had all required explanations. And if it was so hard for *them* to understand what I was all about, what must *others* be saying? In fact, he knew what others in Washington were saying, and it was pretty awful. He then rattled off a list of names and specific comments. [15]

Given the tremendous hostility Moley harbored over the years, not all his stories can be taken at face value. But this one has the ring of truth about it, not least because it is the rare Moley story that puts Corcoran in a neutral, even friendly, light. Corcoran, and presumably Cohen, could feel the political winds blowing to the left, both from the White House and from the young New Dealers flooding Washington. While Moley stood his ground or moved doggedly into the oncoming storm, Corcoran and Cohen moved—or at least seemed to move—with the crowd.

The gap between Moley and Roosevelt widened inexorably as the

1936 election approached. By the summer before the election, Moley was displaced as the lead speechwriter by Samuel I. Rosenman, who had played a similar role in Roosevelt's 1928 campaign for governor of New York. Rosenman had gone on to serve as counsel to the governor in Albany, and Roosevelt had rewarded him with an appointment to the New York State Supreme Court in 1932. Between court engagements, Rosenman continued to advise Roosevelt on various matters, and to assist with speeches. A few days before the Democratic Convention of 1936, the president asked Rosenman to come to the White House as an informal campaign adviser.

From the beginning, Rosenman's chief assignment was speechwriting, starting with the platform and the president's acceptance speech for the 1936 Democratic National Convention. Rosenman worked on a first draft of the acceptance speech with Stanley High, a liberal Methodist lay minister and former magazine editor who had assisted Roosevelt with speechwriting throughout 1935 and 1936. Independently, Roosevelt also asked Moley and Corcoran to work on a draft, presumably with Cohen's assistance. As Rosenman analyzed the situation, the president "was loath to tell Moley that he was about to use other people for his speeches. . . . But Roosevelt hated to make the break cleanly and definitely as he should have."[16] Subsequently, Roosevelt gave the Moley-Corcoran draft to Rosenman and High, with orders to work the two texts together to form a final product.

Not surprisingly, the Moley-Corcoran draft differed from the Rosenman-High draft in both tone and substance. "The Moley-Corcoran draft was a very moderate, conciliatory speech based on the theme of faith, hope and charity as the foundation of a 'nation fighting the fight for freedom in a modern civilization,'" wrote Rosenman. "Our draft, on the other hand, was a militant, bare-fisted statement of the necessity for economic freedom to supplement the political freedom the people had won in the past. It was intended to give battle to the reactionaries in both parties who were now out in full force to stop the New Deal."[17] Moley's implausible account of the story was that Corcoran had written the original version of the Rosenman-High draft, which was "for the most part, an elaborate, involved explanation of the Brandeis little-business philosophy." Moley had therefore gone over the draft "at length, redictating and tossing out great gobs of it."[18]

Roosevelt made an attempt to reconcile the two speech drafts by meeting with all four writers at dinner three days before the speech was to be delivered. At the meeting the president launched into Moley for his conservative views and decried the influence of his "new, rich friends." Angry words were exchanged, and the break between Moley and Roosevelt was complete. (Moley's version of events was considerably different, suggesting that his confrontation with the president was "no different than the rest" of his occasional disagreements with Roosevelt and "had vanished by morning." Given the rapid deterioration of relations between the two men, however, Moley's interpretation seems doubtful.)[19]

Having dispensed with Moley, Roosevelt now embraced the Rosenman-High approach, delivering a stinging speech likening the "economic royalists" of American business to the government of King George III and the "average man" of 1936 to the minutemen of 1775: "We are fighting to save a great and precious form of government for ourselves and for the world." The speech denounced monopoly, praised the small businessman, decried the concentration of economic power, and bemoaned the growth of economic inequality. "Against economic tyranny such as this, the American citizen could appeal only to the organized power of Government," Roosevelt concluded. "Government in a modern civilization has certain inescapable obligations to its citizens, among which are protection of the family and the home, the establishment of a democracy of opportunity, and aid to those overtaken by disaster."[20]

Corcoran escaped the cross fire of the Moley-Roosevelt fallout and soon became a permanent member of Rosenman's team, bringing Cohen with him. Always a fighter, Corcoran found his voice in defending the New Deal and attacking its critics. Corcoran, wrote Rosenman in his book *Working with Roosevelt*, "could always be counted on to insist on fighting words in a speech wherever opponents of the New Deal were concerned. He did not give up easily on his views about what should go into a particular speech." Cohen, by contrast, "was not always at our White House drafting sessions. He preferred to work in his own office long past midnight, reading, studying and writing. For years we urged him fruitlessly to join us, and it was not until the President himself insisted that he began to come regularly. But even by this kind of remote control, his contribution to the thought in many speeches was as great as Tom's."[21]

The speechwriting burden was heaviest, of course, at the height of the 1936 campaign. Rosenman, High, Corcoran, and Cohen would prepare several speeches in advance, in between campaign trips. Most of the speeches, however, "had to be written one after another while the train was making its way around the country." Rosenman was always on the campaign train, joined at times by High and Corcoran; Cohen stayed in Washington, keeping in touch with the campaign through Corcoran. At each campaign stop, the presidential entourage would communicate with the White House by telephone and telegraph. Corcoran's research team would provide facts, figures, news clippings, speech drafts, and other suggestions.[22]

The speeches of the 1936 campaign were brilliantly crafted and elegantly written. Roosevelt continually reminded his audiences of the accomplishments of the first four years, underscoring his administration's bold activism. Corcoran, Cohen, High, and Rosenman worked closely together, and Roosevelt himself contributed to the speechwriting effort, all of which makes it difficult to separate out Cohen and Corcoran's influence. As the election drew closer, moreover, the speechwriting team became increasingly influenced by the competitive and combative atmosphere that surrounds any campaign, and that was especially marked in 1936. Rosenman advocated "fighting" speeches from the beginning, with Roosevelt becoming "more indignant as the campaign continued." By the end of the campaign, the president was taking no prisoners.

That Roosevelt moved to the left at the very time that Cohen and Corcoran moved into the administration's inner circle led many to conclude that the two were in large part responsible for the shift. Those who drew this conclusion assumed, of course, that Cohen and Corcoran were radicals, or at least liberal Brandeisians—an assumption drawn from the publicity over their roles in the stock market and holding company battles. But there is no objective evidence to suggest that Roosevelt's heightened rhetoric toward the end of the 1936 campaign was due to Cohen and Corcoran's influence.

Moreover, Roosevelt's leftward shift can and has been overestimated and misinterpreted. When the president and his speechwriters were in a fighting mood, their target was indeed big business, and their rhetoric was drawn from the well of Brandeisian liberalism. In mid-October, for example, Roosevelt summarized the challenge facing the administration as follows:

> Our job was to preserve the American ideal of economic as well as political democracy, against the abuse of concentration of economic power that had been insidiously growing up among us in the past fifty years. . . . During those years of false prosperity and during the more recent years of exhausting depres-

sion, one business after another, one small corporation after another, their resources depleted, had failed or fallen into the lap of a bigger competitor. . . . This concentration of wealth and power has been built upon other people's money, other people's business, other people's labor. . . . It has been a menace to the social system as well as to the economic system which we call American democracy.[23]

Such rhetoric was pure Brandeis (the phrase "other people's money" derived from the title of Brandeis's 1914 book).[24] But Roosevelt's solution to this problem—big government—ran directly in the opposite direction.

Similar caution must be used in interpreting the last major speech of the 1936 campaign, delivered on October 31 at Madison Square Garden in New York. It was a speech on which, according to Rosenman, the speechwriting team "spent more time . . . than any other." Roosevelt "told us to take off all gloves in the final speech," Rosenman recalled. "We did—and if there was a trace of a glove left when we got through, the President himself removed it." Frankfurter gave Corcoran detailed suggestions on the speech. "My notion for Madison Square Garden is that its central theme should be the great American tradition to which he has been true, "a tradition expressed in the utterances of our presidents who are now outside of party controversy—whose statements as to the purposes to which this country was dedicated defines them." Thus Roosevelt should speak of Jefferson, Lincoln, Theodore Roosevelt, and Woodrow Wilson. Frankfurter suggested the usual emphasis on concentrated wealth, "the plain everyday American citizen," "the men and women who labor in stores and shops and factories." But the solution, once again, was centralized government power. "The wrought and neglect of government from 1921 to 1933 had to be righted. . . . Then go on and quickly summarize the main directions of the New Deal, relief, reconstruction, security, fair dealing . . . , conservation of natural and human sources [sic], the right of men to associate together . . . , public and not *private* control of public finance . . .—and all with full observance of the ancient liberties regarding freedom of speech, freedom of press, and freedom of ballot."[25]

Roosevelt and his speechwriters did not follow all of Frankfurter's advice. But the law professor's approach was mainly consistent with the final product, which stressed the administration's record and the need for an aggressive and efficient national government. "I should like to have it said of my first administration that in it the forces of selfishness and of lust for power met their match," Roosevelt said. "I should like to have it said of my second administration that in it these forces met their master."[26]

Perhaps Cohen, Corcoran, and the other speechwriters were thinking of themselves when they wrote the concluding paragraphs of Roosevelt's final campaign speech.

> Sometimes men wonder overmuch what they will receive for what they are giving in the service of a democracy—whether it is worth the cost to share in that struggle which is a part of the business of representative government. But the reward of that effort is to feel that they have been a part of great things, that they have helped to build, that they have had their share in the great battles of their generation.

However large or small our part, we can all feel with Theodore Roosevelt who said many years ago: "It is not the critic who counts; not the man who points out how the strong man stumbles, or where the doer of deeds could have done them better. The credit belongs to the man who is actually in the arena; whose face is marred by dust and sweat and blood; who strives valiantly; who errs and comes short again and again; who knows the great enthusiasms, the great devotions, and spends himself in a worthy cause; who at the best knows in the end the triumphs of high achievement; and who at the worst, if he fails, at least fails while daring greatly; so that his place shall never be with those cold and timid souls who know neither defeat nor victory."[27]

Cohen's deep involvement in Roosevelt's reelection effort did not keep him from carrying out his various other duties. Throughout 1935 and 1936 his attention was primarily directed toward defending the Public Utility Holding Company Act against a broad-based legal challenge by the utility industry. "Once the act passed in the summer of 1935," recalled Joseph L. Rauh, "every holding company in the country brought suit to upset the law, to have it declared unconstitutional."[28] The government's defense of the Holding Company Act fell to a team of lawyers from several government agencies, including the Justice Department and the Securities and Exchange Commission. Although Assistant Attorney General Robert Jackson and SEC general counsel John J. Burns led the team on paper, Cohen—who along with Corcoran was named a special assistant to the attorney general for purposes of the holding company litigation—was generally regarded as the de facto leader of the government's defense team.

The cases began on September 15, 1935, when the trustees of the bankrupt American States Public Service Company filed a petition in the United States District Court for the District of Maryland, alleging that the Holding Company Act was unconstitutional; on the same day, two creditors of the same company filed their own petitions, one creditor supporting the trustees' position and the other—Burco, Inc.— opposing it. The "Burco case," as it was known, was heard before federal judge William Coleman in Baltimore on the 27th of September.[29]

The timing and nature of the Burco case clearly exposed the utility companies' legal strategy in opposing the holding company act. Burco's support of the act was purely artificial, designed to allow the utility company lawyers (led by former presidential candidate John W. Davis) to frame the litigation in their own terms and to put the government on the defensive. Judge Coleman, moreover, was a staunch opponent of the New Deal and strongly sympathetic to the utility companies' case. Cohen, therefore, adopted the strategy of trying to defuse the case rather than win it. Taking the position that the proceedings were nonadversarial, premature, and collusive, the government appeared before Judge Coleman and argued that the court had no jurisdiction to consider the case.[30]

Rauh, who assisted Cohen on the public utilities litigation, recalled the scene: "It was pretty dramatic. Here was a former Democratic presidential candidate arguing a case against the New Deal. You couldn't get into the courtroom unless you were part of the machinery. My role wasn't bad. I was told to find the bondholder that Davis said he represented. He turned out to be a dentist. I found him in Baltimore and asked, 'Would you come down to the court or do I have to bring a subpoena for you?' He came. We put him on the stand and asked, 'Do you have a lawyer here?' He said, 'Oh yes, some guy named Davis,' and he pointed to John W. Davis. It was a great act." Despite Rauh's detective work, however, Coleman eventually ruled against the government, holding on November 7, 1935, that the act was "void in its entirety."[31] The judge's decision emboldened the utility companies to pursue their legal assault with full force, and during late November and early December "over fifty suits . . . were brought by more than a hundred companies in a dozen district courts to enjoin enforcement of the Act."[32]

Burco, Inc.—having nominally lost the case—now appealed to the

United States Court of Appeals for the Fourth Circuit. Cohen held firm, objecting to the jurisdiction of the trial court and refusing even to file a brief or make an oral argument on the constitutional issue. Nevertheless the government did file a brief on the jurisdictional questions, and Tommy Corcoran appeared to argue the case before the court. On February 22, 1936, the Fourth Circuit ruled against the government and held the act invalid.[33] Burco appealed to the Supreme Court, and now the government—in a brief written by Cohen and Corcoran—moved to oppose Supreme Court review. "We said, 'Ben, how can you possibly not review a decision of a court of appeals saying your bill's unconstitutional,'" recalled Rauh. Cohen replied "that it didn't make any difference, 'We want the Supreme Court not to act.'" Cohen wrote and rewrote his brief for three nights before submitting it to the high court, which, despite its lack of sympathy for the New Deal, announced on March 30 that it would not consider the case.[34] The utility companies had won on paper, but their case had no force outside the Fourth Circuit, and for political purposes it was of no effect at all. For the moment, Cohen had prevailed.

The government lawyers, meanwhile, had gone on the offensive. Apparently at Cohen's suggestion, they chose as their test case the Electric Bond & Share Company (EBS), which had pointedly refused to register as a holding company as required by the act. Electric Bond & Share presented a good test case for the government for several reasons. Above all, it was big. As the government put it, the company embraced "utility properties in no fewer than thirty-two states, from Pennsylvania to Oregon and from Minnesota to Florida," and it served 10 percent of all the electricity customers in the United States. Its activities and those of its subsidiaries were clearly interstate in character, not only in terms of the interstate transmission of energy but also in its use of the mails and other means of interstate commerce. Its offices and the principal offices of all its subsidiaries were based in the state of New York, which gave jurisdiction to the District Court of New York and allowed the government to bring its case before none other than Julian Mack, Cohen's friend and mentor. (According to one account, James Landis, then chairman of the SEC, called Mack "within minutes of receiving the information of Electric Bond's formal refusal to register.")[35] But Cohen must also have found EBS an attractive target on account of its chairman, Wendell Willkie, with whom he had sparred repeatedly during the negotiations on the bill and with whom he exchanged some diplomatic but still sharply worded correspondence.

With its own case in progress, the government moved to dismiss, delay, or minimize the importance of all the pending suits brought by the various utility interests. Arguing that commissioners of the SEC, the attorney general, and the postmaster general (who was involved because, under the act, nonregistered companies were denied the use of the mails) could be served only in the District of Columbia, they moved for dismissal of all but the seven cases filed in the district. When the utility companies named local postmasters or Justice Department officials in their pleadings, the government simply refused to contest the litigation. As for the seven cases brought in the district, Cohen and his colleagues presented a successful motion to the Supreme Court of the District of Columbia to stay all proceedings pending the resolution of *SEC* v. *Electric Bond & Share.*

All these legal maneuvers certainly outwitted the utility lawyers, who were forced to contest the constitutionality of the Public Utility Act in a case and courtroom of the government's choosing, and who had seen their own cases stopped cold. Cohen has properly received credit for the government's approach, although Rauh's conclusion—"It was possibly as great a legal feat as was ever pulled off"—undoubtedly overstates the case.[36]

Cohen reveled in the praise heaped upon him for his handling of the holding company cases, which after all were the first truly important legal cases in which he had ever been involved. In March 1936, Cohen heard about and passed on to Frankfurter some remarks of John Foster Dulles, who was advising the utilities on the holding company cases; this was after the Fourth Circuit had upheld the lower court's decision in the Burco case but before the Supreme Court's refusal to review the matter. Cohen reported the incident in some detail, and in a manner that belies his reputation for self-effacement: "The Government's strategy in handling the utility cases had been remarkably astute [Dulles said]. He referred to me by name as being responsible for this strategy and called me a 'very bright young man' but 'a misguided idealist'. In selecting the Bond and Share case for a test suit, the Government had selected the best possible case, and he doubted very much whether Bond and Share could prove that the Act as applied to Bond and Share was beyond the Federal Power. The Government had also shown great strategy in refusing to do battle in any of the other cases which the utilities had so temptingly offered them."[37] If Cohen wanted approval, he got it, and more. Frankfurter sent word of the matter to the president, who responded effusively in a note to Cohen. "For weeks I have been intending to write you to tell you of the grand job you did on the Burco case," the president wrote. "To have beaten John W. Davis must have given you a real thrill—I know it gave me one."[38]

In legal terms, the government's case against Electric Bond & Share was narrowly focused on the company's refusal to register as required by law. The registration requirements of the Public Utility Act were contained in sections four and five of Title I. Section five required "any holding company or person purposing to become a holding company" to register with the SEC and to provide various pieces of information required by statute or regulation. Section four made it illegal for any unregistered holding company to engage in a wide variety of activities, including the sale or transportation of electrical energy or natural gas in interstate commerce, the use of the mails or of "any means or instrumentality of interstate commerce," and the offering for sale of any security. Focusing on Electric Bond & Share's refusal to register, the government sought simply to enforce these two sections, arguing that they were constitutional, that they were separable from the rest of the act, and that the resolution of any constitutional question concerning the other provisions of the act required "an advisory opinion on hypothetical facts." The utility companies, for their part, insisted that sections four and five were inseparable from the totality of the act.[39] Which side would win would be largely determined by who won this severability argument, since the most controversial provisions of the act—including the modified death penalty provision—were found outside of sections four and five.

The legal decision as to whether sections four and five were severable from the rest of the statute involved a number of technical issues, including whether the two sections were "so woven into the Title that there is . . . [an] inherent or practical difficulty in enforcing them separately" and whether the legislative history was sufficient to overturn the courts' traditional assumption of severability. Cohen and the other government lawyers argued that Congress intended the registration and enforcement of nonregistration provisions of the law to function independently of the other sections of the law. Their argument was reinforced by the clear parallel between the approach of these two sections and of the Securities Act and the Securities Exchange Act, both of which worked through a registration requirement with penalties for failure to register. The defendant utility companies answered by suggesting that sections four and five were merely incidental to the broader purpose of the statute, which was to regulate the industry by the regulatory system detailed in sections six through eleven.

These technical issues overlapped with a political argument that reflected the long-standing fight between the proponents and opponents of the bill, and particularly between Cohen and Willkie. From the beginning, the utility companies sought to focus attention on the death penalty clause and on what they saw as the government's radical attempt to transfer power from the existing holding companies to "a tyrannical . . . independent Government commission or bureau with wide discretionary powers." Cohen's attempt to narrow the question to sections four and five threatened to take away the companies' strongest argument, and put them in the ironic position of attacking a part of the bill they did not really oppose. As Willkie wrote Cohen in 1937, "I have never objected to any of the provisions of the Holding Company Act except Section 11 [the death penalty provision]. As a matter of fact, I advocated most of them before the Act was introduced."[40]

Cohen had also opposed the death penalty provision from the beginning, of course, and had spent a good deal of effort during the drafting process to moderate its potentially devastating effects. His legal strategy in *Electric Bond & Share* reflected his hope that the death penalty provision would be applied cautiously and carefully. "The Act," as Cohen and his associates wrote in a brief to the district court, "provides the broad framework for an extensive regulatory program which cannot be fairly tested in its constitutional aspects while it still remains a law in the abstract and has not had a chance to operate. . . . A law, particularly a complicated regulatory law, appears quite different in retrospect than in prospect. Actual administration of a law often proves unfounded the unreasoned fears of its antagonists."[41] Cohen's attempt to foreclose discussion of section 11 or of any of the other "control provisions" of the act was thus both sound legal strategy and a reflection of his deepest sense of the political realities of regulation.

Judge Mack, as could be expected, bought Cohen's argument in its entirety. On January 29, 1937, he ruled that sections four and five "can well be given legal effect as a separate, workable act, even though the registration provisions also give to the registered holding company a status which subjects it to such of the other statutory provisions as may be valid," and he rejected outright the utility companies' argument "that the entire act revolves around section 11." Once Mack accepted Cohen's narrowing of the case, the rest was easy; using the precedents of the

Securities Act of 1933 and the Securities Exchange Act of 1934, both of which had been upheld by the Second Circuit, Mack held the registration and nonregistration enforcement provisions to be within Congress's power to regulate interstate commerce.[42]

Mack's ruling was upheld on appeal by the Second Circuit. The majority opinion, written by Judge Martin T. Manton, followed Cohen's line closely, upholding the registration provisions and declining to consider the constitutionality of the remainder of the act. But Judge Learned Hand filed a separate concurrence, in which he expressed doubt as to "whether sections 4 and 5 of the act . . . could stand alone if all the rest of the statute were stripped away." Hand added, "I am by no means sure that all parts of these sections are valid; for example, those which forbid the use of other means ('or otherwise'), than the mails and interstate commerce; again, some of the regulatory discretions vested in the Commission." Hand did agree that sections four and five were constitutional, however, because "when all these doubtful provisions are deleted, a workable system of controls would still be left."[43]

Both Cohen and Frankfurter were furious with Hand's opinion, which they regarded as damaging and unnecessary, and both reacted characteristically. Frankfurter, in the words of Gerald Gunther, "proceeded to lecture Hand rather patronizingly about the flaws in his approach," and urged the judge "to read one of his law-review articles 'about withholding constitutional dicta.'" Cohen wrote not to Hand but to Frankfurter. "My pleasure over the c.c.a. [Circuit Court of Appeals] opinion has been considerably marred by Judge Hand's concurring remarks," he wrote. Concludes Gunther: "Cohen did indeed agree that something had to be said about the validity of other provisions of the act in order to sustain the registration provision," but objected that "Hand had pointed not only to provisions that were clearly constitutional, but also to possibly challengeable ones." Frankfurter's response to Cohen was less than effusive: "I suppose you deserve no credit since the Constitution speaks so clearly," he wired. "But I congratulate you nevertheless."[44]

The final step was the Supreme Court, which heard oral arguments in February 1938 and handed down its opinion less than two months later. The Court that decided *Electric Bond & Share* was not the same Court that two years earlier had gutted major parts of the New Deal. Justices Sutherland and Van Devanter were gone, replaced by solidly pro-Roosevelt judges, Stanley Reed and Hugo Black (Reed, however, did not participate in the case because as solicitor general he had signed off on some of the briefs in the case), and Justice Cardozo was ill. Thus the Court, by a vote of five to one, upheld the court of appeals and with it the constitutionality of the registration provisions of the act. It would be years before the Court would reach the constitutional questions raised by the remainder of the act, but Cohen had accomplished his goal. By the time the Court returned to the Public Utility Holding Company Act, he and the country would have long since directed their energies elsewhere.[45]

9

The Court-Packing Plan

It must be remembered that legislators are the ultimate guardians
of the liberties and welfare of the people in quite as great a degree
as the courts.

— *Justice Harlan Fiske Stone,*

quoting Justice Oliver Wendell Holmes (1936)

The Supreme Court's 1938 decision upholding the Public Utility
Holding Company Act was a major victory for Ben Cohen and for
the Roosevelt administration. But the resolution of the *Electric Bond &
Share* case came as something of an anticlimax: the real battle with the
Supreme Court had been waged and won a year before, during Franklin
Roosevelt's so-called effort to pack the Court.

The Court fight came on the heels of Roosevelt's unprecedented
landslide victory over Alf Landon in the 1936 elections. Roosevelt won
the popular vote by 60.8 to 36.5 percent, and carried the electoral college by a margin of 523 to 8. "Every voter on relief and every voter who is
a member of any trade-union could be eliminated," concluded journalist Dorothy Parker, "and still Mr. Roosevelt would have been reelected.
We have heard the voice of a nation speak." Roosevelt's opponents were
wholly dispirited, reduced to hoping that Roosevelt's second administration "would take a more sane course than the first."[1]

But Roosevelt's victory, however impressive, remained hollow, for
he had still not overcome the opposition of the Supreme Court of the
United States. For nearly two years, a majority of the justices had stood

obstinately in the way of the New Deal program—or so it seemed to the president and his advisers. "Apparently there are at least four Justices who are against any attempt to use the power of the Federal Government for bettering general conditions, except within the narrowest limitations," wrote Attorney General Homer Cummings in 1935. "This is a terrific handicap." The majority of the justices, wrote Ben Cohen near the end of the first term, seemed to have forgotten the advice given to them by Chief Justice William H. Taft more than a decade before: "[I]t is not the function of this Court to hold congressional acts invalid simply because they are passed to carry out economic views which the Court believes to be unwise or unsound."[2]

Sophisticated court-watchers found hope in a case decided in late November 1936, when the justices upheld a lower court ruling upholding New York State's unemployment compensation statute. The vote was four to four, with Justice Stone—one of the Court's most consistent liberals—absent due to illness. Although the tie vote produced no opinion of the Court and provided no precedent for future cases, it was plain to see that a majority of the justices (if Justice Stone were included) was now prepared to vote in favor of such statutes. "The result is encouraging," wrote Cummings in a telegram to the president, "since it indicates increasing liberalism of at least one justice[,] probably Justice Roberts." Still, the decision threw "little light on the constitutionality of the federal social security statute," Cummings cautioned, and even less on other legislation pending before the Court.[3]

In retrospect, the New York unemployment case was indeed a precursor of things to come. Unbeknown to the administration, the justices also decided other key cases in conference votes in the period between the election and the new year. Had key administration officials known what was happening inside the justices' conference room, they might have dropped their plans for aggressive action against the Court and played a waiting game. But even this is doubtful; by November 1936 it would likely have taken far more than just one or two pro–New Deal decisions to dissipate the atmosphere of distrust that had built up between the Roosevelt administration and the Supreme Court.

The Supreme Court had not always been hostile to the New Deal. During their 1933–34 term the justices had upheld two important state laws dealing with the economic emergency—a Minnesota statute restricting mortgage foreclosures and a New York statute fixing a minimum wholesale price for milk. In tone and approach, both decisions seemed friendly to the idea of government regulation of private economic affairs, particularly in times of crisis. "While emergency does not create power," wrote Chief Justice Charles Evans Hughes in the Minnesota case, "emergency may furnish the occasion for the exercise of power." Justice Owen Roberts, writing for the Court in the New York milk case, went further. "So far as the requirement of due process is concerned and in the absence of other constitutional restriction," he declared, "a state is free to adopt whatever economic policy may reasonably be deemed to promote public welfare, and to enforce that policy by legislation adapted to its purpose." Skeptics (and legal scholars then and later) pointed out that the state laws at issue in these cases were not constitutionally analogous to the federal legislation of the New Deal, and noted the extremely narrow five-to-four majority in both cases. But these early signs at least pointed in the right direction.[4]

The congressional legislation of the early New Deal did not find its way to the Supreme Court until the early days of 1935, when the justices considered the constitutionality of the Gold Clause Resolution, a congressional enactment that permitted Roosevelt to devalue the dollar under the gold standard (from $20 an ounce to $35), while at the same time abrogating all contracts—including private agreements and federal bonds—that promised payment of debts in gold specie. Administration officials viewed the *Gold Clause* cases as extraordinarily important to the nation's economic health (Attorney General Cummings took the unusual step of arguing the cases in person, wearing his presidential gold cufflinks for good luck), and the president awaited the results with great anxiety. In a message drafted for delivery in case of an adverse outcome, Roosevelt was prepared to take the extreme step of announcing that he would refuse to comply with the justices' decision:

> The actual enforcement of the gold clause against the Government. . . . will increase out national debt by approximately nine billions of dollars. . . . The literal enforcement of this opinion would . . . put the Government and 125,000,000 people into an infinitely more serious economic plight that we have yet experienced. . . .
>
> I do not seek to enter into any controversy with the distinguished members of the Supreme Court of the United States. . . . [But it] is the duty of the Congress and the President to protect the people of the United States to the best of their ability. . . . To stand idly by and to permit the decision of this Supreme Court to be carried through to its logical, inescapable conclu-

sion would so imperil the economic and political security of this nation that the legislative and executive officers of the Government must look beyond the narrow letter of contractual obligations.[5]

In the end, Roosevelt had no occasion to deliver this extraordinary speech; the Court, in a five-to-four opinion, upheld the government on every meaningful point. Still, Chief Justice Hughes, writing for the majority, took the opportunity to deliver a stern sermon to the administration on the obligation of contracts.[6]

Contemporary observers were not surprised that the Court gave in to the administration on the *Gold Clause* issue; as the *Indianapolis Star* put it, "No power on earth could unscramble the egg the New Dealers handed to the Court."[7] But Court-watchers also foresaw that the decision increased the odds of adverse decisions in future cases. Since the justices "were forced by circumstances and expediency into a clearly reluctant backing of the New Deal in the gold cases," wrote the columnist TRB in *The New Republic*, "the natural tendency of at least one or two of them will be to react in the other direction at the earliest opportunity."[8] That opportunity came on May 6, when Justice Roberts, switching sides and writing for a different five-to-four majority, invalidated the Railroad Retirement Act. A pension scheme for retired railroad workers was "in no proper sense a regulation of the Activity of interstate transportation," Roberts ruled, but was instead "an attempt for social ends to impose . . . upon the relationship of employer and employee . . . as a means of ensuring a particular class of employees against old age dependency." Even the chief justice dissented from Roberts's extraordinarily narrow reading of the Constitution's commerce clause.[9]

After the railroad retirement case, matters went from bad to worse. On May 28 ("Black Monday," to the New Dealers), the Court ruled against the administration in three separate cases. By far the most important was *United States* v. *Schechter Poultry*, which invalidated the National Industrial Recovery Act. Here the Court was unanimous, objecting both to the act's delegation of legislative authority to the executive branch and to its expansive definition of interstate commerce. On the same day, the justices also struck down the Frazier-Lemke Farm Mortgage Act, and ruled against Roosevelt in a dispute over the dismissal of a member of the Federal Trade Commission.[10]

The May 1935 decisions inaugurated an eighteen-month period in which the Court invalidated several key New Deal programs, includ-

ing the Agricultural Adjustment Act of 1933 and the Bituminous Coal
Conservation Act of 1935.[11] In June 1936, in *Morehead* v. *New York* ex
rel. *Tipaldo*, the Court also ruled against a New York State minimum
wage statute, prompting the president to declare that the Court had
established a "no-man's-land" in which neither the states nor the federal
government could act against the nation's social and economic problems.[12] Contemporary scholars disagree as to whether the justices were
motivated by political hostility toward the New Deal or by the compul-
sions of legal doctrine, but the New Dealers had no such doubts.[13] Justice Harlan Fiske Stone, dissenting in the Agricultural Adjustment Act
case, charged the majority with producing "a tortured construction of
the Constitution"; if the Court's decisions were not "met in some way,"
wrote Attorney General Cummings, "it is going to be impossible for the
Government to devise any system which will effectively deal with the
disorganized industries of the country, or root out, by any affirmative
action, manifest evils, sweatshop conditions, child labor, or any other
unsocial or anti-social aspects of the economic system."[14]

The Supreme Court's opposition to the New Deal affected Ben
Cohen on a personal level. High on his list of concerns was the inevita-
bility of a Supreme Court ruling in the *Electric Bond & Share* case, which
at the time of Roosevelt's reelection victory was still wending its way
through the lower courts. Another case for which Cohen felt a personal
connection was the Court's June 1936 decision in *Tipaldo*, which struck
down the New York State minimum wage law. The statute at issue in
the *Tipaldo* case was none other than the one that Cohen had worked
on for so many years as an adviser to the National Consumers' League
(see the discussion in Chapter 4).

The major obstacle facing Cohen and his colleagues as they had
worked on a minimum wage law was the Supreme Court's decision in
Adkins v. *Children's Hospital*. The *Adkins* case, decided in 1923, had invalidated a Washington, D.C., minimum wage law as a violation of both
the employer's and the employee's right of contract. In the wake of the
Adkins decision, Felix Frankfurter and other constitutional experts were
convinced that no minimum wage law could withstand judicial scrutiny;
the only hope was for the Court to reverse itself (a dim prospect at best)
or for the nation to ratify a constitutional amendment explicitly authorizing minimum wage regulation.

Cohen consistently rejected this line of reasoning, arguing that a
properly designed minimum wage statute could be brought into line

with the *Adkins* ruling. The Court's concern in *Adkins*, he argued, was
that the District of Columbia law at issue required employers to pay
women a minimum wage based not on the value of the services rendered
but only on the need "to supply the necessary cost of living to women"
and "to maintain them in health and to protect their morals." Because
the District of Columbia law focused only on the needs of the worker,
wrote Justice Sutherland for the *Adkins* Court, the District of Columbia statute "undertakes to solve but one-half of the problem. The other
half is the establishment of a corresponding standard of efficiency." The
crux of Justice Sutherland's position, as Cohen saw it, was expressed in a
single sentence: "To the extent that the sum fixed exceeds the fair value
of the services rendered, it amounts to a compulsory exaction from the
employer for the support of a partially indigent person, for whose condition there rests upon him no peculiar responsibility, and therefore,
in effect, arbitrarily shifts to his shoulders a burden which, if it belongs
to anybody, belongs to society as a whole." To correct this deficiency,
Cohen added to his New York statute the requirement that New York
employers pay a "fair wage" based on "the fair and reasonable value of
the services rendered," and to that end he laid out a complex administrative mechanism designed to investigate particular industries and to
determine fair wage values.[15]

The importance of the fair value clause in the New York statute was
not lost on Chief Justice Hughes, who dissented from the Court's opinion in *Tipaldo*. "That the difference is a material one, I think is shown
by the opinion in the *Adkins* case," he wrote, and quoted Justice Sutherland's 1923 opinion at length:

> The feature of this statute which, perhaps more than any other,
> puts upon it the stamp of invalidity is that it exacts from the
> employer an arbitrary payment for a purpose and upon a basis
> having no causal connection with his business, or the contract
> or the work the employee engages to do [Sutherland wrote].
> . . . A statute requiring an employer to pay in money, to pay
> at prescribed and regular intervals, to pay the value of services
> rendered, *even to pay with fair relation to the extent of the bene-
> fit obtained from the service*, would be understandable. . . . But a
> statute which prescribes payment without regard to any of these
> things and solely with relation to circumstances apart from the
> contract of employment, the business affected by it and the

work done under it, is so clearly the product of a naked, arbitrary exercise of power that it cannot be allowed to stand under the Constitution of the United States.

"As the New York act is free of that feature," Hughes concluded in his *Tipaldo* dissent, "the question comes to us in a new aspect." [16]

Justice Pierce Butler's majority opinion in *Tipaldo*, however, made short work of Cohen's elaborate efforts to reconcile his statute with the Court's language in *Adkins*. "The [*Adkins*] decision and the reasoning upon which it rests clearly show that the State is without power by any form of legislation to prohibit, change or nullify contracts between employers and adult women workers as to the amount of wages to be paid," Butler concluded. "If the State has power to single out for regulation the amount of wages to be paid to women, the value of those services would be a material consideration. But that fact has no relevancy upon the question whether the State has any such power. And utterly without significance upon the question of power is the suggestion that the New York prescribed standard includes value of services with cost of living whereas the District of Columbia standard was based upon the latter alone." [17]

The majority's absolute refusal to take seriously the differences between the New York statute and the District of Columbia law at issue in *Adkins* profoundly affected Ben Cohen's views on how to deal with the Court. As long as the Court took such an overtly hostile approach, Cohen and his colleagues could find little reason for hope.

From the president's point of view, there were three ways to deal with the Court's intransigence. The first, and safest, was simply to wait for one or more of the justices to leave the bench, whether by death or resignation. Given the advanced age of many of the justices, there was a near certainty that Roosevelt would have several appointment opportunities over the next four years. But the sheer obstinacy of justices like James McReynolds and Willis Van Devanter made the possibility of new appointments seem remote. Moreover, the nation's continued recovery from the Depression and the necessary reforms of the economy hung in the balance, with key statutes—especially the Social Security Act and the National Labor Relations Act—still awaiting their day in court. To the president, at least, the Court problem cried out for a quicker, and surer, solution.

That left only two alternatives: amending the Constitution, or forcing the Court to change its mind by direct congressional action. Attorney General Cummings championed the latter approach, advocating a plan to enlarge the Court, adding a sufficient number of justices to ensure decisions favorable to the New Deal. Cummings developed his plan in great secrecy, keeping even his aides in the dark by dividing it into small packages and letting no one in on the larger picture. The plan itself provided inducements for the justices to retire at the age of seventy, and allowed the president to make one additional appointment for every justice above the age of seventy who did not retire. In theory, congressional approval of the proposal could have given Roosevelt six new high-court appointments, with the Court growing (assuming no retirements) to include as many as fifteen justices.

Cummings did not invent the "Court-packing" approach. The size of the Court had been changed before in American history, and had even been used specifically to influence the Court's constitutional decisions.[18] The specifics of the Cummings proposal had been borrowed from an idea championed in the 1910s by Woodrow Wilson's attorney general, James McReynolds. That McReynolds was now one of the four most conservative justices on the high bench gave the plan a wonderfully ironic twist and made it particularly appealing to the president.

Cummings was not the first official in the Roosevelt administration to think of enlarging the Court as a way of breaking the constitutional stalemate. The idea had been circulating rather widely for some time, and was frequently mentioned in newspapers and in private correspondence among the New Dealers. In September 1936, for example, Dean Charles E. Clark of Yale Law School had written to Professor Edward S. Corwin, of Princeton, that "I do think that the possibility of increasing the size of the Court ought to be more considered in Congress than apparently it has." Immediately after the election, likewise, the New York *Daily News* editorialized on the desirability of solving the constitutional problem "by packing the Court with additional justices friendly to the New Deal."[19]

Whether the idea was original or not, Roosevelt found Cummings's plan immensely attractive. Above all, the plan avoided any sort of constitutional amendment, an approach that Roosevelt firmly and consistently opposed. The president's refusal to consider a constitutional amendment stemmed in part from his political and constitutional philosophy; along with others of a progressive disposition, he deeply believed that the broad provisions of the Constitution were flexible enough to cope with the changed realities of modern life. Conceding the necessity of amending the Constitution in order to accommodate the New Deal, therefore, was tantamount to an admission that progressivism was inconsistent with the American political and constitutional tradition.

Moreover, many New Dealers were convinced that amending the Constitution was impractical. "If we come to the question of a constitutional amendment," wrote Homer Cummings to Roosevelt in January 1936, "enormous difficulties are presented. No one has yet suggested an amendment that does not do either too much or too little, or which does not raise practical and political questions which it would be better to avoid." Among the objections to amending the Constitution was that the process would take too long; that the outcome would be uncertain; that it would be difficult to reach a consensus on precisely what language to use; and that, in the end, any new constitutional provision would be interpreted by the very same justices who had caused the problem in the first place. Tommy Corcoran was known to tick off from memory a list of the thirteen states "that would naturally be against a broadening amendment or in which money could be used to defeat it."[20]

Roosevelt's coolness toward the amendments approach also reflected political factors. The innovative and unorthodox nature of many of the New Deal programs left the administration open to, and the president sensitive to, charges of radicalism. His political critics lost no opportunity to criticize the New Deal as out of line with American traditions and values, and Roosevelt well knew that any amendment proposal would play into the opposition's hands. "The proposer of an amendment would be heralded as a monster," one congressman remarked in 1936. "The gentlest proponent imaginable would be greeted by three-fourths of the Nation's papers as 'Wants to Smash the Constitution.'"[21]

Despite these philosophical and practical obstacles, at the start of the 1936 campaign it seemed to many New Dealers that the Supreme Court's increasingly conservative decisions made a constitutional amendment the only feasible alternative. The final blow came in *Tipaldo*, in June 1936. *Tipaldo*, wrote Stanley High to Roosevelt, "more than any other previous decision—may solidify opinion in favor of an amendment." With the Democratic national convention fast approaching, momentum built for the adoption of a platform plank specifically endorsing an amendment. "There seems to be a growing conviction amongst our friends that the Democratic Platform should contain some affirmative statement dealing with a constitutional amendment," observed Cummings. "No doubt . . . that the way has been opened up for such a course, by the recent decision in the minimum wage case." [22]

But as disturbing as *Tipaldo* was to the Democrats, it was even more devastating to the Republicans. The GOP, which met in convention just days after the Court announced its judgment, had long since committed itself to supporting various New Deal–style initiatives at the state level while opposing them in Washington, and its leaders had already approved a platform plank calling for "state laws and interstate compacts to abolish sweatshops and child labor, and to protect women and children with respect to maximum hours, minimum wages and working conditions." The Court's decision in *Tipaldo* apparently made such a plan unconstitutional, and several prominent Republicans—including presidential candidate Alf Landon—called for a constitutional amendment to overrule the Court. By doing so, Landon compromised any future attempt to use the Constitution issue against Roosevelt. "For months [the Republicans'] . . . chief battle cry has been 'stand by the Court,'" observed the *New York Times* in advance of Landon's decision. "To advocate . . . [a constitutional amendment now], merely because public opinion has been disturbed and distressed by a single decision of the Supreme Court, would be inviting Republican orators to swallow their own words." [23]

The Republicans' predicament no doubt delighted Roosevelt, and he would not give away his newfound advantage by supporting a constitutional amendment of his own. Instead, the president turned the issue on its head, casting the Republicans, and not the New Dealers, as the constitutional radicals. In a speech at Little Rock, Arkansas, on June 10 —while the GOP convention was still in session—Roosevelt tacitly contrasted his own constitutional philosophy with that of the amendment-happy Republicans:

> The Constitution provided the best instrument ever devised for the continuation of . . . [the Framers'] fundamental principles. Under its broad purposes we intend to and we can march forward, believing, as the overwhelming majority of Americans believe, that the Constitution is intended to meet and fit the amazing physical, economic and social requirements that confront us in this modern generation.

The problems that the New Deal was "commencing to solve," Roosevelt added—"prices, wages, hours of labor, fair competition, conditions of employment, social security"—were "in short the enjoyment by all men and women of their constitutional guarantees of life, liberty and the pursuit of happiness."[24]

Roosevelt's now-solidified opposition to amending the Constitution carried over into the drafting of the Democratic Party platform in late June. A majority of the delegates, and some of Roosevelt's advisers, backed a plank calling for an amendment. This created a problem for the candidate because, as Attorney General Cummings wrote the president, "if we attempt to deal specifically with the problem we must go further than the Republican Platform, or its candidate." In the end, Roosevelt agreed to a compromise, crafted by Donald Richberg, which called for a "clarifying amendment" if "pressing national problems could not be solved within the Constitution." In his acceptance speech, Roosevelt kept up the pressure on the Republicans, and underscored his own commitment to the Constitution. Calling his opponents "economic royalists," he accused them of forgetting "what the Flag and Constitution stand for. Now, as always, they stand for democracy, not tyranny; for freedom, not subjection; and against a dictatorship by mob rule and the overprivileged alike."[25]

If there was any doubt as to whether Roosevelt would back down from his opposition to an amendment once the campaign and the election were over, it was dispelled on January 6 in his State of the Union address. "During the past year there has been a growing belief that there is little fault to be found with the Constitution of the United States as it stands today," the president told the nation. "The vital need is not an alteration of our fundamental law, but an increasingly enlightened view with reference to it. Difficulties have grown out of its interpretation; but rightly considered, it can be used as an instrument of progress, and not as a device for prevention of action. . . . Means must be found to adapt our legal forms and our judicial interpretation to the actual present needs of the largest progressive democracy in the modern world." Though buried deep inside a long and wide-ranging message, these remarks were not lost on his audience. "Basic Law Upheld," ran a subheadline in the *New York Times*, which added: "In placing himself in opposition to any immediate amendment of the Constitution the President demanded instead a more liberal interpretation by the Supreme Court of the economic and social legislation enacted by Congress, and implied that if these interpretations do not come Congress should look into its own powers to see what curbs could be put on the judicial branch."[26]

A month later, Roosevelt turned implication into reality, formally submitting his "Judicial Reorganization Act" to Congress on February 5. The proposal was accompanied by a presidential message and by an official letter from the attorney general. Following Cummings's advice, the Court-enlargement feature of the bill was carefully concealed within a major reorganization of the federal judiciary; similarly, the president's message downplayed the overtly political nature of the plan by stressing the "incapacity of aged justices and the need for additional appointments to get the Court abreast of its work."[27]

Roosevelt's attempt to dress up his plan in the mantle of judicial reorganization fooled no one. Critics in the press and in Congress immediately labeled the plan an effort to "pack the Court" and charged the president with coming "perilously near to a proposal to abandon Constitutional Government." "Surely Mr. Roosevelt's mandate was to function as the President, not as Der Fuehrer," wrote the columnist William Allen White. "How long will the people be fooled?" The unpopularity of the proposal was evident to many observers, including Secretary of the Treasury Henry Morgenthau. "Certainly, the sentiment is rolling up against him," he wrote in his diary a few days after the bill was introduced. "I hear it on every side. I have not met anybody who thinks well of it."[28]

Despite these early signs of trouble, the administration was determined to marshal an all-out effort to secure congressional approval of the plan. It was the kind of fight that Tommy Corcoran loved, and though Ben Cohen was motivated less by zeal and more by duty, he nevertheless fell quickly into line. On the very day the plan was announced, Corcoran—with Roosevelt's permission—called on Justice Brandeis and delivered advance copies of the bill and the speech. According to Corcoran's account, which has never been corroborated, Brandeis "expressed sorrow at the President's move against the court and regret that Roosevelt had not 'waited a little while' longer." Later, Corcoran looked back on this statement and connected it with the impending retirement of Justice Van Devanter, which was already known to Brandeis and judicial brethren.[29]

Cohen and Corcoran were by now leading members of the administration's "general staff," the small working group that planned the administration's overall strategy on the Court fight and that directed its troops. "Both Corcoran and Cohen worked closely with [Robert] Jackson," wrote journalists Joseph Alsop and Turner Catledge. "The trio formed a sort of intellectual bloc."[30] Corcoran was assigned primary responsibility for directing the administration's efforts in the Senate, a role he shared with Joseph Keenan of the Justice Department. In this capacity, he was on the front lines of the White House offensive; although seventy-six of the ninety-six senators were Democrats, the outcome of the Court fight in the Senate—in sharp contrast to the more rigidly controlled and thus more reliable House—was highly uncertain. Cohen's contributions, as usual, were made behind the scenes, largely through his assistance with speechwriting and the preparation of congressional testimony.

From early on, Cohen, Corcoran, and Jackson—along with others —pushed the president to take on the Supreme Court directly and vigorously. Roosevelt's initial effort to present his plan as a kindly effort to assist the overburdened justices had clearly failed, and even his most loyal supporters in Congress were becoming uneasy. In early March, Roosevelt at last accepted the advice of the Cohen-Corcoran-Jackson bloc and delivered two speeches—both drafted by Cohen, Corcoran, Donald Richberg, and Sam Rosenman—directly attacking the justices and depicting the Court as the primary obstacle to the success of the New Deal. "If three well-matched horses are put to the task of ploughing a field where the going is heavy, and the team of three pull as one, the field will be ploughed," Roosevelt told a group of Democrats in Washington, D.C., on March 4. "If one horse lies down in the traces or plunges off in another direction, the field will not be ploughed." He concluded: "We gave warning last November that we had only just begun to fight. Did some people really believe we did not mean it? Well—I meant it, and you meant it."[31]

A fireside chat, broadcast on March 9, continued in the same combative style. The Court had "improperly set itself up as a third house of the Congress," Roosevelt declared, "reading into the Constitution words and implications which are not there, and which were never intended to be there." Quoting Justice Stone, Roosevelt denounced the Court majority for endorsing a "tortured construction of the Constitution" and for reading their "personal economic predilections" into the fundamental law of the land. "We have, therefore, reached the point as a nation where we must take action to save the Constitution from the Court and the Court from itself. We must find a way to take an appeal from the Supreme Court to the Constitution itself. We want a Supreme Court which will do justice under the Constitution and not over it."[32]

In the March 9 speech, Roosevelt took on directly his critics' charge that he was seeking to "pack the Court":

What do they mean by the words "packing the Supreme Court"? . . . If by that phrase . . . it is charged that I wish to place on the bench spineless puppets who would disregard the law and would decide specific cases as I wished them to be decided, I make this answer: that no president fit for his office would appoint, and no Senate of honorable men fit for their office would confirm, that kind of appointees to the Supreme Court.

But if by that phrase the charge is made that I would appoint and the Senate would confirm justices worthy to sit beside present members of the Court, who understand modern conditions, that I will appoint justices who will not undertake to override the judgment of the Congress on legislative policy, that I will appoint justices who will act as justices and not as legislators—if the appointment of such justices can be called "packing the Courts," then I say that I and with me the vast majority of the American people favor doing just that thing—now.[33]

Roosevelt also challenged those who advocated the constitutional amendments approach, arguing that the amendments process was unnecessary, slow, and uncertain. "When the time comes for action, you will find that many of those who pretend to support you will sabotage any constructive constitutional amendment which is proposed." Moreover, there was no guarantee that a constitutional amendment, even if approved, would have its desired effect: "And remember one thing more. Even if an amendment were passed, and even if in the years to come it were to be ratified, its meaning would depend upon the kind of justices who would be sitting on the Supreme Court bench. For an amendment, like the rest of the Constitution, is what the justices say it is rather than what its framers or you might hope it is."[34]

Roosevelt's fireside chat, like the Mayflower speech, was an artistic success but a political failure. "A few letters and telegrams came in to senators of the opposition," Alsop and Catledge reported; "there was the usual deluge of mail at the White House, but there were no signs that the speeches had changed the situation in any important fashion." This lack of movement was immediately apparent in the Senate Judiciary Committee, which opened hearings on the bill on the day after the fireside chat. When the administration's witnesses began to testify, opposition senators—supported by researchers supplied by the American Bar Association—tied them up with time-consuming cross-examinations. At the end of their allotted two weeks, Corcoran and Keenan had managed to put fewer than half their scheduled witnesses on the stand. At that point, according to Alsop and Catledge, "The opposition was not quite ready. [Senator] Burke suggested that the administration take another week, give the opposition two weeks, and go on thereafter, each taking alternate weeks. Corcoran spurned the suggestion, in which he saw an effort to trap the administration into helping the opposition with its suspected filibuster. Corcoran and Keenan irritably closed the administration case on the spot—a serious error, for it allowed the opposition to hold the headlines for an unconscionably long time."[35]

The opposition, moreover, was brilliantly organized and executed its plan flawlessly. On the Monday after Corcoran ended the administration's formal presentation, Senator Wheeler led off the opposition case by reading a letter from Chief Justice Hughes. The letter— which Wheeler had procured after an intense lobbying effort, and to which Justice Brandeis did not object—calmly and convincingly refuted Roosevelt's claim that the justices were behind in their work and in need of assistance. The administration had already abandoned all pretexts that the Court-packing bill was aimed at efficiency, and had in fact spent the previous three weeks attacking the Court and its politics directly. But that was just the point; by refocusing attention on the administration's original approach, the Hughes letter effectively undermined the administration's monthlong effort, directed by Cohen, Corcoran, and Jackson, to change the subject. Having done that, Wheeler and his colleagues marshaled a long parade of witnesses in support of the Court and the Constitution. As March came to an end, the administration was in disarray and the Democratic Party was deeply divided. The Republicans, meanwhile, were content to lie low and enjoy the show as Roosevelt's once unstoppable field army disintegrated before their eyes.

Roosevelt's announcement of the Court-packing proposal in early February put Cohen and Corcoran in an uncomfortable position. Privately, they had opposed the plan. In December and January, at the request of Solicitor General Stanley Reed, they made their views clear in a "comprehensive memorandum on the constitutional situation." The memorandum, which went through several drafts and which was apparently reviewed by Felix Frankfurter, provided a detailed survey of the Court problem and an analysis of proposed solutions. In the end, it called for the passage of a constitutional amendment designed to reestablish the balance of power between Congress and the courts.[36] "If an Act of the Congress or of a state legislature is found to conflict with the federal Constitution," proposed Cohen and Corcoran, "Congress should have the power by two-thirds vote of both Houses as existing at time of the decision or a majority vote of both Houses of a succeeding Congress to reenact the federal statute or resuscitate the state statute provided its action is accompanied by an express declaration that the legislation in question in the judgment of the Congress does not contravene the Constitution. . . . Such declaration should have the same effect as a decision of the Supreme Court overruling its prior decisions." Only such an approach would succeed in "retaining our Constitution in substance as it is and retaining our accustomed form of judicial review but providing means for correcting judicial action which denies to the Constitution the flexibility and elasticity necessary to maintain it," they concluded. "The remedy proposed retains the safeguards of judicial review and yet does not subject a democratic people to the tyranny of an irresponsible judiciary."[37]

Cohen and Corcoran's proposed solution was radical even in the context of the remedies endorsed by other members of the administration. Cummings's Court-enlargement plan, for example, would have resulted in only a temporary shift of power from the Court to the political branches. Cohen and Corcoran's amendment, by contrast, would have permanently altered the constitutional balance of power. That Cohen and Corcoran were driven to such a position reflected, above all, Cohen's outrage at the way the Supreme Court had treated his New York minimum wage statute in the *Tipaldo* case. "[T]he decision of the Court in the *Tipaldo* case invalidating the New York minimum wage legislation involved issues so clear that no legal legerdemain could conceal them from the public," he and Corcoran wrote. "It was clear, as a minority of the Court has frankly and repeatedly charged, that the majority was reading into the Constitution their own personal economic predilections." That same majority was also likely to read their own personal economic predilections into a substantive constitutional amendment. "To taunt us with the knowledge that the Constitution can be amended [to overturn specific decisions] is no answer," argued Cohen and Corcoran; "[t]he difficulty is not with the Constitution but with the spurious and arbitrary constructions never intended by its makers." An amendment could give Congress the power to regulate labor conditions, for example, but such an amendment "would not necessarily prevent the Court from continuing to hold minimum wage legislation invalid on the grounds of due process." The problem, put simply, was that "few of the proposed amendments carry any guaranty against tortured constructions thereof by the courts in the future."[38]

In their December–January memorandum, Cohen and Corcoran also attacked the idea of enlarging the Court. While conceding that newly appointed justices would likely approach "the problems of the day" in a "somewhat different" way "from that of several of the present incumbents," Cohen and Corcoran were not convinced that all the new appointees would automatically support the New Deal:

> Time and circumstances change and it is impossible to say that those who remain the longest upon the Court are necessarily the most arbitrary in their judgments or the most unsympathetic with the needs of the present. Some men grow more truly objective with age, others grow more opinionated. The zeal of many a supposed young liberal has proved to be nothing more than dogged persistence in a job which at the time attracted liberal sympathies. Placed upon the court, such a liberal is obstinately persistent in his neglect of other men's senses with which he has not been active and is smugly satisfied that what is not reasonable in his "liberal" eyes cannot be reasonable to anyone.

"At best," Cohen and Corcoran concluded, "enlarging the Court is a temporary expedient which may fail of its purpose."[39]

Cohen and Corcoran's explicit discussion of the Court-enlargement idea was no coincidence. Although they later denied any knowledge of the Roosevelt-Cummings plan, in fact they wrote their memorandum on the constitutional situation with full knowledge of the Justice Department's pending proposal to enlarge the Court. Their contact was Warner W. Gardner, a junior official in the Office of the Solicitor General who had worked closely with Reed and Cummings on the preparation of the Court bill. As Gardner recalled years later, before the end of December Cohen and Corcoran visited the Justice Department, and heard Cummings and Gardner explain "the provisions and expected operation of the bill." Knowing that his account contradicted other historical accounts, Gardner went to great lengths to defend his version of events:

> Some scholars have expressed doubt as to whether they [Cohen and Corcoran] knew of the bill at this time. My memory is entirely clear that one day toward the end of December, while I

was still active as Cummings' assistant in this area, we discussed the bill at some length in the Attorney General's small office, he seated at his desk, Cohen and Corcoran on a sofa to the right of the desk, and I on the chair in front of the desk.

Gardner cannot have mistaken the timing of this conference by more than a few days, since, as he explained, "I dropped out of regular contact with the project at the end of December."[40]

Both at the time and later, Cohen and Corcoran specifically denied that they had any knowledge of the Court-packing plan prior to early February. "I saw neither the President's message nor the bill which accompanied it until I read them in the newspaper," Cohen wrote in a letter to Justice Brandeis in July 1937. "Tom likewise did not see the bill before it was released to the public. He was shown a draft of the message a day or two before it was sent to the Congress, but he was not asked or given the opportunity to make any substantive suggestions." Cohen also explicitly denied any prior knowledge of the proposal in a telephone conversation, overheard by David Ginsburg, with Felix Frankfurter.[41]

Corcoran did not admit to learning about the Court proposal until shortly before the formal announcement. On February 2, according to Sam Rosenman,

> with the President's consent, I talked with Corcoran about the proposed message. This was the first Tom had heard of it. . . . I do not know what Cummings had said to the President, if anything, about Tom in connection with this message, but the President told me that Tom should stay out of these conferences. He also told me to make sure that Cummings did not know that Tom was taking any part in the discussion or preparation of the message.

At a dinner the night before Roosevelt's announcement, according to Rosenman, the Court-packing plan was "the sole topic of conversation. . . . Tom kept talking about the terrible effect it was going to have on 'old Isaiah'—meaning Justice Brandeis."[42] As Corcoran recalled the events in a conversation with Harry Hopkins,

> No one saw the draft or the rewriting [of the president's message] so far as I know but Cummings—Richberg and Sam Rosenman. The latter acquainted me with some of the statements which I was sure were wrong—notably the one about the crowding of the Court calendar—I tried to see the President to cau-

tion him . . . but Rosenman said the President was determined
to send the message at once. I did get in to see him the morning the message went to the hill—I urged him to tell Brandeis
in advance, hoping to soften the blow on him—the President
told me to see him at once—I crashed the sacred robing room—
he walked with me in the hall while the balance of the Court
filed by—not knowing of the bombshell that was awaiting them.
Brandeis asked me to thank the President for letting him know
but said he was unalterably opposed to the President's action
and that he was making a great mistake.[43]

Cohen's claim to have been left in the dark was even more complete,
and his alibi more elaborate. As Joseph Lash recounts the story, "Ben
. . . had gone to New York City; arriving in Penn Station he picked up
a paper and read about the President's press conference and the plan's
introduction. He turned around, got on a train, and went back to Washington in order to be with Tom." This story is patently false; Cohen
might have made it up, or it might have grown up as an elaboration of
his flat denial of prior knowledge of the plan. It would not have been
the first time that false rumors about Cohen were spread about Washington, nor the first time that Cohen allowed such rumors to circulate
if they served his purposes.[44]

     Both Cohen and Corcoran were playing a game of liar's poker, and
holding their cards very close to their vests. Other evidence besides
Warner Gardner's testimony makes it clear that both men knew of the
Court proposal well in advance. On January 24, for example, Cummings wrote in his diary that "the President also told me that he had
tried it [the Court-packing plan] on Tommy Corcoran and the latter
agreed it would work."[45] The explicit discussion of Court enlargement
in Cohen and Corcoran's memorandum of December-January also sup-
ports Gardner's account of a meeting in the same time frame.

     If Cohen and Corcoran did know about the plan in advance, why
did they go to such great lengths to conceal their involvement? It seems
unlikely that they were motivated simply by their disagreement with the
proposal; once the plan was announced, both Cohen and Corcoran became enthusiastic supporters (at least in public), working hard to secure
its approval. A more plausible explanation is that, given their reputation
as "radicals," Cohen and Corcoran thought the plan would have a better
chance of passage if they were not associated with it. This would not ex-

plain why they so publicly and enthusiastically embraced the plan after its announcement, however, nor would it explain why they concealed their prior knowledge of the proposal even from their friends and associates—including, among others, Sam Rosenman and David Ginsburg.

The most likely explanation is that Cohen and Corcoran tried to distance themselves from the plan in order to protect Felix Frankfurter, who was a likely future Supreme Court nominee and whose association with the plan would have been a great handicap. Just two days after the president's public announcement of the Court-enlargement scheme, Cohen wrote Harold Laski in England about Frankfurter's judicial aspirations:

> History will judge the President's proposals by their works, and their works will depend on the quality of the new appointees. I don't know any one more suited than Felix for the difficult and important tasks of adapting constitutional doctrines to present-day conditions while still preserving their value as a symbol of the orderly continuity of our national life. There is a subtly instigated movement over here to create the impression that Felix is too radical to win confirmation and that the President would defeat his own purposes by taking on the fight. . . .
>
> Tom Corcoran tells me that you had a talk with the President some time ago and he expressed to you his desire to put Felix on the Court. Do you not think that it might be helpful if you wrote a note to the President commending the courageous statesmanship of his proposals but warning him of the forces which will be at work to devitalize and discredit his proposals after their acceptance by pressing the claims for judicial preferment of second-rate aspirants over men like Felix who will bring real vision and statecraft to the Court? The perspective and disinterestedness of distance should add weight to your advice."

Certainly any hint that Frankfurter knew of the Court plan in advance would have played into the hands of those who tried to depict him as "too radical to win confirmation." And Cohen and Corcoran's close association with Frankfurter might have made them reluctant even to admit their own limited involvement in the plan's development.[46]

Frankfurter also played his hand carefully. On January 15, Roosevelt had written to Frankfurter: "Very confidentially, I may give you an awful shock in about two weeks. Even if you do not agree, suspend final judgment and I will tell you the story." Frankfurter responded three days later: "Are you trying to find out how well I can sit on top of Vesuvius by giving me notice that 'an awful shock' is in store for me 'in about two weeks?' " In mid-February, Frankfurter sent a carefully worded message to the president elaborating on his views. "Dramatically and artistically you did 'shock' me. But beyond that—well, the momentum of a long series of decisions not defensible in the realm of reason nor justified by settled principles of constitutional interpretation had convinced me, as they had convinced you, that means had to be found to save the Constitution from the Court and the Court from itself." There was "no easy way out," Frankfurter added. "Risks had to be taken." As Ben Cohen commented later, Frankfurter's response contained "a little implication . . . that perhaps he did not agree with the action taken."[47]

It would be pure speculation to suggest that Frankfurter also knew about the Court-packing plan in advance. Certainly he was in contact with Cohen and Corcoran as they prepared their December-January memorandum, however, and they were in the habit of keeping him informed of important events. Frankfurter also had the opportunity to meet with Cohen and Corcoran in person when he came to Washington for Roosevelt's inauguration on January 20. There might be some signs that all three men—Cohen, Corcoran, and Frankfurter—were protesting too much in their denials of any foreknowledge of events. At a minimum, it is highly suspicious that Frankfurter was apparently content to "sit on top of Vesuvius" for two weeks without pressing Cohen and Corcoran for more information.

But whatever the reality of Cohen and Corcoran's prior knowledge of the Court-packing plan, Washington insiders lost no time in zeroing in on them as key players in its development. "Two comparatively young New York lawyers are known to have had much to do with shaping the President's Supreme Court plan and, possibly to have drafted it," wrote a columnist for the *Washington Star* on February 9. But what really brought Cohen and Corcoran back into the public eye was a statement by Sen. Burton K. Wheeler (D-Wyo.), a onetime solid "Roosevelt man" (he had been a co-sponsor of the holding company bill) who now became a leading critic of the Court-packing plan. In testimony before the Senate Judiciary Committee on March 22, Wheeler revealed that the Court-packing proposal is not new to me. It may be new to many of the members of the committee. I appreciate the fact that the administration did not take into its confidence any of the members of the Committee on the Judiciary or the leaders among either the Democrats or Progressives; but a proposal was submitted to me at the last session of Congress to increase the Supreme Court. The proposal was not made to me by the President of the United States, and was made probably without his knowledge or consent, but it was made by men who were close advisers to the President and who are now working day and night to see that this proposal is enacted into law. I said to these young men at the time that I was opposed to it; I thought it was wrong in principle, and that the American public would never stand for it.[48]

Three days later the *New York Times* established that the "young men" in question were Cohen and Corcoran. "In the cloakrooms and corridors of Congress," Arthur Krock subsequently commented, "it is not doubted that Senator Wheeler had the famous duo, his old cronies, in mind . . . since he was the legislator they would be most likely to approach with a plan aimed to change the majority interpretations of the Supreme Court."[49]

Wheeler elaborated on his charges in his autobiography, which was published in 1962:

That the President for some time had been fuming at the High Court for reversing much of his New Deal legislation was widely known. I was one of the very few persons who knew the administration had toyed with the idea of doing something about it as far back as 1936. Tommy Corcoran and Ben Cohen, the White House's legislative liaison team, had come to the office of the Senate Interstate Commerce Committee, of which I was chairman, with a speech which they hoped I would deliver. They left the speech with Joe Wright . . . who was secretary of the committee . . . because I was out of town. The speech criticized and—by implication—warned the Court to watch its step. When Wright showed it to me, I told him I was not interested in delivering such a speech.

In May, Corcoran came to me and urged me to introduce a bill which would add three members to the Supreme Court. I told Tom . . . that if he wanted to defeat the President in the

1936 election a proposal to tamper with the Court would be the surest way to do it.[50]

In a private letter to Justice Brandeis written after the Court-packing controversy was over, Cohen flatly denied Wheeler's charge that there was a bill involved. "What we gave to Senator Wheeler was not a bill but material for a speech which he told Tom he would like to make attacking the Supreme Court for a series of decisions which the Senator regarded as wholly unwarranted," he wrote. "Although the Senator never used the material I never heard directly or indirectly that he took any exception to the suggestion therein for a temporary increase in the size of the Court." Moreover, Cohen continued, the president "had nothing whatever to do with, nor had he any knowledge of, the material which Tom and I prepared for Senator Wheeler."[51] Years later, Cohen explained the episode to an interviewer: "I had been thinking of the problem, and the fact that in the past the Court had been packed to effect a change in views. I wrote a speech for Wheeler to give on the Senate floor—this was in 1936—suggesting that the Court should be mindful that the country will not submit to a denial of powers that the Constitution conferred on [the] government. . . . If [the] Court does not mend its ways, it will be faced with changes it does not like. While it did not call for packing of [the] Court, it suggested the Court should remember that Congress had authority to enlarge the Court."[52] Although neither Cohen nor Corcoran spoke out publicly when Wheeler made his charge, they managed to get a different story out to the press. "[I]ntimates of Mr. Corcoran and Mr. Cohen deny that they were the 'bright young men'" to whom Wheeler referred, reported Arthur Krock, "and present instead the names of Robert Jackson, Assistant Attorney General, and Carl McFarland, a Department of Justice official."[53]

Read carefully, Wheeler's account of the affair makes reference to two separate encounters with Cohen and Corcoran. In the first—which Cohen confirmed—the two men approached him with a speech draft in which the idea of enlarging the Court was at least hinted at, if not threatened directly. In the second—which Cohen ignored—Corcoran approached Wheeler with the draft of a Court-enlargement bill. If Corcoran did approach Wheeler on this second occasion, it is not likely that he did so without Cohen's knowledge and consent. It is even possible that Cohen wrote the bill in question himself, particularly since the incident allegedly took place in May 1936—before *Tipaldo*, and thus before Cohen moved away from the Court-enlargement approach and toward his procedural amendment.

Less than a month after his devastating letter was read to the Senate Judiciary Committee and the nation, Chief Justice Charles Evans Hughes looked down from his center seat on the high bench and announced the Supreme Court's decision in *West Coast Hotel* v. *Parrish*, a case that presented "the constitutional validity of the minimum wage law of the State of Washington." The case, Hughes declared, required the Court to confront explicitly its 1923 decision in *Adkins* v. *Children's Hospital*, which held that minimum wage laws violated the "right to contract" enshrined (or so the *Adkins* Court had said) in the due process clause of the Fifth and Fourteenth Amendments. Summarizing his opinion for a five-to-four majority, Hughes dismissed *Adkins* as a "departure from the true application of the principles governing the regulation by the State of the employer and employed." Those principles made it clear that the state legislatures—and, by implication, Congress as well—were "clearly entitled to consider the situation of women in employment, the fact that they are in the class receiving the least pay, and that they are the ready victims of those who would take advantage of their necessitous circumstances." *Adkins*, Hughes concluded, "should be, and is, overruled."[54] The difference between the liberals' victory in *Parrish* and their defeat a year before in *Tipaldo* was the vote of one justice—Owen Roberts—whose "switch in time" had, at a stroke, rewritten the Constitution. Ironically, the key conference vote on the *Parrish* case had taken place weeks earlier, before Roosevelt had announced the Court-packing plan. The president had already won the game, but he did not know it.[55]

Although scholars have debated whether Roberts's vote in *Parrish* was motivated by political or legal considerations, his decision to uphold the Washington State minimum wage dramatically altered the politics of the Court-packing fight. With the justices apparently now on board the New Deal bandwagon, the administration's case for a drastic remedy suddenly became far less compelling. The equation changed even more on April 12, when the same five justices who had formed the majority in *Parrish* voted to uphold the constitutionality of the National Labor Relations Act. The chief justice, again writing for the Court, suddenly abandoned the logic of two years' worth of anti–New Deal decisions. "Although activities may be intrastate in character when separately considered," he wrote in *National Labor Relations Board* v. *Jones & Laughlin*

Steel Corp., "if they have such a close and substantial relation to interstate commerce that their control is essential or appropriate to protect
that commerce from burdens and obstructions, Congress cannot be denied the power to exercise that control."[56] Having weakened the grip
of the due process clause in *Parrish*, Hughes and his brethren now relaxed the limitations of the commerce clause. Congress, if these decisions held, was now free to impose broad regulations on the national
economy.

With the logic of hindsight, it seems clear that Roosevelt should
have accepted his victory gracefully and withdrawn from the Court
fight, or at least sought a face-saving compromise. Friends of the president both inside and outside the administration proposed just such a
course. Senate Majority Leader Joseph T. Robinson (D-Ark.), for example, suggested to Joe Keenan that Roosevelt "say he's won, which he
has, agree to compromise to make the thing sure, and wind the whole
business up." As Sen. James F. Byrnes (D-S.C.) put it, "Why run for a
train after you've caught it?"[57]

Joe Keenan pushed Robinson's compromise plan inside the White
House, but found little support. For one thing, Roosevelt himself was
opposed to backing down; he regarded the Supreme Court's latest decisions as further manifestations of the chief justice's penchant for politics, and he had little faith that *Parrish* and *Jones & Laughlin Steel* marked
a permanent shift in the Court's thinking. In this view he was apparently joined by Cohen, Corcoran, and Jackson. "As they saw it," wrote
Alsop and Catledge, "if any court bill was passed it would make the administration responsible for the future actions of the high bench. They
did not believe that the mere addition of two extra justices would produce a dependable high bench. They foresaw that a time might come
when the new Court of eleven would render an unpopular decision, and
then, they predicted, the whole business would rebound sharply into
the President's face."[58] Two other factors argued against compromise.
The Supreme Court had yet to hand down a decision on the constitutionality of Social Security, a case Jackson had argued and the outcome
of which was still uncertain, and the White House had promised the
first new Supreme Court appointment to Joe Robinson, whose political
loyalty was unquestioned but whose reliability once on the bench was
thoroughly doubted.

In the end, however, the president's refusal to compromise was
based more on emotion than on political calculus. Roosevelt, like the
Cohen-Corcoran-Jackson trio, had become personally involved in the

Court fight; he and his advisers had built up such resentment toward the opposition justices that they were unwilling, or unable, to see the constitutional revolution for what it was. On the day after the *Parrish* decision, for example, Cohen wrote a long letter to his old friend Charles Burlingham denouncing Justice McReynolds's views on civil rights and civil liberties. That McReynolds was in the minority—on these cases as well as on the minimum wage issue—did not seem to matter. "Only six years ago in *Near* v. *Minnesota*," he wrote, "there was only a bare majority of the Court that found that the constitutional guaranty of the freedom of the press was violated by a permanent injunction suppressing a newspaper merely because it had negligently charged officials of a state with neglect of duty and corruption. Neither Justice McReynolds nor any of the other justices who dissented in yesterday's minimum wage case cast their votes with the liberal majority to uphold the freedom of the press in that case." A bare majority on the Court, in Cohen's view, was not enough. Just a few months before, he had advocated a constitutional amendment stripping the Court of its power of finality in constitutional cases, in part because he feared what even a reconstituted Court might do in future cases. If the Court were to be neutralized instead by Court-packing, the job would have to be done right. As Robert Jackson put it, "If you're going to pack the Court at all you've got to really pack it."[59]

For all these reasons, the administration was not yet ready to give up on the Court proposal. It continued to fight hard for the bill, with Tommy Corcoran, as always, at the center of the struggle. "What we need to do on this Court proposal is to analyze as clearly down to fundamental issues and to act as directly in relation to those issues as did the Revolutionary Fathers on the issues of their time," he wrote in a memorandum after the Supreme Court's decisions in *Parrish* and *Jones & Laughlin Steel*. In early May, in preparation for the congressional debates, Corcoran requested his speechwriting team to prepare drafts of eight different speeches, "which can be used as themes for elaboration in many other speeches." These included "a speech showing the necessity of having a type of mind on the Supreme Court with enough imagination to allow Government to begin to handle the problem as soon as the problem begins to show its head"; "a speech on civil and religious liberties and how they are not affected or even probably better safeguarded by the President's proposals"; and a "King Edward speech" suggesting "that the President's method of statutory reform is wiser than constitutional amendment because it affords the shortest way out and that there are too many opportunities for division in this country to risk having a long political row over amendment." To supporters outside the government, he gave explicit advice and instructions. "In my opinion, the most effective speech you can make for us should have two parts," he instructed New York lawyer John J. Burns: "The first should be built around . . . the concrete statutes that impinge upon the life of the average man and woman and the difference in their timing implied in the President's plan and in amendment plans. That's good political stuff for your audience and for all liberals. The second half of the speech ought to be directed squarely at the Catholic worry about religious liberties." Corcoran also continued to monitor the rapidly changing political situation in the Senate, counting and recounting votes and estimating and reestimating the likely outcome.[60]

The fortunes of the president's Court bill slumped yet again in early June, with the release of a sharply worded majority report of the Senate Judiciary Committee. "It is a measure which should be so emphatically rejected," the report concluded, "that its parallel will never again be presented to the free representatives of the free people of America." But just when all seemed lost, Roosevelt rallied his forces, inviting all 407 Democratic senators and representatives to a picnic on Jefferson Island, in Chesapeake Bay, in mid-June. "The meeting of the Democratic Congressmen on Jefferson Island . . . had rather surprising results," reported the British ambassador to Washington, "for the Roosevelt charm was turned onto them as through a hose pipe and they have returned to the Capital in a far more malleable spirit. . . . The feelings which induced seven Democratic Senators to sign the adverse [Judiciary Committee] report . . . are no longer in fashion."[61]

More important than FDR's legendary charm in reviving support for the bill among Democrats was his eventual decision to override the judgment of Cohen, Corcoran, and Jackson and accept a compromise that included, among other points, a limit of only one additional appointment to the Supreme Court per calendar year. The president's decision to abandon the hard line was prompted by the obvious failure of his original proposal; the resignation of Justice Van Devanter, which allowed him an immediate appointment in any event; and the intercession of Senator Robinson, who told the president on June 3 that he could not win with the original plan but that he could with the revised one.

Throughout the month of June, Robinson worked to revive the bill; by the end of June, he appeared to have secured a slim majority in favor of the president. Robinson opened the floor debate on the proposal in

July with a passionate speech, then struggled to keep his forces together over the next several days. But the opposition rallied its own troops and gained the momentum; at least one senator who had been in Robinson's camp announced his opposition to the bill, and others threatened to follow. On the afternoon of July 13, the majority leader left the Senate; "his faced seemed drawn and . . . he was breathing hard." He went home to rest, and the next morning was found dead in his apartment, the victim of a heart attack.[62] The Court bill was probably doomed by then anyway, but Robinson's death sealed its fate. On July 22, the full Senate voted to return the bill to the Judiciary Committee, effectively ending a battle that had consumed nearly half the first year of Roosevelt's second term.

One by-product of Roosevelt's efforts to revive the Court-packing bill was the introduction of the proposed Fair Labor Standards Act in May 1937, which was put forward in part to divert attention from the faltering Court plan and in part to strengthen the administration's crumbling support on Capitol Hill. Roosevelt's proposal included the establishment of minimum wages, maximum hours, and other protections for workers. A version of the bill had been introduced in the Senate in 1935 by Hugo Black, and promptly defeated; during or shortly after the 1936 campaign, Roosevelt asked labor secretary Frances Perkins to revive the bill. In early 1937, Cohen and Corcoran took time from the Court fight and worked with Robert Jackson to revise the measure.

The constitutional obstacles in the way of the Fair Labor Standards bill in early 1937 were considerable. Less than a year earlier, the Supreme Court had invalidated not only the state minimum wage law at issue in the *Tipaldo* case, but also a federal law intended to regulate the conditions of labor in the bituminous coal industry.[63] Also still on the books was the Court's 1918 decision in *Hammer* v. *Dagenhart*, striking down an earlier attempt by the federal government to regulate child labor. If Congress were allowed to regulate such matters of local concern, Justice William R. Day had written for a narrow majority in *Dagenhart*, "all freedom of commerce will be at an end . . . and thus our system of government [will] be practically destroyed."[64]

In the bituminous coal case, known as *Carter* v. *Carter Coal*, Justice Sutherland had made it clear that Congress's authority under the commerce clause did not extend to the regulation of local production. "We have seen that the word 'commerce' is the equivalent of the phrase 'intercourse for the purposes of trade,'" he wrote. "Plainly, the incidents leading up to and culminating in the mining of coal do not constitute such intercourse. The employment of men, the fixing of their wages, hours of labor, and working conditions, the bargaining in respect of these things—whether carried on separately or collectively—each and all constitute intercourse for the purposes of production, not of trade."[65]

Earlier cases suggesting that Congress could regulate local activities having a "direct" impact on interstate commerce did not help the Bituminous Coal Act, the Court concluded, because "the controversies and evils, which it is the object of the act to regulate and minimize, are local controversies and evils affecting local work undertaken to accomplish that local result. Such effect as they may have upon commerce, however extensive it may be, is secondary and indirect."[66]

By the time the revised labor standards bill was submitted to Congress in May, the constitutional climate had changed considerably; the Court's decisions upholding the Washington state minimum wage and the National Labor Relations Act (NLRA) made judicial approval of the Fair Labor Standards bill much more likely. As Chief Justice Hughes had written in upholding the NLRA, "It is a familiar principle that acts which directly burden or obstruct interstate or foreign commerce, or its free flow, are within the reach of the congressional power."[67] Making too much of these decisions might compromise the Court bill, however, so Roosevelt's message accompanying the Fair Labor Standards focused instead on the need to overturn *Hammer* v. *Dagenhart* outright.

Cohen, Corcoran, and Jackson were well aware of the significance of the Court's recent decisions, and in their bill they stuck closely to the logic and language of *West Coast Hotel* and *Jones & Laughlin Steel*. As summarized in the accompanying Senate report, the first section of the proposal "recites the adverse effects upon interstate commerce of the employment of workers under substandard labor conditions in occupations in and affecting interstate commerce. It contains also a declaration that the correction of such conditions affecting interstate commerce requires congressional action prohibiting the shipment in interstate commerce of goods produced under such substandard conditions, and providing for the elimination of substandard labor conditions in occupations in and directly affecting interstate commerce."[68]

The overall approach of the Cohen-Corcoran-Jackson bill was twofold. First, the bill directly imposed across-the-board restrictions on substandard labor conditions. Such conditions included the employment of children under the age of sixteen; the use of labor spies or professional strikebreakers to deny to workers the right of self-organization; the payment of wages below a certain level; and the stretching of the workweek past a certain number of hours. In addition, labor standards could be imposed on specific industries or under certain conditions by the newly created Labor Standards Board.[69]

Cohen and Corcoran sent their bill to Hugo Black, the Alabama senator (and future Supreme Court justice) who chaired the Senate Committee on Education and Labor. The three men met several times, with Black's assistant Lee Rhoads acting as secretary. "I was the markup man, taking notes," Rhoads recalled. "They would play Harvard lawyer, using legalese. Black told them he thought these things could be said in simpler language. Neither got his full way on the bill. The Senator said he couldn't get through everything they wanted. They'd question him on that, and he'd look at them with a smirk, as if to say 'you guys don't know what you're talking about here.' They didn't see eye to eye on everything and discussed things pretty strongly sometimes."[70] Above all, Black objected to the virtually unlimited discretion that the original draft placed in the Labor Standards Board to impose minimum wages and maximum hours.

Black held hearings in June, meanwhile gathering support for the bill. The bill that the Education and Labor Committee approved in early June excluded a number of categories of workers, including "persons employed in a bona-fide executive, administrative, professional, or local retailing capacity, persons employed as seamen or fishermen, railroad employees . . . [and] persons engaged in agriculture." It also barred the labor board from imposing minimum wages above forty cents an hour or a standard workweek at under forty hours, and allowed children under sixteen to work in employment that did not "interfere with their schooling" and was not "detrimental to their health."[71]

The Senate approved the revised Fair Labor Standards bill on July 31. "Ben and I worked with it day and night, and day and night," reported Corcoran, with typical aplomb, "and that's why I got my great and tremendous admiration for Hugo." Cohen and Black also became close friends, and, in later life, tennis partners. Black agreed to expanded exemptions for agriculture, and additional concessions requiring the Fair Labor Standards Board to take into account transportation costs and "local economic conditions" in fixing minimum wages. The full Senate also weakened the bill's restrictions on child labor, especially by exempting agricultural employment altogether.[72]

The House Committee on Labor approved the bill, with various amendments, on August 6, 1937. Victory on the House floor now seemed likely, but first the bill had to get past the House Rules Committee, which consisted of five southern Democrats, five northern Democrats, and four Republicans. Both the southern Democrats and the northern Republicans objected to the bill and refused to vote it out of committee. Congress would pass a different version of the Fair Labor Standards Act a year later, but for 1937 at least, that bill too had gone down to defeat.

Congress's failure to pass a labor standards bill was yet another disappointment for the New Dealers. The first session of the Seventy-fifth Congress, which had started with such promise for the Roosevelt administration, ended in an atmosphere of defeat and gloom. For all its efforts, the administration had achieved practically nothing of real substance.

In the long term, of course, Roosevelt won his war with the Supreme Court. The justices' "switch in time" proved permanent, and their threat to the New Deal and to economic regulation in general dissipated. But the fight proved very damaging to the president and to the course of the New Deal. As the historian William E. Leuchtenburg has written, the Court-packing fight blunted the president's reform agenda and squandered the advantages of the 1936 election. It deeply divided the Democratic Party; helped unite opponents of the New Deal in both parties; cut into the president's popularity; and helped bring an end to the Democrats' overwhelming majorities in both houses of Congress. The Court fight also had implications for American foreign policy, for it distracted Roosevelt from the growing crisis in Europe, rekindled Americans' fear of executive power, and weakened the president's power at a time he needed it most.[73]

For Cohen and Corcoran, the Court-packing fight was no less disastrous. Their highly public role in the controversy exposed them to publicity—both positive and negative—as never before. Never again would they enjoy the practical advantages of low-profile operatives, as they had since the days of the holding company battle. Moreover, the Court fight reinforced their reputation as left-wing radicals (for how else to describe the supposed architects of Roosevelt's grab for power?) while identifying them as White House insiders with connections and influence that led to the president himself. This close association with the president increased their reputation for power—no small commodity in Washington circles—but it also exposed them to attack from all those who were now alienated from the president.

Corcoran's more highly public role in the Court fight made him the more frequent target, but Cohen could not avoid being tarred with the same brush. "Who is Tommy Corcoran?" asked a widely read piece by Alva Johnston in the *Saturday Evening Post* in July of 1937. Johnston went on to give the answer: "[H]e is White House Tommy. 'Tommy the Cork' is President Roosevelt's pet name for him. Through an extraordinary combination of qualities—many of them admirable—Tommy, at the age of thirty-six, has risen to a position of power vaguely resembling that which the Duke of Buckingham held under James I, or which Olivier the Barber held under Louis XI."[74] The *Literary Digest* provided a similar portrait:

> Corcoran and Cohen exist only to make life easier for the Boss in the White House. This is how they do it:
>
> The President's brow is knit over a problem. Perhaps he wants a law. He calls in Corcoran, who later consults with Cohen. Together they draft a general outline of desired objectives. Then they marshal a small army of "young brains," discovered by Corcoran in various governmental offices. RFC, SEC, PWA, TVA bulge with "young brains." . . .
>
> The "brains" snap into action. Legislative blue prints are made, passed back to Corcoran & Cohen. Finally, the blueprints, blue-penciled by the C. & C. team, are rushed to the President, ready for Congress. Such New Deal agencies as the Electric Farm and Home Authority, RFC (new style), SEC, TVA were set up in this way.[75]

As in 1935, the publicity tended to depict Cohen and Corcoran as wild-eyed radicals. "For several years . . . [Cohen] has been allied with the more aggressive faction in the power controversy," wrote a columnist in the *Washington Star* just days after the Court fight began. "It was he who drafted the holding company act and who insisted on its more lethal provisions. . . . [W]hen any sweeping new legislation is proposed, he is quite likely to appear somewhere in the picture."[76]

In the short term, such publicity increased Cohen and Corcoran's influence in Washington. In the long term, it was detrimental. As Drew Pearson and Robert S. Allen wrote in late July, Cohen and Corcoran's experience in the Court fight "illustrates what every White House Brain Truster is up against, and the more effective he is, the more he is up against it." The problem, Pearson and Allen concluded, is that "[t]he minute he gets into the limelight, he gets pulled to pieces."[77]

10

Domestic Politics, 1937–1938

They call themselves catalysts.

—*Caption on the cover of* Time *magazine, September 12, 1938*

The publicity surrounding Cohen and Corcoran's involvement in the Court-packing controversy amplified their reputations as Washington power players and cemented their close association with the New Deal's liberal wing. When Roosevelt moved to the left in 1937, and especially when he did so again in 1938, commentators assumed that Cohen and Corcoran were responsible, and their reputations grew to even more extraordinary heights.

But Cohen and Corcoran were not nearly as influential—nor indeed as liberal—as both contemporaries and historians have suggested. The eighteen months after the defeat of the Court-packing plan were not so much the high-water mark of Cohen and Corcoran's influence as the beginning of their long, slow drift away from power. By late 1938, they (and especially Corcoran) had absorbed so much of the venom and vitriol aimed at the White House that they had become a political liability for Roosevelt. At the same time, they were about to be eclipsed by a new generation of White House insiders who would help Roosevelt lead the nation in the coming war.

Certainly Ben Cohen felt anything but influential as the congressional session came to a close in August 1937. His advice on the Court issue had been ignored, and his support for the plan had strained his relationships with Justice Brandeis, Senator Wheeler, and Felix Frankfurter. Whatever the press might say, Cohen had reason to doubt the extent of his power within the White House. Once the president had decided on a course of action, Cohen could influence his tactics; but he had little influence on Roosevelt's strategic thinking and, when the chips were down, little real clout.

Even while Cohen was making an all-out effort on behalf of the Court plan, for example, he was rebuffed by the president on a major issue at the core of Cohen's official responsibilities at the Interior Department. The dispute concerned the development of a national power policy; it came to a head when Congress turned to the consideration of legislation providing for the administration of the Bonneville power project, near Portland, Oregon. The Bonneville Dam had been under construction since 1933, and as it neared completion, Congress and the administration faced the need to agree on legislation to provide for management of the site and to establish ground rules for the distribution and sale of the power produced there. Earlier attempts to push forward on such legislation had been made in 1935 and 1936, but had been held up by conflicts between those whose priority was the distribution of power to industry and those who were more concerned with the provision of cheap electricity to the inhabitants of the region. There was also a major fight brewing within the administration between the War Department and the Interior Department, each of which wanted control of the overall project, and a dispute over whether the cost of electricity should be allocated on a uniform basis (the "postage stamp" model) or should be based in part on the actual costs of transmission to a given location.

On January 16, 1937, Roosevelt moved to break the deadlock and go forward on a Bonneville bill, appointing the Committee on National Power Policy (CNPP) to bring forward a recommendation within two weeks. Roosevelt also asked the committee for broader advice on a national power policy. In terms of membership, the new committee was practically indistinguishable from the existing National Power Policy Committee, and Cohen was again appointed to serve as counsel.[1] On January 25, Roosevelt met with members of the committee at the White House and proposed the creation of regional power cooperatives, modeled on the Tennessee Valley Authority, across the country. These new cooperatives quickly became known as "little TVAs."

The actual drafting of the Bonneville bill was a cooperative effort, with Cohen playing a major role. The draft, officially submitted to the president on February 9, was a modified version of a bill introduced in the previous session of Congress by the four senators from Oregon and Washington. Whereas the 1936 version had vested administrative authority in the War Department, the new draft gave administrative responsibility to a civilian "Columbia River administrator," who would be "appointed by and responsible to the Secretary of the Interior"; the War Department was left with only "the responsibility for completing the dam, locks, power plant and appurtenant works" and for the actual operation of the locks. The bill also made it clear that in disposing of the power produced by the project, "the Administrator shall . . . give preference and priority to public and cooperative agencies . . . not organized or doing business for profit but for the purpose of supplying electrical energy to their members as nearly as possible at cost." As for the allocation of electricity costs, the draft bill merely offered the suggestion that the rate schedule, which was to be fixed by the administrator, "may provide for uniform rates or rates uniform throughout prescribed transmission areas with a view to distributing the benefits of an integrated transmission system and encouraging the equitable distribution of the electric energy developed."[2]

At a meeting with northwestern senators and congressmen on February 18 and in a message to Congress a week later, Roosevelt endorsed the approach of the CNPP bill. As the bill progressed through hearings in the House, however, controversy erupted once more over whether control of the project should be vested in a civilian administrator responsible to the Interior Department, or in the Army Corps of Engineers. The question involved much more than a turf battle between executive agencies; as the historian Philip J. Funigiello has written, "The implication, which everyone understood, was that the victor would determine the rate schedule, thereby fixing policy for years to come."[3]

Although Roosevelt had appeared to endorse Cohen's draft in late February, he now refused to support the Interior Department on this vital question. Instead, he informed the chief of the Army Corps of Engineers that the army could supervise the generation of power at the plant, delivering it to the civilian administrator for distribution; a few weeks later, he informed Harold Ickes that either the civilian or the military arrangement was acceptable, "whichever was finally agreed upon." Eventually, Senator Homer Bone (D-Wash.) worked out a compromise arrangement incorporating the president's idea of split control, but with sufficient safeguards and controls to bring the final legislation much closer to the CNPP's original concept. Under this arrangement the War Department would operate the dam and the power station, but the civilian administrator would have the power to set rate schedules and control the amount of power produced. In addition, the Bone amendment followed the CNPP proposal in giving preference in the distribution of power to public agencies and nonprofit cooperatives.[4] So modified, the Bonneville bill passed the House in July and the Senate in August, and was signed into law on August 20.

Ickes, Cohen, and their Interior Department colleagues had won a substantial victory, but the Bonneville bill was a short-term fix and no substitute for a clearly articulated national power policy. More important, Roosevelt's refusal to give them his full support rankled, and contributed to Cohen's increasing sense of personal and professional unhappiness. With Corcoran, too, growing weary of his role in the administration, Cohen and Corcoran began to think seriously of leaving Roosevelt and Washington, perhaps returning to New York to open their long-discussed law practice.

It did not take long for rumors concerning Cohen and Corcoran's future to leak into the press. In August, when it looked as if Congress would approve the executive reorganization bill, Arthur Krock speculated that one of the new presidential assistants would surely be Corcoran, whose job would be "to put a lawyer's eye on all matters requiring decision by the White House" and to "tie together all the other lawyers in the Federal service, striking a balance of their views and making his own recommendations." Cohen, however, was not on Roosevelt's short list for the new positions. "That omission is comprehensible," Krock wrote. "Dissident Democrats in Congress would probably mutter if Mr. Corcoran is offered one of the places, and takes it." But Cohen, with his reputation as a "crafty young" radical, was a different story. "If Mr. Cohen went to the White House also, to work under its potent aegis and with its wide facilities, his anonymity protected as now it cannot be, the roars of Democrats would probably be heard across the continent, and the Republicans would have another gift from the President."[5]

For the moment, Congress's failure to pass the reorganization measure made all such discussion moot. But in the meantime there was considerable speculation that Cohen and Corcoran would in fact resign from public service and open a private law practice in New York; in late July, the *Washington Times* reported Cohen and Corcoran's departure as an established fact. Such reports may have been wishful thinking on the part of those unfriendly to Roosevelt and his agenda, but like many such rumors they contained a germ of truth. Corcoran did inform his father that he had received "a very tempting offer" via Joe Kennedy, one that would offer real money in the private sector. Cohen was less forthcoming but did not dismiss the possibility of ending his association with the government. "Despite all reports," he wrote Jane Harris on August 1, "Tom & I really have made no definite plans for the coming year. And I am not sure what we will do or ought to do. I'll talk things over with you when [you] are better, although I do think it is probably best for both of us to stick together and that neither of us can be as effective working alone as we can be together."[6] The *Washington Herald* quoted Cohen as saying that their departure was more or less a question of whether than of when. "We are contemplating such a move, but not immediately," Cohen said. "When we lose the government as our client we expect to continue our partnership in private practice and we expect to get other clients."[7] One barrier to an immediate move was that the public utility holding company case, with which Cohen was still deeply involved, was scheduled to go before the Supreme Court the following February (see Chapter 7).

When Congress recessed at the end of the summer, Cohen took time off to visit his mother in California. His physical distance from Washington gave him time to reflect, and, as usual, his mood grew bleak. "It was good of you to remember my birthday," he wrote Jane Harris from Los Angeles in late September. "I am sorry that we can't celebrate . . . together. I am getting very old, 43 years. What a long time and so little of wisdom or of value to show for them." He had lived in Washington long enough that he longed for the comfort of its familiarity, but both professionally and personally he was approaching another crossroad. "I am anxious to get back," he wrote Harris, "but don't really know what I want to do when I get back."[8]

After a brief side trip to the Pacific Northwest to visit the Bonneville Dam and the Grand Coulee power project, Cohen at last returned to the capital.[9] There were several small projects awaiting his attention, starting with the preparation of a presidential speech marking the 150th anniversary of the ratification of the Constitution. But most of Cohen's energy was directed toward dealing with yet another political crisis, this one over the brand-new appointment of Hugo Black to the Supreme Court of the United States.

Roosevelt had nominated Black in August to fill the vacancy created by the retirement of Justice Willis Van Devanter, one of the "Four Horsemen" who had consistently opposed the New Deal. The nomination had been promised originally to Sen. Joe Robinson, who had led the Court fight in the Senate, but Robinson's death from a sudden heart attack had thrown open the field—the first list compiled by the Justice Department included some fifty-four names. As for the press, almost any lawyer with sufficient loyalty to the New Deal was considered fair game for speculation. "The names of a score of Federal and State officials and former judges figured tonight in a widespread guessing contest as to Justice Van Devanter's successor on the Supreme Court bench," reported the *New York Times* on the day of Van Devanter's retirement in May. On the *Times*'s top-ten list were some of the best-known names in legal Washington, including James Landis, Homer Cummings, Stanley Reed, Robert Jackson, Felix Frankfurter, and, of course, Cohen and Corcoran.[10]

In reality, the administration did not settle on a shortlist until early August. The president wanted "a thumping New Dealer, easily confirmable and reasonably young, and from the South or West since neither section was well represented on the Court."[11] Only three names were now in play: Solicitor General Stanley Reed, and Senators Sherman Minton and Hugo Black. Minton soon bowed out in favor of Black.

Reed had strong credentials and strong support, including the backing of Felix Frankfurter, but Roosevelt, after some hesitation, gave the nod to Black.[12] The president's decision was partly intended as a reward for loyalty, but it also served broader political purposes. By nominating Black, Roosevelt aimed to secure the appointment of a solid liberal while avoiding another debilitating fight with the Senate; Black, as a fellow senator, would be subject to virtually automatic confirmation. The Black appointment was also a way of getting even with the Southern conservatives who had emerged as the most influential opponents of Roosevelt's second-term agenda. "To give the rebels' part of the country so important an appointment," commented Joseph Alsop and Turner Catledge, "yet give it to one of the two or three left-wingers in the Senate was a neat and cruel irony to the rather vengeful president."[13] With the end of the session looming, the Senate confirmed the appointment within five days of Roosevelt's announcement of the nomination.

Black and his wife took off on a celebratory trip to Europe, but the real fight over his appointment to the high court was just beginning. Controversy centered on Black's alleged membership early in life in the Ku Klux Klan. Allegations of Black's membership in the Klan had circulated even before the Senate confirmation vote, and were taken seriously enough that the members of the Senate Judiciary Committee dispatched William Borah (R-Idaho) to discuss the matter with Black. Black neither admitted nor denied any past involvement with the Klan, telling Borah only that he was not currently a member. That was good enough for the Judiciary Committee, which refused even to hold hearings. In September, however, the Pittsburgh *Post-Gazette* carried a series of articles, reproduced in papers across the country, proving in great detail that Black had once been a member of the Klan and that he had never resigned: "He holds his membership in the masked and oath-bound legion as he holds his high office in the Nation's Supreme Tribunal— for life." [14]

Black cut short his European vacation in late September and prepared to address the American people in a nationally broadcast radio speech. Cohen and Corcoran had developed a strong friendship with Black throughout the legislative battles of the New Deal, and stood ready to help. They read Black's draft speech, pronounced it "terrible," and wrote their own version, replete with "abject repentance . . . and a plea for forgiveness, along with an indictment of Klansmen, past and present." Black rejected the Cohen and Corcoran approach and stuck with his own version, in which he simply admitted his brief membership in the Klan. "I did join the Klan," he said. "I later resigned. I never rejoined." [15] He did not apologize, nor did he explain further. Instead, he stressed his long record of public service and his commitment to liberal principles. Whether Cohen and Corcoran's speech would have been more or less effective is a moot point, since the speech Black did deliver was convincing enough to serve its purpose. Black kept his seat on the Court and remained there for more than thirty years, until he retired (one week before he died) in 1971. He and Cohen remained friends, and avid tennis partners, for life.

The Black controversy was yet another stumbling block for an already troubled administration. Nevertheless, Roosevelt took steps in late September to salvage his tattered legislative program and regain some part of the lost momentum. First, he took off across the country on a campaign-style trip that included, among many similar events, the dedication of the Bonneville Dam. The president drew confidence from the "panorama of cheering crowds, bounteous crops, and mighty public works" throughout the trip, returning to Washington in a fighting mood. He immediately issued a call for a special session of Congress, to meet in November, and proclaimed an agenda that included all the unfinished business of the previous summer—including the Fair Labor Standards Act, executive reorganization, and the expansion of the TVA concept to other parts of the country—as well as some new ideas, most important a revision of the nation's antitrust laws.

Roosevelt accompanied his formal charge to Congress with a fireside chat, delivered on October 12, 1937. The usual speechwriting team —Cohen, Corcoran, and Rosenman—worked on both the message and the speech. The general approach of the chat was to depict Congress as opposing, instead of representing, the American people. "The people of the United States were checked in their efforts to prevent future piling up of huge agricultural surpluses and the tumbling prices which inevitably follow them," Roosevelt said. "They were checked in their efforts to secure reasonable minimum wages and maximum hours and the end of child labor. And because they were checked many groups in many parts of the country still have less purchasing power and a lower standard of living than the nation as a whole can permanently allow." Roosevelt also attacked "private monopolies and financial oligarchies," and announced that "we are already studying how to strengthen our antitrust laws in order to end monopoly." And, for the first time, he devoted a substantial part of the fireside chat to the growing prospect of war and the danger of isolationism. "I want our democracy to be wise enough to realize that aloofness from war is not promoted by unawareness of war. In a world of mutual suspicions, peace must be affirmatively reached for. It cannot just be wished for. And it cannot just be waited for." [16]

Having regained the initiative, the president had reason to be optimistic about the upcoming special session. Others were not so sure. Correspondents on the Western trip, reported *Time* magazine, "found the West's preponderant farm populace devoted to Mr. Roosevelt, indifferent to crop control, opposed to the wages-hours bills, and in doubt about the Supreme Court issue." And the president, both on the trip and in a press conference upon his return, seemed keenly aware of stubborn economic problems back East. "A sickly stock market, onerous corporation taxes, and a dislocated budget frazzled the nation's financial nerve centers," *Time* commented. Although for the moment "these circumstances only fueled the President's determination to press ahead for his program," within a week the pessimists would be proven right, and the president's agenda would be sidetracked.[17]

The big blow to Roosevelt's attempted resurgence came from Wall Street. Stocks had been in a general decline since mid-August, but on Monday and Tuesday, October 18 and 19, the decline turned briefly into panic. In a scenario that recalled October 1929, the sudden price break forced thousands to sell shares to cover margin calls; by one estimate, some 40,000 to 50,000 accounts were closed out on Tuesday morning alone. The Dow Jones Industrial Average, which had climbed to over 190 in mid-August, stood at just over 137 on Monday morning; at one point on Tuesday, it dropped below 116. In percentage terms, the market plunged 15 percent in approximately twenty-four hours.

Wall Street steadied itself by Tuesday afternoon, regaining all the morning's losses, but the psychological damage to investors and the political damage to Roosevelt would not be so easily erased. The "recession of 1937" probably started in mid-summer, and several economists had been pessimistic since the spring. For most Americans, however, the bad economic news did not hit home until the October stock market panic.[18]

The onset of the recession put the administration in a quandary. On the one hand, the economic downturn gave new urgency to the president's legislative program. On the other, the White House knew well that the president's power and popularity depended on his ability to claim the success of the New Deal. In his October fireside chat, Roosevelt himself seemed to acknowledge the awkwardness of his position. "For most of the country this has been a good year," he said, "better in dollars and cents than for many years and far better in the soundness of its prosperity." Everywhere he went on his western trip, Roosevelt reported, "I found particular optimism about the good effect on business which is expected from the steady spending by farmers of the largest farm income in years." A president's duty, however, was to "think not only of this year but of future years," and to "look beyond the average of the prosperity and well-being of the country, because averages easily cover up danger spots of poverty and instability." Above all, he reminded the people, a president "must not let the country be deceived by a merely temporary prosperity."[19]

Caught between a desire to extend the reform program of the New Deal and an unwillingness to acknowledge the depth or extent of the recession, Roosevelt hesitated. By November, he could no longer ignore the economic crisis; he characterized the marked decline in industrial production as "a matter of definite concern," but he did not follow up such comments with a bolder legislative program. Without strong presidential leadership, and with Congress still in an uproar over the events of the previous spring and summer, the special session was a nonstarter. Congress adjourned in December without having passed a single item on the president's original agenda.

Roosevelt's indecisiveness in the fall of 1937 was paralleled by a growing split within the administration over how to cope with the economic emergency. On one side were the so-called conservatives, led by Henry Morgenthau, who pressed the president to focus on "restoring business confidence" by balancing the federal budget. On the other were a loosely allied group of "liberals"—known, at the time, simply as the "New Dealers"—who urged a more aggressive approach. Yet the liberals, as historian Alan Brinkley has demonstrated, were deeply divided on how to proceed. Some saw combating the recession as the main goal, while others viewed the crisis merely as an opportunity to extend the New Deal's emphasis on reform. Some followed British economist John Maynard Keynes in arguing for massive public spending, while others saw a crackdown on monopolies as the more pressing concern. What they shared, as Brinkley has written, was the conviction that one way or another the "government must exercise an increased level of authority over the structure and behavior of private capitalist institutions."[20]

It took until April 1938 for the president to make up his mind. When at last he did, he embraced the liberal approach with all his rhetorical might. Within weeks, he called for spending increases to "prime the pump" and thus restart the national economy, and for a "thorough study of the concentration of economic power in American industry and the effect of that concentration upon the decline of competition." With the recession deepening and the president at last returning to political form, Congress approved both proposals, and topped off the session by passing a modified Fair Labor Standards bill as well. The liberals, it seemed, were at last ascendant.[21]

According to press accounts, Cohen and Corcoran's influence on Roosevelt was evident well before the president's April 1938 move to the left. "The role of chief adviser is undoubtedly held at present by Thomas Corcoran—'Tommy the Cork,'" wrote Stanley High in November 1937. But he immediately corrected himself: "It might be more accurate to say that it is held jointly by Corcoran and his even more anonymous associate Ben Cohen." High continued:

> Cohen and Corcoran constitute a shadowy, fantastic team entirely unique, I should say, in the annals of American government. No one would dare to predict how long they will last, but while they last most informed observers will agree that they exercise more influence at the White House and, through the White House, are more of a force throughout the entire reaches of government than any pair of statesmen in Washington, in the Cabinet, in Congress, or anywhere else. . . .
>
> Of the two Tom is the more entertaining and Ben the more dependable. If Ben were free to consult his own preferences

—which, under Tom's unrelenting drive, he is not—he would probably jump at a chance to return to the quiet life of a bona fide government lawyer or get out of the government entirely. He has an extraordinary legal mind.

His ambition, I think, is to use his legal ability in the business of the law, undisturbed by the boisterousness and the risks of politics or the nocturnal brain-storms of his partner and room-mate. He belongs to the New Deal left wing but he is not a Frankfurter product. . . . His radicalism, therefore, is less evangelical than Tom's. Left alone, Ben Cohen could probably circulate, unsuspected and with a free conscience, among the members of the Chevy Chase Club or enter a New York legal firm and find a considerable measure of satisfaction in the company of his conservative associates at the bar.

Such a course, however, was not likely, "so long as Tom Corcoran chooses to make Washington his Happy Hunting Ground. . . . Tom would be scintillating without Ben but he would be much less useful."[22]

Roosevelt's April 1938 endorsement of the liberal approach on spending and corporate monopolies served to confirm High's characterization of Cohen and Corcoran as "the new chief advisers." The story line was simple: liberals and conservatives had waged a six-month war for the president's ear, and the liberals—led by Cohen and Corcoran—had won. Journalists Joseph Alsop and Robert Kintner thus described the events of late 1937 and early 1938 as a "palace struggle over depression policy" whose outcome "left the New Dealers lords of all they surveyed." Now that the liberals were in charge, wrote Alsop and Kintner, their goals were clear:

The purposes of the New Dealers are those of American left-liberals. It has already been pointed out that the great majority of them are merely very aggressive old-fashioned trust-busters, with heavy trimmings of theory on social welfare, business regulation and similar matters. . . . Being intellectuals, seeing their ideas become facts excites them more than anything else could do. And thus, however unsound you may think their ideas, the New Dealer's first interest is in doing a good job according to their lights.

"They are interested in every governmental matter," Alsop and Kintner concluded, "from the Treasury tax programs to the rate of lending at the

RFC. . . . They are always working together, and on scores of different projects."[23]

At the top of the list of "New Dealers," of course, was Corcoran, with Cohen following closely in his shadow. "Sometimes Corcoran is at the White House daily for weeks on end, slipping in by a back way with his brief case overflowing with papers. Sometimes the President will tell him, 'Do this,' and he will not return until he can say 'It's done,' or 'It can't be done.' His duties are so many and the President's reliance on him is so continuous that wherever he is, all day long, he always makes it possible for the White House to reach him. Every evening, no matter how late he has played or labored, he always makes a last call to the White House operator to be sure there are no more orders." Meanwhile, "the New Deal's special thinker, the brilliant and contemplative Cohen," along with Isadore Lubin, Leon Henderson, and Laughlin Currie, "watch economic trends together, forecast new developments, suggest corrections."[24]

As the purported leaders of the liberal coup, Cohen and Corcoran took on celebrity status. On September 12, 1938, they found themselves on the cover of *Time* magazine, above the caption "They call themselves catalysts." In the cover photograph, Cohen sits, pen in hand and broad smile on his face, peering through his glasses at what looks to be a new piece of legislative draftsmanship; Corcoran stands over his partner's left shoulder, also smiling, as if in approval. They are "the Administration's unofficial legal firm, Cohen & Corcoran," according to the accompanying article, constituting "with one or two more . . . what in President Jackson's time was called the Kitchen Cabinet."[25]

Part of what made Cohen and Corcoran such good copy in the national press was the seeming incongruity of their relationship. "Conjunctions of dreamy, intellectual Jews and effervescent Irishmen may have occurred before," wrote *Time*, "but never more effectively than in Cohen & Corcoran." This emphasis on their ethnic backgrounds made stereotyping inevitable. Corcoran was gregarious and loyal—but also a political "operator"; Cohen was brilliant and scholarly—but also Machiavellian in his scheming. Corcoran, wrote the *Washington Star* in August 1937, is the New Deal's "minstrel," toting his accordion to White House functions, where he "bubbles good fellowship and tells anecdotes which amuse the President," all the while working "14 hours a day furthering the President's program." Corcoran's personality "is the master key to the success and fame of Corcoran & Cohen," echoed *Time* magazine. "Historic is the White House party at which Tommy the Cork, playing his accordion and singing his ballads, charmed the Great Charmer. His tenor voice is honey smooth. . . . He handles people as a virtuoso plays the violin." All of this makes " 'Tommy the Cork' (as the President calls him) sound like a shrewd, insinuating schemer— which he is—but for reasons more tough-minded and lawyer-like than his critics credit." The "shy, cool" Cohen, by contrast, was "brilliant and contemplative," content to pull strings from behind the stage. If Corcoran and Cohen held important offices, *Time* concluded, they "would have to observe rules of the game. As it is, Corcoran and Cohen are beyond the rules. They are engaged in making them." [26]

By the summer and fall of 1938, press accounts of Cohen and Corcoran's exploits had, as one letter-writer to *Time* put it, "gotten out of hand." When Cohen returned from a European trip in late September, even the *New York Times* became feverish with excitement. Calling Cohen "one of the two young lawyers said to wield more influence with President Roosevelt than any other Americans," the *Times* reported that his arrival on the liner *Manhattan* was "surrounded by a system of security and protection more elaborate than any remembered in the port by customs men and others who have met ships for the last generation."

> Cohen was met down the bay by his reputed partner in power, Thomas Corcoran, who left the Federal barge office a half hour ahead of the usual cutter which carries customs inspectors, immigration agents and newspaper men. It was reported that the special cutter also carried a handful of special Treasury agents, but if there were any they disappeared on the ship, and Mr. Cohen denied knowing of them. . . .
>
> Pursers, assistant pursers, stewards and other members of the Manhattan's crew denied that Mr. Cohen was on board, but he was found by reporters standing on the after end of the promenade deck, talking with friends.
>
> The purser's staff even prepared two sets of passenger lists, one with Mr. Cohen's name on the "additional" group of those who booked late. The other did not show his name.

Cohen denied that anything special was going on. "He carried a bulging brief case containing, he said, not official papers but neckties, pajamas and a toothbrush." Asked if he had returned from Europe with any new ideas, Cohen replied, " 'No, nothing in the way of new ideas. I have simply been on vacation' . . . . He said he had asked for 'privacy' on the liner because he wanted to return quietly." [27]

A reporter on board the ship seemed to sum up the press frenzy that surrounded Cohen and Corcoran in 1937 and 1938. "You are credited," he told Cohen in the lead-in to a question, "with being one of the two men—three including President Roosevelt—who run the affairs of the country."[28]

Ironically, Cohen and Corcoran's reputation as power players peaked just as their real influence began to decline. Despite their high visibility in late 1937 and 1938, and despite the apparent triumph of the "liberal" New Dealers, Cohen and Corcoran's major contributions to the president's domestic agenda were already behind them.

The Congress that convened in January 1938 did pass the revised Fair Labor Standards Act. It also approved sharp increases in federal relief spending, ratifying the administration's new, "Keynesian" approach to fiscal policy, and authorized the creation of the Temporary National Economic Committee (TNEC) to investigate the concentration of economic power in the United States. The administration also won victories on naval spending, agricultural adjustment, and flood control. But the congressional session was hardly a completely successful one from the liberal perspective. The 1938 Congress killed, held up, or buried much more legislation than it approved. Among the casualties were an anti-lynching bill (blocked by a Senate filibuster), the executive reorganization bill (defeated in the House), and the "little TVAS" proposal (allowed to die in committee). For the liberals, as the historian William Leuchtenburg writes, "1938 was a discouraging year. They had scored some successes in Congress, a surprising number given the strength of the bipartisan conservative coalition, but they had suffered some mean setbacks too."[29]

The triumph of liberalism in 1938, in short, was more a matter of politics than of public policy. Sensing the president's hesitation and vulnerability in the winter of 1937–38, Cohen and Corcoran teamed once more with Robert Jackson to craft a political strategy designed to regain the momentum Roosevelt had sacrificed in the Court-packing fight. The centerpiece of that political strategy was at first the attack on monopoly, then later an attempt to "purge" the Democratic Party of its most conservative elements. At the same time, Cohen and Corcoran strongly supported, though they did not lead, the growing movement among the administration's economists to promote public spending as the only way to revive the slumping economy.

The campaign against monopolies began in late 1937. On its front lines were Harold Ickes and Robert Jackson, both confirmed anti-monopolists who, following the teachings of Louis Brandeis, deeply felt that the concentration of economic wealth in a relatively few hands posed a serious threat to the very survival of American democracy. After a Cabinet meeting on November 4, Ickes passed Roosevelt a note comparing the New Deal's struggle against monopoly to Andrew Jackson's fight against the Bank of the United States. "At that time [Bank president Nicholas] Biddle forced a panic on the country in his effort to keep money supreme, and money is acting the same way now," Ickes wrote in his diary. "Of course, the finances of the country are not in the control of one man as they were in the days of Biddle, but, on the other hand, there is more money, it is well organized, and it has been at the top of the heap for so long that it is not disposed to brook opposition." Jackson's views on the subject were, if possible, even more strident. "There is no doubt he is a real liberal," wrote Ickes of Jackson. "He sees what the big corporations and big businesses generally are doing to the country."[30]

For Cohen and Corcoran, by contrast, the antimonopoly campaign was more about strategy than substance. In mid-December the "liberal crowd," as Corcoran put it, badly needed "a center around which to rally—just so they may touch each other and feel that it is not too desperately lonely in the front line trenches." Corcoran's idea of such a center was physical ("What they need is an unending series of little dinners and five o'clock drinks where they can meet in small but shifting combinations," he wrote Frankfurter, perhaps thinking of the days of the "Little Red House"), but the liberals also needed to come together in a metaphorical sense. A strong anti–big business campaign fit the bill perfectly.[31]

Cohen, unlike Jackson and Ickes, was not opposed in principle to the concentration of economic power. As his approach to holding company regulation demonstrates, he opposed bigness and monopoly for reasons grounded in economic theory rather than political ideology: where monopolies did in fact result in artificially inflated prices, consumer purchasing power was hurt and the recession deepened. But he did not believe that the recession of 1937 had been caused by the excessive concentration of wealth, or by an economic conspiracy of the moneyed interests. While Ickes was comparing the recession to President Jackson's fight over the Bank of the United States, Cohen was trying to convince Ickes to argue in favor of Keynesian spending—a policy he had advocated to no avail in 1933 and 1934.[32] However, with Ickes and

Corcoran committed to the antimonopoly campaign (albeit for different reasons), Cohen's involvement was a foregone conclusion.

Jackson kicked off the antimonopoly campaign with a December 26
radio address and a December 29 speech to the American Political Science Association; Ickes followed with his own radio speech on December 30. Cohen and Corcoran played a major role in drafting all three
speeches, with assistance from Leon Henderson and others. Jackson
and Ickes used much of the same rhetoric, both blaming the recession on
the deliberate actions of America's richest "Sixty Families." The Sixty
Families had contrived the recession, both men declared, as part of "a
strike of capital . . . a general strike—the first general strike in America
—a strike against the government—a strike to coerce political action."[33]

President Roosevelt himself echoed the antimonopoly theme in his
annual message to Congress on January 3, 1938—not surprisingly, since
Tommy Corcoran had a hand in writing the speech. The "concentration of economic control to the detriment of the body politic," Roosevelt wrote, "gives us food for grave thought about the future." In many
cases, "such concentrations cannot be justified on the ground of operating efficiency, but have been created for the sake of securities profits,
financial control, the suppression of competition and the ambition for
power over others." The president was not quite ready to declare open
warfare on business; unlike Ickes and Jackson, he merely observed that
"the ownership of vast properties or the organization of thousands of
workers creates a heavy obligation of public service," and advised that
"the power should not be sought or sanctioned unless the responsibility
is accepted as well."[34]

Politically, the antimonopoly campaign paid large dividends. The
Jackson and Ickes speeches played well in the press; indeed, Jackson
found himself on the cover of *Newsweek*.[35] Within weeks, "trust busting" emerged as the primary alternative to a more business-friendly
regulation approach to federal economic policy. The general question
"Which way is Roosevelt headed now?" commented *Newsweek*, could
be more precisely phrased as, "Is the Roosevelt administration going in
for trust busting or for the opposite course of recognizing monopolies
and regulating them?"[36]

So stark a dichotomy between regulation and antimonopoly vastly
overstated the differences between the two approaches. The antimonopoly rhetoric of Ickes and Jackson was never linked to a specific
legislative program; there is no indication that even they ever intended

federal policy to be taken to the logical limits suggested by their over-heated rhetoric. Those on the pro-regulation side, similarly, recognized the need for government action to limit the power of monopolies—such as the electrical power holding companies—that could not be justi-fied in terms of economic efficiency. Nor was there a clear line between the trust-busters and the Keynesian spenders. By forcing up prices, the Keynesians realized, monopolies could artificially depress con-sumer purchasing power, potentially negating the benefits of govern-ment spending.

Perhaps more than any other figure, Ben Cohen demonstrates the futility of any effort to divide the New Dealers into two neat groups. Public opinion placed him squarely within the antimonopoly camp, a view reinforced by his close association not only with Ickes and Jackson, but also with Louis Brandeis himself. (The view that "large industrial units" were "a thing essentially dangerous, not to say evil," was held, wrote Raymond Moley, "by many leading statesmen and students of public affairs, including Borah, Brandeis, and a number of satellites of these men, chiefly young lawyers who are operating in responsible posi-tions in Washington."[37]) In reality, however, Cohen's perspective was far closer to the Keynesians and the regulators than it was to the Bran-deisians.

The liberals' reluctance to embrace trust-busting as anything more than a rhetorical device helps explain why the antimonopoly campaign did not result in a meaningful legislative proposal, much less actual legislation. Cohen was directly involved in drafting the antimonopoly message that Roosevelt sent to Congress in late April; he and Cor-coran had written the first draft in early April, and Cohen had trav-eled to Atlanta to join the presidential train en route to Washington to present it to Roosevelt. The final draft—completed with contributions by Jackson, Thurman Arnold, and others—was submitted to Congress on April 29. After denouncing monopoly in the strongest terms ("Fas-cism. . . . That heavy hand of integrated financial and management con-trol . . . banker control of industry . . . blindly selfish men. . . ."), the message called for a program of almost comically small proportions. "To meet the situation I have described," Roosevelt concluded, "there should be a thorough study of the concentration of economic power in American industry and the effect of that concentration upon the decline of competition."[38]

Even the Seventy-fifth Congress could accept so cautious a recom-mendation, and in June Roosevelt signed into law legislation creating the Temporary National Economic Committee (TNEC), a twelve-member group with representatives from both the legislative and executive branches. Over the next three years, "five hundred and twenty-two witnesses produced thirty-one volumes of testimony, and 188 government economists prepared forty-three monographs under the committee's supervision." But no specific action resulted from this impressive pile of research. For real trustbusters, the TNEC was, as the title of one scholarly article put it, "A Study in Frustration."[39]

Aside from the TNEC, the administration's modest successes in 1938 came over the strenuous objections of powerful conservative Democrats in the House and Senate. Southern conservatives especially opposed passage of the Fair Labor Standards bill, both on general principles and because they believed that a minimum wage would nullify the competitive advantages of their region's low pay scales. With Southern Democrats controlling nearly all the key leadership positions in the House and Senate, and with both the Speaker of the House and the majority leader on record in opposition, Washington-watchers had pronounced the bill virtually dead on arrival.

The administration forged ahead despite these obstacles, following a strategy devised in large part by Tommy Corcoran. Corcoran's plan, in effect, was to turn the upcoming Florida senatorial primary into a "demonstration project" for the New Deal. The primary pitted a staunch Roosevelt loyalist—incumbent Sen. Claude D. Pepper—against two opponents of the New Deal. Corcoran convinced Pepper to focus his campaign on the wages and hours bill, and threw behind it the full weight of the administration's political machine and of his own connections. (Corcoran personally raised over $10,000 from the United Fruit Company for the Pepper campaign.) When Pepper won, the administration hailed the victory as a personal triumph for the president.

The effects of the Pepper victory were seen immediately. Within days, 218 members of the House of Representatives came forward to sign a discharge petition, circumventing the Rules Committee to allow a floor debate on the wages and hours bill. Among those signing the petition were twenty-three Southern Democrats. Three weeks later, the bill passed the House. After the differences between the House and Senate bills were reconciled, the measure was sent to the White House, where it was signed into law on June 25, 1938.

The Pepper project had been so successful that Corcoran and his colleagues tried the same strategy elsewhere. Various administration officials publicly endorsed pro–New Deal candidates in Democratic primaries in Pennsylvania and Oregon. In the California primary, Sen. William McAdoo produced a "Dear Mac" letter of endorsement from the president himself. Then, in June, Harry Hopkins entered the political fray in his home state of Iowa, coming out in favor of Rep. Otha Donner Wearin in his primary fight against the incumbent senator, Guy Gillette. The administration's decision to fight in Iowa was odd; Wearin and Gillette had similar voting records, showing mixed support for the New Deal. Corcoran explained that the administration "needed to make a show of strength," but that need was hardly obvious. The national press seized upon the one major difference between the two candidates—Wearin had voted in favor of the Court bill, Gillette against it—and concluded that the White House had targeted those who opposed the Court bill in a general "purge" of the Democratic Party.

Despite the administration's endorsement of Wearin, the local Iowa Democratic machine carried Gillette to victory by a margin of almost two to one. But instead of backing down, Roosevelt accelerated his efforts to rid the party of those who would not support the New Deal. On June 24, 1938, the president threw down the gauntlet in a fireside chat. "As the head of the Democratic Party . . . charged with the responsibility of carrying out the definitely liberal declaration of principles set forth in the 1936 Democratic platform," he declared, "I feel that I have every right to speak in those few instances where there may be a clear issue between candidates for a Democratic nomination involving these principles, or involving a clear misuse of my name."[40] As it happened, Roosevelt intervened in more than a "few instances." Beginning in early July, he personally delivered speeches urging Democratic voters to defeat Happy Chandler in Kentucky, Walter George in Georgia, "Cotton" Ed Smith in South Carolina, Millard Tydings in Maryland, and John J. O'Connor in New York. The White House political machine also became involved in campaigns in Texas, Oklahoma, Colorado, and Connecticut.

Despite these presidential efforts, the results of both the late-summer primary elections and the general election in November were devastating. Of all the candidates targeted for primary defeats, only one—John J. O'Connor of New York—was defeated. Infighting among the Democrats contributed to the party's loss in November of eighty-one House seats, eight Senate seats, and eleven governorships.

Corcoran bore the brunt of the criticism for the purge operation. Early on, he had been identified as a leading member of the "elimination committee" guiding the effort, a group that included Harold Ickes,

Jimmy Roosevelt, David Niles, and Joe Keenan. (Ben Cohen's name was conspicuously absent from the list.) To the press, Corcoran was the "generalissimo" of the purge campaign, a leader of the administration's "general staff," a "hatchet man." Corcoran became "persona non grata" at the White House, at least according to the rumors; when he was dispatched to New York to run the anti-O'Connor campaign, journalists opined that he had become a liability in Washington. " 'Tommy the Cork,' " speculated one newspaper, "May Be on the Way Out."[41]

Ben Cohen was not as directly involved in the purge campaign as his partner; his forte had always been policy, not politics. He did work with Corcoran and Rosenman on many of the president's speeches, however, including the fireside chat that introduced the purge, and he provided other, similar services in the background. But precisely what Cohen did or did not do is beside the point; in the public eye, he and Corcoran were inextricably linked, and the politicians who had been the targets of the purge effort—and their supporters in the newspapers—were happy to reinforce the association. "The little group that was undertaking to drive me from public office were Communists," thundered Georgia's Senator George. "That group includes . . . Tommy Corcoran and Benny Cohen, two little New York Wall Street lawyers who have arrogated unto themselves the power of saying who shall be a senator and who shall not be a senator." Millard Tydings echoed the sentiment: "Against whom am I running," he asked. "David J. Lewis, or Drew Pearson, Tommy Corcoran, Ben Cohen and another group of New Yorkers?" If Corcoran's star was falling, it seemed, Cohen's was destined to fall with it.[42]

Despite his closeness to Corcoran both personally and politically, Cohen had increasingly less to do with his friend's political activities as 1938 wore on. And as Corcoran's role took him out of the White House, Cohen's relationship with Roosevelt, and his place in the inner circle, began to fade. At the end of August, while Corcoran was in New York helping to defeat John J. O'Connor, Cohen departed for a trip to Europe, ostensibly on power policy business, but also on a mission for his Zionist colleagues. Over the course of the previous year or so he had become deeply worried about the growing crisis in Europe, and above all about the increasingly precarious position of European Jewry. Cohen expressed his sense of concern in a letter to Jane Harris written aboard ship on the outbound voyage. "We can only hope for the best," he wrote, "without knowing what the best may be."[43]

11

Waiting for the War

As early as 1937, I remember Ben telling Justice Cardozo he wished he
could take a year off and study world affairs because international
disaster was at hand.

—*Joseph L. Rauh, Jr.*

Cohen had begun to worry about foreign policy as early as the winter of 1937–38. According to his friend Joe Rauh, Cohen complained
early on that "the real problem now is that most of the people in the
New Deal don't have any experience in foreign affairs."[1] His own experience in such matters was not all that extensive either, but his outlook
tended to be cosmopolitan, and he was as well placed as anyone to begin
to turn his attention to the threat of war. Within a few years, and for
the rest of his life, Cohen would direct most of his energy and attention
to matters of war and peace.

Cohen was drawn to the foreign policy arena for personal as well
as professional reasons. His sympathies were aroused by the plight of
the Jews in Germany and by the increasingly difficult predicament faced
by his friends in England; prime among these was Margery Abrahams,
whom he had kept in touch with since his Zionist days and who had
become active in the effort to rescue Jewish children from Nazism. Undoubtedly Cohen was also influenced by Frankfurter, who had close
connections in British academia and among the European Jewish leadership. Adding to the mix was the fact that Cohen's circle of friends in
the United States was generally anti-isolationist. "I was very much concerned with the rise of Hitler from the beginning," he recalled later. "By

sheer law of imitation, if Hitler succeeded, there would be reverbera-
tions here. Felix had some of the same feeling." Cohen watched anx-
iously over events in Europe and attempted to expand the jurisdiction
of his own National Power Policy Committee to include defense power
matters.[2]

The crisis in Europe, and in particular the plight of the Jews, worsened throughout 1938. On March 12, Nazi troops marched into Austria; one day later, Hitler announced a formal annexation (or *Anschluss*).
The Anschluss brought 190,000 Austrian Jews under Nazi control and,
by signaling Hitler's aggressiveness toward the goal of a "Greater Germany" free of Jews, indirectly threatened millions of Jews living in
neighboring countries. Germany's increasingly hostile attitude toward
its Jewish population also encouraged those who favored the adoption
of similar legislation elsewhere, including Romania and Poland.

The Roosevelt administration responded to what it called the "refugee crisis" in Europe by calling for an international conference, to be
held at the French resort city of Evian in July 1938. More a gesture than
a serious effort to help the embattled Jews of Europe, the Evian Conference had little chance of achieving tangible results. Even before the
delegates arrived at Evian, the State Department made it clear that "no
country"—including the United States—"would be expected to receive
a greater number of emigrants than is permitted by its existing legislation."[3] The United Kingdom attended only on the condition that there
would be no discussion of the Palestine question. Germany was not invited; Evian was not to be a forum for negotiation with the Nazi government.

The results of the conference were in line with expectations. None
of the major powers signaled a willingness to accept significant numbers of resettled Jews. American efforts to convince other nations to accept refugees—including, in particular, several Latin American republics—failed completely. After nine days, the delegates produced little
more than an agreement to establish a new organization, to be called
the Intergovernmental Committee on Political Refugees (IGC), to continue its work. Leadership of the committee was split between the
United States and Great Britain, with Roosevelt's friend George Rublee
selected as director and Earl Winterton as chairman. The IGC agreed
to meet in London on August 31, but the new agency had little support
from its member nations and, consequently, little real influence.

Ben Cohen was not involved in the planning of the Evian Conference, nor was he a member of the American delegation. From all ac-

counts, the idea for an international meeting on the refugee problem
was Roosevelt's alone; in any event, despite his growing interest in foreign policy Cohen as yet had no foreign policy responsibilities or connections. In September 1938, however, Cohen did travel to England in
connection with the refugee issue. He did so not as a representative of
the United States government, but as a private citizen; he spoke for,
or at least relayed information from and to, his colleagues among the
leadership of the American Jewish community.

The details of Cohen's trip remain obscure, largely because Cohen
himself kept the details close to his vest. Ostensibly he was on vacation,
and he explicitly denied to reporters that the trip served any business
purpose whatsoever. For the record, he was on official business for the
National Power Policy Committee, and at least part of the trip was paid
for by the Interior Department. Probably there was a germ of truth in
both these explanations, though Cohen neglected to mention that his
trip was also connected with the Jewish crisis.

Because of its mandate over Palestine, Great Britain was in a special position with respect to the Jewish refugees of Europe. Although
before Evian the government had explicitly ruled out an increase in the
Palestine immigration quotas, the growing crisis nevertheless led Jewish activists to increase their efforts to persuade the British government
to relent. Britain was also under intense pressure from the Arab states,
however, and was adamant in its refusal to take any steps that might be
regarded as encouraging efforts to bring about the creation of a Jewish state. Thus at this critical moment the British government moved in
precisely the opposite direction from that urged by the Jewish community, signaling its decision to repudiate a 1937 plan to partition Palestine into Arab and Jewish sections and replace it with a "unitary Palestinian state." Given the existing Arab majority in Palestine and the strict
immigration quotas, this approach meant a de facto abandonment of
the British government's commitment—expressed in the Balfour Declaration of 1916—to a Jewish national home in Palestine. The British,
far from contemplating an increase in the number of European refugees allowed into Palestine, were on the verge of shutting the gates altogether.

Exactly what Cohen hoped to accomplish on his trip is unclear.
With events evolving so rapidly, it is most likely his American Zionist
colleagues sent Cohen to London not so much to pursue specific negotiations, but simply to be on the ground at a critical place and time.
Whatever his purpose, Cohen sensed in advance that it was a vain one.

"I sort of feel that I am on a fool's errand," he wrote Jane Harris while en route to Europe. "I am sure that there is nothing that I can really accomplish and I can't just regard this journey as a pleasure trip somehow."[4]

While in Europe, Cohen traveled to Paris to meet with David Ben-Gurion, then chairman of the Jewish Agency for Palestine and later the first president of the State of Israel. It is unclear from the historical record whether the Cohen–Ben-Gurion meeting was planned in advance, or whether either man even knew that the other would be in London. Ben-Gurion had reached the conclusion that the Jewish community in Palestine (or Yishuv) could no longer count on British support or rely on British intentions; the only hope for the eventual creation of a Jewish state, therefore, was in an aggressive policy of armed resistance. At his meeting with Cohen, Ben-Gurion floated this idea and tried to gauge the prospects for American support of such a course. Cohen, however, "discounted the possibility of American support for an aggressive line by the Yishuv . . . against British policy. Ben-Gurion reached the conclusion that neither a U.S. administration nor the Jewish community there would support a Zionist policy that might lead to a violent confrontation with Britain." As a fallback, Ben-Gurion turned to persuading Cohen "to act with other leading American Zionists to bring about Roosevelt's intervention in favor of their cause." Cohen, however, was hesitant and noncommittal.[5]

During Cohen's visit to Europe, the leaders of the American Zionist movement took steps to prevent a complete shutdown of Jewish immigration to Palestine. On September 14, Cohen received word from Julius Simon in Jerusalem advising him that meetings were in progress to determine "whether it would be advisable at this juncture that a limited number of representative Jews in various countries (Zionists and non-Zionists) submit to the British government a short statement in which another solution of the Palestine problem is suggested." The specific idea was to ask the British government "to adopt as its policy the establishment of a Palestine State with two nationalities of equal status, the Jews and the Arabs, and to declare that this is the primary reason for the presence of Great Britain in Palestine." The proposal also suggested that "during the next 10 years the Jewish population shall become no more than 40% of the entire population."[6]

Cohen's analysis of the proposal and his suggested modifications shows the keen sense of political strategy he had developed in his five years in Washington. Above all, Cohen urged, "the statement should be so issued as to avoid its apparent repudiation by the Arabs by their words or by their action." Thus the proposal should be signed by "representative Jews, but not too many," and should be "submitted to the Colonial Office but not published." As Cohen explained a few weeks later, "we should avoid making a public statement expressing our belief that Jews and Arabs can reach a satisfactory understanding, when there is danger that the Arab leaders under existing circumstances might repudiate the statement by issuing a counter public statement of their own to the effect that they would enter into no arrangements with the Jews countenancing further Jewish immigration into Palestine." Cohen also advised against the 40 percent cap on the Jewish population. Such a concession "would make it difficult for the Jews to ask more and it would make the Arabs feel that a smaller percentage should be conceded." Instead, Cohen suggested that Jewish immigration be limited only by the "absorptive capacity" of the land, provided that the Jewish population "should not be allowed to exceed the number of Arabs or a prescribed ratio to the entire population." Finally, Cohen suggested that the proposal be applied not only to Palestine proper but also to Trans-Jordan, Syria, and even other Arab countries. "From both the Jewish and Arab point of view it is desirable that the areas available for Jewish settlement should be spread over a larger rather than a smaller territory. In this way more Jews can be settled without outnumbering the Arabs."[7]

As the British moved toward a decision on the future course of their Palestine policy, the American Zionists carried out a well-organized but low-profile campaign to convince President Roosevelt to bring pressure to bear on London. The commanding presence behind the campaign was Louis Brandeis; when told that "telegrams were coming in at the rate of ten thousand a day and more to the State Department," he told Rabbi Stephen S. Wise, "Keep it up. Have another hundred thousand sent." Wise added, "He urged also that we remember the smaller towns and the Quakers." Brandeis, however, was reluctant to go to Roosevelt personally, and it was left to Frankfurter and Cohen (who, by then, was back in Washington) to arrange for the justice to be summoned by the president for a conference. "I think he was unhappy about being sent for by the Skipper," Wise told Frankfurter, "understanding perfectly, of course, that it was due to the intervention—or shall I say intercession—of you and Ben. What he said was 'He has sent for me only to defend himself; to use me as a shield.'" But Brandeis's meeting with Roosevelt went better than the justice expected. "F.D. went very far in our talk in his appreciation of the significance of Palestine," Brandeis reported to

Frankfurter afterward. "He was tremendously interested—and wholly surprised—on learning of the great increase in Arab population since the War; and on learning of the plenitude of land for Arabs in Arab countries, about which he made specific inquiries."[8]

For a brief period in November—especially after the brutal Nazi terrorism of Kristallnacht—the efforts of the Zionists and the Jewish activists seemed at last to be making some headway in Washington and London. "[T]he wholesale confiscation, the atrocities, the increasing attacks . . . have aroused public opinion here to a point where if something is not done there will be a combustion," wrote one State Department official. To reporters, President Roosevelt exclaimed that he "could scarcely believe such a thing could occur in a twentieth century civilization," and, as a temporary step, he ordered an extension of visitor's visas for German refugees. At long last, Rabbi Stephen Wise and other American leaders could dare to hope that their efforts on behalf of the Jews of Europe were beginning to pay off.[9]

Within a few months, Wise and his colleagues would be cruelly disappointed. Roosevelt made grand statements condemning the German government, and he made diplomatic efforts to convince other countries to accept Jewish refugees. But he did not advocate easing up on the nation's rigid immigration quotas, nor did he make a serious effort to dissuade the British from closing off Jewish immigration to Palestine. In May 1939, Great Britain essentially closed the matter by issuing a white paper restricting Jewish immigration to a total of 75,000 over the next five years. Years later, Cohen downplayed his disappointment. "To imagine that Roosevelt could have come up with a magic wand to solve the Jewish problem," he told an interviewer, "might be expecting too much."[10]

Cohen's growing interest in foreign policy was also reflected in his speechwriting role, which he continued to share with Sam Rosenman and Tommy Corcoran. Roosevelt's speeches in 1939 and 1940 resounded with clear and straightforward rhetoric, as if to suggest the president's clarity of purpose and certainty of course. "We have learned that survival cannot be guaranteed by arming after the attack begins," Roosevelt declared in his January 1939 message to Congress. "We have learned that God-fearing democracies of the world . . . cannot safely be indifferent to international lawlessness anywhere." When the war began in Europe, Roosevelt addressed the nation in even more direct terms. "I have said not once, but many times, that I have seen war and that I hate war," he began in a fireside chat. "I say that again and again." But the war would not go away. "It is easy for you and for me to shrug our shoulders and to say that conflicts taking place thousands of miles from the continental United States, and, indeed, thousands of miles from the whole American Hemisphere, do not seriously affect the Americas— and that all the United States has to do is to ignore them and go about its own business. Passionately though we may desire detachment, we are forced to realize that every word that comes through the air, every ship that sails the sea, every battle that is fought, does affect the American future." America would remain a neutral nation at law, the president concluded, "but I cannot ask that every American remain neutral in thought as well. Even a neutral has a right to take account of facts. Even a neutral cannot be asked to close his mind or his conscience."[11]

Cohen also worked with Rosenman and Corcoran on the president's May 16, 1940, request for additional defense appropriations. Writing less than a week after the German invasion of France, Roosevelt asked Congress for more than $1 billion in cash and contract authorizations for the army and navy. "Our task is plain," he declared. "Our defenses must be invulnerable, our security absolute. But our defense as it was yesterday, or even as it is today, does not provide security against potential developments and dangers of the future." Although "our objective is still peace," Roosevelt wrote, "we stand ready not only to spend millions for defense but also to give our service and even our lives for the maintenance of our American liberties."[12]

Although Cohen continued to keep one eye on Europe, there was still work to be done at home. But Cohen's involvement in domestic affairs from 1938 to 1940 was unfocused and sporadic, a reflection not only of the administration's lack of focus but also of his own changing role within the Washington power structure. Now in his mid-forties, he had suddenly become an elder statesman, known and respected by a host of younger colleagues scattered throughout the government. His advice was routinely sought on a wide variety of matters, some wholly outside his ordinary scope of interests. It was a role he would continue to play throughout the 1940s and, indeed, for the rest of his professional life.

At the same time, Cohen had amply demonstrated his loyalty and usefulness to the president, and Roosevelt took advantage of Cohen's proximity to ask him to carry out various routine tasks. "The President asked me to get him a memorandum from Leon Henderson before he sees Senator O'Mahoney and Congressman Sumners about the Monopoly Investigation," Cohen wrote to Missy LeHand on one occasion. "I hope you will see that the President has a chance to read the enclosed memoranda from Henderson before the President has his conference with O'Mahoney and Sumners." When Roosevelt asked Cohen to "work out the mechanics" by which the White House could send a New York Power Authority report to the Hill so that it could be printed as a congressional document, Cohen responded with a statement "which contains certain suggestions which might be useful in commenting upon the Report at your press conference tomorrow" along with "a summary . . . for your information of the essential feature of the Report. . . . [and] Two copies of the report . . . with identic [sic] letters of transmittal to the Chairman of the Senate and House Committees on Military Affairs." [13]

Cohen's easy access to the White House made him a natural conduit for information intended for the president and for requests for presidential action. Thus when (then Representative) Lyndon Johnson sought to release an "exchange of letters" with the White House requesting and authorizing the takeover by the Lower Colorado River Authority of various properties owned by the Texas Power and Light Company, he acted through Cohen. Cohen transmitted to Roosevelt a copy of Johnson's letter proposing the takeover, endorsed the idea in a cover memorandum to the president ("Lyndon Johnson . . . has done an admirable job in working out the problems of Texas' little TVA . . ."), drafted a reply, and urged quick action: "Lyndon hopes to release the interchange of letters with you and hopes he may have your reply when he sees you tomorrow." [14] Typical of Cohen's wide range of contacts and confidantes is a June 1939 memorandum to Missy LeHand transmitting three separate requests to the president:

> Mr. McNinch thinks the Federal Power chairmanship can be best handled by the President speaking personally to Seavey rather than sending word through any intermediary. He suggests that the President call in Seavey for a short interview, express the wish that Olds be named Chairman and Seavey, Vice Chairman, and compliment Seavey on the way he has handled the Commission during McNinch's absence.
>
> 2) The Senate has attached an amendment to the appropriation for the Department of Justice requiring appointments calling for salaries in excess of $5000 to be confirmed by the Senate. The Attorney General is very much disturbed. I should think the President would want to instruct the Congressional

leaders Monday to see that this vicious amendment is eliminated in conference.

3) Senator Wheeler told me that he would appreciate some
help from the President to get his two railroad bills out of the
House Judiciary Committee. He thought some word to Rayburn and to Chandler and to McLaughlin would help.[15]

Several leading members of the Jewish community—including
Rabbi Stephen S. Wise—continued to use Cohen as a channel to Roosevelt. One of many such requests came in June 1939, when Wise sent
Cohen information about the fate of the Jews in Germany and Austria.
"I send it to you for your own sake," Wise wrote, "but I have been thinking about it—would it not be well to let the Chief see it? It is not so long
as to be intolerable, and it would be immensely valuable for the Chief
to get this particular glimpse of what is happening." Cohen, however,
was not always obliging of such requests. When Wise asked Cohen to
arrange a meeting between Roosevelt and representatives of the World
Jewish Congress and the Jewish Agency for Palestine in 1940, for example, Cohen demurred. "I appreciate your position," he wrote, "but
I don't feel I should push myself into Jewish matters when the skipper
does not ask my advice. . . . Why don't you speak to LDB & FF about it.
They are high moguls and I am only a no-body." [16]

The death of Justice Benjamin Cardozo on July 9, 1938, gave Ben
Cohen the chance to use his White House connections to lobby for the
appointment of Felix Frankfurter to be Cardozo's successor. Although
the tensions that had crept into Cohen's relationship with Frankfurter
in the mid-1930s had not gone away, Cohen's desire to see his mentor
placed on the high bench was genuine. "I still want to see the Holmes-
Cardozo succession maintained," he wrote Charles Burlingham in August, 1938, "and I see no one who would commend himself to the President as within the reach of that tradition so much as F.F. Certainly the
post should be above race or geography and I think the skipper would be
glad to take that view if supported sufficiently by public opinion. And
so far at least F.F. seems to have public opinion heavily with him rather
than against him." [17]

As a highly respected law professor and the nation's leading "public interest" lawyer, Frankfurter received widespread support, not least
from within the administration. Among those who lobbied Roosevelt
on his behalf were Cohen, Corcoran, Harold Ickes, Harry Hopkins, and
Robert Jackson. Although Frankfurter affected surprise when officially

informed of the appointment in January 1939, he was well aware of all this activity on his behalf. "I don't know why Felix was so surprised," Cohen recalled later. "Tom was vigorously lobbying for his appointment and would call him every night to report what had been done. And he did it all on my phone!"[18]

Cohen also kept busy in this period with a range of domestic policy concerns. In the spring of 1940, for example, he approached Roosevelt about a plan to promote "useful public works" by linking together work relief grants and Reconstruction Finance Corporation loans. Cohen had been an advocate of using federal money for "useful" projects since at least 1933, when he proposed that work relief money be spent on upgrading railroad crossings. Now he suggested that the federal government encourage state and municipal agencies to pursue "useful" projects by allowing the RFC to issue loans to be used in conjunction with Federal Works Agency grants, in a ratio of seven to three. Such loans would not require additional congressional appropriations, which gave the proposal "unusual attractions" in a year "when political considerations may complicate the handling of our economic problems." Roosevelt expressed interest in the idea, which Cohen put into the form of a legislative draft.[19]

In early 1938, Cohen weighed in on proposed legislation to eliminate tax exemptions on income derived from securities issued by the federal government or by the states. In a draft of a presidential message on the subject, Cohen argued that "the reciprocal tax-immunity accorded such income . . . constitutes a serious menace to the fiscal systems of both the states and the nation." The essential problem was that such tax exemptions provide a greater benefit to those with higher incomes than to those with lower incomes, thus defeating the purpose of a progressive tax system. That the income on government securities was exempt from tax was wholly the result of an outdated and untenable interpretation of the Constitution, Cohen believed; the remedy was for Congress to pass new legislation and allow the Supreme Court to overturn its contrary precedents. "I feel very strongly that the President should recommend legislation and not a constitutional amendment," Cohen wrote Jackson. "It is an issue on which I think the President should wish to take a stand." Cohen also advocated the passage of legislation, originally proposed by Carter Glass, to "require tax-exempt income to be taken into account in determining the surtax applicable to taxable income" under federal law.[20]

The Temporary National Economic Committee (TNEC), which

grew out of Cohen and Corcoran's antimonopoly activism in 1938, also occupied some of Cohen's attention. He was close to many of the members of the TNEC, including Isadore Lubin, William O. Douglas, and especially Leon Henderson, who served briefly as the committee's executive secretary, and Robert Jackson, who had moved up in the meantime to solicitor general but who was still an active antimonopolist. Cohen was also involved with the National Resources Committee, a group headed by the president's uncle, Frederic A. Delano. Parallel to these inquiries, Cohen and Corcoran worked briefly on a revision of the nation's antitrust laws, trying to "reorganize or agglomerate 27 different laws" passed over a span of fifty years.[21]

Another 1939 project involved proposed legislation to provide for the insurance of loans to business. "There has been persistent and widespread feeling," Cohen wrote in a memorandum, "that business enterprise, particularly small enterprise, has been hampered by want of adequate credit, particularly credit for capital developments which cannot be liquidated within a short term."[22] Small businesses lacked access to the big-money channels of investment banking, Cohen explained, and commercial banks frequently avoided such loans because of the inherent risks and the need to maintain liquidity. The solution was to limit the banker's risk by developing a system of insurance for business loans. In Cohen's bill, the Reconstruction Finance Corporation was authorized to insure business loans against losses above 10 percent of the loan value, at a cost of between 0.25 and 1 percent of the loan value per year.

Cohen and Corcoran remained highly useful to the president throughout 1938 and 1939, but there was no question that their brief reign as "chief advisers" was coming to a close. The beginning of the end came in 1939, when Roosevelt at last won congressional approval of the long-awaited executive reorganization plan, which authorized him to appoint six new presidential assistants—men who were to have the "passion for anonymity" that the Brownlow commission had suggested two years before. Significantly, the president declined to appoint either Cohen or Corcoran to one of the new posts.

Roosevelt's decision to leave Cohen and Corcoran out of the new reorganization plan was widely regarded as evidence of an effort by the administration to move in a more "moderate" direction. This impression was greatly strengthened by the comments of the president's press secretary, Stephen Early, when he released to the press copies of the executive order implementing the reorganization legislation. The order "definitely defines" the duties of the president's new assistants, Early said, "and I see nothing in the Order that will permit those old much heralded and celebrated creatures of the imagination to have a place in the new set up. For the first time the President specifically designates the duties to be performed by authorized officials of the White House Offices." When a reporter asked, "How about Corcoran and Cohen?" Early replied, "They are not creatures of the imagination and I refer only to creatures of the imagination. Really there never was a Brain Trust but much has been written about one—that is out the window now."[23]

Although Early tried to dismiss his comments as not applying to Cohen and Corcoran, the press would have nothing of it. The *Baltimore Sun* ran a picture of Cohen and Corcoran alongside its report of Early's comments under the caption, " 'Out the Window' For Them?" A day later the *Sun* reported on Early's "further explanation" of the status of Cohen and Corcoran. " 'Cohen and Corcoran,' he stated, 'are not in the White House. They never have been. One (Corcoran) is employed by the RFC and the other (Cohen) by the National Power Policy Committee. I see no change in their status.' " Asked "how seriously the reports about tossing the 'Brain Trust' out the window should be taken," Early replied by asking "whether there was a 'Brain Trust,' and where it might be."[24]

The mini-furor created by Early's comments elicited a response from Roosevelt himself one day later. Although the president stressed that Cohen and Corcoran's status was "unchanged," his remarks amounted to less than a complete endorsement. Roosevelt said "that not only had there been no change in the status of Messrs. Corcoran and Cohen and their relations to the White House," reported the *New York Times*, "but that they never existed as White House advisers except in the minds of newspaper men who had created this double-headed banshee and had finally decided that the ghost should be buried."[25]

All discussion of ghosts aside, Cohen and Corcoran were in fact on their way out. Corcoran's role in the intense political infighting of the Court-packing and purge campaigns made him more of a burden than a benefit to Roosevelt. Cohen "might have toiled unknown and unscathed as an important but anonymous member of the New Deal circle if his name had not become associated with that of his more active friend," wrote journalist Heywood Broun. "Whenever Tommy Corcoran moved into the limelight the ghost of his friend came spiritually along."[26]

But the president had another reason to distance himself from Cohen and Corcoran. As the 1940 campaign came into focus, Roosevelt began serious consideration of the possibility of seeking an unprecedented third term in the White House. The movement for a third term had been started by Ickes and Corcoran, and was strongly supported by the administration's liberals. By late 1939 it was clear that the Court-packing plan and the purge attempt had backfired, greatly strengthening the "regular" leadership of the Democratic Party. The possibility of a liberal candidate winning the nomination now seemed remote, and momentum shifted to the candidacy of James Farley, whose leadership of the national party committee gave him strong grassroots support.

Roosevelt would not directly oppose Farley's candidacy, nor would he openly campaign for a third term. Privately, however, he encouraged Corcoran's efforts to rally support behind the third-term effort. This Corcoran did by fighting the established Democratic Party machinery and organizing pro-Roosevelt forces in a number of key states, and by attempting to orchestrate a public relations campaign "debunking the Third Term myth from any scientific, historical basis" and arguing that "the American people can choose whom they want for their immediate reasons without violating their own 'way of life.' "[27]

As long as Corcoran was closely associated with the White House, it was impossible for Roosevelt to create the impression that he was merely a passive onlooker in the third-term campaign. Roosevelt's unwillingness to make any public effort to secure a third term extended all the way until the 1940 convention, which began with the president still refusing to commit himself publicly and ended with the delegates "spontaneously" drafting the president to run again. To successfully pull off this charade, Roosevelt needed Corcoran on the outside. But all these political machinations required to secure the nomination for Roosevelt only worsened Corcoran's relationship with the party regulars, and by mid-1940 he really was "out the window," exiled to New York City to run an "Independent Voters for Roosevelt" organization wholly outside the regular campaign machinery.

Corcoran had made a great sacrifice for Roosevelt and for the country, and it was inevitable that he would grow to resent his removal from power. The focal point for Corcoran's disaffection came in early 1940, when he married his former secretary, Peggy Dowd. Neither Roosevelt nor Felix Frankfurter fully approved of Dowd, who, they felt, was socially beneath her husband. As Corcoran told the story (which has never been substantiated), he and his bride had gone to the White House to be "received" by the president; Peggy had even bought a new

hat and dress for the occasion. After a long wait, Harry Hopkins informed the new couple that the president was unable to make room in
his schedule to see them. Although Corcoran would work for the president through the 1940 campaign, his future with the administration was
now in grave doubt. When Corcoran left the government, Cohen too
would be forced to reevaluate his role in Franklin Roosevelt's third-
term White House.

12

Destroyers for Bases

There is no reason for us to put a strained or unnecessary

interpretation on our own statutes contrary to our own national

interests. There is no reason to extend the rules of international laws

beyond the limits generally accepted by other nations to the

detriment of our own country.

—*Benjamin V. Cohen, July 1940*

In the summer of 1940, the presidential campaign and even his own future took a back seat to Ben Cohen's growing concerns about the crisis in Europe. The Roosevelt administration's sympathies were clearly with Britain, but with public opinion opposed to American involvement in the war and a presidential campaign ahead, the president was unwilling to risk a bold move on the foreign policy front. After Hitler's invasion of Poland in the fall of 1939, Roosevelt did convene a special session of Congress and asked for repeal of the Neutrality Act of 1935, which prohibited the shipment of "arms, ammunition, or implements of war" to any and all belligerents. Characteristically, however, Roosevelt tried to portray neutrality repeal as a moderate and cautious act, and not as a move toward involvement in Europe. In a speech drafted in part by Corcoran and Cohen, he suggested that existing law actually increased the chances of American involvement in the war— first, by permitting the raw materials or component parts of armaments to be shipped to belligerent nations in American ships, and second, by permitting the extension of wartime credits to belligerent nations. Neutrality Act reform, he suggested, would allow the direct shipment of American armaments to belligerent nations only on a "cash-and-carry" basis, banning war credits, and would ensure the safety of American vessels by prohibiting them from entering war zones. After a bitter congressional and public debate, Congress adopted Roosevelt's proposal.[1]

The overall effect of the neutrality revision was minimal. For one thing, both the British and French hesitated to purchase large amounts of weaponry, even though they had the money to do so—a reflection, as the historians William L. Langer and S. William Gleason noted, "of the hesitation, confusion and false optimism with which Britain and France were to confront the first winter of war." The lack of actual fighting throughout the winter of 1939–40 convinced both countries that the war would last long enough for them to produce their own arms, thus reducing the need to purchase American weaponry. In some respects, the new law was actually counterproductive to those who wanted to increase America's support for the allies. The prohibition on American ships in war zones, for example, actually assisted the German naval blockade of Britain by eliminating the traffic of American ships into and out of British ports.[2]

With the war on temporary hold in Europe, and American public opinion still refusing to commit itself one way or the other, Roosevelt kept up the facade of neutrality while revealing an increasing tilt toward the allies. In his 1940 State of the Union address (also partly written by Corcoran and Cohen), he reminded the nation that "whether we like it or not, the daily lives of American citizens will, of necessity, feel the shock of events in other countries." Those who "in innocence or ignorance or both" think otherwise were like ostriches. And, he concluded, "It is not good for the ultimate health of ostriches to bury their heads in the sand." In the spring of 1940, Roosevelt briefly explored the prospects of a peace settlement, but even if his attempt was serious there was no hope. When Undersecretary of State Sumner Welles returned from a tour of Rome, Berlin, Paris, and London to gauge prospects for a peace effort in late March, for example, he was convinced that there was not "the slightest chance of any successful negotiation at this time for a durable peace." In any event, within a few weeks none of this would matter; the "Phony War" that had lasted through the autumn and winter was about to become a very real one.[3]

First, on April 9, 1940, Germany invaded Denmark and Norway. Denmark fell immediately; despite a British counteroffensive, Norway followed by the end of the month. Then, on May 10, the Germans invaded Holland and Belgium, opening up the western front. The Dutch surrendered quickly, the Belgians were driven back, and by mid-May the Nazis had driven across the Meuse River and into France. The German advance brought down not only the Allied defenses but also the British government; Neville Chamberlain resigned on May 10, to be replaced by Winston Churchill. Belgium surrendered on May 28 (as the British and French armies made their miraculous evacuation at Dunkirk), the Germans entered Paris on June 14, and three days later the French government asked for armistice. One measure of the speed and extent of the German advances is that, over a period of three months, American access to Europe was reduced to the Pan American clipper into Lisbon.

The Allied collapse put England in a desperate position. As Churchill put it a few years later, by early July "it became clear to all countries that the British Government and nation were resolved to fight on until the last. But even if there were no moral weakness in Britain, how could the appalling physical facts be overcome? Our armies at home were known to be almost unarmed except for rifles. There were in fact hardly five hundred field guns of any sort and hardly two hundred medium or heavy tanks in the whole country. Months must pass before our factories could make good even the munitions lost at Dunkirk. Can one wonder that the world at large was convinced that our hour of doom had struck?"[4] German troops were less than thirty miles from the English coast, and England was left to face them alone.

Under such circumstances, the British could look for assistance only to the United States. On May 15, Churchill cabled Roosevelt asking for immediate aid, including "the loan of forty or fifty of your older destroyers to bridge the gap between what we have now and the large new construction we put in hand at the beginning of the war." In mid-June, Churchill repeated the request in more urgent terms: "Nothing is so important for us," he wrote, "as to have the thirty or forty old destroyers you have already had reconditioned." Roosevelt was able to comply with several of Churchill's requests, but on the destroyers he was firm. "As you know, a step of that kind could not be taken except with the specific authorization of the Congress and I am not certain that it would be wise for that suggestion to be made to the Congress at this moment. Furthermore, it seems to me doubtful, from the standpoint of our own defense requirements, which must inevitably be linked with the defense requirements of this hemisphere and with our obligations in the Pacific, whether we could dispose even temporarily of these destroyers. Furthermore, even if we were able to take the steps you suggest, it would be at least six or seven weeks as a minimum, as I see it, before these vessels could undertake active service under the British flag." "I understand your difficulties," Churchill responded, "but I am very sorry about the destroyers. If they were here in six weeks they would play an invaluable part."[5]

As Roosevelt suggested in his letters to Churchill, the argument against sending U.S. destroyers to England was grounded in practical, political, and legal arguments. Above all, the president had at least one eye on isolationist sentiment, both in Congress and in the country. The public's lack of enthusiasm for the war in Europe posed a great risk in the upcoming presidential campaign, and Roosevelt would do nothing that would give his opponents a chance to brand him as a warmonger. The Republican nomination of interventionist Wendell Willkie on June 28 dispelled some of these concerns, but by no means all of them. The British press exulted in the belief that Willkie was an "Aid-Britain" man, but as late as early August the president was unsure of Willkie's real sentiments or how he might respond under the pressures of campaign politics.[6]

Further complicating matters was the fact that increased aid for England threatened to work at cross-purposes to Roosevelt's major policy initiative of the early summer, which was a dramatic buildup in U.S. defense programs. It was awkward to part with fifty destroyers—even outdated ones—while at the same time asking Congress to appropriate huge sums for American armaments, including new ships. In mid-July, Congress in fact passed a huge navy bill described as "by far the largest naval expansion ever authorized," a measure that set in motion plans to develop a two-ocean navy. While fifty old destroyers were hardly worth mentioning compared to the 1.3 million tons of shipping authorized in the act, their symbolic significance was tangible.[7] Moreover, as a former assistant secretary of the navy, Roosevelt was undoubtedly more attached to naval vessels than to airplanes or other armaments.

The legal problems with a destroyers deal were perhaps even more intractable. At least two statutes seemed to outlaw such a transfer: the Espionage Act of 1917 and a revised version of a 1794 statute designed to protect American neutrality. The Espionage Act made it unlawful, during a war in which the United States is a neutral nation, to "send out of the jurisdiction any vessel built, armed, and equipped as a vessel of war, or converted from a private vessel into a vessel of war, with any intent or under any agreement . . . that such vessel shall be delivered to a belligerent nation." The 1794 statute, as amended, stated that "whoever, within the territory or jurisdiction of the United States, fits out and arms, or procures to be fitted out and armed, or knowingly is concerned in the furnishing, fitting out, or arming of any vessel with intent that such vessel shall be employed in the service of any foreign prince, or state . . . shall be fined not more than $10,000 and imprisoned not more than three years." Airplanes and other armaments might be shipped to the British under existing law, it seemed, but the transfer of naval vessels appeared to require new congressional legislation.[8]

Both the legal and political problems inherent in the British request for destroyers came to a head in mid-June, when word leaked of an arrangement to furnish England with twenty lightly armored motorboats (known variously as submarine chasers, mosquito boats, or suicide boats). The proposed deal—under which the United States would have deferred delivery on the vessels, allowing the Electric Boat Company to sell them to the British—was promptly attacked in Congress and in at least a few newspapers. "Swarms of Congressmen who talk and vote for f.d.r.'s defense moves in public are fuming in cloakrooms to the effect that 'this man is surely leading us to war,'" reported *Newsweek*. "Nothing in a long time has equaled Congressmen's privately expressed anger over the attempt to send Britain U.S. 'mosquito boats.'" The congressional attack was led by Sen. David I. Walsh (D-Mass.), chairman of the Senate Naval Committee, who promptly introduced explicit language into the naval expansion bill to make such sales illegal.[9]

By late June, fdr gave up on the mosquito boats. Bowing to congressional opinion and to Attorney General Robert H. Jackson's informal opinion that the sale of the mosquito boats "would seem to be prohibited" by the Espionage Act of 1917, Roosevelt canceled the deal. The president's actions came too late to prevent the adoption of Senator Walsh's amendment to the naval expansion bill, which Roosevelt signed on June 28, but the new law—which declared in part that "no military or naval weapon, ship, boat, aircraft, munitions, supplies, or equipment, to which the United States has title . . . shall hereinafter be transferred, exchanged, sold, or otherwise disposed of in any manner whatsoever unless the Chief of Naval Operations in the case of naval material . . . shall first certify that such material is not essential to the defense of the United States"—seemed suddenly superfluous.[10]

While the political drama played itself out in Washington, the crisis in England grew even more desperate, and Churchill's pleas for the destroyers became stronger and more insistent. On June 15, the prime minister cabled Roosevelt, "We must ask therefore as a matter of life or death to be reinforced with these destroyers." On July 31, he wrote, "The whole fate of the war may be decided by this minor and easily remediable factor." Churchill's apparently futile appeals were reinforced by his ambassador to the United States, and by William Bullitt, Roosevelt's ambassador to France.[11]

But pressure in favor of a destroyers deal was also building on the home front. In June, a group of New York lawyers and business leaders came together to form the Century Group, the purpose of which was to argue that "all disposable air, naval, military and material resources of the United States should be made available at once to help maintain our common front." The Century Group included in its membership such men as Charles C. Burlingham, Dean Acheson, Joseph Alsop, and Robert S. Allen, all of whom had close ties to key members of the Roosevelt administration, including Ben Cohen. A much larger group with greater grass-roots support, founded by the journalist William Allen White, was the Committee to Defend America by Aiding the Allies. By July, White's group had attracted considerable support and financial resources, and had begun to make an impression on public opinion. By late summer the committee had more or less absorbed the Century Group, which remained as a sort of outspokenly interventionist subcommittee.[12]

Over the course of the summer, Roosevelt's political problems would begin to lessen as American public opinion swung toward aid for Britain in the wake of Nazi victories and British suffering. The legal barriers that stood in the way of a destroyers deal, however, would not go away. In fact, with the passage of the Naval Expansion Act in late June, events had taken a very decided turn for the worse.

On July 1, Ben Cohen received a message from the columnist (and Century Group activist) Joseph Alsop, who had received it from a member of the staff of the British embassy in Washington. Cohen immediately passed the message on to Harold Ickes, who by then had easier access to the president. "The Britisher said to Alsop," as Ickes recorded it, "that he had no right to divulge it to him but that a cable had come from Great Britain to the Embassy saying that without more boats England could not hold the Channel against Hitler. Great Britain desperately wants some of our old destroyers." Ickes dutifully passed the message along to Roosevelt, urging FDR that "by hook or by crook, we ought to accede to England's request." But Roosevelt, citing the June 28 statute, replied that such a deal would be impossible unless the chief of naval operations could certify that the destroyers were useless for defense purposes, and that "it would be difficult to do this in view of the fact that we were reconditioning more than a hundred of them to use for our own defense purposes."[13]

Despite this presidential rebuff, Cohen began work in mid-July on a memorandum arguing that the sale of fifty old destroyers to England was in fact congruent both with existing statutory law and with international law principles. Cohen's effort reflected the depth of his concern over the rapidly worsening situation in Europe, and its successful completion would require all his considerable legal and political talents. Yet the effort was of immense importance, for without a legal justification for acting without congressional authority the destroyers deal—and, as it appeared to some, Great Britain itself—was doomed.

In essence, Cohen argued that the sale of destroyers to Great Britain was consistent with Congress's will and intent, justified under existing law, and entirely in keeping with the attorney general's opinion on the mosquito boat question. Therefore, he suggested, the destroyers could be transferred to England without statutory authorization from Congress. By July 19, Cohen was ready to send his memorandum to the president.[14]

In a cover letter to FDR, Cohen recognized that "even if Congressional approval is not required, Congressional opinion would have to be taken into account," and his memorandum began on a decidedly political note. "In the present state of the world, the maintenance of British sea-power is of inestimable advantage to us, in terms of our own national defense," he wrote. Given such a premise, "it cannot be lightly assumed that statutes designed to safeguard our national defenses were intended to block action dictated by a realistic appreciation of the interests of our national self-defense." Thus the statutes had to be interpreted, if possible, to permit the sale of the destroyers.[15]

And, of course, it was possible. The June 28, 1940, statute, designed to prevent the sale of mosquito boats or any other naval vessels, permitted an exception if the chief of naval operations certified that the vessels were "not essential to the defense of the United States." It would not be necessary, Cohen added, "to have them stricken from the register as actually unfit for further service." A 1916 statute, moreover, permitted the secretary of the navy to sell "any or all of the auxiliary ships of the Navy classified as colliers, transports, tenders, supply ships, special types, and hospital ships, which are over eighteen years of age, which he deems unsuited to present needs of the Navy and which can be disposed of at an advantageous price." Since a 1901 law gave the president the authority "to establish and from time to time modify . . . a classification of vessels of the Navy" he could classify the old destroyers as auxiliary vessels, and then the Secretary of the Navy could then declare them "unsuited to the present needs of the Navy" and release them. As an alternative, the ships could be first transferred to the army, as permitted by law, and then released by the secretary of war, who would not be bound by the apparently stricter rules governing the secretary of the navy.[16]

In this way the navy could "trade in" the destroyers, presumably to private corporations, in return for an advantageous price. But could those private corporations in turn sell them to the British? The key statutes, again, were the Espionage Act of 1917 and the amended version of the 1794 law banning the sale of vessels of war to other nations. But Cohen did not begin with these. Instead, he digressed to matters of international law, establishing the principle that citizens of neutral countries had the right to sell arms to belligerents, as long as the neutral country did not become "a base of hostile operations against a country with which it is at peace." Quoting several authorities on international law, Cohen interpreted these principles to permit the *sale* of armed vessels to belligerent nations as long as they were not "built, fitted out or armed to the order of the belligerent"—because in that case the neutral citizen "prepares the means of naval operations, since the ships, on sailing outside the neutral territorial waters, and taking in a crew and ammunition, can at once commit hostilities." Though there was authority for these arguments, they were by no means apparent or uncontroversial. Nevertheless, Cohen concluded that international law did not prohibit the "*sale* to a belligerent of vessells [*sic*] of war which were not built, fitted out or armed to the order of the belligerent"—which of course fit the case of the destroyers, which had been built years ago to the order of the United States Navy.[17]

Cohen interpreted the American statutes in the light of these principles. The 1794 statute made it a criminal act only to be "concerned in the furnishing, fitting out, or arming of any vessel with intent that such vessel shall be employed in the service of any foreign prince." It did not, in terms, ban the sale of a ship even if the seller knew such ship would be used as an instrument of war, unless the seller actually furnished, fit out, or armed the ship for that purpose. Cohen even suggested that an 1822 Supreme Court opinion by Justice Joseph Story seemed to indicate the sale of an armed vessel would be prohibited only if there was "intent that it should cruise or commence hostilities before it reached a home port of the purchaser."[18]

The last and most serious obstacle to the sale was the Espionage Act, which Cohen admitted disingenuously "might have a direct bearing upon the sale of our old destroyers to Great Britain." That law made it a crime "to send out of the jurisdiction of the United States any vessel built, armed, or equipped as a vessel of war . . . with intent . . . that such vessel shall be delivered to a belligerent nation." There were two ways to interpret this provision: first, that no vessel of war could be sent out of the jurisdiction of the United States with intent that it be delivered to a belligerent nation; and second, that no vessel could be sent out of the jurisdiction of the United States that had been "built . . . as a vessel of war" with the intent that it be delivered to a belligerent. In other words, the provision could be interpreted to permit the sale of a vessel of war provided it had not been *built* with the intent that it be delivered to a belligerent—an interpretation happily consistent with international law, as Cohen read it, and with his reading of the 1794 statute as well.[19]

Confined to a footnote was the argument that Attorney General Jackson's opinion concerning the mosquito boats was not inconsistent with Cohen's view of the law. The mosquito boats were being built for the United States, and were not finished. The legal question in that case, therefore, was "whether they could be released to the builder to enable him to complete and fit them out to the order of the British government. The question did not relate to boats which had been completed and equipped before any sale to a belligerent was contemplated."[20]

The destroyers deal, Cohen argued, was fully legal, because "it cannot by the farthest stretch of the imagination be said that . . . [the destroyers] were built, armed or equipped to the order of any belligerent, or with the intent that they should enter the service of any belligerent." It was only necessary that the United States be assured by the British that such ships would not engage in hostilities until they reached British or "near-by neutral" ports and "with only such crew and supplies as may be necessary to navigate to such near-by ports." He concluded: "There is no reason for us to put a strained or unnecessary interpretation on our own statutes contrary to our own national interests. There is no reason to extend the rules of international laws beyond the limits generally accepted by other nations to the detriment of our own country."[21]

Brilliant and creative as Cohen's memorandum was, its legalistic arguments at first made little impact. Despite its tightly drawn logic, the memorandum ran counter to a commonsense interpretation of the statutes, and went completely against any reasonable interpretation of Congress's mood, whether in 1940, 1917, or 1794. Moreover, Cohen's arguments were not immune from criticism even on legal grounds, particularly as they related to international law principles. Ickes was unimpressed, as was Corcoran. "I told Ben very frankly," Ickes wrote, "that in view of the Jackson opinion the President could not now reverse himself. He couldn't get away with it in public opinion. I continue to advocate an amendment to the Neutrality Act."[22]

Nevertheless, Roosevelt read the memorandum personally and sent it along to Frank Knox, the new secretary of the navy, with the comment that "in view of the clause in the big authorization bill I signed last Saturday, which is intended to be a complete prohibition of sale, I frankly doubt if Cohen's memorandum would stand up. . . . Also I fear Congress is in no mood at the present time to allow any form of sale." The most Roosevelt would do was to hold out the possibility of congressional action "at a little later date." Even Joe Alsop considered the distinction between destroyers and mosquito boats to be a legal "shenanigan." A lone ray of hope came from Oscar Cox, a lawyer at the Treasury Department who had assisted Cohen by making several suggested improvements in an early draft of his memorandum. "It looks as if the memo may have its effective uses in the near future," Cox predicted.[23]

Once again, events were moving quickly. The British naval situation continued to deteriorate, and advocates of a destroyer deal redoubled their efforts to find a way out. To the two existing options—new legislation or something along the lines of the Cohen memorandum—were added others. One suggestion was that Roosevelt and Willkie act together to forestall political opposition. The Century Group also suggested that, in exchange for the destroyers, the British government provide the United States with "immediate naval and air concessions in British possessions in the Western Hemisphere."[24]

The idea of trading destroyers for the right to use British naval bases was conveyed to Frank Knox, who broached the question to the British ambassador, Lord Lothian, on August 1. Three members of the Century Group, in turn, brought the idea to Roosevelt. The following day's Cabinet meeting produced a consensus that, in Roosevelt's words, "the survival of the British Isles under German attack might very possibly depend on their getting these destroyers," but that "legislation to accomplish this is necessary." It was agreed that the administration would use William Allen White to ask Willkie and other key Republicans to approve such a plan, then send a "definite request to Congress for the necessary legislation." Churchill immediately approved the indefinite lease of British naval bases in return for the destroyers.[25]

The next two weeks were full of behind-the-scenes negotiations and fevered attempts to influence public opinion. Willkie refused to commit himself as to his personal views on the destroyer deal, and flatly evaded any commitment to help influence congressional Republicans. "The implication, according to [Secretary of the Treasury Henry] Morgenthau, was that Willkie "wouldn't give much trouble on this matter but would in no way guarantee that he wouldn't." The isolationist press, at the same time, picked up the tempo of their criticism of the deal, while the Committee to Defend America by Aiding the Allies began its own counteroffensive. With opinion in the country deeply divided, it was unclear whether Congress would go along; according to one poll, seven senators favored the deal while twenty-three opposed it, with some thirty-nine awaiting word from FDR or Willkie and twenty-seven undecided or unknown.[26] (Eventually, both Willkie and his vice presidential nominee informed Roosevelt through third parties that they could not publicly support the agreement, but that they would make no objection if "plausible grounds" could be found to proceed without congressional approval. Later, Willkie broke this agreement, an action he later regretted.)

At this point Cohen entered the picture once more, recasting his memorandum to the president as a lengthy letter to the *New York Times*, to be signed not by himself but by four prominent lawyers: Dean Acheson, Charles Burlingham, Thomas D. Thacher, and George Rublee. The group, though small, was carefully chosen to appear balanced and nonpartisan. Burlingham had opposed FDR's Court-packing plan; Thacher had served in the Hoover administration (and had argued against Cohen at the Supreme Court on the Holding Company case). Acheson was a respected Washington lawyer and former law clerk to Louis Brandeis, who had briefly served Roosevelt as undersecretary of the treasury, while Rublee had served in various diplomatic capacities, including a stint as chairman of the Intergovernmental Committee on Refugees. The final form of the letter was prepared by Cohen and Acheson, and published by the *Times* on Sunday, August 11. "I have very rarely joined in a letter which I had no part preparing and with so little consideration as I gave ours this time," Burlingham wrote Cohen. "I feel rather embarrassed, but having embarked on this voyage I rely on you to carry me through."[27]

The Acheson-Burlingham-Thacher-Rublee letter tracked the arguments in Cohen's original memorandum closely, though there were changes in the order of the presentation and in emphasis. It consigned the more technical arguments to the latter portion of the document, and heavily emphasized recent political and legal developments. The letter suggested that moving without congressional approval was necessary only to save time, since its authors believed that "preponderating opinion both in and out of Congress favors such action." It emphasized that Congress's actions on June 28 did not supersede other laws designed to broaden the power of the secretary of war to authorize such transfers, but merely assured "that the technical heads of the Army and Navy might veto the release of ships, equipments or supplies deemed by them essential to our own safety." And it more explicitly took on the attorney general's mosquito boats opinion, moving it out from the confines of Cohen's original footnote. Still, the essential legal arguments were identical to those in the original memorandum, and much of the language was taken verbatim. "The transfer of our old destroyers to Great Britain," it concluded, "may help very materially to keep the dangers of war from our own shores." Seeking new congressional authority would only "allow a few dissident senators and representatives the chance to delay, and by delay possibly to frustrate, the carrying out of the will of the people to keep war from our own shores."[28]

The impact of the Cohen-Acheson letter in specific terms is difficult to measure. Langer and Gleason, in their respected *Challenge to Isolation*, concluded that "this highly competent legal opinion evidently clinched the matter." The letter was frequently cited in the public debate, though it was only one piece of what was, in effect, a public relations campaign on behalf of the agreement. In any event, FDR's mood shifted within a few days of the letter's publication; on August 14, he met with Morgenthau, Secretary of War Stimson, Knox, and Sumner Welles, and seemed concerned only about "whether he should conclude the deal with the English first and tell Congress afterward or tell Congress first." Morgenthau recorded in his diary that "for the first time that I have discussed the destroyers with the President, he seemed to have made up his mind."[29]

The final outline of the destroyers deal was concluded after a few more weeks of negotiation. Lord Lothian, Welles, Morgenthau, Arthur Purvis (Britain's supply officer in Washington), Stimson, and Knox worked out the details of the transfer of destroyers and other equipment and the terms of the leases on the British bases. Churchill and Roosevelt traded cables on various issues. The objections of Secretary of State Cordell Hull were overcome. Roosevelt let it leak out first that negotiations were under way for the acquisition of British bases, denying any connection to the destroyers, though in such a way as to imply that such a connection might in fact exist. Cohen played little role in these proceedings, although he did continue to supply the president with arguments designed to justify the agreement under international law.[30]

All that remained to seal the deal was to convince Admiral Harold R. Stark, the chief of naval operations, that the destroyers were "not essential to the defense of the United States," and to persuade Attorney General Jackson that the agreement was consistent with his earlier mosquito boats opinion. The key figure was Jackson, since Stark was apparently willing to go along if advised he could do so by the attorney general.

Jackson reached his decision on or about August 17. On that date he sent to Admiral Stark a brief memorandum concluding that Stark had virtually complete discretion to determine that the destroyers were not "essential to the defense of the United States." Congress had explicitly rejected language to the effect that the chief of naval operations certify that any material to be transferred "is not essential and cannot be used in the defense of the United States"; thus it was clear that "Congress did not intend to impose any arbitrary limitation upon the judgment of the highest staff officer as to whether the release of any material would or would not impair our essential defense." The phrase "essential to the defense of the United States," therefore, "must be regarded as relative and not absolute, and should not be constrained in relation to our total defense requirements." "It is my opinion," Jackson concluded, "that the Chief of Naval Operations may, and should, certify . . . that such destroyers are not essential to the defense of the United States if in his judgment the exchange of such destroyers for strategic naval and air bases will strengthen rather than impair the total defense of the United States."[31]

Apparently there were last-minute doubts on the part of Stark or Jackson, or perhaps Army Chief of Staff George C. Marshall, for on August 21 these three met with Navy Secretary Knox, Secretary of War Stimson, and Undersecretary of War Welles in Jackson's office for final approvals. Whatever the objections, they were overcome by Stimson's enthusiasm. With the legal and military men on board, Roosevelt was ready to conclude the details with Churchill. The final agreement was signed on September 2; the next day, the attorney general released his formal opinion on the legal issues involved. Jackson's opinion, dated August 27, certified that the proposed exchange of destroyers for bases could be accomplished by executive agreement (and hence without a treaty requiring Senate approval); that the president had authority to "alienate the title to such ships and obsolescent materials"; and that existing statute law did not prohibit the transfer of the destroyers to Great Britain. On the still-open mosquito boats question, however, Jackson would not budge. The sale of such vessels, Jackson added, was still prohibited.

Jackson's arguments in his August 27 opinion, as in his August 17 memorandum to the secretary of the navy, closely followed Ben Cohen's July memorandum and his August letter to the *Times*. Several passages, in fact, were quoted verbatim. In preparing his opinions, Jackson relied not only on Cohen's arguments directly but also on an analysis of the *Times* letter prepared by Newman A. Townsend of the solicitor general's office. Unquestionably Cohen's arguments provided a necessary element in the process by which the administration changed its mind on the legality and political viability of the destroyer transfer. As Cohen put it later, with characteristic modesty, "Many people feel that that letter made enough impression on him [Jackson] to have him take up the problem again."[32]

It is certainly an exaggeration to suggest that the fifty destroyers "saved England." The British did find ample uses for the destroyers, which for months and years to come played a vital role in escorting merchant ships and tankers transporting critical war supplies to Britain. But the destroyers did not arrive soon enough to play a role in deterring a German invasion; indeed, by September the threat of an immediate German offensive across the Channel had largely passed.

Indirectly, however, the destroyers deal had an enormous influence on the future of the war. The agreement paved the way for the Lend-Lease program, which created a statutory mechanism for transferring huge amounts of war materiel to the Allies. The idea that American aid was "lent" to the Allies in return for items of tangible value proved a useful public relations technique, and Roosevelt continued to use it even after America's entry into the war. But the impact of the destroyers agreement was more profound, and more fundamental. In both theory and practice it marked the end of American neutrality in Europe and the beginning of American involvement in the anti-Nazi alliance. Though America would not enter the war until December 1941, Roosevelt's agreement to send the destroyers was a decisive step. There is even some evidence that Churchill's impassioned pleas for the destroyers were motivated at least in part by a desire to force the Americans to take "a decidedly unneutral act" that would lead, he hoped, to "a long succession of increasingly unneutral acts in the Atlantic which would be of the utmost service to us."[33]

Cohen's contribution to the destroyers-for-bases program transcended his creative (if disingenuous) legal argument. From the beginning, Cohen was well aware that the legal issues were subordinate to the political, and that his major task was to convince not only the American people and Congress but also the administration itself that sending destroyers to England was both legally possible and practically necessary. In early July, when he began his efforts, not a single major player in the Roosevelt administration believed the deal could go through, legally or politically, without congressional approval, nor did anyone believe the deal could be sold to Congress or the American people without grave political risk. In mid-July, the president himself rejected the idea that the administration could act independently; the attorney general had dismissed the idea in June, and even Cohen's closest friends, Ickes and Corcoran, thought his efforts a waste of time and energy. Singlehandedly, Cohen began the ball rolling in the other direction, and although he cannot be given sole credit for the outcome, he was the crucial catalyst.

The destroyers agreement marked a personal watershed for Cohen as well. For perhaps the first time in his public life, he had taken on a crusade of his own, bucked his nominal superiors at every turn, and won. No longer was he doing Roosevelt's work, or Ickes's, or even Frankfurter's, for though the justice was obviously supportive of his efforts and provided key advice, especially on the *New York Times* letter, he was at best a minor player. Cohen worked with others—Oscar Cox, Joe Alsop, and Dean Acheson especially—but he became a leader instead of a follower, and he succeeded brilliantly.

He had also come around fully to foreign affairs. Although he remained at the National Power Policy Committee for a short while longer, he would soon be sent to London as counselor to the new American ambassador, John Winant. He would then work throughout the war on war mobilization and reconversion, with his attention and responsibilities increasingly focused on Europe. The remainder of his career would be in the realm of foreign policy, first at the State Department and then at the United Nations.

Years later, toward the end of his career, Cohen presented the destroyers agreement as a model of presidential responsibility and leadership. Downplaying (even concealing) his own role in the affair, Cohen argued that the agreement showed how Roosevelt guarded against "the aberrant exercise of Presidential power" by refraining "from committing himself definitely or completely to a specific course of action, whether it was executive action, national legislation, or international engagement, until he had some idea of the support he might expect or the strength of the opposition he might encounter." In making this deal, Cohen wrote, Roosevelt waited until he was sure that public opinion supported the idea and that the Republicans—especially Willkie and Senator Charles L. McNary of Oregon—would not raise a fuss.[34]

Cohen's nostalgic view of the destroyers agreement reflected the concerns of the 1970s, an era in which the abuse of executive power seemed a far greater danger to American democracy than did any external threat. In 1940, however, especially from Cohen's perspective, the real danger was not the bold exercise of executive power but timidity in the face of the growing Nazi menace. Like the expansion of the president's domestic powers during the New Deal, the expansion of executive authority in the realm of foreign policy would provide later presidents with a blueprint for ignoring Congress, manipulating public opinion, and bending domestic law to fit the exigencies of foreign policy. Cohen, as the motive force behind the destroyers-for-bases agreement, was thus a principal architect of the Imperial Presidency.

13

London

I don't feel that I have been doing much to win the war. . . . And that
is all that matters.

—*Ben Cohen to Jane Harris, April 1941*

It was clear by the fall of 1940 that Great Britain had survived the
initial Nazi assault and was in for a long-term struggle, and that the
United States was committed to at least a supporting role. Roosevelt's
reelection in November 1940 ratified the president's limited moves to
aid the British, and gave Roosevelt considerably more room to maneu-
ver in his dealings with both Congress and the American people. But
the overall situation in Europe remained grim, and Ben Cohen longed
to be closer to the action. His opportunity came with the resignation
of Joseph P. Kennedy as the American ambassador to Great Britain.

Kennedy's resignation was announced on December 1, 1940, and
dated November 6—the day after the election. The ambassador had become increasingly unhappy in London, and was particularly wounded
by Roosevelt's habits of dealing through special envoys and of failing to inform him on important matters. Although Kennedy supported
Roosevelt for reelection and gave a rousing endorsement on national
radio a week before election day, differences between the two on America's role in the European war had developed over the summer and were
growing wider. Kennedy was generally pessimistic about England's
chances against the Nazis, and was passionately opposed to American
involvement in the war—points he made clear in a conversation with
reporters on November 9. Although the major papers quoted him out

of context as saying that "democracy is all done in England," his actual remarks were no better. He praised the extreme isolationist Charles Lindbergh, opined that England was fighting not for democracy but for "self-preservation," and declared that "I can't say we aren't going in [to Europe]. Only over my dead body."[1]

With Kennedy out of the picture, Roosevelt selected as his successor the progressive Republican and former New Hampshire governor John G. Winant. Despite his partisan affiliation, Winant had been linked with the New Deal since 1935, when Roosevelt appointed him the first head of the Social Security Board; subsequently he was sent to Geneva as Roosevelt's voice on the board of the International Labor Organization (ILO). Still, Winant was an odd choice; he had little experience and would cut a poor figure in London high society. "His friends marvel at Ambassador Winant's dress," one reporter observed, "wonder how he manages to keep his trousers so unpressed, where he finds so many pale blue shirts with frayed cuffs and collars."[2] At this critical moment in Anglo-American history, critics wondered if Winant was up to the job.

Yet Winant was not without qualifications. For one thing, Roosevelt trusted him, and knew that he would not balk at being kept out of the loop on various negotiations and initiatives. For another, he was the virtual antithesis of Joseph Kennedy, being a solid liberal and strongly in the pro-British camp. Moreover, Winant's ILO connections guaranteed a solid relationship with the British Labour Party, a useful hedge against an eventual British drift to the left. "Mr. Roosevelt believes that Britain's Minister of Labor Ernest Bevin and other British labor leaders will grow increasingly powerful during the war, [and] be still more powerful after it," commented *Time* magazine. "Ambassador Winant . . . has their confidence as no career diplomat or wealthy businessman like Joseph Kennedy could hope to gain it."[3]

When John Winant sailed for London in March 1941, he took Ben Cohen with him, in the capacity of a new position labeled "counselor to the ambassador." The exact circumstances of Cohen's appointment—like much else about his service in London—is lost in the fog of history. Neither Cohen nor Winant kept a diary. Any records left behind at the American embassy in London were subsequently lost or destroyed, as the State Department makes little effort to preserve internal consular documents. There was considerable speculation about Cohen's specific duties, of course, and a good deal of circumstantial evidence. But there is very little in the way of hard facts.

The first question is whether the initiative for Cohen's appointment came from Winant, from Cohen himself, or from a third party. Joseph Lash reports, without attribution, that "Winant enlisted the help of Ray Moley in New York to persuade Ben to accompany him to London." Harold Ickes also recorded that "Winant wants Ben." Given Winant's lack of direct foreign policy experience, the idea of having an assistant with Cohen's connections and talents must have been appealing. Their personal relationship was cordial, and Winant surely had tremendous respect for Cohen's abilities.[4]

If the initiative did come from Winant, it was a happy coincidence. As Ickes put it, "all of Ben's real interest now is in England."[5] The move to London also gave Cohen the chance to escape from the political intrigues of the third term, which were beginning to hit painfully close to home. The problem was not so much Cohen's own status, which had been recently solidified by his work on the destroyers agreement. The problem, as before the election, was Tommy Corcoran.

By early 1941, the possibility that Corcoran would play a major role in the third Roosevelt administration seemed remote. Corcoran's personal relationship with Roosevelt had deteriorated badly. At the same time, Corcoran's new status as husband and father-to-be increased his longing for personal and financial security. With his myriad Washington and New York connections, a private law practice promised to be both lucrative and interesting. Moreover, Corcoran's Washington career, despite its early glamour and high profile, was going nowhere. He had never achieved rank or status, and was now without any job at all, having left government service in 1940 to work on Roosevelt's presidential campaign.

From Roosevelt's point of view, Corcoran was not nearly as useful as he had been in the mid-1930s. Years of service as an administration "hatchet man" had earned him as many opponents in the capital as he had friends. "Tom's disregard for bruised feelings had made him a lot of enemies," wrote Sam Rosenman, "and his ruthlessness and aggressiveness had aroused the antagonism of important political leaders such as Jim Farley and Ed Flynn. . . . And it is true that Tom's zealousness was sometimes embarrassing to the President." It did not help that Corcoran was widely blamed for both the purge of 1938 and the Court-packing plan. Nor was it a good sign that any future role for Corcoran was opposed by Harry Hopkins, who had quickly become the new presidential favorite. Exactly what role Hopkins had in Corcoran's demise is unclear, but Rex Tugwell thought it obvious "that somehow he was responsible for Corcoran's departure."[6]

By late January 1941, Corcoran had more or less made up his mind to enter private practice, probably in New York, and he wanted Cohen to go with him. Characteristically, Cohen found it difficult to make a decision; he found it hard to say no to Corcoran, but he had never been comfortable with the kind of law practice Corcoran was likely to pursue. "Tom complained that he had already wasted two or three months waiting for Ben to make up his mind and that if he did not want to form a law partnership with him it was Ben's to decide," Ickes recorded in his diary on January 26. "However, he felt that he had a right to a decision." Despite his reservations, Cohen did seriously consider the offer; a week earlier, he had asked Ickes to keep him on as a special counsel if he did make the move to New York. Whether Cohen wanted the Interior Department position as a source of income, as a way of keeping his hand in politics, or simply as a way of avoiding a clear-cut decision is hard to tell.[7]

Both Ickes and Felix Frankfurter were convinced that Corcoran should stay in the government. The problem was to find a specific job that would keep Corcoran happy, give him an opportunity to use his talents, and, not least of all, assuage his bruised feelings. Yet at the same time, Corcoran needed to be kept within a narrow political compass, lest his liabilities outweigh his potential contributions to the administration. In December 1940, Ickes had urged Roosevelt to find Corcoran "some position of prestige" within the administration, but even Ickes could not figure out exactly where Corcoran belonged. The best he could come up with was for Corcoran to help Lyndon Johnson raise money for congressional Democrats in the 1942 elections—hardly the sort of "prestige" position Corcoran wanted.[8]

Cohen, too, was active in trying to help his friend find a suitable administration post. Working with Jim Rowe at the White House, Cohen drafted a letter from Roosevelt to Corcoran urging him to stay on. Corcoran, of course, had no idea of Cohen's involvement in this enterprise. Written as a letter of congratulations upon the birth of Corcoran's daughter, the letter combined conciliation, ego-stroking, and an appeal to duty. "I know you are troubled about your family responsibilities," the letter noted. "But this is the most critical year in our country's history and you simply cannot leave me now." Roosevelt/Cohen continued:

You must know that I understand fully how much your front-line fighting has put you "on the spot," and that you can no longer contribute effectively without portfolio. As our plans unfold, National Defense will have positions of rank and responsibilities where your great talents will be desperately needed.

All this, as you will be the first to appreciate, takes time. And so, as your Commander-in-Chief, I instruct you to enroll within the next week as a Special Assistant to the Attorney General to await a definite assignment. I need intelligent, devoted and selfless men. You have been one of those few and must continue. . . .

You have been fond of quoting Holmes as your great exemplar. Fundamentally, he was a great soldier in life and not merely on the battle field. Ask yourself how he would have answered this call.[9]

In late January, Corcoran reported to Ickes that the president, despite opposition from Navy Secretary Frank Knox, had offered him the post of assistant secretary of the navy. This was the post that Roosevelt himself had held in World War I, and, to Roosevelt at least, it commanded a level of prestige far above its intrinsic value. But Corcoran refused to commit himself, and eventually turned down the offer.[10]

By early February, the odds that Corcoran would stay on in Washington were dropping fast, and Cohen knew he would have to make a decision on the law partnership soon. There was also a more personal issue playing on Cohen's mind. "When Tom and Peggy set up house-keeping together on Garfield Street," as Lash explained, "they found a place for Ben." But when Margaret Corcoran was born in January 1941, "Ben realized he had to establish his own household as well as decide what he was going to do."[11]

Winant's offer of a job in London solved all Cohen's problems at once. He could put off a decision on the law partnership with Corcoran while moving closer to the war and perhaps into a position where he could do something about the plight of the European Jews. As Ickes put it, "I suspect that [Cohen's] . . . soul is in constant agony over the plight of Jews in the world today and the possibility of the greater harm that may reach them if England falls."[12]

Before he left for London, Cohen completed one or two projects still on his desk. He played a small role in the drafting and passage of the

Lend-Lease Act, designed to permit various creative funding mecha-
nisms for allowing the British to purchase American arms and materiel.
The primary goal of Lend-Lease was to address the British need for
arms and munitions. The revision of the Neutrality Act in 1940 had
made it easier for American firms to sell war materials to England, but
by restricting the extension of wartime credits made it more difficult for
England to pay for them. By November 1940, the British government
faced a serious financial crisis and was quickly running out of dollars.
When the British ambassador arrived in New York on November 23, he
put the issue plainly to the American people. "Next year . . . we know
will be long and hard," he declared. "England will be grateful for any
help. England needs planes, munitions, ships and perhaps a little financial help."[13]

At a December 17 press conference (as usual, for background only),
Roosevelt casually suggested an idea he had developed while at sea,
namely, that the United States assist the British by "leaving out the dollar mark in the form of a dollar debt and substituting for it a gentleman's
obligation to repay in kind." On December 29, the president made the
concept official, revealing it in a nationally broadcast fireside chat in
which he committed the United States to becoming "the great arsenal
of democracy." The public responded favorably, and a bill was drawn up.

The Treasury lawyers' draft of what became the Lend-Lease Act of
1941 had already been reviewed by the secretary of the Treasury when
Ben Cohen was called in for a consultation. There is no evidence that
Cohen was involved at an earlier point, either at the Treasury or at the
White House. Cohen's suggestions were minor, but they pointed in the
direction of increasing the flexibility of the statute. He suggested eliminating an explicit section prohibiting "any transactions in violation of
international law," and clarifying a provision on the use of American
repair facilities to allow the repair of vessels actually owned by Great
Britain.[14] Cohen also participated in later drafting sessions—including
once in his own office—but he made no really important contributions.

Because Cohen had played a major role in the negotiations leading to the destroyers agreement, it is natural to assume that he had a
similar part in Lend-Lease. But the circumstances of the two episodes
were not at all comparable. Cohen was a dominant figure in the destroyers agreement because the rest of the administration, from the president on down, had dismissed the possibility of sending ships to England
under existing law; only Cohen saw the legal loopholes that would do
the trick. Moreover, in the summer of 1940 public support for aiding

England was uncertain at best. The circumstances surrounding Lend-Lease were entirely different. The president himself had conceived the idea and had announced it publicly; all that was left was to write the actual statute. Cohen's advice and experience were helpful, but they were hardly essential.

Once Cohen had agreed to accompany Ambassador Winant to England, the obvious question was what he would actually do once he was there. The exact nature of Cohen's responsibilities generated considerable speculation at the time, especially at the British Foreign Office, which assumed that Cohen (like Averill Harriman and Harry Hopkins) had been sent to London for some specific "mission" or purpose. Although this assumption was hardly unreasonable, it was apparently unjustified. On balance, the evidence suggests that Cohen's duties were vague and ill-defined. Perhaps Winant believed that Cohen's role would grow and evolve depending on circumstances.

Cohen's official title was counselor to the ambassador. This position, carefully distinguished from the traditional post of counselor to the embassy, was established especially for Cohen, and as the British Foreign Office noted, "is something of an innovation as far as London is concerned," although Lord Halifax, the British ambassador in Washington, did have a legal adviser on a temporary appointment. Nonetheless the British found a precedent for a permanent legal adviser in its own embassy in Cairo, and made no technical objection. Following the practice of the Egyptian government in the Cairo case, the British accorded Cohen the diplomatic rank of counselor.[15]

Cohen's appointment was deliberately made outside of State Department channels. Funding for the position came from the president's emergency fund, from which was allocated a total of $10,000 for salary and expenses. The alternative was the State Department emergency fund, but Rowe advised Roosevelt against drawing on it. "The State budget officials tell me this has never been used for such a purpose, that it is an extremely useful fund and that they are fearful of Congressional criticism. At one time every Department had such a fund but because of abuse Congress took it away. State could pay expenses but it would be an involved 'red tape' procedure."[16] Left unstated was the obvious fact that the appointment of a Jew to this sensitive post might have met with State Department criticism. Certainly Cohen's experience in later years reinforces the suggestion that it was advisable to work around, rather than through, the State Department.

But what specifically was Cohen expected to do? At the most basic level, he would serve as Winant's personal assistant, writing speeches, analyzing complex issues, providing his insights on British economic and political life. Cohen was comfortable with such a role and played it well, but if those were his only duties, he was vastly overqualified for the job.

What else, then? An obvious assumption—made by many who thought about the question only casually—was that Cohen's duties involved Lend-Lease, or perhaps the final negotiations over the destroyers agreement. Another possibility involved Jewish issues, about which Cohen still maintained a keen interest. Still another theory, although more fanciful, is that Cohen was involved in some top-secret mission—perhaps, in retrospect, having to do with the Atlantic Charter or other confidential negotiations.

For better or worse, the only one of these theories supported by the slightest bit of direct or circumstantial evidence is that Cohen's mission involved Lend-Lease. It is apparent from correspondence between Cohen and Lord Keynes (then serving in the British Treasury) that Cohen played some small role in working out the details of the program, but by itself that does not prove that Cohen went to London for that purpose. In fact, what evidence there is points directly away from the conclusion that Cohen's main mission was Lend-Lease, or the destroyers agreement, or Zionist matters. Finalizing the details of Lend-Lease was the primary responsibility of Averill Harriman, whose mission to London coincided with Cohen's tour of duty. Cohen was of course an expert on the destroyers issue (or at least on certain of its legal aspects), but the duty of negotiating the details was entrusted to the capable Charles Fahy and his delegation. And although Cohen did follow Jewish and Zionist matters while in England, he never did so in any official capacity, and it would be dubious in the extreme to suppose that the president had sent him there with such questions in mind. Finally, there exists not a single piece of evidence to suggest that Cohen was involved in the negotiations over the Atlantic Charter, or on any other secret or sensitive matter at the highest levels of the Anglo-American relationship.

The British Foreign Office continued to speculate on Cohen's appointment even after his arrival in London. One theory was that he had been sent to serve as a bridge to the British left wing. From Washington, Lord Halifax wrote that "Mr. Cohen has been described as a left-wing New Dealer, very friendly to [the] British cause, very close to the President and likely to repay cultivation." Whatever FDR's purpose in sending Cohen to London, Halifax was told that Cohen "himself is more interested in winning the war." At least one Foreign Office official dismissed out of hand the idea that Cohen was sent for some ulterior purpose. "Mr. Roosevelt is not Lenin," commented T. North Whitehead, "and it is highly improbable that he would attempt to interfere with our internal politics in the manner suggested. . . . No doubt Mr. Cohen has been appointed because he is thought to be a competent legal adviser." Still, London did accept Halifax's suggestion on one point. "If the American Dept. will put me in touch with Mr. Cohen on arrival," noted one hand in the Foreign Office, "I will do my best to 'cultivate' him." [17]

Cohen and Winant arrived in Bristol, England, early in the morning of March 1, 1941, on a British ferry plane, having crossed the Atlantic on the Pan American clipper to Lisbon. Cohen described both flights as swift and smooth, not mentioning that the ferry plane passed a German Fokker on its way to Switzerland. The British provided a glorious welcome, complete with honor guard, a planeful of notables including the Duke of Kent, and a royal special train. "I am glad to be here," Winant said by way of greeting. "There is no place I'd rather be than in England." Halfway to London, the train stopped to pick up King George himself, dressed in the uniform of a field marshal, with hand outstretched. "I am glad to welcome you here," said the king. Later they all had tea with Queen Elizabeth.[18]

Cohen, in typical manner, played down the pomp and circumstance. "London has been very quiet since we have been here," he wrote Lou and Jane Harris a few days after his arrival. "I have seen a few people, but have not as yet got seriously down to work." He did record that the ambassador had been warmly received, and seemed to be genuinely liked by the people. But already Cohen was lonely, and missed home. "It was a little tough leaving," he admitted. "To tell the truth I feel just a little bit lost and out of the main currents since I left Washington."[19]

There is little record of Cohen's activities while in London. Surviving material presents only a cross section of his duties, and may or not be representative. The Oxford historian Arnold J. Toynbee noted on May 7 that Cohen's "particular job at the embassy . . . is to advise the Ambassador on questions connected with Peace Aims and Reconstruction," though whether Cohen's responsibilities in this area really did constitute his main focus of concern or were only a side interest is unknown. In any event, Cohen spent the weekend of May 3–4 with Toynbee and others at Oxford who were dealing with such matters under the auspices of the Foreign Research and Press Service (FRPS), and asked to receive "from time to time memoranda or articles which may be prepared by your group on some of the problems we discussed." Toynbee referred the matter to the Foreign Office, and certain papers were cleared for distribution to Cohen and other Americans.[20]

The papers Toynbee did send to Cohen hardly dealt with matters of state. "The first instalment [*sic*] consists of papers on very general subjects which do not trench very deeply on to the more dangerous political and economic issues," wrote a member of the Foreign Office staff. Even so, the Foreign Office directed Toynbee to inform Cohen that "the papers are to be regarded as showing how the minds of the authors are working, and not in any sense indicating the trend of thought of His Majesty's Government, to whom the papers have not even been submitted." The papers sent to Cohen included such enthralling titles as "The Causes of the Failure of the League [of Nations]," "The Time-Factor in Peacemaking," and "The Role of Law in International Reconstruction."[21]

Though Cohen's request for FRPS material does suggest at least one of his areas of interest, the papers were of little real diplomatic or other value. As F. Ashton-Gwatkin of the British Foreign Office noted in an internal memorandum, the material was not first-rate "on the Economic side," and did not reflect the government's policy. In fact, Ashton-Gwatkin pointed out, "H.M.G.'s [His Majesty's Government's] future economic policy is not laid down and cannot be laid down at present," and, in any event, "if and when H.M.G. communicate their official views on economic policy to the U.S. Government, it will not be through F.R.P.S."[22]

By late May, the British government began to appreciate the idea of using Cohen as an official but relaxed channel for communicating with the U.S. government on postwar and reconstruction matters. The Reconstruction Committee of the British government had established only the most limited and formal relationship with its counterpart at the State Department in Washington, which was headed by an official named Leo Pasvolsky. "It might help to smooth a path which has become a little thorny if [Harold] Stannard [of the War Cabinet staff] were authorised to tell . . . Cohen of our wish here to get into friendly touch with Pasvolsky and generally to inform Cohen of what we are doing," suggested a British Foreign Office official. "Stannard could then ask Dr. Cohen to let him know the matters on which he would like to be kept informed of our progress." Using Cohen in this manner would allow the British to have "liaison with the United States in Reconstruction matters which is at once cordial and discreet."[23] Before the War Cabinet's plan could be implemented, however, Cohen had already given up his appointment in London and returned to Washington.

Cohen, as noted earlier, did play some role in working out at least one detail of Lend-Lease. He met on more than one occasion with Lord Keynes over Great Britain's inability to pay for commitments made prior to the passage of the legislation. On March 17, Keynes sent Cohen a list of such obligations. "It looks therefore as if . . . we shall need to be relieved of commitments on existing orders in the u.s.a. to the amount of £360 million," Keynes wrote, "and to receive reimbursements in respect of advance payments and capital of £195 million, or at any rate a large proportion of this assistance, in order to be able to bridge the gap." Cohen suggested (as Keynes reported) that the British develop a "fresh constructive proposal," since the director of the budget had directly promised not to use Lend-Lease to fund past transactions. Keynes took Cohen's advice, developing an idea that involved the use of Reconstruction Finance Corporation funds to achieve the same purpose. Cohen was "greatly attracted to the plan," Keynes told his colleagues, but suggested leaving out the rfc. The matter was left unresolved, to be taken up by Keynes and others in Washington.[24]

Cohen was also contacted by the British government in connection with a related question that concerned a request for American assistance in increasing the credit balances available to the government. Cohen referred the matter to Winant, who cabled an endorsement of the idea to Washington. "It occurred to me that . . . special British situations will arise in which it might be simpler for a country at war to be able to meet financial contingencies rapidly and from its own coffers," wrote Winant in words either written or inspired by Cohen. "In the present circumstances shortage of funds might not only weaken England as a first line of defense but be a sufficient threat to prompt us to find the money to meet a special situation that would be hard to explain to Congress in the time which an emergency allowed and might be particularly embarrassing to handle without Congressional action."[25]

As for Cohen's other duties in London, there is remarkably little evidence. He appears to have helped Winant with a speech delivered at the Pilgrim's Luncheon, and, given Cohen's experience in speechwriting, it is likely that he wrote or helped write others. The Pilgrim's speech is of some interest, because in it Cohen laid out the first stages of the philosophy that would guide the remainder of his public career.

Winant used the opportunity of the luncheon to thank the British for their warm welcome, reaffirm the Anglo-American friendship, and underscore the great purposes of the war against tyranny. Then, in words written by Cohen, Winant urged greater cooperation among nations in the eventual postwar order. "We must recognize that the well-being of men and of nations has become interwoven with the well-being of other men and other nations in a degree that would have been inconceivable a few short decades ago." Sounding the call for what sounds very much like an international New Deal, Winant declared, "In an interdependent world men must cooperate, dominate or perish."[26]

If Cohen performed any other significant duties at the embassy, there is no record of them. As always he was well informed on a range of matters, and met "many interesting people." But he was overwhelmed by feelings of uselessness and frustration. "I dont [sic] feel that I managed somehow to be of sufficient help to you," he wrote Winant in August, tendering his resignation. Frankfurter elaborated in a confidential note: "He felt he wasn't much use to you because he was out of things. It's true that's a foolish feeling but you know how diffident and unself-assertive he is." To Jane and Lou Harris, as always, Cohen was most candid. "I don't feel that I have been doing much to win the war," he wrote in May. "And that is all that matters."[27]

In retrospect, it seems clear that Cohen's position was ill-conceived and poorly defined from the start. Winant's role in London was to be a politician, not a policy maker. His primary task was to repair the damage done to the Anglo-American relationship under Joseph P. Kennedy and to convince the British people and their government of America's commitment to the war effort. Specific policy initiatives—on which Cohen's talents would have been most useful and where he could have made an impact—were not high on Winant's official or unofficial agenda.

Moreover, Cohen's lack of State Department credentials and connections was a serious handicap. Whatever dealings he did have with the British government overlapped with the more official avenues of communication, whether through the embassy in London or through Washington. Such back channels are common in modern diplomacy, and they were used to great advantage in the British-American relationship. But neither Roosevelt nor Hopkins had any intention of using Cohen in such a manner, and thus his lack of official connections simply got in the way of any meaningful contribution.

Ironically, it was the British government that saw Cohen as a useful alternative to official channels, as indicated in the War Cabinet's effort to use Cohen to improve the discussion on reconstruction and postwar planning. Cohen left too early for such a relationship ever to develop, but it is doubtful that the British would have found him a useful conduit. At one time, Ben Cohen was the man to know in Washington. By the spring of 1941, however, no one at home was paying him much attention.

Cohen made no secret of his frustrations in England. "The letters that . . . [Tom Corcoran] has been having from Ben Cohen indicate that Ben is not altogether happy in London," Ickes recorded in his diary in April. "Apparently he is being sidetracked and Tom believes this is being done deliberately by the tories of our embassy under orders from the State Department here." A month later, Ickes noted that "Jim Forrestal came back from London and he said that Ben had nothing to do, was lonely, and, as Ben had indicated . . . to me, wanted to get back to his work." Cohen spent some time with Margery Abrahams, whom he had known since the early 1920s and who had remained a friend. But Abrahams's daughter, who was a young girl at the time, recalled in an interview that Cohen was extraordinarily quiet and withdrawn, speaking only when Abrahams drew him out.[28]

Cohen returned to Washington with Winant on a routine visit in early June. He never resumed his duties in London, although it was not until late August that he made his resignation official. "After much thought and not a little heartbreak I have decided [to] remain here for the present," he informed Winant. "I plan to resign end of month and take a little time out to think things over outside official harness." He had no plans for the future. "I plan to hang around for a while just as I have done the last couple of months, but I shall be technically on leave. I think I have about 60 days' accrued leave. By the time that runs out I should know better whether there is any work about for me."[29]

While Cohen waited, his friends made serious efforts to bring him back into the administration in an official capacity. These efforts began while Cohen was still in London, and continued throughout the summer and into the fall. Finding the right spot proved a difficult and delicate matter, however, and was made more so by the lingering problem of Tommy Corcoran's status. As long as Corcoran remained in limbo, it seemed, Cohen was unwilling to make a definite commitment himself. And if in the end Cohen felt that his friend had been misused, it was unlikely that he himself could function effectively in a top administration post.

The one job Corcoran wanted was that of solicitor general, the Justice Department official with primary responsibility for conducting the government's business before the Supreme Court. As such, the position required not only Senate confirmation but also the informal consent of the Court itself. Using the skills that had made him a Washington legend, Corcoran orchestrated a mini-boom for his candidacy. Along with endorsements from a variety of political figures, Corcoran lined up letters of recommendation from four members of the Supreme Court: Stanley Reed, Hugo Black, William O. Douglas, and Jimmy Byrnes.

The stumbling blocks to a Corcoran nomination were twofold. The first was that Corcoran was seen as simply too political for the job. Despite the flow of endorsements to the White House, there was tremendous concern that Corcoran could not change overnight from the political operator that he had appeared to become to the neutral judicial statesman he would have to be in the solicitor general's post. The second problem was that Corcoran's nomination was aggressively opposed by Felix Frankfurter.

Corcoran's relationship with Frankfurter had been disintegrating for several years. Like Cohen, Corcoran had grown to political manhood in the 1930s and had outgrown his student-professor relationship with Frankfurter. Tensions between the two men were evident as early as 1935, and had grown more acute thereafter. They had clashed openly more than once, most recently when Frankfurter had rejected Corcoran's recommendation of Stuart Guthrie to be the administrator of the federal courts. What really poisoned the Frankfurter-Corcoran relationship, however, was the outbreak of war in Europe.

In the early days of the European war—while Frankfurter was doing everything possible to draw the United States toward the conflict—Corcoran took a detached, even isolationist approach to American involvement. Frankfurter's feelings were intensified not only by the Jewish crisis but also by his extraordinary love of England; he and Marion had even adopted two English children. Like Cohen, therefore, Frankfurter expressed his support for American involvement in the war in terms of helping Great Britain. Corcoran, who keenly felt his Irish heritage, had of course precisely the opposite view of the English.

Two events led to the final break between the two men. At one point, Frankfurter enlisted Corcoran's help as an envoy to the Irish community in America, charging him with using his influence to end Irish neutrality vis-à-vis Germany (the most immediate concern was to get the Irish to adopt a blackout, because the lights in Ireland helped

German pilots navigate over England). Corcoran accepted the assignment, but he had no success. When he told Frankfurter of his failure, the justice blew up, accusing Corcoran of "halfheartedness" and "for behaving like Synge's *Playboy of the Western World* and murdering his father." Whether or not Frankfurter's charge was justified, the result was the same; Corcoran ended the interview by storming out of Frankfurter's chambers. The other occasion was of a more personal nature. Corcoran had gone to Frankfurter's apartment with his accordion, intending as usual to sing his trademark Irish songs. Marion, overcome with rage at all things Irish, ordered Corcoran to stop and forbade him from ever playing Irish songs in her home again.[30]

Frankfurter's opposition to Corcoran's appointment as solicitor general thus came as no surprise, and Corcoran did not ask his erstwhile friend for a letter of endorsement. But Frankfurter did more than simply refuse to support Corcoran; he worked actively against him. Early on, the justice called Jim Rowe to his chambers and asked him directly whether the president would appoint Corcoran to the job. As Rowe informed Roosevelt, "I told him I had no idea but I was, frankly, doubtful. . . . F.F. cited a similar case in which Lincoln wanted to appoint someone to the Supreme Court but hesitated for months because the man in question had Presidential ambitions and was not the kind to give them up. He finally exacted a promise of 'no politics' and made the appointment. Two weeks later the distinguished Justice was again running for President at top speed. . . ." Frankfurter also expressed doubt over whether Corcoran could win Senate confirmation without a "public quarrel" that would hurt the Court.[31]

Frankfurter made his views even more clear in a letter to Corcoran that he wrote but never sent. Frankfurter's opposition had nothing to do with "your silly behavior toward me," the justice wrote. "Nor do I think you are wanting in the intellectual qualifications that a Solicitor General ought to possess." Rather, the problem was that the Solicitor General's job required a full-time commitment. "If you tell me that you would make the technical functions of the solicitor generalship your exclusive job, I am bound to tell you that no man can promise away his temperament." It was precisely because Frankfurter himself could not make such a commitment, he told Corcoran, that he had himself refused the position eight years before.[32]

Inside the White House, at least, it became obvious that Corcoran would never get the solicitor general's job. In late June, Jim Rowe summarized the situation for the president. In an artful memo, Rowe began and ended with an endorsement of Corcoran, to whom he owed his success in Washington and with whom he would later establish a law partnership. In the heart of the memorandum, however, Rowe systematically laid out the case against Corcoran. "If Tom Corcoran would be a real Solicitor General," wrote Rowe, "he would be the best this Administration has ever had. He would make Stanley Reed look silly. He would be considerably better than was Bob Jackson, which is indeed high praise." But Corcoran would never be a "real" solicitor general. Echoing Frankfurter, Rowe pointed out that "in Tom's present frame of mind, I don't know whether" a promise to eschew politics, "even if made, would stick." In any event, Rowe advised, "if this matter were held up a month or so, it may die of its own weight." Despite all this, Rowe concluded somewhat disingenuously that "the best Solicitor General since [Thomas] Thacher, and including him, would be Tommy Corcoran."[33] In the end, Roosevelt delayed the nomination until the fall, and then named Charles Fahy, who had most recently served in London as the chief negotiator on the details of the destroyers-for-bases agreement.

Despite the problem of finding a place in the administration for Corcoran, Cohen's numerous friends in Washington continued to try to find a suitable position for him. At the forefront of the effort was Ickes, who had never wanted Cohen to leave in the first place and had been trying to get him to come home ever since. While Cohen was still in London, Ickes urged him to return to his Interior Department position as a freelancer "who can turn his very extraordinary abilities in that direction where they can best be used." In July, Ickes succeeded in convincing the president to appoint Cohen to full membership on the National Power Policy Committee, to which he had been counsel throughout the New Deal. Roosevelt agreed, but Cohen declined the appointment.[34]

Others were seeking a more prestigious position for Cohen. In April, Roosevelt once again came close to naming Cohen to the Securities and Exchange Commission, this time as chairman; Frankfurter was convinced that "it was the President's intention to make the nomination shortly." But both Frankfurter and Ickes opposed this appointment, for different reasons. Ickes felt that Cohen "is not an executive and to sit at a desk signing papers and struggling with personnel questions would not only get him off of his fine edge, but he could not do the job thoroughly in any event."[35] Frankfurter was ostensibly more interested in keeping Cohen in London, but it is also possible that his conflict with Corcoran had spilled over into his feelings for Cohen.

Corcoran's suggestion was that Cohen be made assistant to the attorney general. This position, as Rowe explained to Roosevelt, involved three sets of duties. First, he was the "patronage dispenser of the Department." Second, he was the " 'contact man' on the Hill for Justice and also in important battles for the White House; exercising influence with Congress, of course, was closely bound up with the patronage aspects of the job. Finally, he served as "a general *administrative* clearing house for Department of Justice detail[s]. The most prominent part of this function is the liaison between the F.B.I. and the other positions."[36]

Rowe's advice on such an appointment was unambiguous. "It is perfectly obvious that Ben Cohen should do none of these three things," he wrote. "He is neither interested nor, in my opinion, fitted by temperament for any of them. . . . He is certainly not the man to indulge in the rough and tumble patronage work, in which it is impossible to satisfy anybody. . . . Even if Cohen wanted to do it, it would probably kill him." Furthermore, Rowe argued, Cohen was "not a good man to handle F.B.I.," a job that required someone "tough enough to get along with [J. Edgar] Hoover."[37] Probably Corcoran's suggestion was designed not so much to fit Cohen's talents and interests, but as a way of allowing Corcoran to exercise influence in these key areas.

Rowe's countersuggestion was that FDR name Cohen attorney general. "During the next few years, the Attorney General will be, next to the Secretary of State, the most important official in Washington," he wrote.

> If we are to keep the forms and much of the substance of our Government in the coming crisis, it is important that what we do be at least traditionally legal. If asked who was the best lawyer in Washington, probably ninety-nine out of one hundred lawyers would unhesitatingly answer "Ben Cohen." You of course know that he is a technical master. But far more important is the fact that he uses the law purely as an instrument. The opinion on the destroyers-bases deal, which was really written by Ben, is a case in point. It was rather hard going but from what I have heard approximately two-thirds of the disinterested international lawyers said the opinion was correct.
>
> From the nature of things, there will be many steps you will

want to take and it will take a brilliant lawyer to make them legal. I think Ben is that lawyer.[38]

Predictably, the Cohen-for-attorney-general boom went nowhere, and by late August Rowe was recommending that Cohen be named one of the president's special assistants. "As time goes on, more and more people in the government would go to Ben for his advice, as they always have," Rowe wrote. "In a few months he will have all the work any one person can handle." Whatever Roosevelt was going to do, Rowe argued, it was necessary to move fast. "I do know however that when Tommy Corcoran does not get the Solicitor Generalship, 'all Hell' is going to break loose and I fear the effect on Ben. I do think it is better to get Ben in a position of stability before Tommy knows he will not be Solicitor General."[39]

All these difficulties in finding Cohen a place in the administration were considerable, but they do not reach the heart of the matter. The real problem was Cohen himself, who throughout 1941 was gradually sliding into what can only be described as an episode of full-scale depression. Ickes's diary entries from the summer and fall of that year provide an almost step-by-step record of Cohen's worsening condition, and are worth quoting in some detail:

> [June 8] Ben Cohen got back from London the latter part of last week and he dropped by to see me for few minutes. . . . Ben looked well, but his mind is still far from being at ease. He is anxious that we get more materials of war to England before it is too late.
>
> [July 5] Ben Cohen came in to see me late Monday afternoon. He was looking for comfort but I could give him none. He is terribly distressed about the rudderless course that our ship of state seems to be pursuing these days. Apparently Ben can think of nothing else and broods over the fate of the world as a mother does over her sick child.
>
> [July 12] Ben Cohen came in late Thursday to go home with me to dinner. I feel deeply sorry for Ben these days. He is almost hopeless about the situation. . . . The poor fellow is thoroughly licked and it is the worse because he is licked spiritually. . . . He is in the unhappy and disturbing situation of not being able either to get in or really to get out and forget all about it so far as possible. . . . Ben Cohen was one of those present [at an affair

honoring Robert Jackson on his appointment to the Supreme
Court] and he didn't even go up to shake hands with Bob. . . .
When I drove him and Tom back with me to the department
afterwards, Tom kidded him about this. I relate this merely as
showing the depths to which dear Ben's spirits have fallen. . . .
The tragedy of the world situation, especially as it affects the
Jews, has literally seared his soul. I would give a good deal if I
could discover some way to bring him out of this.

[August 2] The fact is that Ben has been going to pieces
spiritually. He won't take any job and he won't do any work,
although he needs such an anchor to keep him from going completely to pieces. . . . He is so engrossed in the war that he can't
even do anything about that. All that he can do is worry.

[September 20] Ben's state of mind has not improved.

[November 15] Ben Cohen came in late in the afternoon.
I had never seen him so downhearted. He told me that he was
so hurt over the treatment accorded him by the President that
he can think and talk of nothing else. . . . Of course, the best
thing for Ben right now, and the only thing that he needs, is a
steady job that will keep his mind off of his very just grievance.
But he won't take a job. He doesn't want to go to New York and
he doesn't want to practice law with Tom Corcoran. He doesn't
like the kind of reputation that Tom has made for himself since
he started in to practice law. He feels ill at ease about using the
office that he has had in the Interior building for so long. He
wanders up to New York once or twice a week and then back
again. He is all at sixes and sevens and his friends are very much
concerned about him.

[December 21] Tom Corcoran and Bill Douglas have been
urging Ben for Chairman of the SEC. Ben was quite emotional
about it. He said that he wouldn't take the place if the President
offered it to him and he wanted me to urge the President not to
make the offer. . . . So after Cabinet on Friday I waited to speak
to the President. Apparently he had Ben in mind for this place,
but he said that Francis Biddle had already told him that Ben
did not want to be considered and that Francis had added that
Ben was "psychopathic these days." . . . I don't think it was very
kind of Francis Biddle to say what he did. . . .

[December 28] [Abe] Fortas had come in on Monday to tell
me that Cohen was in a terrible mental state the preceding Fri-

day, which was the day I asked the President not to offer him the appointment of Chairman of SEC. According to Fortas, Ben broke down and cried and his friends were afraid that he might commit suicide.[40]

There is considerable other evidence of Cohen's emotional instability in this period. Rowe, in his August 1 memorandum to Roosevelt supporting Cohen for attorney general, observed that "Ben . . . is emotionally very low. . . . In other words, he is very unhappy and—after all these years—just a little temperamental. He has been for many years a steadying force in the Administration and now he is becoming just a bit of a prima donna himself. It would be his ill fortune to pick just the wrong time." In October, Cohen himself wrote Winant without elaboration, "I have been very unhappy, as most of us are these days, for divers reasons." Most seriously, at one point in 1941 or 1942 Cohen called Felix Frankfurter and actually threatened suicide.[41]

There is also a noteworthy exchange of correspondence between Cohen, Robert Szold, and Rabbi Stephen Wise in late October and early November of 1941. Cohen's letter is worth reproducing at some length, because its tone and form are as revealing of his state of mind as is its substance. Cohen's letter was cast as a formal memorandum addressed to "Dr. Wise and Mr. Szold"—a salutation perhaps appropriate for Wise but hardly so for Szold, who had been Cohen's close friend for some two decades. The full text of Cohen's letter is as follows:

> I have been told that rumors are circulating widely in Washington that I am not returning to London because of a quarrel which I am supposed to have had with Ambassador Winant about Zionism and that these rumors emanate from Zionist sources.
>
> The reasons which have influenced my decision not to return to London at the present time are my own concern and I do not propose to talk about them. But I resent deeply any suggestion that my decision was influenced by any quarrel or differences with the Ambassador about Zionism as such is not the case and the suggestion is utterly without foundation. It is painful to me and cannot but be harmful to the Zionist cause.
>
> I did suggest to Justice Brandeis last June that I thought it was advisable for him to have a talk with Ambassador Winant about Palestine in view of discussions which had occurred and which were likely to occur in London on that subject, since I

thought it important that Ambassador Winant be informed of the Justice's views (for which I know he entertained great respect) particularly as this was a subject which I did not feel that I could or should discuss freely with the Ambassador.

I hope that I may rely upon you to put an end to these false rumors about the reasons which have influenced my decision not to return to London because I am afraid that if I find anyone continuing to circulate these rumors I may in my wrath forget the Sixth Commandment.

Benjamin Victor Cohen

P. S. I am reliably informed that these false rumors are being spread by a Mr. Shulson [*sic*], who has some connection with the Zionist organization.

Wise's reply suggests that Cohen's response to this incident was wholly disproportional. "I have your memorandum of the 29th," he wrote, "but I cannot understand it. You speak of a widely circulated rumor in Washington. That rumor has not reached me [in New York], nor can I understand why it should have reached anybody. . . . I cannot understand why Mr. Schulson would choose to be responsible for such rumors, which, I repeat, had never come to my attention." Wise concluded: "Unless you permit Bob [Szold] and me to talk to Schulson and give denial [to] such rumor—even though it [be] unknown to me—I don't know what can be done."[42]

Cohen was not completely immobilized during the summer and fall of 1941. He continued to follow public events, particularly the war effort. He provided occasional advice and commentary to those who sought him out, and involved himself with various matters that he felt needed attention. In July, for example, he worked with Col. Bill Donovan on Donovan's "new organization"—the agency that eventually became the Office of Strategic Services. (In September, Roosevelt asked Cohen to attach himself to the organization formally, but Cohen refused.) Cohen's contribution was to draft an executive order for the new agency; in this enterprise, he followed Donovan's views to the letter, proposing a military-style organizational structure and even suggesting that Donovan be promoted to major general.[43] On the whole, however, Cohen's level of activity and involvement in this period was far below what might have been expected in the critical period before and after America's formal entry into the war.

Further documentation on Cohen's mental state in 1941 and 1942 is unavailable. Cohen's own papers—never particularly complete—are especially thin for this period. The very nature of his depression, of course, kept him from his usual level of public activity and interaction. Understandably, Cohen's friends were not keen to discuss his condition, either in writing or in later interviews. Then, too, America's entry into the war kept several of Cohen's closest friends, including Joe Rauh, away from Washington (and away from Cohen) in this period.

Taken in its totality, however, the available evidence establishes beyond question that Cohen's condition at this time was not simply a reflection of his usual melancholic temperament. His refusal to take on meaningful work; his heightened sensitivity to real or perceived slights; his generally low mood; his immobility in the face of the growing world crisis; and, above all, his talk of suicide all point to a depressive episode of the most dangerous proportions.

That Cohen's response to both his personal troubles and the world crisis was disproportionate, of course, does not mean that there was no basis for his unhappiness. The implications of the impending Holocaust for European Jewry, though still in its early stages, were already apparent. In addition, Cohen had had serious disagreements with Roosevelt and his new advisers, especially as regards the treatment of Corcoran. But as disturbing as these developments were, many others in similar and worse positions were able to cope with them and continue their daily business. As Ickes put it in early July, "I do not feel any more hopeful than he does but I have gotten down to bedrock of something approaching fatalism. . . . I do not believe that poor Ben has these qualities."[44]

Likewise, Cohen's personal crisis underscores but does not fully explain his psychological response. At forty-seven, having completed eight years of service to the Roosevelt administration, he found himself underappreciated and without substantial influence in the White House. The jobs that he wanted were never offered, and those that were offered were not the ones he wanted. Tommy Corcoran, his closest friend, had been treated even more shabbily. Cohen's attempt to escape from the internecine politics of Washington into the frenzy of the Anglo-American war effort had resulted only in disillusionment and disappointment. After nearly three decades of public service, Cohen could only sit by and watch while others were given positions of prominence and public recognition.

Cohen would come out of his depression, and by 1942 was again ready to make extraordinary contributions to the war effort and the postwar settlement. His public career would extend another ten years, and his involvement with the worlds of politics and ideas would continue until the end of his life. But 1941 marked a turning point. Had events turned out otherwise, he might have taken the decisive step toward the highest levels of public life. As it was, he would remain permanently in a subordinate, and underappreciated, capacity.

Franklin D. Roosevelt signs the Public Utility Holding Company Act in August 1935. Behind the president, from left to right, are Senators Alben W. Barkley (D-Ky.), Burton K. Wheeler (D-Mont.), and Fred H. Brown (D-N.H.); Dozier Devine of the Federal Power Commission, Rep. Sam Rayburn (D-Tex.); Ben Cohen; and Tommy Corcoran. Courtesy AP Wide World Photos.

Ben Cohen, age two or three,
c. 1897. Courtesy Bernard
Freund.

Ben Cohen, in high school or college,
c. 1910. Courtesy Bernard Freund.

Ben Cohen, age seven or eight, c. 1901, with sisters Bess (left) and Pearl (right). Courtesy Bernard Freund.

Ben Cohen, approximately age ten, with his family, c. 1904. Back row, from left to right: Moses Cohen, Ben Cohen, Sarah Cohen. Front row, left to right: Bess Cohen, Daniel Cohen, Pearl Cohen, Frank Cohen. Courtesy Bernard Freund.

Cohen and family outside their Chicago apartment building, c. 1915. From left to right: Frank, Ben, Bess, Dan, Sarah, Pearl, Moses. Courtesy Bernard Freund.

Ben Cohen, c. 1935. Courtesy
Bernard Freund.

Ben Cohen at his desk c. 1945. Courtesy Bernard Freund.

Ben Cohen and Tommy Corcoran, 1969. Courtesy Bernard Freund.

Ben Cohen at age seventy-five. Courtesy Bernard Freund.

Jane Harris, c. 1920. Courtesy Isaac Harris.

Jane Harris, c. 1950. Courtesy John L. Keiser.

FIFTEEN CENTS

September 12, 1938

TIME

The Weekly Newsmagazine

Color photograph for TIME *by Paul Dorsey*

Volume XXXII

COHEN & CORCORAN
They call themselves catalysts.
(See NATIONAL AFFAIRS)

Number 11

"They Call Themselves Catalysts," *Time*, September 12, 1938. TIME/Timpix.

14

World War II

The angel or friend of frustration seems to hover over Washington to plague and make most of us wretched. War is the great frustrator and I should not complain.

—*Benjamin Cohen to Archibald MacLeish*

Cohen's hiatus from government lasted until the fall of 1942, when he accepted the position of general counsel to the newly created Office of Economic Stabilization (OES). The OES had been established under the Emergency Price Control Act of 1942 "to formulate and develop a comprehensive national economic policy relating to the control of civilian purchasing power, prices, rents, wages, salaries, profits, rationing, subsidies, and all related matters." Roosevelt appointed as director the former South Carolina senator James F. Byrnes, who resigned his lifetime appointment on the Supreme Court to take up the post. To symbolize the importance of Byrnes's position and its "unique status," the director and his small staff moved into the new west wing of the White House, then still under construction.[1]

The responsibilities of the OES cut across the duties of several agencies involved with the war effort. Part of Byrnes's job, as Roosevelt conceived it, was to relieve the president "of the problems on the home front and the jurisdictional disputes which increased with the creation of every new agency." When Roosevelt offered him the position, Byrnes recalled, he told him that "in these jurisdictional disputes I want you to act as a judge and I will let it be known that your decision is my decision, and that there is no appeal. For all practical purposes you will be assistant President."[2]

The OES was a small agency, limited to Byrnes and a staff of five. For all intents and purposes the agency was Byrnes's personal preserve, with Cohen and the other staff members advising their chief but exercising little independent authority. Cohen was used to such a role, of course, and was comfortable working with Byrnes, whom he had known since the early days of the New Deal. Over the years, the two men had developed a close personal relationship, which they maintained through the war years and beyond.

Although Roosevelt conceived Byrnes's role on domestic policy in broad terms, the official task of the OES was a fairly narrow one. As its name suggests, the agency was charged with the responsibility of coordinating the government's effort to check the onset of wartime inflation. The position of general counsel therefore called for expertise in law and economics, both of which were well in line with Cohen's background and abilities. But given Byrnes's broad role as "assistant president" and the agency's proximity to the Oval Office, it was inevitable that a wide range of domestic policy issues would eventually cross Cohen's desk. Toward the end of the war, both Byrnes and Cohen became increasingly concerned with foreign policy issues as well.

As for the administration's anti-inflation efforts, the focal point was the president's "hold-the-line" order of April 1943, which froze most wages and prices at current levels and authorized the Office of Price Administration to roll back others to prewar levels. The order was generally successful in taming inflation, but it precipitated a number of internal problems for Byrnes and his staff. By stripping the War Labor Board of its authority to grant wage increases in cases involving alleged inequities, for example, Byrnes gained tighter control of wages but was forced to deal with opposition from several members of the board, including the powerful representatives of organized labor. After the labor representatives threatened their collective resignations, Cohen and others convinced Byrnes to agree to a compromise that restored some, but not all, of the board's discretionary power.

Byrnes's hard line on wages and prices also put the OES in the middle of several bitter and protracted labor disputes, including threatened walkouts in the coal and rail industries. The coal dispute amply demonstrates the close working relationship between Roosevelt and Byrnes and the intense cooperation between Byrnes's staff and the White House proper. When the miners began a series of walkouts in April

1943, Byrnes lost no time in orchestrating a presidential-level response. First, Roosevelt sent the labor leaders a message ordering them to call off the strikes; then he signed an executive order (prepared by Byrnes's staff) ordering Secretary Ickes to take control of the mines and operate them on behalf of the United States. Roosevelt followed this with a nationally broadcast radio address urging the miners to go back to work. (Cohen, as in earlier days, helped Robert Sherwood to prepare the speech.) All these efforts paid off, at least in the short run, as the miners—for the time being—returned to work.[3]

As 1943 wore on, it became more and more difficult for Byrnes to cope with his dual position as director of the OES and as "assistant president" for domestic policy. For one thing, the OES's mandate was simply too narrow to give the agency the kind of formal authority it needed to coordinate the myriad and overlapping activities on the home front. Also, the specific duties of the OES director compromised his ability to serve as the president's top adviser on domestic affairs. As Byrnes explained, "[M]y wholehearted efforts to make stabilization work were beginning, in my view, to impair my usefulness as the President's assistant in other vital matters on the home front." As the court of last resort for decisions on price and wage levels, for example, Byrnes continually found himself beseeched for special favors by senators and congressmen, "and my refusals to accommodate them were liable to impair good relations between the President and them"—and thus could jeopardize the administration's broader domestic policy goals.[4]

But the crux of the matter was Byrnes's growing sense that his responsibilities as OES director were mundane when compared with the nation's urgent need for increased coordination on the home front. As he wrote the president, "I have presented to me daily by the departments and by members of Congress matters of far greater importance to you than the price of potatoes and beans. I feel that I can render you a greater service by trying to assist in such matters. The effort to do these things and then hear the claimants for increased wages and prices is an impossible task." The solution, Byrnes argued, was to appoint a new OES director with limited responsibilities, move the agency to offices in the Federal Reserve Building, and reconstitute Byrnes and his staff as an umbrella agency within the White House with full responsibility for the war mobilization effort.[5]

The result was the Office of War Mobilization, established by executive order on May 27, 1943.[6] The order was drafted by Ben Cohen and Donald Russell, Byrnes's assistant at the OES and former law part-

ner, with the help of Wayne Coy of the Bureau of the Budget. The form
and content of the executive order were clearly influenced by Byrnes's
desire to avoid a repetition of his experiences at the OES. But the order
also reflects the lessons that Cohen had learned and applied during the
long New Deal.

To begin with, the order preempted congressional efforts to establish the Office of War Mobilization by statute. The leading congressional proposal sought to create a "giant administrative body"
comprising all or part of fourteen preexisting agencies. Such an arrangement was both unwieldy and inflexible. "The constantly shifting
exigencies of war had already indicated the urgent need for adaptability
in policy, structure, and administration," concluded political scientist
Herman Miles Somers. "An agency established by Congress could not
have the complete elasticity required, while one established by executive
order could be remodeled, expanded, curtailed, or abolished whenever
the President saw fit."[7] This need for flexibility was demonstrated just
two months after the creation of the agency, when a second executive
order was issued to expand the OWM's jurisdiction to include the coordination of "foreign supply, foreign procurement, and foreign economic
affairs."[8]

The substance of the executive order, like Cohen's 1934 statute
establishing the Securities and Exchange Commission, was likewise designed to give the new agency the maximum degree of flexibility. The
agency's mandate was broad and sweeping: it was authorized

> (a) To develop programs and to establish policies for the
> maximum use of the nation's natural and industrial resources
> for military and civilian needs, for the effective use of the na-
> tional manpower not in the armed forces, for the maintenance
> and stabilization of the civilian economy, and for the adjust-
> ment of such economy to war needs and conditions;
>
> (b) To unify the activities of Federal agencies and depart-
> ments engaged in or concerned with production, procurement,
> distribution, or transportation of military or civilian supplies,
> materials, and products and to resolve and determine contro-
> versies between such agencies or departments. . . .
>
> (c) To issue such directives on policy or operations to the
> Federal agencies and departments as may be necessary to carry
> out the programs developed, the policies established, and the
> decisions made under this Order.[9]

The order thus "appeared to comprehend virtually all home-front functions of the executive branch and was generally so accepted," Somers concluded. "It appeared to omit only foreign, diplomatic, and strategic military considerations."[10]

The agency created by the executive order was to be, in form and function, an extension of the White House. Byrnes's power as director stemmed entirely from the authority delegated to him by the president, and extended only so long and so far as he continued to enjoy the president's confidence and support. Because the director's power came directly from the president, it could not be delegated further down the line, as the political scientist V. O. Key (then at the Bureau of the Budget) recognized. "When department and agency heads request a decision from the OWM, they expect and should have a firm decision by the Director," Key concluded.[11] Finally, the OWM arrangement marked a concentration of power in the executive branch that was not only especially justified in time of war but also consistent with Cohen's early New Deal philosophy. In all these ways, the OWM was a model for the postwar consolidation of executive power, especially in foreign affairs.

Cohen stayed at the Office of War Mobilization throughout 1943 and the first part of 1944, and continued as counsel when the agency was transformed by act of Congress into the Office of War Mobilization and Reconversion in October 1944. Cohen's formal duties at the OWM and OWMR were similar to those he had performed at the OES, and consisted mainly of advising Byrnes on the many and intricate problems of managing a wartime economy. The problems involved were highly complex, both technically and because of the inevitable bureaucratic infighting that marked both major and minor disputes. "I must say that I have difficulty understanding the situation in the War Production Board," Cohen complained to Vice President Henry Wallace in May 1942. "It seems that private companies give data to the War Production Board as an agency of government, and such data is available only to a limited group within the War Production Board, some of whom have business affiliations with private companies, and is not available to wholly disinterested government experts in other departments working on the same problem."[12]

Having at last achieved an important role in the war effort and pleased to be working with Jimmy Byrnes, Cohen recovered significantly from his bout with depression. He was so content during his early days with Byrnes, in fact, that Ickes remarked specifically upon it in his diary: "Ben is much happier these days now that he has a regular job in connection with the war," he wrote in November 1942. But the stresses of the job quickly took their toll. "The angel or friend of frustration seems to hover over Washington to plague and make most of us wretched," he wrote a month earlier in a note to Archibald MacLeish. "War is the great frustrator and I should not complain." The following summer he unburdened himself along similar lines to Charles Burlingham. While the military situation was "much further ahead than we dared hope a year ago," he wrote, "I feel much less comfortable about our progress, or lack of it, on the civilian work. Labor is much more sullen and resentful than most editorial writers think. . . . The labor representatives just won't face the facts of life on the imminent danger of inflation. . . . I really fear that if we don't do a better job in holding down the cost of living we are going to have great domestic trouble at the close of the war which may greatly jeopardize the chances of creating a good peace."[13]

On one or two occasions during the war, Cohen seemed to relapse into the kind of behavior that marked his earlier episodes of depression. One example occurred during the negotiations over the "hold-the-line" order of May 1943, when Cohen clashed with Byrnes over proposed restrictions on the discretionary authority of the War Labor Board (WLB) to authorize wage increases in exceptional cases. Given the board's highly publicized clash with labor leader John L. Lewis, Cohen feared (as Ickes recorded it) that the order "might be regarded as a retreat by the Administration." Cohen thus proposed a modification of the order so as to give the board the power to determine "minimum tested and going rates" for specific jobs in particular industries and regions, and then grant increases when necessary to bring wages up to these levels. Byrnes at first refused to consider any such change, but after the order was published he acceded to intense pressure and changed his mind, reserving the "right to review all cases that would increase prices or production costs."[14]

Cohen's objection was reasonable, and his advice was sound—had Byrnes followed his suggestion originally, he would have avoided the need to reverse himself a few days later. But Cohen's reaction, as in earlier episodes, was disproportionate. "Ben was so worked up over the situation that he was really emotional," wrote Ickes. Just before a White House meeting between Byrnes, Ickes, and Roosevelt, Cohen "tried to thrust a copy of his statement . . . into Byrnes' hand, for him to submit to the President. Jimmy said rather shortly that he would not do it. In a breaking voice Ben complained that Jimmy 'would not even submit it,' and said that, in such circumstances, he could not be of further use to Byrnes." Cohen was still "unhappy about the episode" a few days later, but after the intercession of Ickes and Tommy Corcoran he agreed not to resign "at this time anyway." This would not be the last time that Cohen would overreact to disappointment and rejection. For the moment, however, the episode had little impact; Byrnes apparently forgot all about the episode within a matter of days.[15]

Cohen's physical location in the White House, his growing reputation as a seasoned expert, and his far-reaching network of friends and associates all but guaranteed his involvement with a variety of important issues not directly related to his work with Byrnes. Cohen was directly involved, for example, with the Roosevelt administration's now infamous decision to remove thousands of Japanese Americans from their homes on the West Coast and intern them in concentration camps throughout the western states. In the immediate aftermath of Pearl Harbor—during the period between Cohen's return from London and his decision to sign on with Justice Byrnes—he worked with Joseph Rauh and Oscar Cox to prepare a memorandum on "The Japanese Situation on the West Coast." Although signed by all three men, the memorandum, Rauh stated in an interview, was predominantly Cohen's work.[16]

The memorandum, Rauh explained forty years later to the federal Commission on Wartime Relocation and Internment of Civilians, was inspired by Cohen's concern that the government would overreact to the potential security problems posed by the presence of Japanese Americans on the West Coast:

> Almost immediately after Pearl Harbor, Benjamin V. Cohen . . . took up with the late Oscar Cox and me . . . his extreme concern over the then anti-Japanese hysteria on the West Coast and in the Congress and we discussed ways and means for alleviating the dangerous situation. An immediate, temporary nighttime curfew seemed to all three of us not only an effective means of handling the explosive situation, but also the least infringement on civil liberties possible in the wake of the post–Pearl Harbor fright and General DeWitt's extreme position [which called for the outright exclusion of Japanese Americans from the West Coast and their internment in camps]. . . . Our suggestion was not well received. . . . But in the interest of preventing evacua-

tion, we continued to press for the curfew and other limited measures.

According to Rauh's account, the Cohen, Rauh, and Cox memorandum, prepared in mid-February 1942, "was the final effort by the three of us to prevent evacuation and internment." If so, the memorandum was spectacularly unsuccessful. As Rauh explained, the memorandum was either "too late to be considered . . . or was not deemed a satisfactory compromise between positions of the Justice and War Departments or simply because it was not adequately persuasive for other reasons."[17]

Throughout the 1950s and 1960s, Rauh devoted considerable time and energy to the effort to persuade the federal government to acknowledge the wrongs committed against Japanese American citizens, and to pay compensation and reparations to the victims. From such a vantage point, as he wrote the Commission on Wartime Relocation, "I look back on the role of seeking a compromise in such a surcharged public situation as an unhappy one that obviously satisfied neither side then and does not satisfy me today." But Rauh was even more concerned that the memorandum not be used to sully the reputation of Ben Cohen. "I want to record how deeply Mr. Cohen felt against the evacuation," he wrote. "When I went into his office one night a couple of months later, he showed me a newspaper picture of a little Japanese American boy leaning out the evacuation train window and waving an American flag. Mr. Cohen had tears in his eyes."[18]

The plain language of the memorandum itself tells a story quite different from the version that Joe Rauh recalled years later. Written just days before President Roosevelt's initial executive order authorizing the establishment of "military areas . . . from which any or all persons may be excluded," the main purpose of the memorandum was to justify the independent exercise of executive power without specific congressional authorization. Although "unusually harsh action is not justified just because the legal power to take such action exists," wrote Cohen and his colleagues, "it is important to bear in mind that action truly necessary for the national safety cannot lightly be assumed to be barred" under the Constitution. Eschewing "constitutional constructions which would make our Constitution in time of war either unworkable or non-existent," Cohen, Rauh, and Cox argued that "the Japanese situation on the West Coast should be met by action reasonably calculated to preserve the national s[a]fety without causing unnecessary harm to persons within our jurisdiction be they citizens or aliens." They made it clear, however, that in balancing the public interest against the interests of those individuals, "any reasonable doubt should be resolved in favor of action to preserve the national safety." In any case, they believed that the president's power to act in such a case was clearly conferred by the commander-in-chief clause, and by existing statutes. "In view of the speed and striking power of modern weapons, and the urgent need for action to meet the Japanese situation on the West Coast, the President would be fully justified in acting under his war powers without further legislation."[19]

Cohen, Rauh, and Cox left no doubt as to the propriety and necessity of quick and certain action. "It is a fact and not a legal theory that Japanese who are American citizens cannot be readily identified and distinguished from Japanese who owe no loyalty to the United States," they wrote. "It is a fact and not a legal theory that the unrestricted movement of Japanese, American citizens as well as aliens, in certain defense areas may lead, and has led in some instances, to bloodshed and riot which cannot readily be controlled by police protection and which could be injurious to our defense effort at a most critical juncture." Moreover, "no one can tell a resident citizen or alien from a Japanese soldier landed by parachute from the air or from small boats along the coast. Since the Occidental eye cannot readily distinguish one Japanese resident from another effective surveillance of the movements of particular Japanese residents suspected of disloyalty is extremely difficult if not practically impossible."[20]

Having established these points, the memorandum proposed "precautionary measures" that were "reasonably adapted to need," and urged that "every effort should be made to relieve unnecessary hardship." In particular, Cohen, Rauh, and Cox recommended the establishment of "special defense areas" in which "the right to enter or move freely in such areas should be restricted to classes of inhabitants expressly designated in the order and such other persons as may be specially licensed. In such areas persons of Japanese extraction should be allowed to enter only under special license." Other areas would be designated as "limited defense areas," in which persons not specially licensed would be denied the right "not to enter, but to move freely in such areas," and would be subject to "curfew, blackout, and other restrictions as the military from time to time find necessary."[21]

The memorandum did suggest four measures "to alleviate hardship." These included the enlistment of American citizens of Japanese extraction into the armed forces; the establishment of "home guard patrols" for rural districts in order to avoid compelling "any general migration of the Japanese" from such areas (such migration was to be avoided not only for "humanitarian reasons" but also "because of the serious effect it would have upon vegetable crops"); the provision of "special reservations at safe distances from the West Coast" where American citizens of Japanese ancestry "could go voluntarily and where they could be usefully employed and live under special restrictions" ("Their transportation and subsistence cost when they cannot find useful work should be bourne [*sic*] by the government," the memorandum added. "Of course, such citizens would be free to go to other places which are not restricted, at their own expense, subject to appropriate provision for reporting their whereabouts"); and the creation of "special reservations" within the West Coast area in which the Japanese "may continue to live and work if they wish under special guards and restrictions." (Such areas "might be roped off," the memorandum added, "and all others than the registered Japanese inhabitants of such reservations might be debarred from entering such areas except under special licenses, while the Japanese inhabitants would be forbidden to leave . . . without special permit.")[22]

Both the timing and the substance of the memorandum on "The Japanese Situation" argue against Rauh's benign interpretation. The memorandum was written just days before Roosevelt's executive order of February 19; as Rauh himself pointed out, "the President wanted to know whether there was any Supreme Court decision which made the War Department's position (in favor of the creation of special defense areas) unconstitutional." Although Rauh was correct in pointing out the memorandum's claim that the validity of such an order "depended on its being 'reasonably related to a genuine war need,' " the memorandum also makes it clear that "any reasonable doubt must be resolved" in favor of the national safety.[23] Assuming that it reached Roosevelt in time and that the president gave it due consideration, the memorandum would have served to reinforce his decision to exclude and intern Americans of Japanese descent—especially since the February 19 order was couched in general terms and did not call for any specific measures to be taken.

Viewed against the backdrop of the wartime hysteria of early 1942, the Cohen-Cox-Rauh memorandum is a moderate document, and justifies Rauh's later claim that it was part of an effort to find a suitable compromise with those who demanded even stronger measures. By proposing an executive order instead of an act of Congress, the three lawyers hoped to minimize the blow to Japanese Americans and to reduce the value of the exclusion program as a precedent for future action. Cohen, Cox, and Rauh repeatedly noted that any such program could not be based on a desire to punish those affected and could not "under the guise of national defense discriminate against any class of citizens for a purpose unrelated to the national defense." The memorandum's suggestions that those excluded from the West Coast be provided with useful employment, and that steps be taken to allow Japanese Americans to be "ghettoized" within their own communities, were, in the context of the times, progressive. Furthermore, despite its evident racism (which, again, must be interpreted in context) the memorandum displays no malice toward Japanese citizens or aliens.[24]

Even so, the Cohen-Cox-Rauh memorandum was part of, and not an effort to stop, the federal government's exclusion and internment policy. As such, its significance for understanding Benjamin Cohen is twofold. First, like the destroyers agreement and the executive order establishing the Office of War Mobilization, it underscores Cohen's tendency to favor a broad reading of executive power under the Constitution and, when possible, to favor flexible administrative remedies over specific legislation. Second, it suggests the depth and passion of Cohen's commitment to the war effort, which, as with many Americans both in and out of government, was his predominant and at times only concern.[25]

Another critically important area of wartime policy involved efforts to aid the Jews of Europe and to interfere with the machinery of the Nazi extermination camps. Although Cohen maintained sporadic contact with many prominent members of the Jewish community and with key officials in several governmental agencies, there is no real evidence that he played a significant role in trying to influence the administration's policy in these area. Cohen's emotional and physical energy was instead directed toward his demanding duties at the Office of War Mobilization, and at the nascent effort to establish the United Nations. For Cohen, as for many American Jews, the best way to help the victims of Nazi genocide was to win the war, and quickly.

The question of whether America and its allies could or should have done more to help the Jews of Europe has generated intense debates among both scholars and the general public. Much of the controversy has centered on two specific questions: whether the western democracies did enough to aid and accept Jewish refugees from Nazi-occupied or threatened Europe in the late 1930s, and whether the Allies could or should have bombed the railway lines running to the Auschwitz death camp or Auschwitz itself. Even where scholars have been able to concur on the basic facts surrounding these episodes, they have not been able to agree on a single interpretive framework from which they should be judged.[26]

There is relatively little disagreement on the number of Jewish refugees from Europe who were admitted to the various western countries in the decade after 1933. All the admitting countries kept careful records and (at a time when social Darwinism had not yet died out) paid particular attention to the ethnic and national status of would-be immigrants. These figures are not completely accurate, of course, but they are roughly correct. They show, for example, that the United States admitted a total of 161,051 Jews between July 1, 1933, and June 30, 1942. It is more difficult to obtain precise data on how many of these individuals came from Germany, but such imprecision has had little effect on the larger historical issues. Nor is there any disagreement on the facts surrounding such well-publicized episodes as the long voyage of the SS *St. Louis*, with 936 people aboard (930 of whom were Jewish) in search of a port that would accept its passengers.[27]

Much more difficult to judge is whether these basic facts reflect an adequate western response to the plight of European Jewry. Every western country imposed strict immigration quotas, generally based on nationality. Objections to increasing the quotas were based on hostility less toward Jews than toward immigrants in general. (Jews constituted more than a third of all immigrants accepted to the United States between 1933 and 1942.) The question thus becomes why such quotas were not raised, a subjective judgment that must take into account not only government policy and public opinion in the western countries, but how many European Jews actually sought to emigrate and in what periods.

The voyage of the *St. Louis* presents a microcosm of the difficulty of resolving these historical debates. Critics of American and western policy stress the duplicity of the Cuban government (which granted and then refused to accept immigration certificates), the refusal of the American government to allow the ship to land its passengers in the United States, and the compelling image of stateless refugees wandering the oceans in search of a friendly port. But those who defend the western governments point out that the passengers were eventually admitted to western European countries—288 to England and the rest to France, Belgium, and the Netherlands. Those who use the story to underscore the inadequacy of the western response note that the passengers who were landed on the European continent ultimately fell under Nazi control and were eventually murdered. Those on the other side suggest that the governments of France, Belgium, and the Netherlands had no way of knowing that their countries would be overtaken by German military forces within little more than a year after the landing of the *St. Louis* passengers.

Whether Allied military forces should have bombed the Auschwitz death camp or the railroad lines leading to it is a question that is mired in even deeper controversy, because there is no agreement even on the basic facts. Consider, for example, the most basic question— whether Allied air forces could have reached and bombed Auschwitz. Certainly such a bombing mission was technically feasible, at least late in the war; Allied bombers did in fact attack an I.G. Farben plant located within a few miles of the Auschwitz complex. More difficult questions are whether the Allies had, or could have obtained within a reasonable time frame, the intelligence data necessary for carrying out such a mission; when and how strongly the recommendation to bomb Auschwitz or the railway lines was made to Allied military and political leaders; and whether such a mission would have in fact saved the lives of any of the Jewish prisoners.

Finally, there is no agreement whatsoever on how historians should approach the larger questions. Is it enough, for example, to judge these questions in historical terms, attempting to evaluate what decision makers knew, when they knew it, and how such questions fit into contemporary value systems? Or should modern analysts look to what such decision makers *might* have done had they known more, or had they been more willing to act? These latter questions are of great importance, because they allow us to extract from history vital lessons for future conduct, but they should be kept separate from questions more narrowly within the sphere of historical analysis.

If it is difficult to understand and evaluate the western response to the Holocaust, it is even more difficult to analyze Ben Cohen's attitudes and actions in this area. Cohen's role during the refugee crisis of 1938 has already been discussed; although he was deeply concerned and wanted to do something to alleviate the problem, he did very little in the way of taking concrete action. As for the bombing of Auschwitz and other Holocaust-related issues, there is, unfortunately, almost no useful and contemporary evidence. For the most part, the hard evidence of Cohen's attitudes on these issues comes from a single interview conducted more than fifteen years after the end of the war.

Cohen's response to the interviewer's question on this subject was blunt and direct. "To imagine that Roosevelt could come up with a magic wand to solve the Jewish problem might be expecting too much," Cohen explained. "When you are in a dirty war, some will suffer more than others," he added. "The question was whether you could reduce the suffering without a sacrifice on your part. . . . Things ought to have been different, but war is different, and we live in an imperfect world."[28] The best way to help the Jews of Europe, in other words, was to win the war as quickly as possible. Every moment's delay in winning the war gave the Nazis further opportunities to conduct their campaign of genocide.

In any event, there is no real evidence that Cohen was in a position seriously to affect American policy in this regard. Although he was working in the west wing, he no longer had the kind of direct access to Roosevelt that he had enjoyed when Tommy Corcoran was still a White House favorite. The Office of War Mobilization and Reconversion was focused primarily on matters of domestic policy, and had little influence on foreign policy and no influence on military policy. Cohen had few contacts in the agencies of the government responsible for foreign and military policy, and little expertise in these areas. And, finally, he was conscious then as always of the vulnerable status of American Jews— especially those in the higher echelons of government—and extremely cautious not to appear to be exercising undue influence on the administration's policy toward the Jews. During the Holocaust, as before the war, Cohen could do little more than worry and wait.

The plight of European Jews may well have strengthened Cohen's commitment to human rights, both at home and abroad. In general, civil liberties and civil rights issues were of relatively little importance to Cohen before the war, and of great interest afterward; the war years mark the beginning of Cohen's growing support for efforts to protect fundamental freedoms (especially freedom of speech and due process of law) and to defend the constitutional commitment to equality for blacks and other racial minorities. This commitment to civil rights and civil liberties would lead in the late 1940s to a founding role in the Americans for Democratic Action, and would characterize his political philosophy in the last four decades of his life.

Cohen's evolving awareness of the importance of civil rights and civil liberties issues was hardly unique. On such issues, he followed the trend among New Deal judges and lawyers, whose interests, at least in the area of constitutional law, were evolving away from economic regulatory issues after 1937. The classic expression of the liberals' new point of view came from Justice Harlan Fiske Stone, in the 1938 case of *United States* v. *Carolene Products*. The case itself is hardly noteworthy, but in a widely quoted footnote, Stone observed that the presumption of constitutionality applied to laws involving economic relationships might be less applicable "when legislation appears on its face to be within a specific prohibition of the Constitution, such as those of the first ten Amendments," or when legislation discriminates against "discrete and insular minorities" such as particular religious or racial groups.[29]

Following the new liberal philosophy, Cohen objected to the Supreme Court's decision in *Betts* v. *Brady*, which held that the Constitution did not require the government to provide counsel to an indigent defendant accused of a serious but non-capital crime. In a lengthy letter to the *New York Times* written with Erwin Griswold of the War Labor Board (and, later, dean of Harvard Law School), Cohen urged an expansive and evolving interpretation of the Bill of Rights. "History in the making is fluid," he and Griswold wrote, "and must take account of historical growth. . . . Certainly a hundred and sixty years of experience justifies an expanding rather than a contracting recognition of what the right to counsel means in a democracy in the twentieth century." In addition to a variety of narrower arguments, the two lawyers appealed to a more general understanding of human rights. "The decision in Betts v. Brady comes at a singularly inopportune time," they wrote. "Throughout the world men are fighting to be free from the fear of political trials and concentration camps. From this struggle men are hoping that a bill of rights will emerge which will guarantee to all men certain fundamental rights. . . . In a free world no man should be condemned to penal servitude for years without having the right to counsel to defend him. The right to counsel, for the poor as well as the rich, is an indispensable safeguard of freedom and justice under law."[30]

Cohen's growing support for civil rights and civil liberties paralleled his increasingly troubled relationship with Felix Frankfurter, who despite his close ties to Holmes and Brandeis became a staunch advocate of "judicial restraint" and turned against his liberal friends and colleagues in a number of important cases. Although Cohen and Griswold did not mention it in their letter to the *Times*, for example, Frankfurter joined with the majority in *Betts* v. *Brady*; two years before, likewise, he had written the Court's majority opinion upholding compulsory flag salutes for schoolchildren.[31] Cohen's substantive differences with Frankfurter on these legal issues gave him the opportunity to vent some of his personal grievances against the justice, which of course had been developing for some time. These included Frankfurter's manipulation and betrayal of Tommy Corcoran (as Cohen saw it), and his longstanding complaint about Frankfurter's habit of treating him as a young subordinate instead of an accomplished colleague.

In January 1944, for example, Cohen and Frankfurter exchanged a series of letters on the value of dissenting and concurring opinions. Cohen's letters were motivated by his concern — or perhaps irritation — at Frankfurter's tendency to file separate opinions for what Cohen regarded as insufficient cause. The letters to Frankfurter suggest Cohen's growing efforts to reverse the student-professor relationship that had for so long dominated their interactions. "Accepting the same general principles, judges can honestly differ as to their application in particular cases," Cohen lectured. "The life of the law is not logic but experience, and judges are naturally and rightly affected by their experience in reaching their judgments. I do not think — and this cuts both ways — that fellow judges should be bitter with one another because their experience drives them to different viewpoints. . . . Because their varied experience and training impel judges to differ, need not make them either judicial reactionaries or judicial demagogues."[32]

Despite Cohen's continued interest in these and other areas of domestic policy, his attention was becoming increasingly focused on foreign affairs. In October 1943, for example, he became a member of the Informal Political Agenda Group, a small committee of senior advisers charged with developing plans for a postwar international organization. The Group was organized at the request of Secretary of State Cordell Hull by Leo Pasvolsky, who as special assistant to the secretary had dealt with Cohen on Lend-Lease and other matters while Cohen was in London. Cohen's appointment marked the beginning of his long-lasting involvement with what would become the United Nations.[33]

The Informal Political Agenda Group eventually prepared a "Plan for the Establishment of an International Organization for the Maintenance of Peace and Security," the basic outlines of which were approved by Roosevelt in 1944 and became the basis for the detailed discussions and negotiations that would follow. Cohen's involvement with the group made him a natural selection as a member of the American delegation to the Dumbarton Oaks Conference, held in Washington from August to October 1944. Even with his friends, however, Cohen was coy; in September, Ickes recorded that Cohen "thinks it was the State Department that put him on the American delegation that is taking part at Dumbarton Oaks."[34]

Cohen was one of a great many participants at Dumbarton Oaks, which brought together American, British, Russian, and, later, Chinese officials to refine plans for a new international security organization. The American, British, and Russian participants in the early stages of the conference agreed on the basic outlines of the new organization, which would comprise a general assembly in which all member states would be represented; a smaller council (later named the Security Council); an international court; and a secretariat. All agreed that the "Big Three" powers (the United States, England, and the Soviet Union) should play a predominant role, especially on the Security Council, where they (and perhaps China and France) would serve as permanent members.

The main issues played out at Dumbarton Oaks involved the makeup and powers of the United Nations Security Council and the rules under which it would operate. The Soviets insisted that the permanent members of the Security Council have a veto power over all proposed decisions; the Americans argued that no state should be permitted to vote on issues to which it was a party. Also on the table was a Soviet proposal to create an international air corps, which would be under the direction of the Security Council, and for the independent representation of the Soviet Republics in the General Assembly. The Soviets withdrew the international air corps proposal after intense American opposition (Cohen, with others, believed that a U.N. charter that allowed American forces to be placed under international command would never pass the Senate); the other areas of controversy were put off to another day.[35]

Cohen's involvement with the creation of the United Nations left a profound impression. For the rest of his government career, he would be focused most intently on the problem of establishing and maintaining world peace, in large part through this new agency of international cooperation and conflict resolution. During much of the Truman administration he served as a delegate or an alternate at the United Nations, and in 1950 he would argue the first American case before the new Court of International Justice at The Hague.

Cohen's deep commitment to the evolving concept of the United Nations provides the backdrop for his involvement in the political machinations that lay behind Franklin Roosevelt's decision on whether to pursue a fourth term in office. As early as January 1944 Cohen became concerned that Roosevelt's continuation in office past the end of the war posed grave problems, not only for the Democratic Party, but also for the welfare of the nation and the future of world peace. Cohen's first idea was to propose a constitutional amendment that would have added one year both to Roosevelt's third term and to the terms of all members of Congress; this extended third term would allow Roosevelt to wrap up the war effort without the intercession of politics. It would be attractive to the Republican Party, he told Ickes, because "while it would mean another year of Roosevelt, it would mean that there would not be more than another year of Roosevelt." From the Republican point of view, such a scheme would mean "almost a dead certainty that they would be back in power in 1945." Ickes regarded Cohen's proposal as a "rather clever idea," but nothing came of it.[36]

A few weeks later, Cohen abandoned his amendment proposal in favor of a new approach, which he outlined in early March in a confidential "Memorandum Concerning the Fourth Term." Cohen now believed (with most political analysts) that if Roosevelt stood for re-election he would win, and that Congress would remain at least nominally in Democratic hands. But "the real difficulty," Cohen wrote, lay in the "probability that the President will not be able to command working majorities sympathetic with his general policies and programs in either House, particularly with reference to important domestic issues." Moreover, "these difficulties on domestic issues would in various ways, logically and illogically, be carried into the foreign field."[37]

The background of Cohen's concern about FDR's relationship with Congress was the so-called Barkley Affair, which occurred in late February. Senator Alben Barkley (D-Ky.) was the majority leader of the Senate and, by all accounts, a loyal if not passionate supporter of the president. The issue that sparked the controversy was Roosevelt's decision to veto a $2 billion tax bill that had cleared both houses of Congress. The president announced his decision in a contentious but essentially friendly meeting at the White House, but one day later he forwarded to Congress a bombastic veto message aimed at Republicans and Democrats alike. "It is not a tax bill," the president declared, "but a tax relief bill providing relief not for the needy but for the greedy." Among the words in FDR's veto message, *Time* magazine pointed out, were " 'unwise,' 'inept,' 'indefensible special privileges to favored groups,' 'dangerous precedents for the future,' " and " 'disappoint and fail the American taxpayers.' "[38]

The president's stinging message led Barkley to resign as majority leader, and the president quickly issued a conciliatory statement. By prearrangement, the Democratic senators accepted Barkley's resignation and then reelected him as majority leader; then the entire Congress answered with an override of Roosevelt's veto. But the whole affair made many Americans—including Cohen—question Roosevelt's ability to get along with Congress. "The Administration lacks even a sufficiently solid basis as a coalition government to command the unified support of its own members in the executive branch," he wrote in his memorandum, "and energetic and articulate support of working majorities within the Congress for any program sponsored by the Administration is sadly wanting." The relationship between the legislative and executive branches was likely to be even worse in a fourth term, and the stakes would be higher: it was imperative that the government and the country be unified "behind the war and the organization of world peace."[39]

For Cohen, who was a student of history and who had been present at the Paris peace talks in 1919, it was impossible to consider the possibility of a fourth term without thinking of the tragic outcome of Woodrow Wilson's quest to secure American ratification of the League of Nations Treaty. Like Wilson, Roosevelt would face a divided Congress and a skeptical nation; he would need all his energy and resources to secure a positive result. And Roosevelt, like his predecessor, was in poor health; he had been sick much of the winter, and his condition had become the subject of discussion and speculation in Washington circles and in the press. From Cohen's point of view, a fourth term could easily turn into a repeat of the Wilson debacle—a weakened or incapacitated president, a hostile Congress, and, ultimately, a doomed effort to create an organization for world peace.

The only viable alternative to a fourth term, Cohen concluded, was for the Republicans and Democrats

> to adopt a common foreign policy platform sufficiently clear and comprehensive to remove from the election of [*sic*] any controversy about America's position in the war and at the peace table. It is a little doubtful, however, whether the spirit of such an agreement would carry through the campaign unless the agreement was accompanied by some tangible act demonstrating to the country and to the world that the agreement was more than a formula of words. The best means of giving vitality to

the agreement and safeguarding its performance would be to have both parties pledge themselves and their nominees to the support of the suggestion that President Roosevelt accept an invitation to become the Chief Executive Officer of the new international organization to maintain the peace.

"This would, it is true, deprive America of President Roosevelt's leadership during the critical period of peace negotiations," Cohen admitted. "But it would demonstrate to the world, perhaps more effectively than a victorious but bitterly contested fourth term election, the confidence of the country in President Roosevelt and his foreign policy."[40]

Cohen's memorandum may have been a thinly veiled suggestion that the Roosevelt presidency had run its course, and that the time had come for a new leader to take over the fight. Certainly Roosevelt would have regarded the memorandum that way; although there is no specific evidence that the president read Cohen's memorandum, it seems inconceivable that he was unaware of it. The memorandum more than likely played a role in worsening Cohen's already strained relationship with Roosevelt, and was probably a factor in the president's refusal to appoint Cohen to high office at the beginning of 1945.

The memorandum on a fourth term must also be read against the background of Cohen's growing sense of fatigue after years of wartime work. Dumbarton Oaks was a welcome distraction, but his role there was admittedly a minor one.[41] Overall, as he explained to Charles Burlingham, he was "getting very weary of the sort of work I have been doing." With the war mobilization work winding down, and with Byrnes and Roosevelt at odds over the president's decision to choose Harry Truman over Byrnes for vice president, Cohen faced yet another decision on the future. In November, the Justice Department proposed to Roosevelt that Cohen be appointed to the United States Court of Appeals for the District of Columbia, replacing Fred M. Vinson, who had resigned in 1943 to become Byrnes's replacement as director of the Office of Economic Stabilization. Roosevelt agreed, but Cohen hesitated. "I have been very much troubled about what I should do," he wrote Burlingham. "I have been offered a place on the CCA here, but I have held the commission up and probably won't take it. I just don't know that I would like to be benched, particularly when so much of one's time would be taken up trying to guess what the Johnnies on the high court will or won't do."[42] Burlingham's advice was noncommittal. "I guess you would make a good judge but nobody could ever tell. But you would be cribb'd, cabined and confined, and to my mind and [former Solicitor General Thomas] Thacher's and [Court of Appeals Judge] Gus Hand's an Instance Court is far more interesting than an appellate one. . . . Well, who am I to advise you? I once had a chance to be a District Judge but I knew I was unfit, I didn't know enough and I didn't want to learn enough, so I went on my way. But you know plenty." Ickes and Corcoran pushed Cohen to accept the post, but, as Ickes wrote, "he insisted that he wanted to be 'free.' We both urged that he could resign at any time but we did not seem to have any effect on him." By the end of December, Cohen had officially withdrawn his name.[43]

Cohen's problem, as he explained to Burlingham, was his consuming interest in the evolving negotiations over the postwar settlement. "I should like to be more active in the peace," he wrote, "but I don't know whether that is in the cards." By late November, Cohen did know that Jimmy Byrnes was actively lobbying Roosevelt to be appointed secretary of state, and that, if appointed, Byrnes would push for Cohen to be named counselor to the State Department. Roosevelt passed over Byrnes once again, however, instead promoting Undersecretary Edward R. Stettinius to the top State Department position. Subsequently, according to a lengthy account of the affair by Edward F. Prichard, Harry Hopkins "told Ben that he had been slated for appointment as one of the Assistant Secretaries, but that after it was decided to appoint General Holmes no additional appointment was available." Hopkins then proposed to Jimmy Byrnes that Cohen be named an assistant legal adviser. Byrnes thought it unlikely that Cohen would accept the position, and when he mentioned it to Cohen, "Ben was indignant and stated many times that he regarded the offer as an insult." At this point, Stettinius, who had served as the chair of the American delegation at Dumbarton Oaks, stepped into the picture. When Cohen told Stettinius "that he would accept no position except that of Counsellor, accompanied by the traditional rank and dignity of the office," Stettinius agreed to take up the matter with the president. On January 2, Stettinius consulted with Roosevelt, and shortly afterward informed Cohen that the president had refused to make the appointment.[44]

That afternoon, Cohen drafted a letter of resignation from his position at the Office of War Mobilization and Reconversion. At dinner the same evening, according to Prichard, "He appeared to be deeply agitated, and showed bitter resentment at the President and Mr. Hopkins." Frankfurter advised Prichard "that the resignation should not be insisted upon," but Corcoran, who blamed Frankfurter and Hopkins for the affair and who "stated that the administration was in a state of political and moral collapse," sought to find a way to get Cohen named solicitor general instead. On January 4, *PM* revealed Cohen's resignation, reporting that Roosevelt's rejection of Cohen was based on his view "that the New Deal viewpoint was already adequately represented in the Department and that the selection of Cohen would create unwanted public complications."[45]

Cohen once more had taken a bold stand against what he regarded as a personal injustice but—as before—he seemed to back down. According to Prichard, Roosevelt told Cohen "that he had always wanted Ben to be Counsellor but that the appointment could not be made until it had been cleared with the Senate and House committees. . . . He told Ben that he would not let him resign and that he wanted to see him more frequently." That night, Byrnes's office released a statement affirming that Cohen had submitted his resignation "for many reasons wholly unconnected with his work with the Office of War Mobilization and Reconversion and his relations with Justice Byrnes. . . . At Justice Byrnes's request he has withdrawn his resignation." The formulation of Byrnes's statement was interpreted in the press "as evidence of Cohen's refusal to resume his post without at least a clear gesture of protest. . . . According to traditional Washington protocol, Cohen should have agreed to return quietly, permitting Byrnes to announce that reports of the resignation were without foundation."[46]

Cohen was deeply hurt by Roosevelt's rejection. "I had known from Ben, himself, that he wanted very much to have this job in the State Department," wrote Ickes. "I remarked [to Tommy Corcoran] that Ben must be feeling very much hurt. . . . Ben is tremendously sensitive." A few days later, Ickes advised Cohen "very frankly that I do not think he ought to accept an appointment with the Department of State even if it were offered to him. I said that he would be joining a group, all of the other members of which would go out to lunch leaving him alone and lonely. I told him that the State Department would probably break his heart." But Cohen was unshakable. "The trouble with Ben is that while he realizes that there is much to this there isn't anything else that he wants."[47]

Roosevelt compounded the insult to Cohen's pride in a January 13 letter offering Cohen a position as an assistant to Stettinius but without the title of counselor. "There seem to be a good many difficulties about the particular designation of 'Consellor,' due to lack of appropriations—the fact that Mr. Hull agreed not to fill the job without the approval of the Appropriations Committee—and that departmental regulations put the Counsellor over all Assistant Secretaries in rank." Roosevelt's concern over the appointment of Cohen to a position that was technically higher in rank than the various assistant secretaries hinted at what many believed to be the real reason behind the president's decision, a point Ickes made explicit in his diary. "I also picked up the rumors yesterday," he wrote on January 21, "that the objection to Ben was that as a Jew he should not be appointed to a prominent position in the State Department."[48]

The president, it seemed, still expected Cohen to act as if he had the "passion for anonymity" once falsely ascribed to him in the wake of the Brownlow commission report. "What I wish you would do, Ben, is to get into the [State] Department and give your talents and convictions to making the kind of a peace to which you and I are devoted. The Department needs you and both Ed [Stettinius] and I want you to work with us—on this, the most important task—short of winning the war— that faces the country. I am sure you can do this, even tho [sic] it be as an Assistant to Ed."[49]

Cohen's feelings on the matter were nicely summed up by Raymond Moley. "He has never been a man to complain," he wrote, "but, apparently, 12 years of meager recognition are too much even for this 'patient Griselda.'"[50] On January 16, Cohen wrote the president a full-page letter restating his refusal to accept any position but that of counselor:

> When we talked together I tried to explain to you why I did not feel that I could be effective working in a subordinate position in the State Department. You told me that you wanted me to go in as Counsellor and only technical obstacles which you thought could be removed stood in the way. I expressed grave doubts as to the wisdom of my becoming counsellor after it had become widely known that I had been offered and refused a subordinate position as it would appear that I had brought pressure to bear to secure the appointment. But you were then unwilling to heed my doubts.
>
> It is now abundantly clear to me that I am not really wanted in the State Department unless I wish to accept some undefined, subordinate position and unless I understand that my services do not rank with those holding Presidential appointment. Accepting that judgment on my services, I must respectfully ask

you to accept my judgment that I cannot effectively serve in the State Department under such conditions.

I hope that you will believe me that I have come to this conclusion not without a heavy heart. You know of my work and deep interest in the peace both before and at Dumbarton Oaks. And my interest has not abated, although I have not been invited in any capacity to a single conference on the work growing out of Dumbarton Oaks since the State Department has been reorganized.

As I explained to you in our talk, I have always worked without rank or position, but I have found my work and effectiveness increasingly handicapped by those who do put rank and position ahead of merit and service. In these circumstances I feel, as I have told you, that I can work more effectively out of office than in office for the things for which you stand. I have accordingly submitted my resignation to Justice Byrnes and at my request he has accepted it.

Of course in a private capacity I shall continue to do whatever I can to help in the war and the peace. At Justice Byrnes insistence I have agreed to continue to help him with the understanding I can do so without title or compensation.[51]

Roosevelt's response was warm, but, one senses, pro forma. "Your note of January 16th was a severe blow to me," he wrote. "I can only say how deeply I regret that you felt unable to accept the position in the Department of State which I hoped you would take, and that you have at the same time requested Justice Byrnes to accept your resignation. . . . Your decision means that the Administration is losing one of its most able and conscientious servants and that I am losing one of my most trusted advisors. . . . The services that you have rendered to the government and to the country during the past twelve years have been outstanding. . . . I know that you will continue to serve the country with great distinction and that I shall be able to call upon you as a friend in the future as in the past."[52]

15

Diplomat

Ben . . . has definitely and, in my opinion, permanently gone
"foreign."

—*Walter Brown to James F. Byrnes, March 12, 1945*

Ben Cohen's resignation from government service in January 1945
marked another watershed in his life and career. Cohen had resigned—
or threatened to resign—several times before, but this was different.
This time, he resigned not merely out of pique, nor from an over-
reaction to what was, from his point of view, the president's dismissive and insulting behavior. Cohen's resignation was, instead, a long-
overdue expression of personal ambition and of a desire for recognition
and reward. Three months past his fiftieth birthday, he was a full generation older than the young men who now served as presidential assistants; his "passion for anonymity," if it had ever existed, had long since
disappeared.

Moreover, as Cohen told Roosevelt, his lack of official title and position severely compromised his ability to function effectively in Washington. In the freewheeling days of the early New Deal, Cohen's semi-
official status was an asset, allowing him (along with Tommy Corcoran)
to move easily around the growing bureaucracy and to shuttle effort-
lessly between the White House and Capitol Hill. But trying to play
a role in foreign policy matters was different. Cohen's only points of
access were through official State Department channels—as when he
was asked to participate in the negotiations before and during Dumbarton Oaks—and through Jimmy Byrnes, whose foreign policy role

(at least until January 1945) was extremely limited. Making headway at the State Department had proved almost impossible; with no official post, Cohen knew his standing was shaky, and after Dumbarton Oaks he had simply been excluded from the ongoing discussions of the postwar settlement.

Ironically, Cohen's insistence on an appointment as State Department counselor was itself a measure of his naïveté in foreign policy making. Although many important decisions were made at the State Department, the really big questions—and in particular the outlines of the postwar order—were being decided in the White House, often with the deliberate exclusion of even the secretary of state. Roosevelt's decision to bypass Byrnes and appoint Stettinius as secretary was largely motivated, as the president himself told Stettinius, by a desire to make it clear "who was boss."[1] As counselor, Cohen would have had direct access to the secretary, and thus to whatever lower-level State Department discussions he chose to attend, but he would have been no closer to the top-level decisions than he was at the Office of War Mobilization and Reconversion (OWMR). He had never enjoyed free access to Roosevelt, not even in the early days, and there is no evidence that the president ever consulted Cohen on important matters of foreign affairs.

In January 1945, however, these questions were wholly moot. Cohen, who was now interested only in foreign policy, was excluded even from the low-level policy making that went on in the State Department. After twelve years, he had little of substance to show for his long service to Roosevelt and to the country. His financial situation was now stable—his frugal living habits and steady government salary, combined with the rapidly appreciating stock market, had seen to that. At last, it seemed, the time had come to move on.

But deeply ingrained habits die hard. Faced with another potentially decisive moment in his life and career, Cohen—as before—hesitated to act. He did not return to New York following his resignation from the OWMR; indeed, he did not even leave his office in the White House. As he told Roosevelt, Byrnes had asked him to stay on, and Cohen had agreed. The only material effect of Cohen's resignation was that he no longer received a government paycheck.

Byrnes's "insistence" that his assistant stay on was real. The timing of Cohen's resignation was extremely awkward for Byrnes; just weeks before, Byrnes had agreed to accompany the president to the Yalta Conference, to be held in late January. Byrnes—having been passed over first for vice president and then for secretary of state—was genuinely surprised at the president's request. As the "assistant president," he had been preoccupied with domestic economic issues, and although his office had some jurisdiction over international economic issues, Byrnes's time and energy were focused on the home front. When he left for Yalta, Byrnes would leave behind a number of critical domestic issues, including passage of the president's newly proposed national service legislation. As the *Washington Post* editorialized, "We cannot imagine that the man who is the administrator of the entire home front can have any mission on the foreign front which can justify his absence at this critical moment, legislatively as well as actually, in home-front affairs. The pilot clearly should be with his ship."[2]

Exactly why the president asked Byrnes to go to Yalta has been the subject of much historical debate. In the short term, certainly, Roosevelt sought to use Byrnes to help sell the upcoming Yalta agreements to both the Senate and the public. He may also have been thinking of Byrnes as an eventual secretary of state, or he may have felt pangs of guilt at having twice passed over Byrnes for higher office.[3] Whatever Roosevelt's motivation, Byrnes made the trip and attended the plenary sessions and most of the social functions. He also kept shorthand notes of the negotiations he witnessed. He had little opportunity to discuss policy matters with Roosevelt, however, and was totally excluded from the foreign ministers' meetings and from the critical negotiations on military matters and on the Far East. Whether by accident or design, Byrnes's view of the proceedings at Yalta was distorted, fragmentary, and lacking in context.

Of course, neither Byrnes nor the American public knew this. The Yalta Conference had been subject to a complete news blackout, and the nation knew nothing of the proceedings (not even their location) until the release of the Yalta communiqué on the evening of February 12. At the request of the White House, Byrnes raced home from the conference, taking one plane after another to arrive in Washington on February 13. He was the first member of the American delegation to make himself available to the press and public, and he made the most of it, holding press and radio conference to brief the nation. The whole affair had been carefully stage-managed by the White House, and Byrnes played his part perfectly. His version of the conference—wholly authentic, from his point of view—stressed Roosevelt's dominance of the proceedings and put an upbeat interpretation on the Declaration on Liberated Europe and on the Polish settlement. He also stressed his own role in advising the president and on shaping the final agreement.[4]

Byrnes continued his lobbying effort on behalf of the Yalta communiqué throughout the spring. In addition to his public statements, he also talked personally with most of his former colleagues in the Senate, and "not a few members of the House." It was clear from early on that Byrnes's lobbying efforts would be successful, particularly where they mattered most. "The obstacles to the Senate's commitment to a world security organization that only a few months ago seemed so troublesome," wrote the *New York Times*, "are now crushed, and the rocky path is now assuming the appearance of a broad avenue."[5]

His final mission for Roosevelt accomplished, Byrnes submitted his resignation from the OWMR, effective April 2. With victory in Europe "not far distant," Byrnes wrote, his office was now directing its efforts toward the reconversion to a peacetime economy, and he had no desire, as he told Roosevelt, "to wind up in peacetime as a bureaucrat in a rapidly shrinking reconversion bureau." Left unsaid, of course, was Byrnes's bitter and continuing disappointment at having been passed over for both vice president and secretary of state. The depth of Byrnes's unhappiness became clear when Ben Cohen suggested that Byrnes accept a place on the American delegation to the United Nations conference in San Francisco. Byrnes's aide Walter Brown was merely stating the obvious when he informed his boss, "I told him that had [Cordell] Hull been named chairman and you could go as head of the delegation I would be in favor of that but that I did not believe you would want to go along in a position second to Stettinius."[6]

Cohen, meanwhile, remained unofficially in his White House office, with his mind and heart on other matters. "Ben is no longer interested in OWMR work," wrote Walter Brown in a memorandum to Byrnes.

> He has definitely and, in my opinion, permanently gone "foreign." Domestic matters are minor league stuff for him now. . . . Regardless of whatever question you may submit to Ben he says your own view or statement is perfect. A good example took place this morning. General Clay sent over by Col. Bowie the regulations carrying out your letter to Crowley. He asked him to clear them with Ben, your legal counsel. Ben looked them over briefly, said they looked o.k. to him but suggested he talk with [Donald] Russell. This is an extremely important matter and although Ben is serving without compensation you have an awkward situation. There is a lot of important legal work to be done here and someone should be charged with responsibility.

If Ben is going to continue in his present state of mind then I
suggest you name Donald [Russell] general counsel.

One solution to this problem was for Cohen to be placed on the San
Francisco delegation. "Of course Ben would jump at the opportunity
in my opinion," wrote Brown, "but he does not feel there is a chance
of him getting any recognition like that from the State Department."[7]
But it was getting late for Byrnes to worry about Cohen or about internal matters at the OWMR; he stayed in the capital long enough to see
Fred Vinson confirmed as his successor, and arrived in South Carolina
on April 8.

Byrnes's retirement from government service did not last long. On
April 12, 1945—just four days after Byrnes's return home—President
Franklin D. Roosevelt died at his Warm Springs, Georgia, retreat. The
cause was a massive cerebral hemorrhage. Ben Cohen heard the news
in the White House men's room and cried. Jimmy Byrnes received
word in Spartanburg at a local radio station, and immediately cabled
Harry Truman—now the president—with an offer to help. Truman sent
a Navy plane to South Carolina to bring Byrnes to Washington; the
president had already decided, according to one account, to appoint
Byrnes as secretary of state. On accepting his new assignment, Byrnes
made it clear that, once again, he wanted Ben Cohen at his side. This
time, Cohen would get the designation of counselor.

Exactly why Truman chose Byrnes to become the nation's chief
diplomat is unclear. Truman himself described his rationale as "mostly
personal"—an attempt to make up for the embarrassment surrounding
Roosevelt's choice of Truman for vice president in 1944. But there were
two more compelling reasons. First, by virtue of his experience as the
"assistant president" and his close and numerous contacts on Capitol
Hill, Byrnes was a solid choice for the position that was now (in the absence of a vice president) next in line for the presidency. Second, from
Truman's point of view (and in the opinion of most contemporary observers), Byrnes's trip to Yalta made him the nation's premier expert on
the critical military and foreign policy decisions to be made in the weeks
and months ahead.

Although Truman relied on Byrnes's advice from the beginning of
his presidency, publicly he waited until after the San Francisco conference to announce the appointment. (Truman had asked Byrnes to go
to San Francisco as his "personal representative," but Byrnes had demurred in order to avoid compromising Stettinius and offending the

congressional members of the American delegation.) By then the war in Europe was over, but the difficult negotiations over the peace, as well as the endgame in the Pacific theater, were still to come. From April to June, Truman quietly gave Byrnes new and important responsibilities, including an appointment to the "Interim Committee," which was charged with making recommendations to the president on the testing and possible use of the top-secret atomic bomb, predicted to be ready within four months.

Thus it was not until July 3 that Byrnes took the oath of office as secretary of state. Four days later, he and Truman boarded the U.S.S. *Augusta* for their trip to Berlin and the upcoming Potsdam Conference with Stalin and Churchill. Also on board was Cohen, whose title was special assistant to the secretary, but who was already acting as the de facto counselor. (Truman had privately agreed to make the appointment official, but not until the end of the trip.) "My one assurance that the State Department may work out all right is that Ben will be connected with it," noted Harold Ickes in his diary on July 8. "Ben will be a great restraint there but it remains to be seen just what he will accomplish."[8]

In a matter of weeks, Cohen was thus catapulted to the top and center of American foreign policy making. He had been suddenly transformed, in the words of the *New York Times*, from "a quiet, unassuming man whom anyone might take for a rather aimless sightseer" into "one of the most powerful individuals in the Truman Administration." On the way to Potsdam, Cohen attended frequent briefing sessions with the president and a handful of top advisers, and he met daily with Byrnes and two other top State Department aides to review departmental papers and to prepare proposals for the president's consideration. "About once a day President Truman sat in on our discussions," recalled Byrnes, "and on the last day aboard ship he spent some hours with us studying the various proposals." Among the papers that Cohen helped Byrnes write (though probably before the trip) was a proposal to establish a Council of Foreign Ministers, a plan that was immediately endorsed by the president and that was later approved at Potsdam. At the conference itself, Cohen attended both the plenary sessions and the meetings of the foreign ministers. He took detailed notes of the proceedings, many of which were later published in the official State Department account. He was also appointed by Byrnes to serve on a subcommittee working on German political questions, and to the subcommittee charged with preparing the draft general protocol of the decisions reached at the conference.[9]

Because of his proximity to Byrnes and Truman and his work on the final declaration, Cohen was an important member of the American delegation at Potsdam. On broad questions of policy, however, he was not particularly influential. Neither Byrnes nor Truman was accustomed to sharing key decisions with subordinates, and both men had a penchant for independent action that, at times, bordered on the impulsive. The only major policy issue on which Cohen expressed a recorded opinion was the future of Germany, and here he was utterly out of touch with his two chiefs. On the day before the first "Big Three" meeting between Truman, Churchill, and Stalin, Cohen attended a meeting of the State Department staff and spoke out in favor of the creation of a "Rhur [*sic*] state under international protectorate." This "bombshell," as Walter Brown described it, provoked serious opposition, though Brown, aware of Cohen's relationship with Byrnes and Truman, assumed that the idea had already been "agreed to on boat." The developments at Potsdam did not dissuade Cohen from his support for this idea, a variant of the "Morgenthau Plan" to break up Germany into a collection of agricultural republics. "[I] cannot claim to be behind the wisdom you see in the trend against dismemberment," he wrote to Felix Frankfurter at the end of the conference. "I am not convinced that some sort of trusteeship of the Rhineland and the Ruhr may not be best for the German people and for Europe as a whole." Both Truman and Byrnes had in fact decided against such a plan before the conference had even begun; Truman, in part because of his opposition to the Morgenthau Plan, accepted the treasury secretary's resignation before leaving for Berlin. For his part, Byrnes wrote in an annotation to Brown's diary that "I had already decided against [the trusteeship] proposal and so told Cohen." [10]

Nevertheless, Cohen returned from Potsdam in a rare upbeat mood. While the American delegation was traveling home on the *Augusta*, the president announced the successful use of the first atomic bomb on Hiroshima; three days later, a second bomb was dropped on Nagasaki, and the Japanese surrender followed soon after. Cohen, who had worked so hard to secure America's entry into the war, might have felt a particular sense of satisfaction at its conclusion. Moreover, he was about to be confirmed in the position he had so long coveted, and was already involved in the work he so desperately wanted to do. With perhaps some understatement, Harold Ickes recorded in his diary that Cohen "seemed very satisfied with his own situation in the State Department." [11]

But Cohen's satisfaction would dissipate quickly. In policy terms, his frustration centered on the American-Russian relationship, which entered a new phase once the shooting stopped. The two countries had worked well together during the war, when they needed each other to face a common enemy. Tensions between them were already apparent in Potsdam, however, and they burst into the open just days after the Japanese surrender with a much-publicized argument over control of the Kuril Islands. A month later, at the first meeting of the Council of Foreign Ministers in London, American-Soviet relations took another turn for the worse. Several substantive issues were in dispute, including the Romanian and Bulgarian peace treaties, although Soviet foreign minister Vyacheslav Molotov chose to emphasize a procedural matter, namely whether China and France would be permitted to take part in the Balkan negotiations. With no hope of progress in London, Byrnes pushed for a second meeting—this time with only the British and the Russians in attendance—to be held a few months later in Moscow.

The London conference revealed deep splits not only between the American and Soviet positions on the postwar settlement, but also between the "hard-liners" and "soft-liners" within the American State Department. Although Byrnes arrived in London hoping to use the atomic bomb as leverage to dictate the terms of the peace, he learned quickly that compromise was unavoidable if the two sides were to make progress. "We have pushed these babies [the Russians] as far as they will go and I think that we better start thinking about compromise," he told John Foster Dulles, whom Byrnes had invited to London. Dulles— sounding a theme that would ring clearer and more insistent in the months and years ahead—compared a deal with Stalin to Chamberlain's agreement with Hitler at Munich, and persuaded Byrnes, for the moment at least, to back down from his compromise efforts.

Byrnes's efforts to find a way to deal with the Russians lasted through the Moscow conference. Abandoning his attempt to use the atomic bomb as an anti-Soviet threat, he now held out the hope of international cooperation on atomic energy under the auspices of a United Nations commission on atomic energy. He also managed to forge an agreement on the Far East that included a purely advisory role for the Soviets in the management of the occupation of Japan. To persuade the Soviets to agree to these proposals, of course, Byrnes had to make deals with them in other areas. Above all, he agreed to Soviet demands in the Balkans, salvaging only "some fig leaves of democratic procedure," as the State Department's George F. Kennan put it, "to hide the nakedness of Stalinist dictatorship." [12]

Byrnes—and presumably Cohen—regarded the Moscow conference as a victory. He had at last engaged the Russians in constructive
negotiations, setting the stage for an agreement on Germany and for the
opening of the United Nations, set to meet in January 1946. American
gains in Moscow were real, and the price to be paid was at least partly
met by concessions that were all but inevitable. For Byrnes and his team,
Moscow preserved the American-Soviet alliance forged during the war
and pledged at Yalta, an alliance that could form the basis of a lasting
era of peace and international cooperation.[13]

But while Byrnes and Cohen were in Moscow, the political landscape in Washington was changing rapidly. "Hard-liners" were gaining
ground in Congress, within the State Department, in the newspapers,
and, most important, inside the White House. Exactly when Truman
decided that his secretary of state's attitude toward the Russians was
insufficiently confrontational was hotly debated by both men, and has
since been the subject of considerable discussion among historians.[14] In
any event, by the spring of 1946 Byrnes—whose antennae were always
well attuned to developments in Washington—turned away from his
policy of negotiation and compromise. When the Soviet Union dispatched military forces toward Teheran in an effort to secure the Iranian oil fields, he was ready to confront the Soviets publicly and in no
uncertain terms. The United Nations charter "forbids aggression," he
told the assembled press corps in London in late February, and "we
cannot allow aggression to be accomplished by coercion or pressure or
by subterfuge such as political infiltration." In mid-March, Byrnes was
even more pointed. "The United States is committed to the support
of the charter of the United Nations," he told a New York audience.
"Should the occasion arise, our military strength will be used to support
the purpose and the principles of the charter." This, in essence, was the
Truman Doctrine—the American commitment to "contain" the Soviet
Union, by military force if necessary, within its agreed-to sphere of influence. Byrnes restated his position in a different context in his influential "Stuttgart Speech," which Cohen helped to prepare. In Stuttgart,
Byrnes pledged, in effect, that American soldiers would remain in Germany as a bulwark against possible Soviet aggression.[15]

It was not difficult for Byrnes to transform himself from a soft-liner
in December 1945 to a hard-liner in February 1946. His views on foreign policy were inchoate and fluid, and he was more than willing to
adjust his position in light of political developments at home or abroad.
For Ben Cohen, however, the transformation was more problematic,

and in the end proved impossible. He had little more real foreign policy experience than Byrnes, but his commitment to the principles of international security—and in particular to the United Nations—was far deeper. He had worked on the United Nations Charter from its beginnings in the Informal Political Agenda Group, and had watched it develop at Dumbarton Oaks and Potsdam. Certainly he lacked both the expertise and the temperament to confront the anti-Soviet hard-liners, whether inside or outside the State Department, and, following a lifetime of practice, he acceded to the views of his chief when matters came to a head. But the reason he had chosen a new career in foreign policy was to build the peace, not to wage another war, and he had no stomach for the coming cold war against the Soviets.

Cohen made his views clear much later, in a 1958 letter to Byrnes in connection with the preparation of Byrnes's memoir, *All in One Lifetime*. "At the close of the war we tried, as was expected of us, to work out the problems of the peace in close cooperation with the Russians," he wrote. "At the time the hopes of our people were high and there would have been great disappointment, if not resentment, had we not tried to work with the Russians. . . . It soon became apparent however that despite our efforts it was not going to be easy to work with the Russians. . . . As the harsh realities became better and more widely known, American as well as allied public opinion was sorely troubled. . . . At the same time you were attacked . . . for being the leader of the get-tough with Russia crowd and . . . for continuing to talk with the Russians. It was and remains my view that while keeping the public informed and not raising false hopes or expectations it is better to keep talking in an effort to make, however slowly, step by step progress towards peace than it is to cut all contacts and to increase the risks of war." [16]

Even the machinery of war, Cohen wrote, must be used only in pursuit of a negotiated peace: "It is frequently said that we should only negotiate from positions of strength. I would rather say that we must maintain sufficient strength to hold our own at the conference table. We cannot protect the interests of ourselves and of the free world at the conference table if our power is not on a basis of equality and in fair balance with Soviet power. But we should not allow ourselves to believe that strength or power is a satisfactory substitute or alternative for peaceful negotiation." For Cohen, the bottom line in both 1946 and 1958 was the stark necessity of avoiding another world war. "Both we and the Soviet Union, however great and irreconcilable many of our interests may be, have an overwhelming common interest in guarding against war, which, however it might come, by accident or design, would totally ruin and destroy both of us."[17]

Cohen lasted in the State Department until August 1947, seven months longer than Byrnes himself. Byrnes's resignation was motivated in part by health considerations, but even more so by the growing distance between the secretary and the president, and between the secretary and his own department. For although Byrnes had shifted into the dress of a cold warrior by early 1946, he, like Cohen, never abandoned hope of working with the Soviets. By contrast, those now coming to power both in the White House and in Foggy Bottom were hard-liners of a different type, passionate anti-Communists who saw the hard line not as a means to achieving peace, but as a surrogate for conducting war. George Kennan, for example, who served in the American embassy in Moscow, based his "containment" policy in part on his conviction that the Russian view was that "[t]he USSR still lives in antagonistic 'capitalist encirclement' with which in the long run there can be no permanent peaceful coexistence." Presidential aide Clark Clifford was even more blunt, advising Truman that "the United States must be prepared to wage atomic and biological warfare, if necessary," to frustrate Soviet expansionism.[18]

As the views of the hard-liners became dominant, Cohen became increasingly marginalized as a policy maker. By the time he resigned as counselor, in late July 1947, his influence within the State Department had all but evaporated. His primary role had been to advise Byrnes, who was now gone, and he had built up little in the way of influence or connections with State Department insiders. Moreover, his views were out of touch both with the department as a whole and with those of Byrnes's successor, George C. Marshall. On Russian affairs, Marshall turned not to Cohen but to Charles E. (Chip) Bohlen, who, according to one reporter, had been "functioning as counselor for a long time on the primary foreign policy, namely Russia. In fact, most state [department] authorities agree Bohlen has been the real working level authority behind the development of the Russian and American policies."[19]

Cohen, yet again, was out of a job. Once more there were rumors that he would set up shop in a legal practice with Tommy Corcoran, but there is no evidence to suggest that such an arrangement was seriously considered by either man at this point.[20] As in 1945 and at earlier points in his career, Cohen temporized by taking no action at all. Secure financially and now at home in Washington, he maintained his wide-ranging contacts within the government, consulted informally on a range of issues, and, for the first time, took to writing down his thoughts in the form of a scholarly work, later published in the *Proceedings of the American Philosophical Society,* on "The Evolving Role of Congress in Foreign Affairs."[21]

Cohen's foray into the field of scholarly analysis marks the beginning of the final phase of his public career, during which he would write a small but significant number of essays, lectures, and papers presented from the perspective of a senior Washington statesman. Despite the depth of his involvement in the domestic New Deal, Cohen's postwar writings were almost exclusively dedicated to foreign affairs.

His 1948 paper on "The Evolving Role of Congress" presents a reasoned argument in favor of a bipartisan foreign policy, one in which both the White House and Congress (controlled, at that time, by different parties) share "a general recognition of the need for receptiveness to cooperation and joint action." Thus "so far as is practicable," the executive branch must consult with the congressional leadership of both parties "before and not after important decisions and declarations are made"; congressional leaders and congressional committees, for their part, "should not take a stand on important questions without consultation with the executive branch." Both branches must also take steps to advance "democratic cooperation in the shaping of our foreign policy" by consulting with "groups of representative and specially qualified citizens" on a regular basis.[22]

At least in part, Cohen's call for a more democratically responsible foreign policy was a reaction to congressional opposition to the Truman administration's handling of foreign affairs—above all, perhaps, the congressional "red-baiting" that helped spark Jimmy Byrnes's shift to a confrontational approach to the Soviet Union. But it also reflects Cohen's frustration with the State Department insiders who at first blocked his appointment as counselor and then developed and pushed the "hard-line" approach. "It would probably facilitate constructive democratic cooperation in our foreign policy if [a] more deliberate effort were made to fill the important political or policy-making offices in the State Department and National Defense Department . . . with men of wide and active experience in public affairs rather than those with technical administrative experience or men from the career service," he wrote. "When career men become the final arbiters of policy, their ability to give disinterested and objective advice may be seriously affected; at least, their ability to do so will be subject to serious question."[23]

It was during Cohen's brief hiatus from government service—on May 14–15, 1948—that the Truman administration recognized the new and independent state of Israel.[24] The American recognition was a great victory not only for American Zionism, but also for a small group of White House aides, led by presidential assistant Clark Clifford, who had waged a long and difficult struggle in the teeth of State Department opposition to win the president's favor. After his departure from official government service, Cohen played an important role in defeating his former colleagues at State.

While at the State Department, Cohen's influence on Palestine policy was strictly circumscribed. The main problem was Jimmy Byrnes, who made it clear early on that he wanted nothing to do with the issue. When Cohen tried to set up an interview between Byrnes and David Ben-Gurion in July 1946, for example, Byrnes responded that Palestine was a presidential issue and thus outside the State Department's purview. "Byrnes resented Zionist criticisms of the State Department's Palestine policy and decided that he would no longer take responsibility for it," writes the historian Michael J. Cohen.[25] Unable to convince Byrnes to take a more active position, lacking significant influence on the State Department regulars, and unwilling to take a public or private position in opposition to the secretary, Ben Cohen was effectively forced to the sidelines on the Palestine question.

Cohen did make quiet efforts to sway the State Department officials with primary responsibility for Palestine to a more pro-Zionist (or less anti-Zionist) point of view. In late July 1947, for example, Cohen met with Undersecretary Robert Lovett, a leading force behind anti-Zionism in the State Department. The following day Cohen sent Lovett a memorandum summarizing the conversation. The memorandum reviewed the history of American involvement with Palestine, from the Wilson administration's approval of the Balfour Declaration to a December 1945 congressional resolution "declaring that the United States shall use its good offices with the mandatory power [Great Britain] to the end that Palestine shall be opened for free entry by Jews into that country to the maximum of its agricultural and economic potentialities, and that there shall be full opportunity for colonization and development." Cohen then proceeded to outline the case for the partition of Palestine into Jewish and Arab territories. "The Jewish and the Arab

positions cannot at the present time be reconciled by voluntary agreement. . . . [A]ntagonisms and fears between the two peoples have been
allowed to grow to the point that there is the gravest doubt whether
an integrated and unitary binational state could effectively function in
Palestine for many years to come. . . . The best practical chance of settlement, therefore, seems to lie in some form of partition which would
give each people a high degree of independence within the areas assigned to them, subject only to the obligation of protecting the basic
human rights of the other inhabitants."[26] Whatever the merits of this
argument, Cohen's entreaties were lost on Lovett and his State Department colleagues, who remained unsympathetic, and at times hostile, to
expanding Jewish settlement in Palestine and to the creation of an independent Jewish state.

The future of Palestine, therefore, depended on the ability of the
Zionists to bring Harry Truman around to their point of view. In large
part, the task fell to two key White House aides, Clark Clifford and
David Niles. But there was another key player, one whom Truman himself would credit as the primary force behind his decision to recognize the State of Israel. He was Max Lowenthal, whom Clifford had
brought in as a legal adviser on the Palestine issue, and whose friendship
and working relationship with Cohen stretched back to the early 1920s.
Lowenthal, whom Michael J. Cohen describes as the "unsung hero" of
the American recognition of Israel, was in close contact with Cohen
throughout 1947 and 1948, and relied heavily on Cohen's advice. Moreover, many of the ideas and arguments that Lowenthal put forward in
his legal briefs were supplied by Cohen.

Lowenthal's role in the Truman administration's decision to recognize the State of Israel was unearthed by historians only recently;
Cohen's role, buried even deeper, has never been fully revealed. Lowenthal, like Cohen, habitually played down his own part in making history. "In interviews given to a member of the Truman Library staff in
September and November 1967," writes Michael J. Cohen, "Lowenthal
was discreet to the extreme. He claimed to have heard about Truman's
recognition of Israel in May 1948 'secondhand from someone in the
White House,' whose name he could not recall. Lowenthal added that
he had never discussed Israel with Truman during that period *at all*."
But Lowenthal's role, as Michael J. Cohen revealed in his 1990 book
on *Truman and Israel*, was anything but trivial. His "skillful drafts provided the reasoned, solid argumentation for the Zionist cause, right up
to the highest level. They would prove constantly to dismay the State

Department, whose permanent staff believed that the president's aides were unfairly, even unpatriotically, introducing extraneous factors into the administration's Middle East policies."[27]

One of Michael J. Cohen's contributions to the historical record was to identify Lowenthal as the source of the ideas and arguments used by Clark Clifford in influencing Truman, particularly in the critical days before American recognition. But Lowenthal, in turn, relied heavily on Ben Cohen—as he had on earlier occasions, particularly in the development of the securities legislation of 1933 and on various projects in the 1920s. The two men remained close friends and saw each other frequently.

Clear evidence of Cohen's behind-the-scenes influence on Lowenthal comes from a memorandum prepared by Lowenthal for Clifford's signature in early March 1948. The memorandum was prompted by a speech to the United Nations Security Council by the American delegate, Warren Austin, proposing the establishment of a temporary U.N. trusteeship over Palestine "to maintain the peace and to afford the Jews and Arabs . . . further opportunity to reach an agreement regarding the future government of their country." Austin's speech, in turn, reflected the views of the State Department's leading Palestine experts. The Lowenthal memorandum represented a "last-ditch" countereffort to defeat Austin's suggestion and to replace it with a partition of Palestine into Jewish and Arab sectors.[28]

Several of the arguments incorporated into the Lowenthal-Clifford memorandum were taken, in places verbatim, from a draft speech prepared by Cohen for delivery by an unidentified member of the House or Senate. Some of the same arguments were used in an article written (and signed) by Cohen and published in the New York *Herald Tribune*. In his speech draft and article, Cohen focused on four key points: that, contrary to the "legal sophistry" of Austin and the State Department, the United Nations Security Council had "the right and duty to restore and maintain peace in Palestine if there is a threat to the peace or a breach of the peace"; that "peace and a political settlement in Palestine are one and inseparable"; that the partition plan was "a means to peace"; and that "casting doubt upon . . . that settlement . . . threatens the survival of the United Nations" as well as "our own national interests in the Near East which depend upon peace in the Near East." The Lowenthal-Clifford memorandum built on these points, but changed the emphasis to point out how the withdrawal of support for partition would benefit the Soviet Union, to the detriment of America's national interest. Still, in tone and language the Lowenthal-Clifford text borrowed heavily from Cohen's original draft. Cohen's "The Senator [Austin] . . . seemed more concerned to point out *how little* the [Security] Council could compel a member to do, rather than to point out *how much* the member states could do to enforce law and peace," for example, became Lowenthal and Clifford's "it seemed to be the sophistries of a lawyer attempting to tell what we *could not* do to support the United Nations—in direct contradistinction to your numerous statements that we meant to do everything possible to *support* the United Nations."[29]

Lowenthal's diary entries for spring and summer also reveal that he was in close contact with Cohen throughout this period, frequently relying on Cohen for background information and advice. For example, Cohen briefed Lowenthal on efforts the previous January by James Forrestal and Robert Lovett to convince Jimmy Byrnes "to join with them and help them in breaking up Partition." (Byrnes refused, on the grounds that "he favored having the UN decide how things should be done about Palestine.") The day after recognition, Lowenthal had a "brief lunch with Ben, who tells me that [Senator] Vandenberg got Byrnes last night, was first inclined to be huffy because he was not told about the Palestine recognition in advance, but Byrnes calmed him and helped him draft the statement he issued." Likewise, in early June, Lowenthal asked Cohen "for suggestions on the business of press editorials and press and radio discussions" on the evolving situation in the Middle East.[30]

Thus it is not surprising that on the day Truman recognized Israel, it was Ben Cohen who got a call from Clark Clifford, informing him that the United States would recognize the new State of Israel upon receipt of an appropriate request from the Jewish Agency. (Clifford had earlier agreed with the State Department that the United States would not recognize the new state unless formally asked to do so.) A similar call went from David Niles to Eliahu Epstein, the Jewish Agency's representative in Washington. It is not clear whether Clifford expected Cohen to intercede with the Jewish Agency or whether the call was merely a courtesy. In any event, the request from the new State of Israel came back to the White House before noon, and Truman's official recognition followed four hours later.[31]

Cohen came out of his official retirement in late September 1948, accepting an appointment as an alternate member of the American delegation to the U.N. General Assembly session in Paris. The composition of the American delegation and even the location of the meeting were, from the Zionist point of view, inauspicious; one American delegate, Republican John Foster Dulles, went so far as to suggest that Paris was selected to "reduce to a minimum" the influence of the Zionists, especially those who surrounded President Truman in the White House. Clifford, Niles, and Lowenthal closely followed the process by which the delegates were selected; as Lowenthal recorded on July 22, "I have been hearing from time to time, from Dave Niles, about the proposed delegation of the US to the UN General Assembly meeting in Paris this Sept. Dave tried to get [General John] Hilldring as a delegate, says the Pres[iden]t told him he would appoint H., but up to last word from Dave it had not gone through—those tentatively listed were [Secretary of State] Marshall, Lovett, Dean Acheson; and among the alternates Dean Rusk. [Phillip] Jessup was full or alternate. . . . This evening, early, Ben phoned to say Dave N. phoned him from NY to know whether Ben would consent to be a delegate, and Ben replied: a full delegate, Yes. Of course this Assembly session may deal with Palestine, among other things."[32]

Two weeks later, Lowenthal noted that "Dave told me . . . that State Dept had recommended that Ben be, not a full delegate, but an alternate—reason assigned: he does not speak well in full assembly meeting. The real point is that 4 of the 5 delegates being Marshall, Dulles, Mrs. FDR and Austin, the 5th place would go to Ben or to Jessup, and someone in state Dept felt it should be Jessup. . . . Ben phoned me in mid afternoon, gave me long statement . . . but it was in short: I would be willing to be alternate, but it would be more efficient to make me full delegate; various reasons." There is no evidence to support Cohen's own impression, as he wrote later, that he "felt without being told that the President wanted me here to try to keep us out of hot water on the Palestine problem."[33]

From the Zionist point of view, the drama in Paris centered on a British-American effort to impose a settlement on the parties to the Middle East dispute, one that would force Israel to return most of the Negev valley to the Arabs in exchange for the Galilee, which it had already occupied by military force. On September 21, Secretary of State George Marshall endorsed the ideas in the plan as "a generally fair basis for settlement of the Palestine question," and urged the governments involved and the General Assembly "to accept them in their entirety." Later, the secretary of state made cautious noises about supporting a resolution threatening sanctions against Israel if it refused to comply with the plan. Marshall's position touched off an immediate and forceful reaction from Jewish politicians and lobbyists, and the president, fearful of losing Jewish votes in the upcoming election, eventually distanced himself from the idea. A week before the election, Truman informed Marshall that he was "deeply concerned" about the United Nations' handling of the Palestine issue. "I hope that before this nation takes any position or any statement is made by our delegation that I be advised of such contemplated action and the implications thereof."[34]

Cohen, as in Byrnes's State Department, was once again among hostile forces and unable to contribute meaningfully to developments. His Zionist sympathies were at odds with most of his fellow delegates, except for Eleanor Roosevelt and, to a lesser extent, John Foster Dulles. Any hope of positive action had to come from the White House, on which Cohen, from across the Atlantic, could exert no influence. After seven weeks in Paris he was frustrated nearly to the boiling point, and he poured out his anger in letters to both Felix Frankfurter and Jimmy Byrnes. "I have not had very heavy assignments here and have not been able to contribute very much to the general pool of knowledge or activity," he wrote Byrnes. "I should be content despite the frustrations to coast along until the end of the session, were it not for the despicable manner in which the Palestine question is being handled. I don't know how long I can stay without exploding more than I have already."[35]

Cohen elaborated more fully on the Palestine situation in his letter to Frankfurter, complaining of the "deep sense of humiliation I feel" with respect to Palestine. "I still have no idea as to what our real position re Palestine is," he wrote. "Marshall has been led to believe that the [State] department's position whatever it is is beyond reproach, that all criticism is unfair and based on ignorance or base political motives or rank special pleading. Everyone who talks to the President against the Dept's position is assumed to fall in one or the other of the above categories. Any wavering of the President who, he assumes, completely shares the dept's position whatever it is, is due to the above influences imposed by outrageous pressures. . . . I feel only embarrassed and compromised by the piece-meal knowledge that is grudgingly accorded to us." With no particular role to play in Paris, Cohen was even reluctant to bring the Palestine issue directly to the president or to take the issue to the press: "I don't think a public row would help particularly as my position would be ascribed to the fact that I am a Jew." Under such circumstances, Cohen's inclination, as so often before, was to withdraw to the sidelines. "My thought is . . . to try to find at an early opportunity a colorless excuse for quietly going home."[36]

Reduced in rank from the State Department counselor to a mere alternate delegate, and politically far removed from most of the other American delegates, Cohen was desperately unhappy in Paris. "I wish very much you were here," he wrote Jimmy Byrnes in the early days of the session. "I feel somewhat like a lost lamb without you. I have somewhat more freedom—in the sense that I do not have to worry that some casual remark of mine will be picked up as an indication of American foreign policy—but I have much less influence. But as the situation is so confused, I do not know that I should have cause to regret or complain of my position." Cohen's malaise was compounded (at least until election day) by the assumption that Harry Truman would be defeated by the Republican challenger, Thomas E. Dewey, and by a mounting sense of futility and frustration. When press reports pilloried the president for floating the idea of sending Chief Justice Fred Vinson to Moscow for a meeting with Josef Stalin, for example, Cohen was beside himself. "It helps no one," he wrote Jane Harris. "It will make the Russians who are terribly difficult now even more difficult and intransigent. It will only increase the redbaiting and what is worse direct it full force against everything liberal." Besides, "It was the stupidest of politics. . . . It only helps Dewey to open the campaign against him . . . and to make his victory, if it comes to him as it probably will, a victory on national and international issues. The New Deal and liberalism are probably in for a short eclipse," he concluded, "but there is no reason why they should commit hari-kari." As for the larger international picture, Cohen was no less bleak: "The work of the UN goes on—and that is the important thing—progress is slow and insignificant—but that is a reflection on the state of the world," he wrote in another letter to Harris. But "part of the UN's usefulness lies in not letting us forget the state of the world as it is." On top of all this, he was not feeling well. "My sinuses have been bothering me a little," he confided to Harris in December, "probably because of the state of my mind as much as the state of my body."[37]

Cohen's days in Paris, despite all provocations, do not seem to have produced another full-fledged depressive episode. "Mrs R had a lovely thanksgiving dinner with Henry Morgenthau and his new wife the guests of honor," he wrote Harris in December. "Lube [Isadore Lubin] seems happy. I had him and his girl out to dinner last Saturday." All in all, he concluded, "Paris is lovely despite what I write and none too pleasant weather." There was even room, in a December 15 letter to Harris, for a joke. "The story is told here of two Israeli[s] overheard talking together. The one said, our situation is impossible. Yes, said the other, you are right, we must do something. We must declare war on America. Why asked the first, how will that help us? Oh, said the first, Germany did it, Japan did it, and now the US is taking care of both of them. But rejoined the other, what would happen if we won[?]"[38]

Cohen remained at the United Nations through the end of the Truman presidency, at various times an alternate, a full delegate, and a "senior adviser" to the delegation. As a member of the American delegation, he was no longer at, or even near, the center of American foreign policy making. His State Department contacts were meager, and even his White House connections became less valuable as the Truman White House moved away from the influence of the Roosevelt years and struck out on a more independent course. Above all, the outbreak of the cold war made the United Nations less a vehicle for the cooperative solution of the world's problems and more a forum for the continuation—mostly by words, but at times by deeds—of the conflict between the United States and the Soviet Union.

The onset and progression of the cold war especially impeded progress on disarmament, an issue of deep concern to Cohen since at least 1945. In 1952, while serving as an alternate U.N. delegate, Cohen was appointed as the American representative to the U.N. Disarmament Commission. "During my year on the Disarmament Commission, I was constantly trying to find some significant but not too complicated proposal which might be made as a first step," he wrote later. "But I was unsuccessful, although I am by no means convinced that one cannot be found. Still there is danger of an isolated step disturbing adversely the existing balance of power, and there is considerable risk in improvising in this field without the support of experts having full knowledge of our defense position."[39]

Cohen's speeches and writings on disarmament reflect both a near-utopian view of future possibilities and a resigned sense of the limitations imposed by existing realities. As Cohen wrote in a 1954 statement approved by the representatives of some fifty organizations and presented to the American delegation to the United Nations, "We recognize our government's untiring efforts and flexibility in past United Nations conferences to find a workable and effective disarmament plan. Despite obstacles and difficulties we urge our government to persevere vigorously in the quest for universal enforceable disarmament of all weapons of mass destruction and the reduction to a minimum of all other weapons with effective provisions for continuous and simultaneous inspection and control under the United Nations."[40]

The problem, of course, as Cohen admitted in his 1953 memo, was that the Soviet Union would have to be willing to subject itself to such inspections and controls. "Some say that the Kremlin will never raise the iron curtain to permit inspection," he wrote. "Of course they will not if they are not prepared in good faith to disarm. But if the time comes when the Kremlin is prepared to disarm if we do, then we cannot assume that they would be unwilling to accept inspection"; there were no "absolute safeguards," and "certain calculated risks must be taken." When such a time did come, Cohen advocated "drastic limitation of the numerical strength of the armed forces and of the kind of arms to be *permitted* to the point that no state is in a condition of armed preparedness to a major war."[41]

Cohen also took primary responsibility for the battle over human rights in Hungary, Bulgaria, and Romania. On April 2, 1949, the United States formally charged the governments of these three countries with crimes against human rights—including religious persecution and the suppression of free speech—in violation of both the peace treaties signed at the end of World War II and the Universal Declaration of Human Rights, which had been approved in Paris the previous autumn. "We cannot accept the proposition that under the guise of dissolving fascist or subversive organizations a state may suppress the expression of views that are odious or even hostile to it," Cohen declared in a speech to the General Assembly on April 18. "We do not question the right of the state to protect itself from those who endeavor to overthrow the state by force and violence, but that right does not justify the suppression of efforts to seek changes by peaceful means even though those efforts are displeasing to the ruling groups."[42]

Cohen had been involved in postwar diplomacy long enough to realize that there was little the United Nations could actually do about the suppression of human rights in Eastern Europe, and, after laying out the indictment in detail, he called for only modest action on the part of the General Assembly:

> The question before us is—what would be the proper and practicable course of action for the Assembly under the circumstances? We believe that the General Assembly should give its encouragement and support to action under the Treaty proce-

dures for inquiry and determination. It seems to us that such a course is preferable to any other that is available to the Assembly. We hope therefore that the General Assembly will take official note of the charges made and of the steps taken under the Treaty of Peace to ensure that human rights and fundamental freedoms are safe-guarded in accordance with the Treaty provisions. The discussion in the Assembly should impress the Governments of Bulgaria, Hungary, and Rumania with the importance of their compliance in good faith with their obligations to cooperate in the settlement of these issues.

Such a course of action was sufficiently unobtrusive to gain widespread support, and the General Assembly adopted a resolution endorsing the American position. The United States and its allies accordingly followed the provisions of the peace treaty, and called for a joint investigation by the United States, Great Britain, and the Soviet Union. Predictably, the Soviet Union and its Eastern European satellites refused to cooperate, and the United States thereupon called on the General Assembly to adopt a resolution calling for an advisory opinion from the International Court of Justice in The Hague to determine "whether the treaty procedures apply to these disputes, (2) whether the ex-enemy countries are obligated to cooperate in the carrying out of these procedures, (3) whether the Secretary-General is authorized to appoint the third member of a treaty commission if requested to do so by one of the parties to the dispute under the treaties and (4) whether a commission composed of a representative of one party and a third member appointed by the Secretary-General constitutes a commission competent to settle the dispute if the other party fails to appoint its representatives."[43]

Once again, Cohen made it clear that the only remedy available to the United States and its allies—short of war—was publicity. "We realize that this problem as the other great problems of the post-war era is not susceptible to any dramatic speedy solution," he told the assembly. "But there can be no advance towards a solution, however gradual it may be, without a universal recognition that in one form or another, governments to have a moral base must rest on the continued consent of the governed. . . . If in fulfillment of our joint responsibilities to the peoples of Bulgaria, Hungary and Rumania, we could only work together to agree upon minimum common standards of human rights and the dignity of the human person, we might thereby immeasurably strengthen the foundation on which we hope to build enduring peace." The General Assembly approved this resolution as well, and Cohen was selected to present the case to the International Court on behalf of the United States—making him the first American to appear before the newly reconstituted judicial body at the Hague.[44]

Cohen's last four years at the United Nations were disappointing and tedious. "My work on the whole—apart from a few short intervals—has not been very interesting or important," he wrote Jane Harris in early 1952.[45] Although he was sought after for speeches and lectures, and was occasionally the subject of some publicity, he was no longer a major figure in American foreign policy. In fact, he was clearly out of favor with the State Department leadership and increasingly out of touch with the White House. His career, which once held so much promise, was now in a permanent holding pattern.

What was even more discouraging to Cohen was the failure of the United Nations to live up to the grand potentialities he had once foreseen for it. "In the early days of the Charter," he declared in a 1965 lecture in Jerusalem, "it was assumed that if there was a threat to or breach of international peace, the United Nations would in one way or another be activated in an effort to stop the fighting and to restore peace." Instead, Cohen had seen "the lack of genuine effort on the part of the member states[,] particularly the Great Powers, to use the as yet untapped resources of the United Nations to develop processes and procedures for the peaceful settlement of disputes among states." Still, he tried to be philosophical. "Of course what we can do is necessarily limited," he wrote Jane Harris in 1951. But "[t]he importance of the U.N. is that it reflects the state of the world, the strife and the difficulties and divergent points of view which one must know and understand even if one does not like them."[46]

16

Elder Statesman

I don't guess there'll ever be another one like him.

—*A young newsstand operator in Washington,*

  displaying clippings about Ben Cohen, 1983

Cohen resigned from government service for the final time on January 20, 1953, the day Harry Truman left the White House and Dwight D. Eisenhower became the thirty-fourth president of the United States. Cohen had been on the government payroll, with occasional lapses, for nearly twenty years, stretching back to his early work on securities regulation under the Public Works Agency. Occasionally over the next two decades his name would surface as a possibility for another government appointment—to the United Nations under Eisenhower, even to the Supreme Court under Lyndon Baines Johnson. But none of these prospects turned into offers, and Cohen settled into a long, though active, retirement.

During his retirement, Cohen remained in close contact with a wide range of politicians, journalists, civil servants, and academics. He maintained an occasional correspondence with Felix Frankfurter and Jimmy Byrnes, and remained fiercely loyal to Tommy Corcoran. But many of his friendships were now with younger men—some of whom had been his own protégés, and among whom he finally received the private affection and public adulation he had so long sought. "One must love Ben Cohen or one does not know him," wrote his friend and tennis partner Julius C. C. Edelstein. "He has loved, and surely he has been loved.

And always will be."[1] Cohen also formed and maintained close ties to family members, especially his nephew Bernard Freund, who was still in Muncie, and Freund's wife and children.

But the love of his many friends and small family could not fill the void left by Cohen's unrequited love for Jane Harris. When Lou Harris died after a long illness in November 1952, Cohen moved quickly—perhaps too quickly—to win her for himself:

Dearest, darling Jane,

    . . . I will not write you all the things in my heart and in my mind. I know the shock and the pain that you have gone through and the burdens and anxieties which weigh upon you. I want, during this period to help you and not add to your grief and difficulties.

    I probably have failed you somehow and somewhere, but it has not been intentionally. I did not intend to press any decision regarding the future upon you until you had time to recover from the shock and poignant pain of Lou's passing and to help the children in their adjustment to their changed world.

    If I tried to make you understand how dearly I loved you, it was not to force any quick decision on you. On the contrary it was only to dispel a notion which I thought you had [at] times had that somehow my devotion to you was in some peculiar [way] due to the fact that you were not free to return my devotion.

    I have tried perhaps inadequately to subordinate my love to your paramount love for Lou and the children. But surely you know that you have meant more to me than any thing else in my life. Truly I can say that all that I am or can . . . hope to be I owe to you.

    I ask no decision for the future from you now, and I will take none. I have loved you through the years when you could not give me the love which I had for you. I love you now with all my heart and I shall continue to love you with all my heart as long as I live, no matter what you may do or what you may say.

    You remember the Bible story of Jacob. He worked and waited seven years for Rachel and then was disappointed. And he continued to wait and wait for Rachel for another seven

years. I have waited twenty years and if I live I shall wait twenty
more if need be. But I will never cease loving you. . . .

I love you Jane darling. May God bless you and keep you,

Always,

Ben[2]

Cohen, unlike Jacob, waited in vain. When author Joseph Lash asked
Harris years later why she had said no to Cohen's proposal, "she burst
out, 'How could you marry Ben? He's brilliant but. . . .' and her voice
trailed off. Pressed again, she replied reluctantly, 'I could not imagine
him as a lover.'" Lash asked Jean Pennypacker, who knew both Cohen
and Harris, what Harris had meant. "I don't think Ben was the kind of
man that roused women's sexual curiosity," she replied. "Ben always said
to me that if he had it to do all over again he would wish not to have
graduated from Chicago at some terribly early age because he never had
the time to develop the social graces. . . . He always pursued what appealed to him intellectually. I think he always felt a little hesitant with
women. . . . I think Ben really wanted to be closer to people but just
didn't know how."[3]

Cohen had been disappointed before, of course, and he reconciled
himself to this latest rejection. He remained unshakably devoted to
Harris and her two children, as he had promised. He saw her frequently,
managed her legal and financial affairs, and watched with special kindness over her daughter Ann, who suffered for many years from multiple
sclerosis. "Ever since Lou's death, you have assumed responsibility for
my family and beyond that you have reached out to Ann, John and me
with love and caring of such quality that it cannot be adequately described," Harris wrote to Cohen in 1980. "I can never repay you for all
that you have done except to reassure you of my devotion to you and
to reiterate a promise I made, at your request, a long time ago that if
ever you were in need, I would unhesitatingly come to you." But by then
both she and Cohen were in poor health, and neither was in a position to
help the other. Cohen was no longer able to handle Harris's finances (an
error on his part, she informed him, had resulted in a $600 tax penalty),
and she gently urged him to understand her decision to seek the advice
of an investment counselor. "For both our sakes, I know it is wise to
have this investment counselor who will take care of these things. . . .
You can always be called upon for advice, but would be relieved of the
annoying paperwork. It is just foolish to think that at this stage of the

game you can take on your major work and the bothersome details of record keeping and bookkeeping."[4]

Neither personal unhappiness nor declining health could keep Cohen away from foreign affairs, which he continued to follow actively throughout his retirement. He served as an adviser on such matters to Adlai Stevenson during his two presidential campaigns, and as an occasional consultant to the Democratic National Committee. He delivered lectures and wrote books and articles, mainly on the topics that had interested him since the 1940s: the United Nations, the ongoing crisis in the Middle East, and the perennial challenge of disarmament. Cohen's friends and admirers paid him great deference, and marveled at his grasp of complex issues and his commitment to core principles. But his influence on specific policy questions was not great. Even when Democratic administrations were in power in the 1960s and 1970s, Cohen was largely regarded by key policy makers as a relic from the past. And, as always, he remained almost entirely unknown outside his narrow circle of friends and acquaintances in Washington.

It is perhaps because Cohen remained largely outside the public eye that his name was rarely mentioned in connection with the McCarthy-era persecutions of liberals and leftists. It is also worth noting that Cohen had retired from active government service in early 1953, before the anti-Communist frenzy reached its peak. Still, someone with Cohen's reputation as a New Deal radical with "soft" views on the Soviet Union could not entirely escape the anti-Communists' venom, and he was occasionally caught up in their web. The most serious such episode occurred in 1955, when Cohen was briefly considered by President Eisenhower for a position on the United Nations delegation.

The possible Cohen appointment was part of an Eisenhower administration effort to re-create the atmosphere of bipartisanship in foreign policy that had, on occasion, marked the previous Democratic administrations. The leading figure in the effort to draft Cohen into the Republican administration was Secretary of State John Foster Dulles; in the previous administration, Dulles himself had served the cause of bipartisanship in foreign policy, working to maintain Republican support for Truman's postwar policies. In that capacity he had known and respected Cohen.[5] When Dulles asked Cohen to consider joining the American delegation to the United Nations, Cohen expressed interest, but hesitated in order to consult with his friends in the Democratic leadership. Apparently he sought and received the approval of several key Democrats, including Sam Rayburn, Lyndon Johnson, Harry Truman, and Adlai Stevenson. Thereupon Cohen accepted Dulles's offer.

The "matter seemed to be settled," as columnist Joseph Alsop wrote in the New York *Herald Tribune*, but a problem developed: "Evidently rumors of the impending Cohen appointment had reached the ears of the more extreme sort of Republican Right-Wingers. No doubt this faction in the party came down like a ton of bricks on the President's personal chief of staff, Gov. Sherman Adams." For whatever reason, Adams asked Cohen to withdraw from seeking the appointment, and Cohen did so. Dulles expressed his "deep regret" to Cohen, and tried to blame the nonappointment on Senate Democrats. Alsop, at least, put the blame squarely on "the remaining blackmail power of the Republican extremists," and suggested that the conservatives' main objection to Cohen stemmed from his support for the "two-China" policy, under which both Formosa (Taiwan) and Communist China would be given a seat at the United Nations.[6]

With his possible involvement in the Eisenhower administration now a nonissue, Cohen returned to a moderately active role in Democratic politics. He advised Adlai Stevenson on foreign policy issues, particularly disarmament, in the 1956 campaign, going so far as to prepare a draft of the foreign policy provisions of the Democratic platform. His advice to Stevenson and to the party reflected his continued interest in the United Nations, his concerns over the growing threat of nuclear weapons, and his long-term hope that the world would advance in its efforts to resolve disputes by negotiation and compromise rather than through armed conflict.

Reflecting its essentially political purpose, the 1956 platform draft constituted an across-the-board critique of the Eisenhower administration's conduct of foreign policy. (Cohen's proposal was "badly mutilated," as Chester Bowles put it, by the time the platform was adopted in final form, because it was not "sufficiently positive.") Whereas the foreign policy of the Roosevelt and Truman administrations "was the product of the best thinking of the American people," the Eisenhower administration "has deprived itself and the nation of the knowledge necessary for an informed and instructive foreign policy by its own connivance in politically motivated attacks in the name of security against those who have dedicated their lives to foreign service of the United States." Even more seriously, Cohen wrote, the administration had failed "to keep the American people informed of the problems which vitally affect their future peace, security and well-being." He also criticized the Republicans for undermining confidence "in the continuity and the national bipartisan character of American foreign policy" and for a variety of specific foreign policy errors, including an overemphasis on military as opposed to economic aid and for having "frightened and alienated the nations of the world" by talking in unilateral terms of "massive retaliation," "agonizing reprisal," and "the immorality of neutrality."[7]

Cohen's proposed foreign policy for a new Democratic administration presented a mirror image of these failed policies. Although the platform draft called for maintaining "a balance of armed strength for ourselves and the free law-abiding nations of the world," it stressed the hope for "genuine progress in the field of disarmament" and pledged that the Democratic Party would "support wholeheartedly the United Nations." It underscored the need for cooperative security arrangements, and called on the United States to "take a vital interest in the improvement of living standards throughout the world." It expressed support for "the right of self-determination of all peoples" and for the expansion of trade and progress in achieving "greater economic and political unity among the free nations of Europe." It pledged to give the State of Israel "the arms necessary for her defense" and to provide the Arab states with economic aid, while urging "the Arab states and Israel to settle their differences by peaceful means." Finally, the platform draft declared that the Democratic Party "stands and will work for universal, effective and guaranteed disarmament in order to eliminate the danger of war which in this atomic age threatens the survival of civilization."[8]

This last endorsement of disarmament efforts was buried among the other platform planks, but its tone and language suggest Cohen's continued deep concern about the nuclear issue, which he had worked on since at least 1945. In an undated memorandum written during the Eisenhower years, Cohen laid out in detail his approach. Again he linked disarmament to the United Nations Charter, arguing that the development of the atomic and hydrogen bombs "make more imperative the devising of ways and means of making effective the principles" on which the charter was based. Specifically, disarmament "should be considered as a necessary means of making effective the principle of the Charter which require [sic] the elimination of the threat or use of armed forces by states as an instrument of foreign policy." Cohen rejected the idea of unilateral disarmament, which would "strengthen the rule of might not the rule of right," but he also called for taking "the problem of disarmament out of the polemics of the cold war."[9]

In Cohen's view, disarmament could be accomplished only within the context of an overall lessening of tensions between the United States and the Soviet Union; thus progress in disarmament and on political settlements was "inseparable." And it was particularly important "that we endeavor to agree upon the arms to be *permitted* rather than those to be *proscribed*." The ultimate goal was to reduce the armed strength of all countries "to the point that no state is in a condition of armed preparedness for war." Such disarmament carried real dangers, Cohen admitted: "There are no absolute safeguards to guarantee disarmament. Certain calculated risks must be taken. These risks are likely to be less in the case of general disarmament than partial disarmament."[10]

Cohen's views on disarmament reflected the values that had motivated him throughout his year on the United Nations Disarmament Commission. He had enough practical experience to know that his ideas were unlikely to be adopted anytime soon. But he retained a deep commitment to the importance of disarmament, and a resolute faith that, someday, the nations of the world would recognize and act upon the necessity of disposing of their weapons of mass destruction.

From 1948 until the end of his life, Cohen devoted considerable energy to his duties as a trustee of the Twentieth Century Fund,[11] a liberal New York foundation now known as The Century Foundation, established in 1919 by Edward A. Filene. Cohen faithfully attended the fund's quarterly meetings, and served for a number of years as treasurer and as chairman of the finance committee. At the fund, Cohen was surrounded by younger men—powerful and influential figures— and he basked in the glow of his reputation as an elder statesman. "Ben Cohen was already on the board of the Twentieth Century Fund when I joined it in the 1950s," recalled August Heckscher, the fund's director from 1956 to 1967. "He seemed to me then to be of superior wisdom— not only because he was an 'old boy' and I was a new one, but because he had achieved a great reputation as one of Roosevelt's young Brain Trusters." M. J. Rossant, the fund's director from 1967 to 1988, who also served as a trustee, told a similar story. "The longer I knew him, the harder it was for me to believe for just how long Ben had been *engagé*. After all, he had been involved in political battles before the New Deal."[12] Cohen's reputation and his ability to cut to the heart of complex problems gave his words great weight and authority. Even toward the end of his life, when his thoughts were prone to ramble and his contributions to the board's discussions were far from acute, the staff and his fellow trustees treated him with enormous respect and admiration.

As treasurer and as a member of the finance committee, Cohen had direct responsibility for the management of the fund's investment portfolio. "He and Adolf Berle (with an assist from Francis Biddle) ran things very much in their own way in those days," recalled Heckscher, "often to the consternation of our able financial consultants." According to Heckscher, "[t]he latter would come to meetings with a long list of proposals to buy and sell. Ben would brush all these aside, and the great men of the Fund would thereupon embark upon philosophic disquisitions about the present and the future of the world. In the end, if I recall correctly, they would leave the Fund's investments much as they were at the beginning of the discussion." Cohen's reputation as a stock exchange wizard was borne out by the fund's portfolio, which "grew reassuringly." It is worth noting that none of his colleagues on the fund ever knew of Cohen's disastrous losses on Wall Street in the 1920s.[13]

Cohen's involvement with the fund's other activities reflected his paramount interest in foreign affairs and the nuclear issue. On one occasion, for example, he proposed that the trustees consider "a preliminary exploration of whether the Fund might undertake a survey of the plans being made by business and government agencies to meet the crisis which would result from a devastating attack on the United States and of the economic, social and political consequences of such a disaster." Of specific importance were corporate and government plans to address "such questions as preservation of financial and other records, replacement of key officials and possible decentralization of operational authority, and reorganization of distributive channels, sources of supply and centers of production." The committee authorized a small pilot study to determine if a larger study would be feasible.[14]

On many occasions, Cohen's interest turned to issues unrelated to foreign policy. In 1958, for example, he proposed to the executive committee that the fund "use funds, if necessary in substantial amounts, to help secure the opening of unsegregated schools in the South." It was clear that Cohen's fellow committee members had reservations about the proposal; the minutes of the meeting record that "there was general discussion as to whether the Fund could intervene without damaging the cause it sought to advance; whether even a large grant by the Fund could be effective in achieving its aim; whether the commitment could be limited in time; and finally, whether such action as might be decided upon would have significance in terms of the general situation." The committee nonetheless appropriated the sum of $5,000 to allow the staff "to follow closely the developing situation in the South." The full board of trustees agreed that "should circumstances arise which would provide the Fund with a promising opportunity, the Board would be notified and would consider what action it might best take." [15]

In his later years, Cohen's influence on the specific decisions made by the board of trustees waned. But he continued to participate actively, perhaps finding at the board's meetings a respite from a life that was becoming increasingly lonely and isolated. Only in the last year or two of his life was he unable to travel to New York on a regular basis. But even then his friends and associates at the fund provided a critical outlet for his energies. "We would talk on the phone at least once a week," recalled Rossant, "usually starting with a brief discussion about the stock and bond markets. Once that chore was dispensed with, Ben brought up his current obsession—the high cost of health care and his ideas for a national insurance plan to meet them; the need for a new approach to arms control; the best way to reduce interest rates and the national deficit; his plan for restructuring NATO; what to do about the International Monetary Fund, the Bank for International Settlements, or the United Nations, and how to negotiate with the OPEC countries. More than once, I was charged with getting in touch with one or another policy-maker to pass along Ben's latest proposal." [16]

On one issue above all others Cohen was particularly vocal and passionate: from very early on, he opposed America's involvement in the Vietnam War. "Late in 1961 or possibly early in 1962," recalled Harvard Law Professor Milton Katz, he and Cohen attended a State Department reception. "Unexpectedly crossing Ben's path, I turned to greet him and was stabbed by his question: 'What on earth does our government think it's doing in Vietnam?'" [17] Cohen expressed his objections to the war repeatedly and in the strongest terms, both in private conversations and in public speeches. His opposition to the war effectively ended his relationship with Lyndon B. Johnson, whom he had known since the days of the New Deal, and strained his friendships with many of the younger men who supported the war, whether within or outside the government. Eventually, of course, many of those who had disagreed with Cohen early in the Vietnam conflict came over to his side, and praised his long-standing opposition to the war as extraordinarily wise and prescient.

Cohen expressed his objections to the war most clearly in a speech to the Washington area chapter of the United World Federalists on August 11, 1967. The fundamental problem, Cohen argued, was that American policy makers had misconceived the war from the beginning as an "Armageddon where the forces of righteousness are arrayed against the forces of evil"; they regarded the North Vietnamese leader Ho Chi Minh as "a communist, nothing else," as "the advance guard for China, Russia and international communism." But the struggle in Vietnam, according to Cohen, was not at bottom a conflict between the communist and free worlds. Rather, it was merely "a war for the control of South Vietnam" between "rival South Vietnam political-military movements, the one supported and in a high degree directed by the Hanoi government, the other supported and in a high degree directed by the United States."[18]

Because the Vietnam conflict was essentially a civil war, Cohen believed that American involvement was specifically prohibited by the United Nations. As he explained in his 1965 David Niles Memorial Lecture,

> The basic law on which the Charter was constructed . . . is based on principles by which all nations, large as well as small, must live if mankind is long to survive on this planet in the nuclear age. . . . First . . . [the Charter] requires all states, large as well as small, to refrain in their international relations from the threat of force except in individual or collective self-defense against armed attack, and all measures taken in the exercise of self-defense must be immediately reported to the Security Council. Second, the Charter requires all states, large and small, to settle their disputes by peaceful means in such a manner that peace, security and justice are not endangered.

Attempts to justify armed intervention by arguing that the charter "does not forbid the use of force by one state at the request of the recognized government of another state to assist the latter to quell a rebellion"—as the United States claimed was the case in Vietnam—could not be supported. "The armed intervention of one state in the civil war of another state whether at the request of the established government or its rival government is in fact the use of force by the intervening states in its international relations, whether the civil war be called a war of liberation or a war in defense of freedom."[19]

Hanoi's involvement in the southern civil war was equally unjus-

tified, of course, although Cohen believed that "the United States undoubtedly does much more of the actual fighting for Saigon than Hanoi
does for the Viet Cong."[20] But the violence done to the U.N. Charter by
Hanoi was far less than that inflicted by the United States. "It is gravely
disturbing that many devoted friends of the United Nations have failed
to grasp that the failure of the United Nations is threatened as much
or more by the neglect of the Great Powers than by the irresponsibility
of the small states. . . . If Great Powers do not sense their imperative
need of the United Nations to preserve the peace, they will not give
the United Nations the support necessary for its growth and survival.
If the Great Powers do not have confidence in the United Nations, they
cannot expect the smaller powers to have confidence in it."[21]

For Cohen, then, Vietnam was more than just an "unfortunate mis-
adventure in the internal affairs of another country," as he put it in a
speech accepting the Isaiah Award from the B'nai Brith in 1969. It was
more even than a great human tragedy that affected the lives of millions
of individuals, both in Southeast Asia and in the United States. It was
nothing less than a repudiation of the principles for which he and his
colleagues had struggled in the closing days of World War II and in the
early years of the peace. For Cohen, continued American involvement
in Vietnam was as complete a rejection of the principles on which the
United Nations was founded as the Senate's refusal to ratify the League
of Nations Treaty had been a rejection of the principles on which that
institution was based. Thus American withdrawal from Vietnam would
not be "a retreat into isolationism," as he told the B'nai Brith audience.
Nor would it be "an abandonment of any treaty of charter obligation." It
would be, instead, "a retreat from an outmoded colonial foreign policy
which we stumbled into when in the course of the cold war we supported the French return to Indo-China." More than that, American
withdrawal from Vietnam would once again allow the U.N. Charter to
resurface as an instrument of world peace, international cooperation,
and conflict resolution.[22]

By the mid-1970s all of Cohen's mentors and older associates were
gone: Judge Mack had passed away in 1943, Harold Ickes in 1952, Jimmy
Byrnes in 1972. Felix Frankfurter, with whom Cohen maintained a formal though strained relationship, died in 1965; Hugo Black died in 1971.
In their place stood a new generation who had come to the New Deal
when Cohen was already an established figure, and who had themselves
become leading lawyers, academics, and government officials. These in-

cluded civil rights lawyer Joe Rauh and attorney David Ginsburg, whose clients included the State of Israel. And there were many others, ranging from those who knew Cohen only casually to those who had known and worked with him since the 1930s.

Both by nature and by circumstances, Cohen had few real contemporaries. The exception was Tommy Corcoran, just six years his junior and his lifelong friend. In some ways the Cohen-Corcoran relationship was as odd in the 1960s and 1970s as it was in the 1930s. Beyond their differences in background and temperament, the former "Gold-dust Twins" had taken completely different paths since their New Deal partnership. Whereas Cohen had remained in government service and had then worked almost exclusively on matters of public interest, Corcoran built a hugely successful private law practice, with an extraordinary reputation for Washington connections and lobbying expertise. And while Cohen was becoming a liberal icon, Corcoran was representing clients and making friends with those on the opposite end of the political spectrum—including the government of Taiwan, the Korean lobbyist Tongsun Park, and the United Fruit Company. "Ben was the epitome of the public interest lawyer," explained Joe Rauh. "Tom was the epitome of the public interest lawyer who then was working against what he had done. Tom was my hero in the Thirties. . . . I am not dispassionate about the New Deal lawyers who have become establishment lawyers."[23]

Yet the bond between Cohen and Corcoran, however inexplicable, remained intact. They saw each other at least once a week, usually on Saturday for lunch at the Cosmos Club, and Corcoran continued to exercise a protective influence over his old friend. Once, when Cohen was injured in a fall, Corcoran moved into Cohen's apartment until Cohen was well.[24] Cohen remained "Uncle Ben" to Corcoran's children, and Corcoran's admiration for Cohen never faltered. In 1977, when Corcoran introduced Cohen to give the main address at a "New Deal dinner" honoring the forty-fourth anniversary of Roosevelt's first inaugural, Corcoran was effusive. Cohen was a true "super-lawyer," Corcoran declared, and "his legal victories were the most important defense of the whole New Deal." But that was not all:

> [T]here was more to Ben Cohen's contribution to Franklin Roosevelt's New Deal than his exploits as an individual palladin [sic]. More important was a quality of spirit and wisdom by which he contributed that maximum contribution anyone

can make to government—that is multiplying the capabilities of
hundreds of others and energizing their contributions to their
specific tasks. And he is one of the few, if not the only, non-
political figure in public life I have known. . . .

No one from the President down did not seek and benefit from Ben's quiet advice. . . . And he infused all he touched
with the energy of moral purpose—always I felt sure connected
with memory that the Cohens were the high priests in the tribe
of Benjamin. Believing, and still believing, in the perfectibility
of human society and that faith can make the fact, he inspired
in the rest of us minor leaguers [the desire to fight] against the
abuse of those who saw us getting in their way.[25]

"We were the lucky ones," Cohen replied, "caught up—by the wise
and compassionate leadership of President Roosevelt—in the mobilization of the energy, experience, and knowledge of this great nation—to
meet its pressing and long neglected needs. For us it was a time when
'to be alive was joy and to be young was heaven.' "[26]

But even the youngest of the New Dealers was no longer young by
the time of the New Deal reunion dinner. Cohen was already eighty-
two, and Corcoran, despite a new romance with Washington socialite
Anna Chennault, was not much younger. ("I've been reincarnated," he
told a reporter. "I'm so young now that I can't afford to drink whiskey.")
The contrast between the old New Dealers and the new Carter administration could not have been more clearly marked: President Carter, for
reasons that were not entirely clear, chose not to attend the party. Con-
sciously or unconsciously, Cohen seemed to recognize that the new administration might draw inspiration from Franklin Roosevelt's legacy,
but not from his onetime advisers and lieutenants. "We look to President Carter and Vice President Mondale to establish their own 'New
Deal' in their own way and style," he remarked at the end of his speech.
"We believe they will find help and comfort in Roosevelt's words added
in Roosevelt's own handwriting to the last draft of a speech prepared
for a Jefferson-Jackson Dinner—words which because of his death were
never delivered: 'The only limit to our realization of tomorrow will
be our doubts of today. Let us move forward with strong and active
faith.' "[27]

The Carter administration of course moved forward, with or without finding inspiration from Roosevelt's never-delivered speech. But
the administration certainly had no need for the advice of the old New

Dealers. Three years after the New Deal dinner, Cohen offered his assistance to President Carter in dealing with the Iranian hostage crisis. The White House knew enough of Cohen and of his reputation to provide a personal written response from the high-ranking Carter aide Stuart Eizenstat. But although Eizenstat thanked Cohen and assured him that his advice had been relayed "directly to [national security adviser] Dr. [Zbigniew] Brzezinski and to the President," one senses that the letter was little more than a polite dismissal.[28]

Fate was unkind to Ben Cohen in old age. Especially toward the end of his life he became increasingly weak and frail. Still he continued to walk his dog around his Dupont Circle neighborhood, and was easily recognized particularly by the Brookings Institution scholars who lived down the street. As one neighbor observed in a letter to Bernard Freund shortly after Cohen's death in 1983,

> I have lived in the Dupont Circle area for several years, and often observed your uncle (always accompanied by his scotty) walking with great resolve and a cheerful whistle. It was a source of inspiration for me to watch him; I imagined what he must have been like when he was younger, and wondered what gave him his determined, purposeful air.
>
> One day, almost 8 months ago, I saw your uncle struggling a bit as he walked, and, introducing myself, walked with him for several blocks. We talked about his health briefly, but he seemed more interested in discussing world affairs.[29]

The years exacted a cruel toll on Cohen's mind. The severe depressive incidents that had plagued him in his youth and middle age seemed to have become less frequent, but they were replaced by an increasingly chronic melancholia and by a growing tendency toward irascibility and inflexibility. His friends began to notice—or pretended not to notice— occasional examples of behavior that was clearly inappropriate to the circumstances, as when he made an emotional anti-Vietnam speech at a Washington cocktail party. "Unhappily," wrote a friend in a note to David Ginsburg, "his end was darkened by the streak of irrationality that so often accompanies that worst of all ailments, old age." Most tragically, Cohen's advancing years brought an inevitable decline in his once-legendary intellectual powers.[30]

By the early 1980s it was clear that Cohen's physical and mental health had taken a turn for the worse. He continued to take walks around the Dupont Circle area. "With the infirmity that accompanies advanced age, the pace of his steps would become slower as the years passed," recalled Robert A. Katzmann, who lived and worked in the neighborhood. "But his determination to complete his appointed round never wavered. His words of greeting, spoken in a distinct cadence, to those who acknowledged him, brought cheer to our day."[31] Ironically, it was Corcoran, who was younger than Cohen and who had always taken on the role of protector, who died first, in 1981. Cohen, private as always, left no record of his grief and loss.

In early August 1983, less than two months before his eighty-ninth birthday, Cohen was found, weak and dehydrated, in his Massachusetts Avenue apartment. "Get me out of this—heat," he told the ambulance driver who drove him to Georgetown University Hospital. He died there two weeks later, on August 15. After Cohen passed away, a hospital spokesman raised the possibility of neglect, claiming that "a person found in that state could not have been under the attention of people." But those close to Cohen told a different story—of "making meals he would not eat, of days of futile argument to seek hospital treatment finally overcome only by the urgent pleas of a group of old friends, neighbors and his doctor." The official cause of death was pneumonia.[32]

The adequacy of the care provided for Cohen was not the only source of controversy that followed his death. Uncertain where to inter the body, his executors in Washington sought permission for a burial at Arlington National Cemetery, arguing, with some force, that Cohen's contributions to the nation and the world more than justified the honor. But Cohen had never served in the armed forces and thus could not be interred at Arlington without specific presidential approval. While his friends sought vainly to persuade the Reagan White House to go along with the idea, Cohen's nephew Bernard arrived from Muncie to claim the body and return it to Muncie for burial. There, in a private Jewish ceremony, he was laid to rest.

All that remained after the eulogies had been read and the memorial tributes written was for Cohen's executors to dispose of his assets according to his wishes or according to their best guess as to his wishes. His books were sold or given away, his papers—or the few that he had saved, largely folded into the pages of books at more or less appropriate locations—donated to the Library of Congress. Few other items of value, whether monetary or sentimental, were left in his apartment. His investment portfolio, however, amounted to over $3 million, most of it in stocks, and most of its dollar value reflecting the appreciation in the market of the modest assets he had managed to hold onto after the crash of 1929. The distribution of Cohen's assets reflected the values that mattered to him most: except for some small bequests, he divided his estate between his family; his hometown university, Ball State; and Harvard, which had given him so many vital personal and professional connections. Ball State, for its part, used the money to endow the Benjamin V. Cohen Fellows Program, which was established to "memorialize Mr. Cohen's commitment to attaining world peace by focusing on study and discussion of the issues with special emphasis on ways of fostering a universal commitment to justice and encouraging the abandonment of intergroup hostilities."[33]

17

Benjamin V. Cohen
Architect of the New Deal

In all this, Ben Cohen was a superintellectual.

—*Frank Watson*

To contemporaries and historians alike, Benjamin Victor Cohen was a leading intellectual force behind the political philosophy of New Deal liberalism. Cohen's "half-century of influence," as the historian Arthur M. Schlesinger, Jr., put it, "was not the influence of a politician possessing a mass constituency or the influence of a publicist possessing a mass audience. It was the influence of a man possessing a brain; the influence of reason quietly and lucidly brought to bear on public policy." Cohen's influence on the direction of government policy has surely been overstated, but his role as a key figure in the origins and development of the New Deal liberalism has never been doubted.[1]

By all accounts, Cohen fit squarely into the political camp of the aging Justice Louis D. Brandeis. Already nearing eighty when the New Deal began, Brandeis had devoted his career to the fight against "bigness" and the concentration of power. He was particularly concerned about the increasing power of large corporations, and especially of private banks and financial houses in the Northeast. And although Brandeis was no devotee of laissez-faire—he believed the government could play a positive role as a regulator of private monopolies and as an agency of economic planning—he did recognize that the concentration of governmental power in Washington also represented a potentially serious threat to the liberties of the citizenry.

Superficially, at least, Cohen was the epitome of Brandeisian liberalism. The historian Jordan A. Schwarz offers a typical analysis: Cohen, he writes, had worked closely on Zionist affairs with Brandeis and his disciple, Felix Frankfurter; he was the author of the Wall Street reform laws, which were "perhaps the most Brandeisian legislation of the New Deal"; and he "disdained administration, putting his highly valued legal skills to work in service of those who would write and defend laws and thereby make policy." Opposed both to the Wall Street power brokers and to the radical reformers who favored collectivism and centralization, Cohen (in Schwarz's judgment) was "the leading exponent of Brandeisianism in the New Deal."[2]

By the late 1930s, agrees the historian Alan Brinkley, Ben Cohen and Tommy Corcoran "stood at the center of a growing network of liberals in Washington—an increasingly self-conscious group whose members considered themselves something of a vanguard pressing for a revived and more aggressive New Deal."[3] Cohen, Corcoran, and their followers were known by various names; most commonly they were referred to as the "New Deal liberals," though often they were known simply as "the New Dealers." Their philosophy, though not exactly coherent, was well known. As Brinkley writes, at the core of New Deal liberalism was the assumption "that government must exercise an increased level of authority over the structure and behavior of private capitalist institutions. The 'New Dealers' expressed such assumptions particularly clearly in the way they interpreted the 1937 collapse; in their lack of patience with those who talked of the need to restore 'business confidence' and those who continued to urge a cooperative 'partnership' between industry and the state; in their insistence that the recession was the result of unregulated monopoly power in the marketplace. Corporate interests, they believed, had colluded to suppress competition and create what liberals liked to call 'administered prices,' choking off what had otherwise been a healthy recovery." To the liberals, the problem was not "that the New Deal had gone too far in regulating the behavior of capitalist institutions," but that "the New Deal had not gone far enough."[4]

But although Ben Cohen was widely recognized as a leading exponent of this new aggressive liberalism, he did not in fact fully share its assumptions or objectives. Instead, Cohen's liberalism coexisted with deeply held conservative principles, particularly with respect to the role of business in society and the relationship between business and government. For reasons having to do with both personality and politics, Cohen rarely spoke of these core values; yet they appear, unmistakably, in the laws he wrote, in the policies he pursued, and in the legacy he created. They exerted a profound influence on the development of modern liberalism and, in the end, help us to understand that the failure of the New Deal's radical impulse was—from Ben Cohen's point of view, at least—not unintentional.

To begin with, Ben Cohen's place in the Brandeis-Frankfurter circle was largely a matter of happenstance. His education at the University of Chicago gave him an essentially classical view of economics and politics. From Chicago he went to Harvard, where he quickly came under the influence of Frankfurter, and then of Judge Julian Mack, whom he later served as law clerk. After a wartime stint in Washington he was recruited by Mack, in his capacity as the leader of the American Zionists, to work at the Paris Peace Talks. As a Zionist, Cohen was drawn inextricably into the circle of Louis Brandeis, with whose ideas on the evils of bigness and the dangers of monopoly he would be forever associated.

When the American and European Zionists split over the differences in their approach to the resettlement of Palestine, Cohen returned to New York and Wall Street. Throughout the 1920s, he retained his close ties to Mack, Frankfurter, and others in the Brandeisian circle, including Max Lowenthal and Robert Szold. Cohen's efforts on behalf of liberal causes in the 1920s—including his work on the New York State minimum wage law and in defense of the Amalgamated Bank—were undertaken largely at the behest of these men. Meanwhile—at least until 1929—he was a highly successful Wall Street investor.

As late as the winter of 1932–33, the idea that Ben Cohen would become a major player in the Roosevelt administration was farfetched. He had no personal ties to Roosevelt, and no desire to go to Washington. He entered the New Deal not for reasons of ideology or personal ambition, but simply because Lowenthal and Frankfurter had asked him to work on the faltering securities bill. For the first year of the New Deal, Cohen worked in almost complete obscurity, writing the Securities Act of 1933 and settling into a dull routine at the Public Works Administration. He continued to regard his posting to Washington as purely temporary, and looked forward to a speedy return to New York.

Not until the congressional battle over the Securities Exchange Act in 1934 was Cohen identified as a member—and, indeed, a leading force—within the New Deal's liberal wing. Opponents of the proposed law, led by Richard Whitney of the New York Stock Exchange, were intent on characterizing the bill as a radical measure motivated largely, if not exclusively, by hostility to business. Cohen, by now joined with Corcoran, was a primary target, and, at times, even used his new reputation as a radical reformer to political advantage. Within months of the passage of the Securities Exchange Act even Wall Street admitted that the measure embodied no such hostility, but this admission did little to change Cohen's political reputation among his friends, his opponents, or the general public.

The Cohen-as-radical motif became more deeply etched in stone in the drawn-out struggle over the Public Utility Holding Company Act of 1935. The holding company episode, with its highly charged and deeply symbolic fight over the death penalty provision, played directly into the hands of those on both sides of the political divide who saw Cohen as a liberal in the Brandeisian tradition. The utility companies, like Wall Street before them, were anxious to discredit the holding company bill as hostile to free enterprise. Cohen's friends and supporters within the liberal camp, likewise, ramped up their rhetoric against the companies. "The holding companies were responsible for high utility rates," recalled Joe Rauh in language that was typical of those on the liberal side of the New Deal, "and they defrauded their stockholders. They would take operating companies and milk them for the benefit of the holding company. It was a very fraudulent process."[5] But Cohen's role in the holding-company fight reflected a far more moderate and cautious viewpoint. He worked closely with representatives of the industry in preparing the act, privately opposed the death penalty provision until Roosevelt insisted on it, and worked carefully to ensure that the bill allowed maximum discretion for the Securities Exchange Commission to use its best judgment in preserving those holding companies that served a useful economic purpose.

Cohen's reputation as a Brandeisian liberal was strengthened greatly by his association with Tommy Corcoran. Because of his flamboyant style and his gift for incendiary rhetoric, Corcoran was even more susceptible than Cohen to charges of fanaticism for the cause of left-wing liberalism. (It was Corcoran, after all, who had led the campaign against the Supreme Court in 1937, and who had spearheaded the attempted purge of conservative Democrats in 1938.) Yet Corcoran, despite appearances, had never been a liberal crusader. He had gone to Wall Street in the late 1920s with the unabashed goal of making a million dollars; when the crash left him overworked and under-compensated he left New York for Washington—to work not for Franklin Roosevelt but for Herbert Hoover. Corcoran's efforts on behalf of the New

Deal amounted to a kind of grand theatrical performance, and he loved
being in the footlights. "We didn't understand the seriousness of the
problem," he recalled many years later, "but we knew the joy of functioning."[6]

The rhetoric of the 1936 campaign, the Court-packing fight, and
the antimonopoly campaign cemented Cohen and Corcoran's reputation as the leaders of the New Deal's liberal wing. Yet here, too, both
contemporaries and later analysts have mistaken rhetoric for reality.
The speeches of the 1936 campaign were especially notable in this regard, with their frequent references to "economic royalists," "forces of
selfishness and of lust for power," and concentration "of wealth and
power . . . built upon other people's money." The antimonopoly fight
had its share of incendiary rhetoric too—some of it written by Cohen
and Corcoran. But Cohen and Corcoran were also victims of a kind of
guilt by association; since their membership in the liberal camp was by
now taken for granted, it was assumed that they agreed with the principles espoused by other members of the group. When Robert Jackson
announced in December 1937 that "certain groups of big business . . .
have now seized upon a recession in our prosperity to liquidate the New
Deal," it was not surprising that Cohen and Corcoran were assumed to
share the same sentiments. But however Jackson felt about big business,
Cohen and Corcoran understood such words—like the antimonopoly
legislation eventually pushed through Congress—to be more symbolic
than real, useful political devices rather than a well-conceived public
policy.[7]

The historical claim that Ben Cohen was committed to Brandeisian
values is based primarily on his authorship of the three major New Deal
statutes regulating the financial markets: the Securities Act of 1933,
the Securities Exchange Act of 1934, and the Public Utility Holding
Company Act of 1935. On the surface, at least, all three of these laws
seemed hostile to concentrated economic power, especially when held
by large (and unaccountable) corporations. The antibusiness rhetoric
was sounded in private by Brandeis and in public by Roosevelt himself
and a host of official and unofficial spokesmen. "The marines will have
landed on Wall Street," proclaimed journalist John T. Flynn on the eve
of the adoption of the Securities Exchange Act. "The place will be an-
nexed to the United States." The antibusiness rhetoric of the administration and its friends was countered by an equal but opposite outcry
from Wall Street, which left little doubt that the financial community

was engaged in a life-or-death struggle. "I do not believe," intoned the chairman of the New York Stock Exchange, "that the liberalism of today . . . requires the Federal government to operate our exchanges, to control our credit, and to regulate our corporations."[8]

All this rhetoric aside, none of Cohen's statutes were hostile to business, nor were any of the three based on a fundamental hostility to bigness or to the concentration of economic power. The Securities Act and the Securities Exchange Act were designed to stabilize the financial markets, not to destroy them; that Wall Street benefited from regulation in the long run was not a coincidence. Even the Holding Company Act, which seemed to embody the Brandeisian principle of decentralized power, on close examination is seen to prohibit only concentrations of economic power that are economically inefficient and thus indefensible in practice.

In writing the financial legislation of the early New Deal, Ben Cohen was not motivated by a conventionally liberal political philosophy. He was not interested in redistributing either wealth or power. Instead, he believed that it was the government's duty to force the financial markets to operate according to sound economic principles, and to create an institutional and policy framework that would stabilize the markets and, through them, the entire economy. Cohen's own experience had taught him that the markets could not be left to themselves, both because of rampant fraud and abuse and because unregulated markets were prone to exaggerated, and ultimately destructive, boom-bust cycles. In the end, unregulated financial markets were as bad for Wall Street as they were for the country.

The paramount evil against which the securities legislation was directed was not the concentration of economic power but the tendency of unregulated financial markets to foster speculation at the expense of sound investments. An obvious first step was to eliminate fraud and insider trading, along with similar schemes that allowed a privileged few to reap profits in ways that were unrelated to the productive allocation of capital. Another was to require the registration of all securities with federal regulatory agencies, thus guaranteeing the disclosure of a wide range of pertinent information. But there was no way to ensure that all investors would read such materials, or that they would be in a position to understand them if they did. Small and unsophisticated investors were essentially incapable of making sound investment decisions, Cohen believed; the best way to protect them, as Tommy Corcoran admitted in congressional testimony, was to keep them out of the stock markets in the first place. Thus the Securities Exchange Act limited the exposure of small investors (above all by imposing tight restrictions on margin trading) and made it more difficult for small stock exchanges scattered around the country to compete with the big exchanges, especially those in New York. Both the exclusion of mom-and-pop investors and the closing down of regional and small-city stock exchanges flew directly in the face of Brandeisian principles. For Brandeis, though a Bostonian himself, believed that "too much power was concentrated in the Northeast, that independent and small businessmen did not stand a chance of competing against their big brethren," and that a keystone of federal policy ought to be economic development in the southern and western regions of the country.[9]

But the problems that plagued the financial markets went deeper than abusive professionals and naïve amateurs. The fundamental issue was that, on their own, the markets were incapable of stopping the continual repetition of devastating boom-bust cycles, in which stock prices rose to unnatural heights and then plummeted, often taking the economy with them. The problem was simple: the rising prices that marked a bull market attracted increasing numbers of investors and amounts of money, which in turn pushed prices to new heights. At the same time, highly priced stocks could be used as collateral for bank and brokerage loans, which could in turn be poured back into the stock market. In the short term, everyone was a winner; but once the market peaked, disaster was inevitable. Falling prices caused creditors to restrict credit, forcing shares to be sold off to meet margin calls. Soon the markets were falling faster than they had gone up, leaving both investors and the economy as a whole in difficult if not dire straits.

The Securities Exchange Act recognized that the boom-bust cycle could be interrupted only by allowing the government to restrict credit, thus keeping the markets from rising to levels that were unjustified by underlying economic realities. Hence the act imposed strict limitations on margin accounts, and expanded the power of the Federal Reserve Board to regulate interest rates. By keeping stock prices from rising to speculation-driven levels far above what could be justified by the underlying economic realities, Cohen believed, the Federal Reserve Board could prevent the crashes and financial panics that had plagued the economy from time immemorial.

If Cohen's Brandeisian image was established by the stock market fights, it was cemented by his association with New Deal power policy. The fair and efficient distribution of electrical power was of special concern to Brandeis; if power and other key components of a nation's infrastructure were controlled by an elite few or by large corporations, the widespread and equitable distribution of economic power would be impossible. (Such concerns were central to Brandeis's plans for Palestine as well as the United States. As early as 1918, he had written Chaim Weizmann that "the utmost vigilance should be exercised to prevent the acquisition by private persons of land, water rights or other natural resources or any concessions for public utilities. These must be secured for the whole Jewish people." [10]) As Jordan Schwarz suggests, "the experimental political economy inherent in" such new programs as the Tennessee Valley Authority, the Bonneville Power Authority, the Rural Electrical Administration, and the Electrical Home and Farm Authority were "even more heartening to Brandeis than [the] . . . laws which reformed Wall Street." [11] And Cohen, as counsel to the National Power Policy Committee, was involved in one way or another with all these—most especially the Public Utility Holding Company Act.

In symbolic terms, the Holding Company Act was the most significant Brandeisian achievement of the New Deal. Like the stock exchange legislation, the Holding Company Act pitted the virtuous and public-spirited New Dealers against greedy and corrupt corporate bosses. At its most basic level, the act sought to break up a form of economic organization that consolidated company after company into one giant monstrosity, controlled (more often than not) from New York. The symbolic centerpiece of the act was the death penalty provision, which would have given the SEC the power to close down a holding company altogether if it did not serve the public interest.

But Cohen's approach to holding companies was not based on Brandeisian concerns about the centralization of economic power. Nor was he motivated by a desire to create a prosperous class of yeoman farmers who could develop the South and West as a counterweight to the financial and political clout of New York City. He accepted the holding company as a legitimate form of economic organization, recognizing that it could be abused but also that it could promote economic efficiency. He opposed the death penalty provision as based on unsound economics, and did everything in his power to weaken its practical impact. For Cohen, the Holding Company Act was essentially an extension of the Securities Exchange Act, and its goals were similar. It was directed not at destroying corporate power but at reining in its abuses and ensuring that businesspeople found more profit in selling goods and services than in promoting paper investments.

Brandeis sought to use government power to bring about fundamental changes in the American economy and in American society itself. The responsibility of the federal government, he believed, "was to use its power . . . to break up concentrations of power elsewhere and to ensure that society's underdogs were treated fairly." Cohen, by contrast, sought to use the government's power to ensure that the economic system as a whole operated efficiently and for the benefit of the nation as a whole. There was a great deal of overlap in these two agendas, but in the end they pointed in different directions—Brandeis wanted to reinvent the system, Cohen to preserve it. "Although the abuses connected with the holding company have been great," Cohen wrote in the National Power Policy Committee's report on holding companies, "it has been represented that the use of this form has induced economy and efficiency in operations where small and territorially related units have been coordinated." Whatever the merits of Brandeis's backward-looking approach, the costs of radical change were too high to consider. "Whether the increased economy and efficiency which may possibly have been obtained in some instances through the use of the holding company form could have been secured in other ways is a question as to which men may differ," Cohen wrote. "But not only is the holding company a very real actuality today but the huge amounts of capital tied up in holding companies cannot readily be untied." [12]

Cohen diverged from the principles of Brandeisian liberalism not only in the goals he sought to achieve but also in the way he sought to achieve them. Whereas Brandeis opposed the concentration of power in Washington, Cohen reveled in it: only by extending the powers of the national government could the economic order be restored and economic stability achieved. And to be most effective, that power had to be exercised not by Congress but by the executive branch—either by the president himself or by executive agencies empowered by broad and flexible grants of authority from the legislative branch.

Brandeis's fear of centralized authority made him suspicious of much of the New Deal. In 1935, for example, the justice voted with the rest of his colleagues to invalidate the National Industrial Recovery Act, because it impermissibly delegated power from Congress to the executive branch.[13] But Brandeis did not stop there; just after the decision was announced, he summoned Tommy Corcoran to the justices' robing room and delivered a stern lecture, to be delivered to the president. "This is the end of this business of centralization," he declared, "and I want you to go back and tell the President that we're not going to let this government centralize everything. It's come to an end. As for your young men, you can call them together and tell them to get out of Washington—tell them to go home, back to the states. That is where they must do their work."[14]

Brandeis's opposition to the concentration of power also made him suspicious of the vast new executive bureaucracy that the New Deal was creating. Because Brandeis agreed with many of Roosevelt's new policies, he was willing to tolerate a significant increase in the size of the executive branch. But the centralization of power within the executive branch did not fit comfortably with his larger political principles, and, as Philippa Strum writes, Brandeis "could not tolerate turning large and amorphous areas of power over to federal officials," as he believed had happened in the National Industrial Recovery Act case. Brandeis was also uncomfortable with unbridled presidential power, a point he made clear by joining in the 1935 opinion overturning Roosevelt's unwarranted dismissal of a federal communications commissioner. For Brandeis, these decisions were all of a piece; as Strum concludes, they could be taken as "a signal that bigness in government could be every bit as oppressive as bigness in business." More generally, Brandeis objected to "the assumption that a big government could control big business," an assumption that had been made by Theodore Roosevelt—and attacked by Brandeis—in the 1912 campaign. "Franklin Roosevelt, in Brandeis's eyes, was making the same mistake—accepting big business as inevitable rather than scaling it down to size."[15]

Ben Cohen took precisely the opposite approach. Although early on he had expressed concerns about the transfer of power from the states to the national government, almost from the day he arrived in Washington he sensed the necessity of expanding federal authority. Moreover, Cohen understood the need to make broad delegations of power from Congress to the executive branch, whether to the president himself or to presidential or independent agencies. Such delegations were necessary in order to allow the government to achieve its goals as times and circumstances changed. Cohen's belief in strong, flexible executive agencies (unlike his views on state versus federal power) was apparent even before the New Deal, in his establishment of an administrative machinery to justify and implement the New York minimum wage law. It was carried forward in statutes creating or expanding the powers of a host of executive agencies, including the Securities and Exchange Commission, the Federal Reserve Board, and, later, the Office of War Mobilization.

Only powerful governmental agencies, operating under broad and flexible grants of authority, could effectively counteract the inevitable (and at times desirable) concentration of economic power in the private sector. For Cohen, regulating the private sector required a kind of Madisonian balancing act; just as James Madison sought to protect rights not by weakening the institutions of government but by balancing strong governmental institutions against one another, so too did Cohen seek to promote economic efficiency by creating powerful and flexible governmental agencies to regulate strong private institutions. In later years, policy makers would take this formula one step further, by creating strong procedural guarantees for those whose interests were adversely affected by government actions and by authorizing both the federal courts and congressional subcommittees to exercise oversight over agency decision-making.

Cohen's approach to administrative governance was not new; as Brandeis's criticism suggested, similar methods had been used before, particularly in the progressive era. But Cohen went further than his predecessors in two respects. First, he not only accepted the concentration of private economic power as inevitable, but also at times promoted it— particularly in the case of the Securities Exchange Act. Under the appropriate circumstances, the concentration of private economic power could lead to more efficiency and, by reducing the total number of players, could make the job of regulators more manageable. Second, his statutes not only gave the administrative agencies extraordinary powers but also encouraged them to exercise those powers with broad discretion and to use them creatively in order to meet changing circumstances. Again, the SEC is the most obvious example, but in some ways the Office of War Mobilization provides an even better example of the ideal form.

Ben Cohen's influence on the growth of the executive branch extended far beyond the drafting of statutes. The role that he and Tommy Corcoran played in the New Deal became a model for a new kind of presidential adviser, and led to the creation of a new kind of presidency. The manifesto for this "managerial" or "administrative" presidency was the Brownlow committee report, issued in 1937 on the eve of the Court-packing fight. Congress at first resisted the recommendations of the committee, but eventually accepted most of its recommendations.[16]

A handful of presidents before Roosevelt had pursued broad and activist agendas. But strong presidential action had been the exception rather than the rule, rarely exercised except during brief periods of emergency and crisis. The Roosevelt administration, too, was operating under conditions of crisis—first the Depression and then the war—but Roosevelt, unlike his predecessors, transformed both the idea of the presidency and the institutional framework in which it operated. As Roosevelt put it in his message to Congress accompanying the Brownlow committee report, "The Presidency was established as a single strong Chief Executive Office in which was vested the entire executive power of the National Government."[17] If the ever-expanding executive bureaucracy were to be brought under presidential control, a new set of institutional arrangements would be necessary.

Cohen and Corcoran's role in the Brownlow committee report was indirect but important. By their actions and example, they provided a model for the expansion and professionalization of the White House staff. The committee recommended the hiring of a small number of "executive assistants"—probably no more than six—who would function as the president's "direct aides in dealing with the managerial agencies and administrative departments of the Government." These aides, Brownlow and his colleagues suggested,

> would have no power to make decisions or issue instructions in their own right. They would not be interposed between the President and the heads of his departments. They would not be assistant presidents in any sense. . . . Their effectiveness in assisting the President will, we think, be directly proportional to their ability to discharge their functions with restraint. They would remain in the background, issue no orders, make no decisions, emit no public statements.

The men selected for these positions, the commission concluded, "should be men in whom the President has personal confidence and whose character and attitude is such that they would not attempt to exercise power on their own account. They should be possessed of high competence, great physical vigor, and a passion for anonymity."[18]

In making these recommendations, the Brownlow committee had Cohen and Corcoran clearly in view. Neither man actually had a passion for anonymity, or course, and the lack of public recognition and career advancement was a source of great frustration to both. But what they had proved—and what the Brownlow committee had recognized—was the extraordinary value of presidential assistants who could act for the president but who did not exercise official authority. Cohen and Corcoran could not only write statutes; they could work informally with key members of Congress to lobby on their behalf; draft presidential speeches and coordinate public relations efforts to build grassroots support for the president's policies; and construct legal arguments both to defend presidential proposals in court and to legitimate them in the eyes of Congress and the public. No Cabinet officer or federal commissioner was in a position to help the president coordinate and control the wide range of activities that encompassed the new executive branch.

Every president from Roosevelt forward has found it essential to employ young White House staff assistants of one kind or another to fill the roles that Cohen and Corcoran played in the early New Deal. The list of presidential assistants in the Cohen-Corcoran tradition is long, and includes such notables as James Rowe, Clark Clifford, Sherman Adams, Theodore Sorensen, Jody Powell, Hamilton Jordan, David Stockman, John Sununu, and George Stephanopoulos. As the executive bureaucracy grew to a size that made the New Deal alphabet soup agencies seem minimalist by comparison, and as the United States assumed an increasingly significant role in foreign affairs, the White House bureaucracy grew with it. By the 1970s and 1980s, the bureaucracy had grown so unwieldy and the White House staff so large that scholars began to wonder if presidential management was even possible. The roles played by Cohen and Corcoran were separated and institutionalized; entire White House offices were now given over to such functions as speechwriting, congressional liaison, and legal affairs.

The growth of presidential authority also brought with it the possibility and reality of the abuse of power. The presidency, wrote the historian (and former Kennedy adviser) Arthur M. Schlesinger, Jr., in 1973, "has got out of control and badly needs new definition and restraint." A strong presidency had been necessary to meet "the great crises of history," Schlesinger wrote, but

> in our own time it has produced a conception of presidential power so spacious and peremptory as to imply a radical transformation of the traditional polity. In the last years presidential primacy, so indispensable to the political order, has turned into presidential supremacy.

"The constitutional Presidency," Schlesinger concluded, "has become the imperial Presidency and threatens to be the revolutionary Presidency."[19]

Ben Cohen, of course, had been an unwitting but primary architect of the runaway presidency. He had played a key role in virtually every aspect of the expansion of the presidency under Franklin Roosevelt, from the First One Hundred Days through the end of the war. His argument on the legality of the destroyers for bases agreement became a model for the unilateral exercise of presidential power to meet foreign policy emergencies. He wrote and helped enforce the executive orders and statutes that established the wartime White House, with its far-reaching powers over the domestic economy. He defended the legality of the presidential orders excluding Japanese Americans from the West Coast, and helped establish the Office of Strategic Services.

Although he never fully acknowledged the connection between the foundation laid by Roosevelt and the edifice built upon it by later presidents, by the 1970s Cohen too was worried about the growth of presidential power in the Johnson and Nixon years. In 1977, Cohen expressed his concerns in a book chapter, entitled "Presidential Responsibility and American Democracy.": "Since the Vietnam war and the Watergate affair," he began,

> thoughtful Americans have been troubled by the growth of presidential power and the danger of improvident or tyrannical exercise of Presidential authority. Certainly the Founding Fathers who had revolted against George III did not intend to give the President the prerogatives of the British Crown. Possibly they overrated the effectiveness of the checks and balances provided in their constitutional distribution of power among the three branches of government.[20]

The growth of the American economy and the increasingly important role of the United States in foreign affairs led Congress to create "new departments and agencies within the executive branch" and to delegate to them "broad, discretionary powers" to deal with complex problems "in light of changing facts and circumstances." The result, Cohen concluded, was a decline in the power of both the Congress and the Cabinet.[21]

Ironically, Cohen pointed as well to the growing power of the unaccountable White House staff:

> There has been a growing tendency for the President to gather
> about himself a small elite group of advisers and assistants, gen-
> erally with little political experience or standing in their own
> right, personally devoted to the President, eager to help him
> but reluctant to press their objections to a suggested course
> of action once they knew the President is favorably inclined
> toward it. This elite group is not subject to confirmation but is
> chosen because of their aptitude to work easily and on the same
> wave length with the President. They review and revise plans
> and programs submitted by the departments and agencies, and
> develop plans and programs of their own, for the President.[22]

If Cohen recognized even a hint of himself in this characterization
of the new breed of presidential adviser, he gave no sign. But Cohen
himself had had little political experience in the early days of the New
Deal, and little political standing until he had left government service
and become a senior statesman. Neither was he immune from the tendency to trim his political sails to conform to the views of his chief.
During the controversy over the death penalty provision of the Holding
Company Act, for example, as during the development of the Court-
packing plan, Cohen did not stand up for his own views once he knew
where the president stood.

In Cohen's opinion, Roosevelt had avoided the pitfalls of his successors by recognizing that "the right to lead and govern depended on his
ability to explain and convince, not to dictate and coerce—his ability to
enlist, not to command—the support of an informed Congress and an
informed people." He filled his administration with "persons of public
standing and influence, from different parts of the country, with varied
experience and outlook." And he "guarded against improvident action
by encouraging members of his administration to advance controversial
proposals, sometimes rival or even conflicting proposals, to test public
opinion before he would take a definite position"—a practice he abandoned only once, when he pushed forward the Court-packing plan.[23]

The problem, then, was to create an institutional mechanism that
would replicate these aspects of Roosevelt's leadership style in an ongoing institutional framework. Cohen's proposed solution was the creation of an "American Executive Council" consisting of between five
and eight "persons of highest public standing, with great but varied experience and outlook, drawn from varied walks of life, these counsel-
lors to be nominated by the President and confirmed by the Senate."

This body would constitute "a small super-cabinet with authority to participate in the decision-making process *before* important or potentially important Presidential decisions and commitments are made, and before important or potentially important Presidential plans, programs and polices are finalized." The Executive Council not only would advise the president and keep him from undertaking improvident actions, but also would serve as a "bridge facilitating meaningful communication between the President and the departments and agencies and between the President and the Congress."[24]

Cohen's suggestion—like many similar suggestions to reform the presidency—went nowhere. As a practical matter, it is highly unlikely that Cohen's suggestion would have been an effective response to the problem of presidential management in any event. It would be difficult to find men and women who had sufficient political clout to serve on such a body but who did not have political ambitions of their own, or who would not leak inchoate presidential proposals to the press and public at the first opportunity; and it would be almost impossible to find a president who would trust such a body and not regard it with disdain or suspicion. Certainly it is hard to imagine that such a group would have steered Lyndon Johnson or Richard Nixon away from Vietnam or Watergate.

Nor was Cohen's characterization of Roosevelt's presidency particularly accurate. Roosevelt was indeed a leader of public opinion, and a master at communicating with and building support among members of Congress and the public—not least because of the speechwriting and lobbying efforts of Cohen and his colleagues. And on most occasions he did encourage the expression of a wide variety of viewpoints within the administration. But Roosevelt had a darker side. He could manipulate public opinion as well as lead it; he could bully Congress as well as cajole it. When in his view it was necessary, he could act in secrecy or with flagrant disregard both for public opinion and civil liberties and civil rights.

But the value of Cohen's analysis lies not in the usefulness of his ideas or in the accuracy of his historical memory. Its value comes instead from the insight it provides into Cohen's evaluation of a system of government that he himself helped create. For implicit in Cohen's analysis of the modern presidency is his belated recognition that presidential power is a two-edged sword, that the legal, administrative, and political strategies that can save the nation in one administration can threaten it in the next. It was only a small step from the destroyers agreement to the Reagan administration's war in Nicaragua; both were justified by strained legal arguments that flew in the face of the clear intentions of Congress. Aides and advisers can help the president, as the Brownlow committee suggested, but they can also isolate him and destroy his sense of perspective. The president "is a form of king," wrote George Reedy, who once served as Lyndon Johnson's press secretary and whose words Cohen quoted with approval, "and no one argues with a king. He is isolated from the moment he steps into the White House because everyone around him is his subordinate. . . . Isolation leads to the capricious use of power. In turn the capricious use of power breaks down the normal channels of communication between the leader and the people he leads."[25] Cohen, who had been instrumental in building the Imperial Presidency, could find no way to undo his own handiwork.

Ben Cohen's death brought forth an outpouring of eulogies and memorials. He was remembered as a man of wisdom and compassion, of loyalty and commitment. "Ben had many qualities that set him apart," wrote M. J. Rossant, a Twentieth Century Fund director. "There was no one more loyal to his friends or more considerate; he was always willing to listen and to help. He was kind and gentle and wise, the wisest man I have ever known." Many expressed similar sentiments. "Ben was not only our life-long friend but our mentor for all purposes and a role model for values," wrote David Ginsburg for himself and Joe Rauh in a 1991 letter. "I doubt that either Joe or I were ever confronted by a serious problem that we did not discuss with Ben. In the early days, on the rare occasions when we did not accept his advice, we were almost invariably proved wrong and he was proved right. As time passed we learned better; rarely, if ever, did we then reject the gentle tug of his reins."[26]

But Cohen's life had been a public one, and his contributions and legacy were properly remembered in broader terms. "His monument?" wrote Philip Dunne, an author and screenwriter who had worked with Cohen in the New Deal and who had maintained a long-term friendship. "If your money in the bank is a little safer, your pay a little higher, your old age a little more secure, your health a little better, your electricity a little cheaper, your food a little less apt to poison you, your civil liberties a little more seriously protected—then perhaps you owe it to Ben Cohen. That would be the only monument that would interest him."[27] Dunne's list of Cohen's contributions may have left some out and included others for which Cohen could claim little credit, but the sentiment was genuine. "It is hard to think of any American of his generation who was more gifted that Mr. Cohen," agreed the editorial board of the *Washington Post.* "It is harder to think of any who used his gifts better, in the public service, than he did."[28]

For scholars of the New Deal and of post–New Deal America, assessing Ben Cohen's life and legacy is a more difficult, if less emotional, task. It is difficult to sort out Cohen's impact on public policy from that of Corcoran and his other colleagues, still harder to weigh his influence on the long-term course of American political and economic history. Most of what Cohen did was done for others, or with others, or in the name of others. Many of his ideas were borrowed or foreshadowed what later became the conventional wisdom, or merely reflected the emerging New Deal zeitgeist. Counterfactual history is mostly speculation, but even without Cohen's participation, it is highly likely that there would still have been a Securities Act and a Public Utility Holding Company Act; Roosevelt would still have won the 1936 election and run for a third term; America would still have gone to war; the United Nations would still have been created; the Palestine mandate would still have been written; and the United States would still have recognized the State of Israel. The details and timing of all these endeavors would have been different, of course, and one can never be sure that history might not have played strange tricks. But in none of these areas did Cohen exert an obviously decisive influence.

The one event on which Cohen did make the difference was the Destroyers for Bases Agreement of 1940. No one else in Washington— least of all the president and the attorney general—believed that the agreement was possible without an act of Congress, and no one in the administration (including Cohen) wanted the administration to ask for new legislation or expected that Congress would have approved a destroyers bill in an election year. The material impact of the destroyers on the British war effort was small, though the "Fifty Ships" pushed the United States significantly toward eventual entry into the war and provided a model for the Lend-Lease program, which provided critical aid to the nations then at war with Germany. Ironically, Cohen's first foray in the foreign policy field was also his most successful; he made no progress during his lifetime on nuclear disarmament or on the peaceful resolution of world conflicts, and he convinced no one of the folly of American involvement in Vietnam until it was much too late and until many others were already joining the chorus of opposition.

But surely there is some truth to the idea—however impossible it might be to prove it in a scientific sense—that Cohen's contributions to the economic and social policies of the New Deal made a difference. His legislation on securities reform and on holding companies put Wall Street on course for a long-term run that, despite the inevitable ups and downs, has been extraordinary by any historical standard. His brilliance as a legal strategist and litigator helped saved the Holding Company Act and provided a model for other New Deal lawyers to follow. And his constant willingness to provide advice to others in Washington on a wide range of legal and policy issues, his minor corrections and his small suggestions, improved countless laws and solidified innumerable legal arguments. These contributions can never be measured, but they were real, and their cumulative impact was considerable.

Cohen's influence and legacy can be measured in another way as well. As a leading intellectual of the New Deal, Cohen brought coherence and cohesion to the dizzying array of laws, policy initiatives, and experimental programs that constituted Roosevelt's bold experiment in national governance. Despite Cohen's reputation as a Brandeisian liberal, it was he more than any other New Dealer who understood the necessity for the federal government to cooperate with business, while ensuring that the government was made powerful enough, and flexible enough, to regulate business in its own and in the public interest.

The aggressive liberalism that was ascendant in 1937 and 1938, which Cohen was associated with but which he never fully endorsed, dissipated quickly. By 1939, the liberals were no longer dominant, and during the war years their agenda was eclipsed by more pressing concerns. By 1945, as Alan Brinkley notes, the liberal network had been scattered to the four winds—Robert Jackson to the Supreme Court, Tommy Corcoran to a private law practice, Ben Cohen to Potsdam and the problems of postwar foreign policy. As the network broke up, so too did the version of liberalism they had once endorsed, or, in the case of Cohen and Corcoran, the version they had once appeared to endorse.

In the place of this reformist brand of liberalism came a new liberal vision that would shape postwar domestic policy for decades after the war, and that still exerts a considerable force on American public policy. Advocates of this new liberalism retreated from efforts to reform the institutions of capitalism, and instead reached an accommodation with them. "They had done so by convincing themselves that the achievements of the New Deal had already eliminated the most dangerous features of the corporate capitalist system," Brinkley explains; "by committing themselves to the belief that economic growth was the surest route to social progress and that consumption, more than production, was the surest route to economic growth; and by defining a role for the state that would, they believed, permit it to compensate for capitalism's inevitable flaws and omissions without interfering very much with its internal workings." This conception, Brinkley concludes, marked a "broad retreat from many of the commitments that had once defined their politics."[29]

But Ben Cohen had no need to retreat to this newer conception of liberalism; his work had embodied its fundamental premises from the beginning in the New Deal. The financial regulatory statutes of 1934 and 1935, which have long been regarded as the apotheosis of Brandeisian liberalism, were in fact precursors of the newer approach; Cohen's early endorsement of Keynesian economics (which he had argued for as early as 1933) was likewise a foreshadowing of the consumption-based economic policies of the postwar era. More fundamentally, Cohen's economic and political philosophy paved the way for subsequent policy makers to reconcile the core tenets of New Deal liberalism with the practical reality (and even necessity) of large corporations, centralized financial markets, and powerful private banks. In practice, that reconciliation was possible only because the national government (and in particular the executive branch) was given broad and flexible power to oversee the capitalist economy and to exert systemwide pressures to manage (or at least attempt to manage) the economy as a whole.

Much of the history of the New Deal has been a story of the Roosevelt administration's struggle to reconcile the principles of liberalism with the existing reality of big capitalism. Historians have analyzed the internal conflicts between liberals and conservatives within the administration, and the internecine battles among "planners," "regulators," and "reformers" within the liberal camp. They have traced the zigs and zags of Franklin Roosevelt's relationship with big business, and, in part on the basis of this relationship, have divided the New Deal into discrete segments—the "first New Deal," the "second New Deal," even a "third New Deal." These changes and developments were real, but emphasizing this surface turbulence can also obscure the less volatile currents that lay at deeper levels but that moved the New Deal forward on a steady course. Though he had more than his share of involvement in the storms that raged over the surface of the New Deal, Ben Cohen's most enduring contributions were part of this less visible, but ultimately more powerful, pattern of developments.

The enduring question of the New Deal, perhaps, is how the Roosevelt administration managed to steer a middle course between those who sought radical reform of the capitalist system and those who opposed even modest changes. Ben Cohen was one of those who stood squarely in the middle between these two groups. Unlike Justice Brandeis and those who were really his disciples, Cohen saw no value in dismantling the large and powerful private corporations that had made so much progress possible. And unlike his Wall Street colleagues who dug in their heels at even the possibility of government regulation of business, he recognized that government regulation of business was necessary not only for the benefit of the public but for the benefit of business itself. Only a powerful national government could stop the private sector from engaging in practices that were both unfair to those at the bottom of the economic scale and self-destructive to business. And only government, Cohen believed, could establish or maintain a healthy economic system in which business and the public alike could flourish. His goal—and, ultimately, the goal of the New Deal itself—"was not to make a revolution but to make the capitalist system work better, for the benefit of all."[30]

Abbreviations in Notes

BVC	Benjamin Victor Cohen
CCB	Charles C. Burlingham
FDR	Franklin Delano Roosevelt
FF	Felix Frankfurter
F.O.	Foreign Office
HSC	Homer S. Cummings
LC	Library of Congress
LDB	Louis D. Brandeis
NPPC	National Power Policy Committee
OSC	Oscar S. Cox
POF	President's Official File
PSF	President's Secretary's File
SSW	Stephen S. Wise
TGC	Thomas G. Corcoran

Harris Papers	Papers and letters collected by Isaac Harris (in the possession of the author)
Public Papers of FDR	Samuel I. Rosenman, ed., *The Public Papers and Addresses of Franklin D. Roosevelt*, 13 vols. (New York: 1938–1950)

Notes

Chapter 1.
Introduction

1. *New York Times*, February 8, 1938, p. 35.
2. David Ginsburg to FF, February 12, 1938, FF Papers, LC.
3. Ibid.
4. *Newsweek*, February 21, 1938, p. 13.
5. Leslie Gould, "Our Invisible Government—It Is Happening Here!" *New York Journal-American*, May 12, 1939; Heywood Broun, "It Seems to Me," *Washington Daily News*, March 31, 1939, p. 27.
6. *Time*, September 12, 1938; "The Irishman and the Jew Who Are Powers in the Roosevelt Administration in Washington, *Jewish Daily Forward*, August 13, 1937, translation in possession of the author; *Time*, September 12, 1938; "Cohen & Corcoran, Inc.," *St. Louis Post-Dispatch*, May 29, 1937; *New York Times*, September 30, 1938, p. 17.
7. Quoted in "Alumni Profile," *The Law School Record* 29 (Spring 1983), University of Chicago Law School; Edward F. Pritchard, Jr., in *Benjamin V. Cohen, 1894–1983* (New York: The Twentieth Century Fund, 1983).

Chapter 2.
Origins

1. *Emerson's Muncie Directory*, various dates, Muncie Public Library.
2. Ibid.
3. Robert S. and Helen Merrill Lynd, *Middletown: A Study in Contemporary American Culture* (New York: Harcourt, Brace and Company, 1929); Jerome Frank, "Ben Cohen," pl.. 12.
4. Lynd, *Middletown*, pp. 479; Joseph P. Lash, *Dealers and Dreamers: A New Look at the New Deal* (New York: Doubleday, 1988), p. 11. Moses Cohen, it might be noted, was a charter member of one of Muncie's smaller civic clubs, the Twa Twa Tribe No. 145 of the Loyal Order of Red Men (G. W. H. Kemper, ed., *A Twentieth Century History of Delaware Co., Ind.*, Chicago: Lewis Publishing Co., 1908, I: 514).

5. Alexander Feinsilver, "Middletown's Jewry," *Opinion: A Jewish Journal of Arts and Letters* (February 1939), p. 17.

6. Lash, *Dealers and Dreamers*, p. 11.

7. BVC to Jane Harris, August 22, 1931, Lash Papers, FDR Library.

8. BVC to Dick Powell, November 27, 1969. Original in the possession of Bernard Freund.

9. Lash, *Dealers and Dreamers*, p. 13.

10. BVC to Dick Powell, November 27, 1969; Lash, *Dealers and Dreamers*, pp. 12, 453.

11. Interview, Joseph P. Lash with BVC, September 20, 1982, Lash Papers, FDR Library, Box 59; BVC transcript, University of Chicago.

12. Harold G. Moulton, *The Financial Organization of Society* (Chicago: University of Chicago Press, 1921).

13. Edward B. Burling to Major A. A. Hoehling, Jr., October 18, 1918, BVC Papers, LC, Box 1.

14. *Cap and Gown* (Chicago: University of Chicago, 1915), p. 393.

15. Quoted in H. N. Hirsch, *The Enigma of Felix Frankfurter* (New York: Basic Books, 1981), p. 20.

16. Quoted in Michael E. Parrish, *Felix Frankfurter and His Times: The Reform Years* (New York: Free Press, 1982), pp. 65–66, 43.

17. Quoted in Liva Baker, *Felix Frankfurter* (New York: Coward-McCann, 1969), p. 47.

18. Public utility course notes, September 28, 1914, Felix Frankfurter Papers, Harvard Law School, Part III, Reel 21.

19. Quoted in Hirsch, *Enigma of Felix Frankfurter*, p. 43; Helen Shirley Thomas, *Felix Frankfurter: Scholar on the Bench* (Baltimore: Johns Hopkins University Press, 1960), p. 14.

20. Interview with Joseph P. Lash, September 29, 1982, Lash Papers, FDR Library.

21. Hirsch, *Enigma of Felix Frankfurter*, pp. 22–23.

22. Ibid., p. 48.

23. Ibid., pp. 49–50.

24. Harry Barnard, *The Forging of an American Jew: The Life and Times of Julian W. Mack* (Np: Herzl Press, 1974), pp. 24ff.

25. Barnard, *Forging of an American Jew*, p. 49.

26. *Great Lakes & St. Lawrence Transp. Co. et al.* v. *Scranton Coal Co.*, 239 F. 603, at 607–8.

27. Roscoe Pound to Julian Mack, nd, quoted in Lash, *Dealers and Dreamers*, p. 16; Pound to BVC, March 2, 1917, BVC Papers, LC, Box 1; interview with Joseph Lash, September 29, 1982, Lash Papers, FDR Library.

28. "Report of Physical Examination," June 7, 1918; "Physical Examination for Appointment," July 12, 1918, BVC Papers, LC, Box 1.

29. BVC to A. A. Hoehling, October 17, 1918, BVC Papers, LC, Box 1; Burling to Major Brookmiller, July 13, 1918, BVC Papers, LC, Box 1; Roscoe Pound to BVC, March 2, 1917, BVC Papers, LC, Box 4.

30. "A bill to provide workmen's compensation for seamen . . . ," BVC Papers, LC, Box 16, p. 4. The actual draft of the bill provides for compensation up to "sixty six and two-thirds percent," but this is apparently an error.

31. BVC to FF, September 17, 1920, BVC Papers, LC, Box 8.

32. Jerome Frank, "Ben Cohen," TGC Papers, LC, Box 120.

Chapter 3.
Zionist Attorney

1. This description, by Ray Stannard Baker, is quoted in Philippa Strum, *Louis D. Brandeis: Justice for the People* (Cambridge: Harvard University Press, 1984), p. 52.

2. H. N. Hirsch, *The Enigma of Felix Frankfurter* (New York: Basic Books, 1981), pp. 32, 85; Michael E. Parrish, *Felix Franfurter and His Times: The Reform Years* (New York: Free Press, 1982), p. 162. See also Bruce Murphy, *The Brandeis-Frankfurter Connection* (New York: Oxford University Press, 1982).

3. Harry Barnard, *The Forging of an American Jew: The Life and Times of Julian W. Mack* (Np: Herzl Press, 1974), pp. 192, 213.

4. Quoted in Melvin I. Urofsky, *Louis D. Brandeis and the Progressive Tradition* (Boston: Little, Brown, 1981), p. 21; *Liggett Company* v. *Lee*, 288 U.S. 517, at 565 (Brandeis, dissenting in part).

5. Strum, *Louis D. Brandeis*, pp. 78, 176–77, 192.

6. See generally Strum, *Louis D. Brandeis*, pp. 196–223; Urofsky, *Louis D. Brandeis*, pp. 68–86; and Louis D. Brandeis, "The Solution of the Trust Problem," in Louis D. Brandeis, *The Curse of Bigness* (New York: Viking Press, 1935), pp. 127–36.

7. BVC, "Faith in Common Man," *The New Palestine*, November 14, 1941, p. 14.

8. Strum, *Louis D. Brandeis*, pp. 231–32.

9. Ibid., pp. 236–42; 249.

10. Benjamin V. Cohen, Foreword to Julius Simon, *Certain Days: Zionist Memoirs and Selected Papers*, ed. Evyatar Friesel (Jerusalem: Israel Universities Press, 1971), p. 9.

11. David Vital, *Zionism: The Crucial Phase* (Oxford: Clarendon Press, 1987), pp. 293, 325, 338–39.

12. Simon, *Certain Days*, pp. 85–86.

13. Ibid., pp. 88–89.

14. BVC to LDB, January 22, 1920; March 24, 1920; April 14, 1920; April 25, 1920; Lash Papers, FDR Library.

15. BVC to LDB, February 9, 1920; March 29, 1920; Lash Papers, FDR Library.

16. BVC to "Zionists New York," April 1, 1920, Lash Papers, FDR Library; BVC to LDB, April 14, 1920, Lash Papers, FDR Library.

17. BVC to LDB, April 1, 1920; March 24, 1920; April 25, 1920; Lash Papers, FDR Library.

18. BVC to LDB, May 2, 1920, Lash Papers, FDR Library.

19. E. J. Dillon, *The Inside Story of the Peace Conference* (New York: Harper and Brothers Publishers, 1920), pp. 9, 3–4.

20. Julian Mack to BVC, October 1, 1919, Lash Papers, FDR Library.

21. Lincoln Steffens, *The Autobiography of Lincoln Steffens* (New York: Literary Guild, 1931), p. 812; Joseph P. Lash, *Dealers and Dreamers: A New Look at the New Deal* (New York: Doubleday, 1988), p. 21.

22. Ella Winter, *And Not to Yield: An Autobiography of Ella Winter* (New York: Harcourt, Brace & World), 1963, p. 47.

23. Ibid., p. 73; Lash, *Dealers and Dreamers*.

24. Ibid.

25. Author's interview with Dorothea Wallis, Oxford, England, January 1993.

26. Ella Winter and Granville Hicks, eds., *The Letters of Lincoln Steffens* (New York: Harcourt, Brace and Company, 1938), p. 495; Steffens, *Autobiography*, pp. 812–13, 820.

27. Simon, *Certain Days*, p. 93.
28. Walter Laqueur, *A History of Zionism* (New York: Holt, Rinehart and Winston, 1972), pp. 458–59; Simon, *Certain Days*, pp. 93, 96–97.
29. Ibid., pp. 93–95.
30. Ibid., pp. 102–3.
31. Lash, *Dealers and Dreamers*, p. 27.
32. Lash, *Dealers and Dreamers*, p. 23.
33. BVC to Paul Freund, January 20, 19??, Lash Papers FDR Library.
34. Bernard Flexner to Julian W. Mack, October 2, 1920; LDB to Julian W. Mack, October 4, 1920, Lash Papers, FDR Library.
35. BVC to Julian W. Mack, October 13, 1920; Julian W. Mack, October 16, 1920, Lash Papers, FDR Library.
36. Simon, *Certain Days*, p. 118.
37. BVC to Julian W. Mack, January 1, 1921; January 7, 1921; Lash Papers, FDR Library.
38. BVC to Julian W. Mack, January 7, 1921, Lash Papers, FDR Library.
39. Telegram, Julian W. Mack to "Executive, Zioniburo," January 16, 1921, Lash Papers, FDR Library. Punctuation revised and capitalizations supplied for clarity.
40. Telegram, BVC to Julian W. Mack, January 17, 1921, Lash Papers, FDR Library.
41. Telegram, Julian W. Mack to BVC, January 19, 1921; BVC to Julian W. Mack, January 20, 1921, Lash Papers, FDR Library.
42. Julian W. Mack to BVC, February 1, 1921, Lash Papers, FDR Library.
43. BVC to Julian W. Mack, January 31, 1921; Frankfurter to BVC, quoted in Lash, *Dealers and Dreamers*, p. 34.
44. FF to BVC; LDB to BVC; Nehemia de Lieme to BVC, quoted in Lash, *Dealers and Dreamers*, pp. 34–35.

Chapter 4.
Lawyer and Investor

1. BVC to Jane Harris, nd [probably September 1934], Lash Papers, FDR Library.
2. FF to BVC, December 17, 1923, BVC Papers, American Jewish Archives, Box 1.
3. Frank L. Hopkins, "Receivers are 'Repeaters' under U.S. Court System," *New York World*, February 23, 1924; BVC interview with Joseph Lash, September 20, 1982, Lash Papers, FDR Library, Box 59.
4. Joseph P. Lash, *Dealers and Dreamers: A New Look at the New Deal* (New York: Doubleday, 1988), p. 41; Jerome Frank, "Ben Cohen," TGC Papers, LC, Box 120.
5. The financial data in this and subsequent chapters are taken from Cohen's 1929, 1932, and 1934 tax returns from the period (BVC Papers, LC, Box 21).
6. BVC to FF, January 1, 1934, Felix Frankfurter Papers, LC, Reel 70, Container 115, "Benjamin V. Cohen"; BVC to Jane Harris, nd, Lash Papers, FDR Library.
7. Matthew Josephson, *Sidney Hillman: Statesman of American Labor* (Garden City, N.Y.: Doubleday, 1952), p. 246.
8. Ibid., pp. 348–49.
9. Max Lowenthal to Sidney Hillman, June 25, 1934, Lowenthal Papers, University of Minnesota, Box 70–71, "SEC Commission appointments; J. D. Kennedy."
10. Philippa Strum, *Louis D. Brandeis, Justice for the People* (Cambridge: Harvard University Press, 1984), pp. 372–73. On the relationship between Frankfurter and Brandeis in the 1920s see generally Bruce Murphy, *The Brandeis-Frankfurter Connection* (New York: Oxford University Press, 1982), pp. 73–97.

11. See Felix Frankfurter, *The Case of Sacco and Vanzetti: A Critical Analysis for Lawyers and Laymen* (Boston: Little, Brown, 1927), and Frankfurter, "The Case of Sacco and Vanzetti," *Atlantic Monthly* (March 1927), pp. 409–32.

12. The quotation is taken from the league's stationery; see, for example, Josephine Goldmark to BVC, January 19, 1933, BVC Papers, LC, Box 11.

13. H. N. Hirsch, *The Enigma of Felix Frankfurter* (Cambridge: Harvard University Press, 1981), p. 85.

14. *Adkins* v. *Children's Hospital*, 261 U.S. 525 (1923), at 546, 559.

15. Quoted in Michael E. Parrish, *Felix Frankfurter and His Times: The Reform Years* (New York: Free Press, 1982), p. 165.

16. FF to BVC, June 14, 1923, BVC Papers, American Jewish Archives, Box 1.

17. *Adkins* v. *Children's Hospital*, 261 U.S. 525 (1923), at 557–58, 559 (emphasis added).

18. Mary W. (Molly) Dewson to BVC, December 29, 1923, BVC Papers, LC, Box 11.

19. FF to BVC, June 5, 1923, BVC Papers, American Jewish Archives, Box 1, Folder 19.

20. Quoted in Lash, *Dealers and Dreamers*, pp. 39–40.

21. "An act to amend the labor law, in relation to general powers and duties of commissioner," State of New York, Senate, No. 923, February 15, 1928. BVC Papers, LC, Box 11.

22. FF to BVC, December 3, 1928, BVC Papers, LC, Box 11; FF to Mary Dewson, December 10, 1928, BVC Papers, LC, Box 11.

23. BVC to FF, January 11, 1932 [probably 1933], BVC Papers, LC, Box 11; FF to BVC, January 4, 1933, BVC Papers, LC, Box 8; FF to BVC, January 10, 1933, BVC Papers, LC, Box 11; Dewson to BVC, February 6, 1933, and January 1, 1932 [perhaps 1933], BVC Papers, LC, Box 11.

24. BVC to FF, January 3, 1932 [probably 1933], and January 11, 1932 [probably 1933], BVC Papers, LC, Box 11.

25. BVC to Elizabeth Rauschenburgh, January 17, 1933, Lash Papers, FDR Library.

26. BVC to FF, January 18, 1933, BVC Papers, LC, Box 11; BVC to Josephine Goldmark, January 19, 1933, BVC Papers, LC, Box 11.

27. *Morehead* v. *New York* ex rel. *Tipaldo*, 298 U.S. 587 (1936), at 615.

28. FF [?] to Lewis Meriam, December 10, 1929, BVC Papers, American Jewish Archives, Box 1, Folder 19; Meriam [?] to BVC, January 16, 1930, FF Papers, LC, Reel 27; Eugene Meyer to FF, April 10 and May 10, 1932, FF Papers, LC, Reel 51.

29. Lash, *Dealers and Dreamers*, p. 36, 453.

30. BVC to FF, February 23, 1933, FF Papers, LC, Reel 114.

31. Ibid.

Chapter 5.
Newcomer to Washington

1. Joseph Eastman to FF, December 16, 1932; FF to BVC, December 19, 1932, BVC Papers, LC, Box 8.

2. See, for example, FF to BVC and Max Lowenthal, January 27, 1933, FF Papers, LC, Reel 114, Container 179; and BVC to FF, January 27, 1933, FF Papers, LC, Reel 114, Container 179.

3. *Public Papers of FDR*, I: 717–78; quoted in Arthur M. Schlesinger, Jr., *The Crisis of the Old Order* (Boston: Houghton Mifflin, 1957), p. 401.

4. Earl Latham, *The Politics of Railroad Coordination, 1933–1936* (Cambridge: Harvard University Press, 1959), pp. 9–10.

5. Ibid., p. 29.
6. Max Lowenthal, *The Investor Pays* (New York: Knopf, 1933), pp. 112, 131, 132–33.
7. Ibid., pp. 173, 186.
8. Ibid., pp. 370, 374, 389.
9. Max Lowenthal, "Brief Comments on New Draft of Hastings Bill, S. 4921," FF Papers, LC, Reel 114; BVC to FF, January 27, 1933, ibid.
10. Max Lowenthal, "The Railroad Reorganization Act," *Harvard Law Review* 47 (November 1933): 23.
11. Ibid., p. 58; BVC to FF, February 23, 1933, FF Papers, LC, Reel 114, Container 179.
12. *Public Papers of FDR*, I: 861, ibid., II: 12.
13. House Report No. 85, 73d Congress, 1st sess. 2 (1933).
14. Norfolk *Virginian-Pilot*, quoted in *Literary Digest*, June 3, 1933, p. 7.
15. Raymond Moley, *The First New Deal* (Cambridge: Harvard University Press, 1966), pp. 308–11; Huston Thompson Diary, March 13, 1933, Huston Thompson Papers, Box 1, LC.
16. *Literary Digest*, April 8, 1933, p. 5; Michael E. Parrish, *Securities Regulation and The New Deal* (New Haven: Yale University Press, 1970), pp. 47–48.
17. BVC to FF, April 1933, BVC Papers, LC, Box 8.
18. Felix Frankfurter, "Memorandum by Felix Frankfurter Re Conversation with A. Lawrence Lowell," May 11, 1933, James M. Landis Papers, LC, Box 7.; Arthur Schlesinger, Jr., *The Coming of the New Deal* (Boston: Houghton Mifflin, 1958), p. 441.
19. TGC to James Landis, March 20 [1928], Landis Papers, LC, Box 4; TGC to Guy H. Holliday, January 4, 1931, TGC Papers, LC, Box 138; FF to TGC, February 25, 1932, TGC Papers, LC, Box 198.
20. TGC to David Cavers, March 22, 1932. TGC Papers, LC, Box 138. For a discussion of the RFC, see James S. Olson, *Saving Capitalism: The Reconstruction Finance Corporation and the New Deal, 1933–40* (Princeton: Princeton University Press, 1988), pp. 13–24.
21. John Worth Kern IV, "Thomas Gardiner Corcoran and the New Deal, 1932–1940," unpublished senior thesis, Princeton University, 1980; Lash, *Dealers and Dreamers*, p. 74; TGC to FF, January 23, 1933, TGC Papers, LC, Box 198.
22. Parrish, *Securities Regulation*, pp. 5–6n.
23. George E. Barnett, "The Securities Act of 1933 and the British Companies Act," *Harvard Business Review* 13 (October 1934): 6; James M. Landis, "The Legislative History of the Securities Act of 1933," *George Washington Law Review* 28 (October 1959), p. 32.
24. Landis, "Legislative History," pp. 34, 32 (emphasis added).
25. Parrish, *Securities Regulation*, p. 50; Landis, "Legislative History," pp. 32, 35 (see also Parrish, *Securities Regulation*, pp. 63–64); "Memorandum on Proposed Federal Securities Act," prepared by Elizabeth Sanford Epstein, with a marginal note in Cohen's hand, April 1933. Attached to BVC [?] to FF, April 1933, BVC Papers, LC, Box 8; quoted in Parrish, *Securities Regulation*, p. 67.
26. "Memorandum on Proposed Federal Securities Act."
27. Landis, "Legislative History," p. 39; Huston Thompson Diary, April 21, 1933, p. 7, Huston Thompson Papers, LC, Box 1.
28. Landis, "Legislative History," pp. 33–38; Parrish, *Securities Regulation*, pp. 59–64.
29. FF to TGC, October 22, 1933, TGC Papers, LC, Box 198; TGC to FF, September 26, 1933, TGC Papers, LC, Box 198; Parrish, *Securities Regulation*, p. 64.

30. FF to TGC, April 17, 1933, TGC Papers, LC, Box 198.
31. Monica Lynne Niznik, "Thomas G. Corcoran: The Public Service of Franklin Roosevelt's 'Tommy the Cork,' " unpublished dissertation, University of Notre Dame, 1981, p. 84.
32. BVC to James M. Landis, May 5, 1933, Landis Papers, LC, Box 4; Landis, "Legislative History," p. 38; *Congressional Record*, 73d Cong., 1st sess., pp. 2910–55.
33. *Congressional Record*, 73d Cong., 1st sess., pp. 2978–84; 2986–3000.
34. Landis, "Legislative History," pp. 44–45; Parrish, *Securities Regulation*, p. 70. Glass's banking bill eventually became the Banking Act of 1933, 48 Stat. 162.
35. Landis, "Legislative History," p. 47. A detailed discussion can be found in Parrish, *Securities Regulation*, pp. 73–107. See also Landis, "Legislative History," p. 49.
36. BVC to James M. Landis, June 7, 1933, Landis Papers, LC, Box 4.
37. Landis, "Legislative History," pp. 40–41; T.R.B., "Washington Notes," *The New Republic*, April 26, 1933, pp. 308–9.
38. *Congressional Record*, May 5, 1933, vol. 77, pt. 3, 73d Cong., 1st sess., pp. 2913, 2938. The full House debate on the Securities Act can be found on pp. 2910–55.
39. BVC to Jane Harris, June 29, 1933; October 17, 1933; Lash Papers, FDR Library.
40. BVC to Jane Harris, nd [1933], Lash Papers, FDR Library.
41. Ibid.
42. TGC to Max Lowenthal, July 29, 1933, TGC Papers, LC, Box 204; quoted in Schwarz, p. 145; TGC to FF, October [?] 1933, TGC Papers, LC, Box 198.
43. BVC to FF, October 9, 1933, FF Papers, LC, Reel 70.
44. BVC to FF, November 10, 1933, FF Papers, LC, Reel 70.
45. In the 1970s, Cohen and Corcoran recalled that they moved into the Georgetown house in June 1933. However, the documentary evidence suggests that they did not move into the house until the fall.
46. TGC to FF, October [?] 1933, TGC Papers, LC, Box 198; TGC to FF, December 30, 1933, FF Papers, LC, Reel 30.
47. See, in general, Katie Louchheim, "The Little Red House," *Virginia Quarterly Review* 56 (Winter 1980): 119–34.
48. Ibid., pp. 128–29.
49. BVC to FF, November 10, 1933, January 1, 1934, FF Papers, LC, Reel 70.
50. BVC to FF, January 1, 1934, FF Papers, LC, Reel 50.

Chapter 6.
Into the Maelstrom

1. BVC to James M. Landis, Landis Papers, LC, Box 4.
2. Michael Parrish, *Securities Regulation and the New Deal* (New Haven: Yale University Press, 1970), p. 110.
3. BVC to Jane Harris, September 7, 1933; September 21, 1933; Lash Papers, FDR Library.
4. Arthur M. Schlesinger, Jr., *The Coming of the New Deal* (Boston: Houghton Mifflin, 1957), p. 457. See also Parrish, *Securities Regulation*, pp. 116–17.
5. Harold G. Moulton, *The Financial Organization of Society* (Chicago: University of Chicago Press, 1921), p. 185.
6. Ibid., p. 207.
7. Ibid.
8. Securities Exchange Act of 1934, sec. 2 (2), 48 Stat. 882 (1934).

9. U.S. Congress, House, *Stock Exchange Regulation*, hearings before the Committee on Interstate and Foreign Commerce, 73rd Cong., 2d sess. (1934), p. 88.

10. I. N. P. Stokes and Telford Taylor, "Draft of Exchange Regulation," February 1, 1934, SEC, II, Landis Papers, Harvard Law School.

11. Parrish, *Securities Regulation*, pp. 115–20; Senate Banking and Currency Committee, *Stock Exchange Practices*, 73d Cong., 2d sess., 1934, pp. 1–15.

12. Ibid.

13. *Time*, February 26, 1934, pp. 53–54.

14. Ibid., p. 56.

15. Sen. Joseph Robinson, quoted in *Time*, April 16, 1934, p. 70; Richard Whitney, quoted in Schlesinger, *The Coming of the New Deal*, p. 465; *Time*, May 14, 1934, p. 66; Whitney, quoted in Parrish, *Securities Regulation*, p. 130. On the Wirt affair, see Schlesinger, *The Coming of the New Deal*, pp. 457–61.

16. BVC to FF, May 11, 1934, FF Papers, LC, Reel 30.

17. John T. Flynn, "The Marines Land in Wall Street," *Harpers* 169 (July 1934), p. 148; BVC to Jane Harris, June 26, 1934, Lash Papers, FDR Library.

18. BVC and TGC to FF, June 18, 1934, FF Papers, LC, Reel 30.

19. FF to TGC, January 12, 1934, TGC Papers, LC, Box 198; BVC and TGC to FF, June 12, 1934, FF Papers, LC, Reel 30; BVC to FF, May 11, 1934, FF Papers, Reel 30.

20. FF to TGC and BVC, May 15, 1934, TGC Papers, LC, Box 198.

21. Parrish, *Securities Regulation*, pp. 125–7.

22. *Literary Digest*, April 7, 1934, p. 7; *The New Republic*, May 2, 1934, p. 335.

23. Parrish, *Securities Regulation*, pp. 137–38.

24. Ibid., pp. 133–34.

25. Ibid., pp. 126–27; Flynn, "The Marines Land in Wall Street," *Harpers* 169 (July 1934), pp. 148–55. Raymond Moley, *After Seven Years* (New York: Harper and Brothers), p. 286.

26. BVC interviews with Joseph Lash, September 29, 1982; November 9, 1982; Lash Papers, FDR Library.

27. BVC to FF, May 11, 1934, FF Papers, LC, Reel 70; Joseph P. Lash, *Dealers and Dreamers: A Look at the New Deal* (New York: Doubleday, 1988), pp. 167–68.

28. Max Lowenthal to Sen. E. P. Costigan, June 7, 1934, J. N. Frank Collection, Box 10, Folder 56, Yale University (emphasis added).

29. Moley, *After Seven Years*, pp. 289–90.

30. Lash, *Dealers and Dreamers*, p. 167.

31. BVC to Jane Harris, undated [spring 1934], Lash Papers, FDR Library.

32. *New York Times*, June 22, 1934, p. 31; Moley, *After Seven Years*, pp. 286–87.

33. See Lash, *Dealers and Dreamers*, pp. 173–84 and notes there; and Max Lowenthal to E. P. Costigan, June 7, 1934, J. N. Frank Collection, Yale University, Box 10, Folder 56.

34. Thomas K. McCraw, *Prophets of Regulation* (Cambridge: Harvard University Press, 1984), p. 183.

35. "Washington Daily Merry-Go-Round," *The State* (Columbia, S.C.), October 1, 1934, p. 10; Landis quoted in Lash, *Dealers and Dreamers*, p. 174.

36. BVC to Jane Harris, July 26, 1934, Lash Papers, FDR Library.

37. Ibid.

38. TGC to Charles Wyzanski, August 4, 1934, TGC Papers, LC.

39. BVC to Jane Harris, June 26, 1934; BVC to Jane Harris, nd [probably September 1934], Lash Papers, FDR Library.

Chapter 7.
The Public Utilities Holding Company Act

1. "President Expected to Dominate Congress," *The Literary Digest*, January 5, 1935, p. 7.
2. *New York Times*, November 14, 1934, p. 33.
3. *Public Papers of FDR*, III: 454; "Recovery Drive Mapped as New Congress Nears," *The Literary Digest*, December 1, 1934, p. 7.
4. *Public Papers of FDR*, III: 454, 449.
5. *Public Papers of FDR*, IV: 16–19, 21. On Roosevelt's misstatement, see Arthur M. Schlesinger, Jr., *The Politics of Upheaval* (Boston: Houghton Mifflin, 1960), p. 305.
6. *Public Papers FDR*, II: 122–23; Arthur M. Schlesinger, Jr., *The Coming of the New Deal* (Boston: Houghton Mifflin, 1959), p. 319.
7. Schlesinger, *Coming of the New Deal*, p. 325.
8. *Public Papers of FDR*, III: 339–40.
9. See Philip J. Funigiello, *Toward a National Power Policy: The New Deal and the Electric Utility Industry, 1933–1941* (Pittsburgh, Pa.: University of Pittsburgh Press, 1973), pp. 29–30.
10. *Ashwander* v. *TVA*, 9 F.Supp. 965 (1935), 297 U.S. 288 (1936); "Public-Utility Firms Plan Court Test of Power Issue," *Literary Digest*, December 15, 1934, p. 45.
11. *Public Papers of FDR*, III: 461–62, 464.
12. "Minutes of a Meeting of the National Power Policy Committee," August 29, 1934, NPPC Records, GCF 103, Box 10.
13. Robert S. Healy to George C. Mathews, October 12, 1934, NPPC Records, National Archives, Box 10.
14. See Funigiello, *Toward a National Power Policy*, pp. 45–47.
15. David E. Lilienthal, *The Journals of David Lilienthal*, vol. 1, *The TVA Years, 1939–1945* (New York: Harper & Row, 1964), p. 45; Franklin D. Roosevelt, *Complete Presidential Press Conferences of Franklin D. Roosevelt*, 25 vols. (New York: Da Capo Press, 1972), IV: 223–30.
16. Robert Winsmore, "New Optimism Does Not Count on Inflation," *Literary Digest*, December 1, 1934, p. 36.
17. BVC to Robert E. Healy, November 23, 1934, NPPC/BVC, National Archives, Box 10.
18. Louis D. Brandeis, *The Curse of Bigness* (New York: Viking, 1935). Quotations from *Liggett Company* v. *Lee*, 288 U.S. 517 (1933); and "The Democracy of Bigness" (1914) from Brandeis, *The Curse of Bigness*, pp. 140, 169.
19. Harold G. Moulton, *The Financial Organization of Society* (Chicago: University of Chicago Press, 1921), pp. 757, 771, 773.
20. *Complete Presidential Press Conferences of FDR*, IV: 223–25.
21. BVC to Robert S. Healy, November 23, 1934, FF Papers, LC, Reel 113.
22. Ibid.
23. "Minutes of a Meeting of the National Power Policy Comittee," December 20, 1934, NPPC Records, National Archives, Box 10.
24. Funigiello, *Toward a National Power Policy*, pp. 53–54.

25. Ibid., pp. 58, 61.
26. Public Utility Holding Company Act, section 11b.
27. BVC to Jane Harris, January 12, 1935, Lash Papers, FDR Library.
28. Ellsworth Barnard, *Wendell Willkie: Fighter for Freedom* (Marquette, Mich.: Northern Michigan University Press, 1966), pp. 94–97.
29. Quoted in ibid., pp. 90–92.
30. *Journals of David Lilienthal*, I: 46–47.
31. *Public Papers of FDR*, IV: 98.
32. BVC to Ickes, February 8, 1935, NPPC Records, National Archives, Box 10.
33. *Report of the National Power Policy Committee*, House doc. 137, 74th Cong., 1st sess., March 12, 1935, pp. 9, 4, 5.
34. Ibid., pp. 8–9. Emphasis added.
35. BVC to Willkie, March 21, 1935, NPPC Records, National Archives, Box 10.
36. BVC to FF, March 9, 1936, BVC Papers, LC, Box 10.
37. Michael Parrish, *Securities Regulation and the New Deal* (New Haven: Yale University Press, 1970), p. 171; Funigiello, *Toward a National Power Policy*, pp. 88–89.
38. Public Utility Holding Company Act, section 11b(1); memorandum of a conversation with TGC, August 21, 1935, Official File, FDR Library, Box 1560.
39. Ralph O. Brewster, "Personal Explanation," *Congressional Record*, 74th Cong., 1st sess., July 2, 1935, p. 10660.
40. "Statement by Thomas G. Corcoran in Reply to a Charge by Congressman R. O. Brewster," TGC Papers, LC, Box 210.
41. "Lobby Hearing Adjourns in Confusion as Brewster Calls Corcoran a Liar," *New York Times*, July 10, 1935.
42. Schlesinger, *The Politics of Upheaval*, p. 318; "Brewster Acted Lobbyist Role, Senator Insists," *New York Herald-Tribune*, July 12, 1935.
43. Funigiello, *Toward a National Power Policy*, p. 93.
44. Arthur Krock, "Are the Two 'Wunderkinder' about to Re-Emerge?" *New York Times*, April 2, 1937, p. 22.

Chapter 8.
At the Center of Power

1. FF to FDR, March 19, 1935, TGC Papers, LC, Box 198.
2. President's Committee on Administrative Management, "Administrative Management in the Government of the United States" (Washington, D.C.: Government Printing Office, 1937), p. 5.
3. FF to FDR, March 19, 1935, TGC Papers, LC, Box 198.
4. Patrick Anderson, *The President's Men: White House Assistants of Franklin D. Roosevelt, Harry S Truman, Dwight D. Eisenhower, John F. Kennedy and Lyndon B. Johnson* (Garden City, N.Y.: Doubleday, 1968), pp. 42, 44; Alva Johnston, "White House Tommy," *Saturday Evening Post*, July 31, 1937, p. 65.
5. Arthur M. Schlesinger, Jr., *The Politics of Upheaval* (Boston: Houghton Mifflin, 1960), p. 226.
6. Quoted in Anderson, *The President's Men*, p. 50.
7. Arthur M. Schlesinger, Jr., *The Coming of the New Deal* (Boston: Houghton Mifflin, 1959), p. 498.
8. Raymond Moley, *After Seven Years* (New York: Harper and Brothers, 1939), p. 333.
9. "Instructions," November 5, 1935, TGC Papers, Box 264.

10. Johnston, "White House Tommy."
11. Moley, *After Seven Years*, p. 333.
12. *Public Papers of FDR*, III: 414, 415.
13. FF to BVC, September 18, 1934, BVC Papers, LC, Box 13.
14. Russell D Buhite and David W. Levy, eds. *FDR's Fireside Chats* (Norman, Okla.: University of Oklahoma Press, 1992), pp. 54–62; FF to BVC, September 18, 1934, BVC Papers, LC, Box 13; Buhite and Levy, *FDR's Fireside Chats*, p. 53.
15. Moley, *After Seven Years*, p. 295.
16. Samuel I. Rosenman, *Working with Roosevelt* (New York: Harper and Brothers, 1952), p. 104.
17. Ibid., pp. 100–105.
18. Moley, *After Seven Years*, p. 344.
19. Rosenman, *Working with Roosevelt*, pp. 105; Moley, *After Seven Years*, p. 346. See also Schlesinger, *The Politics of Upheaval*, p. 578.
20. *Public Papers of FDR*, V: 230–36.
21. Rosenman, *Working with Roosevelt*, p. 116.
22. Ibid., pp. 121–27.
23. *Public Papers of FDR*, V: 486.
24. Louis Brandeis, *Other People's Money and How the Bankers Use It* (New York: Stokes, 1914).
25. FF to TGC, October 28, 1936, TGC Papers, LC, Box 198.
26. *Public Papers of FDR*, V: 566–73.
27. Ibid., V: 581.
28. Quoted in Katie Louchheim, *The Making of the New Deal: The Insiders Speak* (Cambridge: Harvard University Press, 1983), p. 111.
29. Not, as Joseph L. Rauh recalled, on September 23, which was Cohen's fortieth birthday.
30. In re *American States Public Service Co.*, 12 F. Supp. 667 (November 7, 1935), at 21–22.
31. Ibid., at 163; Louchheim, *Making of the New Deal*, p. 112.
32. The legal background in the case can be found in "Litigation Involving the Public Utility Holding Company Act of 1935," unsigned and undated memorandum in TGC Papers, LC, Box 260.
33. *Burco v. Whitworth*, 81 F. 2d. 721 (February 22, 1936).
34. *Burco v. Whitworth*, cert. denied, 297 U.S. 724 (1936). For Rauh's account, see Louchheim, *Making of the New Deal*, p. 112.
35. Joseph P. Lash, *Dealers and Dreamers: A New Look at the New Deal* (New York: Doubleday, 1988), p. 287.
36. Quoted in Louchheim, *Making of the New Deal*, p. 111.
37. BVC to FF, March 9, 1936, FF Papers, LC, Reel 91, Container 145, "Holding Companies, 1935–36."
38. FDR to BVC, May 14, 1936, in Elliott Roosevelt, ed., *F.D.R.: His Personal Letters*, 4 vols. (New York: Duell, Sloan and Pearce, 1947–50), I: 590–91. That Cohen was an intermediate source of the information on which FDR's letter was based belies Lash's suggestion that "a note from Roosevelt was a sweet accolade, but it was the work that Ben enjoyed." Lash, *Dealers and Dreamers*, p. 287.
39. *Electric Bond and Share* v. *Securities and Exchange Commission*, 303 U.S. 419 (1938), at 433.
40. Willkie to BVC, March 20, 1935, NPPC Records, National Archives, Box 10; Willkie to BVC, September 3, 1937, FF Papers, LC.

41. "Brief for the Plaintiff and Cross-Defendants on the Constitutionality of the Public Utility Holding Company Act of 1935 as Applied to the Defendants," draft, May 7, 1936, NPPC Records, National Archives, Box 9.

42. *Securities and Exchange Commission* v. *Electric Bond & Share Co. et al.* (District Court, S.D. New York), 18 F. Supp. 131 (January 29, 1937).

43. *Securities and Exchange Commission* v. *Electric Bond & Share Co. et al.*, 92 F.2d 580, at 593 (Hand, concurring).

44. Gerald Gunther, *Learned Hand: The Man and the Judge* (New York: Knopf, 1994), pp. 465–66; Lash, *Dealers and Dreamers*, p. 346.

45. Later Supreme Court cases involving the constitutionality of the Public Utility Holding Company Act include *North America Co.* v. *SEC*, 327 U.S. 686 (1946) and *American Power & Light Co.* v. *SEC*, 329 U.S. 90 (1946).

Chapter 9.
The Court-Packing Plan

1. Quotes from "Comment: Election Results Inspire Praise and Gibes from Newspapers and Columnists," *Literary Digest*, November 14, 1936, pp. 9–10.

2. HSC to FDR, May 7, 1935, Cummings Papers, University of Virginia; Box 170. BVC, "The New Problem of Government Under the Constitution," BVC Papers, LC. XN9.21

3. See *Assoc. Industries of New York State* v. *Dept. of Labor of New York et al.*, 299 U.S. 515 (1936) [per curiam]; Cummings to FDR, 24 November 1936, Official File, FDR Papers.

4. *Home Building & Loan Assn.* v. *Blaisdell*, 290 U.S. 398 (1934), at 426.

5. Elliott Roosevelt, ed., *F.D.R.: His Personal Letters*, 4 vols. (New York: Duell, Sloan and Pearce, 1947–50), III: 458–59.

6. *Norman* v. *Baltimore & Ohio Railroad Co.*; *Perry* v. *United States*, 294 U.S. 240 (1935).

7. Quoted in *Literary Digest*, March 2, 1935, p. 37.

8. *The New Republic*, March 6, 1935, p. 100.

9. *Railroad Retirement Board* v. *Alton R.R. Co.*, 295 U.S. 330 (1935), at 374.

10. *A.L.A. Schechter Poultry Corp.* v. *United States*, 295 U.S. 495 (1935); *Louisville Joint Stock Land Bank* v. *Radford*, 295 U.S. 555 (1935); *Humphrey's Executor* v. *United States*, 295 U.S. 602 (1935).

11. The complete list of New Deal laws invalidated by the Supreme Court after May 1935 is as follows: the Federal Home Owners' Loan Act of 1933 (*Hopkins Saving Assoc.* v. *Cleary*, 296 U.S. 315 (1935)); the Agricultural Adjustment Act of 1933 (*United States* v. *Butler*, 297 U.S. 1 (1936)); 1935 amendments to the Agricultural Adjustment Act of 1933, *Rickert Rice Mills* v. *Fontenot*, 298 U.S. 513 (1936)); and the Bituminous Coal Conservation Act of 1935 (*Carter* v. *Carter Coal Co.*, 298 U.S. 238 (1936)).

12. *Morehead* v. *New York* ex rel. *Tipaldo*, 298 U.S. 587 (1936).

13. For a revisionist account arguing that the Court was motivated not by politics but by the law, see Barry Cushman, *Rethinking the New Deal Court: The Structure of a Constitutional Revolution* (New York: Oxford University Press, 1998). But see also William Lasser, "Justice Roberts and the Constitutional Revolution of 1937 — Was There a 'Switch in Time'?" *Texas Law Review* 78, 1347–76 (May 2000).

14. *United States* v. *Butler*, 297 U.S. 1 (1936), at 87 (Stone, dissenting); Homer S. Cummings Diary, vol. 5, p. 65, May 27, 1935, HSC Papers, University of Virginia, Box 234.

15. *Adkins* v. *Children's Hospital*, 261 U.S. 525 (1923), at 557–58.
16. *Morehead* v. *New York* ex rel. *Tipaldo*, 298 U.S. 587 (1936), at 623–64 (Hughes, C.J., dissenting), quoting *Adkins* v. *Children's Hospital*, 261 U.S. 525 (1923) at 558–59 (emphasis added).
17. *Morehead* v. *New York* ex rel. *Tipaldo*, at 611, 613–14.
18. See Henry J. Abraham, *Justices and Presidents: A Political History of Appointments to the Supreme Court* (New York: Oxford University Press, 1974), pp. 115–16.
19. Quoted in William E. Leuchtenburg, *The Supreme Court Reborn: The Constitutional Revolution in the Age of Roosevelt* (New York: Oxford University Press, 1995), pp. 116, 112.
20. HSC to FDR, January 29, 1936, HSC Papers, University of Virginia; see also William Lasser, *The Limits of Judicial Power: The Supreme Court in American Politics* (Chapel Hill, N.C.: University of North Carolina Press, 1988), pp. 150–51, and Leuchtenburg, *Supreme Court Reborn*, p. 110.
21. Elbert D. Thomas, "The Constitution and the Courts," *Congressional Record*, January 18, 1936, p. 644.
22. Stanley High to Roosevelt, June 1936, President's Secretary's File Box 185, FDR Papers, FDR Library; HSC to FDR, June 20, 1936, HSC Papers, University of Virginia.
23. *New York Times*, June 12, 1936, p. 22.
24. *Public Papers of FDR*, V: 200–201.
25. HSC to FDR, June 20, 1936, FDR Library, PSF, File 76; Arthur M. Schlesinger, Jr., *The Politics of Upheaval* (Boston: Houghton Mifflin, 1960), pp. 581–82; *Public Papers of FDR*, V: 234.
26. *Public Papers of FDR*, V: 639–40.
27. Leuchtenburg, *Supreme Court Reborn*, pp. 124–25.
28. Quoted in *Literary Digest*, Feburary 13, 1937, pp. 5–8; Morgenthau Diary, February 15, 1937, Henry Morgenthau Papers, FDR Library.
29. Monica Lynne Niznik, "Thomas G. Corcoran: The Public Service of Franklin Roosevelt's 'Tommy the Cork,'" unpublished dissertation, University of Notre Dame, 1981, p. 287.
30. Joseph Alsop and Turner Catledge, *The 168 Days* (New York: Da Capo Press, 1973), p. 85.
31. Quoted in Samuel I. Rosenman, *Working with Roosevelt* (New York: Harper and Brothers, 1952), p. 157.
32. "A 'Fireside Chat' Discussing the Plan for Reorganization of the Judiciary," March 9, 1937, *Public Papers of FDR*, 1937 volume, p. 126.
33. Ibid., pp. 128–29.
34. "Defending the Plan to 'Pack' the Supreme Court," in Russell D. Buhite and David W. Levy, eds., *FDR's Fireside Chats* (Norman: University of Oklahoma Press, 1992), pp. 88–95.
35. Alsop and Catledge, *The 168 Days*, p. 113.
36. Cohen attributed this proposal to Dean Charles E. Clark of Yale Law School.
37. BVC and TGC, "Memorandum on Constitutional Problems," BVC Papers, LC, Box 7.
38. Ibid.
39. Ibid.
40. Warner W. Gardner, "Memories of the 1937 Constitutional Revolution," *Supreme Court Historical Society Quarterly* 20 (1999): 14.

41. BVC to LDB, July 30, 1937, BVC Papers, LC, Box 13; author's interview with David Ginsburg, August 1999.

42. Robert E. Sherwood, *Roosevelt and Hopkins: An Intimate History* (New York: Harper and Brothers, 1950), pp. 89–90.

43. Rosenman, *Working with Roosevelt*, pp. 149, 156.

44. Joseph P. Lash, *Dealers and Dreamers: A New Look at the New Deal* (New York: Doubleday, 1988). p. 295. Lash provides no source for this story; it was probably told to him in one of his many interviews with Cohen, Corcoran, or another of the New Dealers.

45. Quoted in Lash, *Dealers and Dreamers*, p. 293.

46. BVC to Harold Laski, February 7, 1937; quoted in Lash, *Dealers and Dreamers*, p. 294.

47. FDR to FF, January 15, 1937, and FF to FDR, January 18, 1937; February 15, 1937; and February 18, 1937, in Max Freedman, *Roosevelt and Frankfurter: Their Correspondence* (Boston: Little, Brown, 1967). pp. 381–82, 384.

48. *Reorganization of the Federal Judiciary*, Hearings before the Committee on the Judiciary, United States Senate, 75th Cong., 1st sess., March 22, 1937, I: 486.

49. "Court Commission Urged by Dr. Dodds," *New York Times*, March 25, 1937, p. 20; Arthur Krock, "Are the Two 'Wunderkinder' about to Re-emerge?" *New York Times*, April 2, 1937, p. 22.

50. Burton K. Wheeler, *Yankee from the West: The Candid, Turbulent Life Story of the Yankee-born U.S. Senator from Wyoming* (Garden City, N.Y.: Doubleday, 1962), pp. 319–20.

51. BVC to LDB, July 30, 1937, BVC Papers, LC, Box 13.

52. BVC interview with Joseph P. Lash, September 16, 1974, Lash Papers, FDR Library. For clarity, I have expanded Lash's shorthand notes.

53. Arthur Krock, "Are the Two 'Wunderkinder' about to Re-Emerge?" *New York Times*, April 2, 1937, p. 22.

54. The Court's opinion appears at 300 U.S. 379 (1937). Exerpts of the chief justice's oral delivery of the opinion can be found in Leuchtenberg, *The Supreme Court Reborn*, pp. 170–73.

55. See Cushman, *Rethinking the New Deal Court*, p. 18.

56. *National Labor Relations Board* v. *Jones & Laughlin Steel Corp.*, 301 U.S. 1 (1937), at 37.

57. Alsop and Catledge, *The 168 Days*, pp. 153, 152.

58. Ibid., p. 159.

59. BVC to CCB, March 30, 1937, BVC Papers, LC, Box 13; Alsop and Catledge, *The 168 Days*, p. 159.

60. TGC, "Notes on the President's Plan," nd, TGC Papers, LC, Box 270; TGC to John J. Burns, April 10, 1937, TGC Papers, LC, Box 269; TGC, Memorandum to "Mr. Rowe[,] Mr. Katz [, and] Mr. Weiner, May 6, 1937, TGC Papers, LC, Box 270; Alsop and Catledge, *The 168 Days*, p. 187.

61. Quoted in Leuchtenburg, *The Supreme Court Reborn*, p. 148.

62. Alsop and Catledge, *The 168 Days*, pp. 262–63, 266–67.

63. *Carter* v. *Carter Coal Co.*, 298 U.S. 238 (1936).

64. *Hammer* v. *Dagenhart*, 247 U.S. 251 (1918), at 276.

65. *Carter* v. *Carter Coal Co.*, 298 U.S. 238 (1936), at 303.

66. Ibid., at 308–9.

67. *N.L.R.B.* v. *Jones & Laughlin Steel Corp.*, 301 U.S. 1 (1937), at 31.

68. U.S. Senate Committee on Education and Labor, "Fair Labor Standards Act . . .

Report [to accompany S. 2475]," 75th Cong., 1st sess., report no. 884 (July 6, 1937), pp. 5–6.

69. Roger K. Newman, *Hugo Black: A Biography* (New York: Pantheon Books, 1994), p. 215.

70. Ibid.

71. U.S. Senate Committee on Education and Labor, "Fair Labor Standards Act . . . Report," p. 6.

72. Newman, *Black*, p. 217. Paul H. Douglas and Joseph Hackman, "The Fair Labor Standards Act of 1938 I: The Background and Legislative History of the Act," *Political Science Quarterly* 53 (1938): 505–6.

73. Leuchtenburg, *The Supreme Court Reborn*, pp. 157–61.

74. Alva Johnston, "White House Tommy," *Saturday Evening Post*, July 31, 1937, p. 5.

75. "Necks In: Irishman and Jew Keep Quiet behind To-Day's Rooseveltian Brain Trust," *Literary Digest*, May 22, 1937, p. 7.

76. Lemuel F. Parton, "Cohen Figures in Court Plan," *Washington Star*, February 9, 1937.

77. Drew Pearson and Robert S. Allen, "Washington Daily Merry-Go-Round," *Washington Herald*, July 31, 1937.

Chapter 10.
Domestic Politics, 1937–1938

1. Ickes Diary, January 24, 1937, p. 1929, Ickes Papers, LC. Portions of the Ickes Diary were published as Harold L. Ickes, *The Secret Diary of Harold L. Ickes*, 3 vols. (New York: Simon and Schuster, 1953). Other portions remain unpublished and are located in the Ickes Papers, LC. In these notes, references to the published edition are given as "Ickes, *Secret Diary*"; references to the unpublished edition are given as "Ickes Diary."

2. "Draft . . . [of] A BILL to authorize the maintenance and operation of the Bonneville project. . . ," February 8, 1937, NPPC, Box 7.

3. Philip J. Funigiello, *Toward a National Power Policy: The New Deal and the Electric Utility Industry, 1933–1941* (Pittsburgh, Pa.: University of Pittsburgh Press, 1973), p. 189.

4. Ibid., pp. 189–91.

5. Arthur Krock, "Further Obscurity for the Cabinet Is Seen," *New York Times*, August 10, 1937, p. 18.

6. "Cohen, Corcoran to Resign," *Washington Times*, July 17, 1937; Joseph P. Lash, *Dealers and Dreamers: A New Look at the New Deal* (New York: Doubleday, 1988), p. 314; BVC to Jane Harris, August 1, 1937.

7. "Corcoran-Cohen, Inc.! N.Y. and Washington," *Washington Herald*, July 26, 1937.

8. BVC to Jane Harris, September 22, 1937.

9. "Brain Trust Chief Visits at Bonneville," *Oregon Daily Journal*, September 12, 1937, p. 1. Apparently the visit was merely a courtesy call; Cohen, who met his associate Joel David Wolfson in Oregon, met with neither the governor of Oregon nor the mayor of Portland. He did meet with the engineer in charge of the construction of the dam, and with Dick Neuberger of the Commonwealth Federation of Oregon and the People's Power League. While in Portland, Wolfson "let it be known that in a few days Secretary of the Interior Harold L. Ickes will appoint a Bonneville administrator."

10. "Capital Guessing on the New Justice," *New York Times*, May 19, 1937, p. 18.

11. Roger K. Newman, *Hugo Black: A Biography* (New York: Pantheon Books, 1994), p. 234.

12. Within six months, Reed, too, would join the Court, replacing George Sutherland.

13. Quoted in Newman, *Hugo Black*, p. 236.

14. Newman, *Hugo Black*, pp. 241–4, 249–50.

15. Ibid., pp. 257–58.

16. "New Proposals at Home, Frightening Storm Clouds Abroad," October 12, 1937, in Russell D. Buhite and David W. Levy, eds. *FDR's Fireside Chats* (Norman: University of Oklahoma Press, 1992), pp. 99, 104, 105.

17. "Fall Session: F.D.R. Seeks Spadework on Wages, Crop Control," *Time*, October 18, 1937, p. 14.

18. Lash, *Dealers and Dreamers*, p. 318.

19. "New Proposals at Home, Frightening Storm Clouds Abroad," October 12, 1937, in Buhite and Levy, *FDR's Fireside Chats*, pp. 99, 98.

20. Alan Brinkley, *The End of Reform: New Deal Liberalism in Recession and War* (New York: Knopf, 1995), pp. 49–64, 56.

21. William E. Leuchtenburg, *Franklin D. Roosevelt and the New Deal* (New York: Harper & Row, 1963), pp. 257–62.

22. Stanley High, "The White House Is Calling," *Harpers Magazine*, November 1937, p. 587.

23. Joseph Alsop and Robert Kintner, "We Shall Make America Over: The New Dealers in Action," *Saturday Evening Post*, November 19, 1938, pp. 89, 91.

24. Ibid., pp. 88, 91.

25. *Time*, September 12, 1938, p. 22.

26. Ibid., p. 24; Blair Bolles, "The Nine Young Men: No. 1—Thomas Gardiner Corcoran," *Washington Star*, August 28, 1937; John O'Donnell and Doris Fleeson, "New Deal Probes Anti-Semitic Drive on New Congress," *New York Daily News*, December 15, 1938.

27. *Time*, October 3, 1938, p. 2; "Roosevelt's Aide Returns Secretly," *New York Times*, September 30, 1938, p. 17.

28. Ibid.

29. Leuchtenburg, *Franklin D. Roosevelt and the New Deal*, p. 266.

30. Harold L. Ickes, *Secret Diary*, vol. 2 (New York: Simon and Schuster, 1953), 242–43 (entry of November 6, 1937); 261, 264 (entry of December 6, 1937).

31. TGC to FF, December 15 [1937], TGC Papers, LC, Box 198.

32. Ickes, *Secret Diary*, 243.

33. Quoted in Brinkley, *The End of Reform*, pp. 56–58.

34. *Public Papers of FDR*, VII: 11.

35. *Newsweek*, January 10, 1938.

36. "Direction of New Deal's Course Remains President's Secret," *Newsweek*, January 17, 1938.

37. Raymond Moley, "Perspective," *Newsweek*, January 17, 1938, p. 44.

38. *Public Papers of FDR*, VII: 305–32. The bland nature of the president's proposal was not lost on the press. "Washington wiseacres last week predicted correctly that the message would be mild," commented *Newsweek*, "because Corcoran, an inveterate Trust Buster, was in one of his worst humors, obviously dissatisfied about something." "Monopoly Authors," *Newsweek*, May 9, 1938, p. 7.

39. Leuchtenburg, *Franklin Delano Roosevelt and the New Deal*, p. 258.

40. *Public Papers of FDR*, VII: 399.
41. Monica Lynne Niznik, "Thomas G. Corcoran: The Public Service of Franklin Roosevelt's 'Tommy the Cork,'" unpublished dissertation, University of Notre Dame, 1981, pp. 359, 362, 368; *Newsweek*, June 6, 1938, p. 6.
42. Quoted in Niznik, *Corcoran*, II: 358, 361.
43. BVC to Jane Harris, September 4, 1938, Harris Papers.

Chapter 11.
Waiting for the War

1. Joseph L. Rauh, Jr., quoted in Katie Louchheim, *The Making of the New Deal: The Insiders Speak* (Cambridge: Harvard University Press, 1983), p. 114.
2. See, for example, BVC to Missy Lehand, October 13, 1938, transmitting a proposed message for FDR to send to Neville Chamberlain in regard to Palestine. Max Freedman, *Roosevelt and Frankfurter: Their Correspondence, 1928–1945* (Boston: Little, Brown, 1967), p. 463; Interview, Joseph P. Lash with BVC, April 8, 1974, quoted in Joseph P. Lash, *Dealers and Dreamers: A New Look at the New Deal* (New York: Doubleday, 1988), p. 396; Harold L. Ickes, *The Secret Diary of Harold L. Ickes*, vol. 3: *The Lowering Clouds, 1939–1941* (New York: Simon and Schuster, 1954), p. 22.
3. Quoted in Henry L. Feingold, *The Politics of Rescue: The Roosevelt Administration and the Holocaust, 1938–1945* (New Brunswick, N.J.: Rutgers University Press), p. 23.
4. BVC to Jane Harris, September 4, 1938, Harris Papers.
5. Allon Gal, "Zionist Foreign Policy and Ben-Gurion's Visit to the United States in 1939," *Studies in Zionism* 7 (1986): 37–38.
6. Julius Simon to BVC, September 14, 1938, and September 18, 1938.
7. BVC to Julius Simon, September 19, 1938; BVC to Robert Szold, October 5, 1938.
8. Stephen S. Wise to FF, October 16, 1938; LDB to FF, October 16, 1938, quoted in Philippa Strum, *Louis D. Brandeis: Justice for the People* (Cambridge: Harvard University Press, 1984), p. 385.
9. Feingold, *The Politics of Rescue*, pp. 41–42.
10. Quoted in Saul S. Friedman, *No Haven for the Oppressed: United States Policy toward Jewish Refugees, 1938–1945* (Detroit: Wayne State University Press, 1973), p. 227.
11. *Public Papers of FDR*, VIII: 463, 462.
12. Ibid., VIII: 204.
13. BVC to Missy LeHand, March 7, 1939; BVC to FDR, May 25, 1939.
14. BVC to FDR, July 19, 1939.
15. BVC to Missy LeHand, June 9, 1939, POF 2708.
16. SSW to BVC, June 13, 1939, NPPC Records, National Archives, BVC to SSW, February 7, 1940, NPPC Records, National Archives.
17. BVC to CCB, August 29, 1938.
18. Quoted in Bruce Murphy, *The Brandeis-Frankfurter Connection* (New York: Oxford University Press, 1982), p. 187.
19. BVC to Missy LeHand, March 28, 1940, enclosing "A Proposal to Encourage Useful Public Works by Linking together Work-Relief Grants and R.F.C. Loans."
20. BVC to Robert H. Jackson, March 9, 1938, with enclosures, Robert H. Jackson Papers, LC, Box 84.
21. Lash, *Dealers and Dreamers*, p. 378.
22. BVC, "Memorandum for the Insurance of Loans of Business," Jerome Frank Papers, Yale University, Box 23.

23. "Discard of 'Brain Trust' Viewed as Stressing Moderation Trend," *Baltimore Sun*, September 11, 1939.

24. "Corcoran and Cohen Outsiders, Early Makes It Very Plain," *Baltimore Sun*, September 12, 1939.

25. "President Labels Brain Trust Ghost," *New York Times*, September 13, 1939.

26. Heywood Broun, "It Seems to Me," *Washington Daily News*, March 31, 1939, p. 27.

27. TGC to Archibald MacLeish, July 5, 1939, quoted in Monica Lynne Niznik, "Thomas G. Corcoran: The Public Service of Franklin Roosevelt's 'Tommy the Cork'" unpublished dissertation, University of Notre Dame, 1981, p. 454.

Chapter 12.
Destroyers for Bases

1. Robert Dallek, *Franklin D. Roosevelt and American Foreign Policy, 1932–1945* (New York: Oxford University Press, 1979), pp. 201–2.

2. William L. Langer and S. William Gleason, *The Challenge to Isolation: The World Crisis of 1937–1940 and American Foreign Policy* (New York: Harper & Row, 1952), p. 235; Dallek, *Roosevelt and Foreign Policy*, p. 212.

3. *Public Papers of FDR*, IX: 1–4; Dallek, *Franklin D. Roosevelt and American Foreign Policy*, p. 218.

4. Winston S. Churchill, *Their Finest Hour* (Boston: Houghton Mifflin, 1949), p. 256.

5. Francis L. Loewenheim, Harold D. Langley, and Manfred Jonas, *Roosevelt and Churchill: Their Secret Wartime Correspondence* (New York: Saturday Review Press, 1975), pp. 94–97.

6. Quoted in *Newsweek*, July 8, 1940, p. 18. Several British papers echoed the sentiment. On Roosevelt's (and Ickes's) apprehensions toward Willkie, see Harold L. Ickes, *The Secret Diary of Harold L. Ickes* (New York: Simon and Schuster, 1953), pp. 293–94.

7. Langer and Gleason, *Challenge to Isolation*, p. 676.

8. Espionage Act of 1917, June 13, 1917, c. 30, Title 5, sec. 3, 40 Stat. 222; Act of March 4, 1909, c. 321, sec. 11, 35 Stat. 1090. The original statute was the Act of June 5, 1794, 1 Stat. 383.

9. *Newsweek*, July 8, 1940, p. 7; *New York Times*, June 19, 1940, p. 8; ibid., June 20, 1940, p. 10, 11; *Congressional Record*, June 21, 1940, pp. 8774–78, 76th Cong., 3d sess., vol. 86, pt. 8;

10. *New York Times*, June 25, 1940, p. 10; P.L. No. 671, June 28, 1940, 54 Stat. 676, at 681.

11. Loewenheim, Langley, and Jonas, *Roosevelt and Churchill*, pp. 99, 105, 107. See also Langer and Gleason, *Challenge to Isolation*, pp. 481–82, 746–48, 756–57.

12. Langer and Gleason, *Challenge to Isolation*, pp. 507, 710–11; Walter Johnson, *The Battle against Isolation* (Chicago: University of Chicago Press, 1944), pp. 114–17.

13. Ickes, *Secret Diary*, 3: 233, July 5, 1940.

14. BVC to FDR, 19 July 1940, BVC Papers, LC, Box 7. The final version of the memorandum, along with several draft versions and draft fragments, is entitled "Memorandum Re: Sending Effective Material Aid to Great Britain with Particular References to the Sending of Destroyers" and can be found in BVC Papers, Box 7 (July 19, 1940).

15. Ibid., p. 1.

16. Ibid., pp. 2–3.

17. Ibid., pp. 4–6.
18. Ibid., pp. 6–7.
19. Ibid., pp. 7–8.
20. Ibid., p. 9n.
21. Ibid., pp. 11–12.
22. See, for example, Manley O. Hudson to CCB, November 12, 1940, BVC Papers, LC, Box 7; Newman A. Townsend, "Memorandum for the Attorney General Re: Over-Age Destroyers," August 13, 1940, BVC Papers, LC, Box 7; Ickes, *Secret Diary*, 3:271.
23. Elliott Roosevelt, ed., *F.D.R.: His Personal Letters*, 4 vols. (New York: Duell, Sloan and Pearce, 1947–50), II: 1048–49; Langer and Gleason, *Challenge to Isolation*, p. 747; OSC to BVC, July 22, 1940, BVC Papers, LC, Box 7.
24. Langer and Gleason, *Challenge to Isolation*, p. 747.
25. Ickes, *Secret Diary*, 3:291–94; Langer and Gleason, *Challenge to Isolation*, pp. 750–51.
26. John Morton Blum, *From the Morgenthau Diaries*, vol. 3: *Years of Urgency, 1938–1941* (Boston: Houghton Mifflin, 1965), p. 180; Roger S. Greene to BVC, August 7, 1940, BVC Papers, LC, Box 7.
27. *New York Times*, August 11, 1940, section IV, p. 8; Joseph P. Lash, *Dealers and Dreamers*, pp. 409–10; Langer and Gleason, *Challenge to Isolation*, p. 757; CCB to BVC, August 26, 1940, BVC Papers, LC, Box 7.
28. *New York Times*, August 11, 1940, section IV, p. 8. A draft of August 6, 1940 can be found in BVC Papers, LC, Box 7.
29. Langer and Gleason, *Challenge to Isolation*, p. 757; Blum, *From the Morgenthau Diaries*, 3:180.
30. Franklin D. Roosevelt, *Complete Presidential Press Conferences of Franklin D. Roosevelt*, 25 vols. (New York: Da Capo Press, 1972), XVI: 123–28.
31. "Memorandum, Attorney General Robert H. Jackson to the Secretary of the Navy," August 17, 1940, BVC Papers, LC, Box 7.
32. Townsend, Memorandum for the Attorney General Re: Over-Age Destroyers," August 13, 1940, BVC Papers, LC, Box 7; Lash, *Dealers and Dreamers*, p. 410.
33. Churchill, *Their Finest Hour*, p. 404.
34. Benjamin V. Cohen, "Presidential Responsibility and American Democracy," in Benjamin V. Cohen et al., *The Prospect for Presidential-Congressional Government* (Berkeley, Calif.: Institute of Governmental Studies), pp. 26–27.

Chapter 13.
London

1. Richard J. Whalen, *The Founding Father: The Story of Joseph P. Kennedy* (New York: New American Library, 1964), pp. 330–42.
2. *Time*, February 17, 1941, pp. 15–16.
3. Ibid., p. 16.
4. Joseph P. Lash, *Dealers and Dreamers: A New Look at the New Deal* (New York: Doubleday, 1988), p. 452; Ickes Diary, February 8, 1941, p. 5202. Portions of the Ickes Diary were published as Harold L. Ickes, *The Secret Diary of Harold L. Ickes*, 3 vols. (New York: Simon and Schuster, 1953). Other portions remain unpublished and are located in the Ickes Papers, LC. In these notes, references to the published edition are given as "Ickes, *Secret Diary*"; references to the unpublished edition are given as "Ickes Diary."

5. Ibid.
6. Samuel I. Rosenman, *Working with Roosevelt* (New York: Harper and Brothers, 1952), p. 227; Patrick Anderson, *The President's Men* (New York: Doubleday, 1968), p. 51.
7. Harold L. Ickes to FDR, December 7, 1940, Ickes Papers, LC, Box 97.
8. FDR to TGC, January 20, 1941, PSF 141, FDR Library. A draft of the letter appears in James Rowe Papers, FDR Library, Box 10. The draft includes the following paragraph, omitted from the final version: "The last year has been a rather difficult one for me, and I know it has been for you. Sometimes you may have thought I had not fully appreciated all the difficulties you were up against; I confess I have believed at times that you had no real appreciation of all the countless problems and irritating minutiae with which I deal daily. It would certainly be no miracle in this complex world if both of us were right. But our friendship, if it is of the fair weather kind, should gladly suffer such minor arrows."
9. Ickes Diary, January 26, 1941, p. 5156; ibid., April 20, 1941, pp. 5401–2. James Rowe suggested in June that the assistant secretaryship was "one of Tom's mercurial and brief ideas . . . about which he seems to have lost all interest."
10. Lash, *Dealers and Dreamers*, p. 452.
11. Ibid., p. 51.
12. Ickes Diary, February 8, 1941, p. 5202.
13. Quoted in *Time*, December 3, 1940, p. 13.
14. *Press Conferences of FDR*, XVI:355
15. British Foreign Office, USA Correspondence, F.O. 371, A 1054, February 22, 1941.
16. Rowe to FDR, February 18, 1941, Rowe Papers, FDR Library, Box 9.
17. British Foreign Office, USA Correspondence, F.O. 371, A 1054, February 22, 1941.
18. BVC to Lou and Jane Harris, March 6, 1941, from Isaac Harris; *Time*, March 10, 1941, p. 29.
19. BVC to Lou and Jane Harris, March 6, 1941, from Isaac Harris.
20. Arnold J. Toynbee to F. Ashton-Gwatkin, May 7, 1941; BVC to Toynbee, May 6, 1941, both in F.O. 371/28900 XC 21319, Public Record Office, Kew.
21. F. Ashton-Gwatkin to [?] Ronald, May 14, 1941; Ashton-Gwatkin to Toynbee, May 16, 1941; Toynbee to Ashton-Gwatkin, May 12, 1941, all in F.O. 371/28900, Public Record Office, Kew.
22. Memorandum by F. Ashton-Gwatkin, June 12, 1941, F.O. 371/28900, Public Record Office, Kew.
23. Unidentified author to R. A. Butler, May 28, 1941, F.O. 371/28899, Public Record Office, Kew.
24. Donald Moggridge, ed., *The Collected Writings of John Maynard Keynes* (Cambridge: Cambridge University Press, 1979), pp. 23: 52–53, 58.
25. Telegram, John G. Winant to Secretary of State, April 3, 1941, PSF 6, FDR Library.
26. John G. Winant, Pilgrim's Speech, March 18, 1941, Archibald MacLeish Papers, LC, Box 5. BVC to MacLeish, September 26, [1941?], ibid.
27. Telegram, BVC to Winant, August 23, 1941, John G. Winant Papers, FDR Library, Box 191; FF to Winant, July 21, 1941, ibid., Box 197; BVC to Lou and Jane Harris, May 10, 1941, Harris Papers.
28. Ickes Diary, April 12, 1941, p. 5360; ibid., May 17, 1941, p. 5509; author's interview with Dorothea Wallis, Oxford, England, January 1993.
29. Telegram, BVC to John G. Winant, August 23, 1941, Winant Papers, FDR Library, Box 191; BVC to Harold L. Ickes, September 4, 1941, Ickes Papers, LC, Box 242.

30. Lash, *Dealers and Dreamers*, p. 449.
31. James H. Rowe to FDR, June 25, 1941, Rowe Papers, LC, Box 10.
32. FF to TGC, October 1, 1941 (not sent), BVC Papers, LC, Box 8.
33. James H. Rowe to FDR, June 25, 1941, Rowe Papers, LC, Box 10.
34. Ickes Diary, April 12, 1941, pp. 5360–61; ibid., April 20, 1941, p. 5402, LC; Ickes to FDR, July 31, 1941, Ickes Papers, LC, Box 97; Ickes Diary, August 2, 1941, p. 5841.
35. Ickes Diary, April 20, 1941, pp. 5401-2.
36. Memorandum on "Ben Cohen," James H. Rowe to FDR, August 1, 1941, Rowe Papers, FDR Library, Box 9.
37. Ibid.
38. Ibid.
39. James H. Rowe to Sam Rosenman, August 29, 1941, Rowe Papers, FDR Library, Box 9.
40. Ickes Diary, June 8, 1941, pp. 5577; July 5, 1941, p. 5684; July 12, 1941, p. 5733; September 9, 1941, p. 5814; September 20, 1941, p. 5887; November 15, 1941, p. 6021, LC.
41. Memorandum on "Ben Cohen," James H. Rowe to FDR, August 1, 1941, Rowe Papers, FDR Library, Box 9; BVC to Winant, October 22, 1941, Winant Papers, FDR Library, Box 191; author's interview with Sir Isaiah Berlin, London, January 20, 1993.
42. BVC, "Memorandum to Dr. Wise and Mr. Szold," October 29, 1941; SSW to BVC, November 3, 1941, BVC Papers, American Jewish Archives, Box 2.
43. Bradley F. Smith, *The Shadow Warriors: O.S.S. and the Origins of the C.I.A.* (New York: Basic Books, 1973), p. 67.
44. Ickes Diary, July 5, 1941, p. 5684, LC.

Chapter 14.
World War II

1. Herman Miles Somers, *Presidential Agency: The Office of War Mobilization and Reconversion* (Cambridge: Harvard University Press, 1950), pp. 34–35; James F. Byrnes, *All in One Lifetime* (New York: Harper and Brothers, 1958), p. 155.
2. Byrnes, *All in One Lifetime*, p. 155.
3. On the coal strike, see John William Partin, " 'Assistant President' for the Home Front: James F. Byrnes and World War II," Ph.D. dissertation, University of Florida, 1977. The coal truce broke down in midsummer, and the dispute plagued the administration well into 1944. See also Byrnes, *All in One Lifetime*, pp. 179–82.
4. Byrnes, *All in One Lifetime*, pp. 183–84.
5. Ibid., p. 184.
6. Executive Order No. 9347, May 27, 1943.
7. Somers, *Presidential Agency*, p. 49.
8. Executive Order No. 9361, July 15, 1943.
9. Quoted in Somers, *Presidential Agency*, p. 47.
10. Somers, *Presidential Agency*, p. 47.
11. Ibid., p. 51.
12. BVC to Henry A. Wallace, May 12, 1942, Wallace Papers, LC, XN5.22
13. Ickes Diary, November 4, 1942, p. 7182; BVC to CCB, June 18, [1943]. CCB Papers, Harvard Law School. Portions of the Ickes Diary were published as Harold L. Ickes,

The Secret Diary of Harold L. Ickes, 3 vols. (New York: Simon and Schuster, 1953). Other portions remain unpublished and are located in the Ickes Papers, LC. In these notes, references to the published edition are given as "Ickes, *Secret Diary*"; references to the unpublished edition are given as "Ickes Diary."

14. Ickes Diary, May 9, 1943, p. 7709; Partin, " 'Assistant President' For the Home Front," p. 85.
15. Ibid., May 9, 1943, pp. 7709, 7712, 7720.
16. BVC, SC, and Joseph L. Rauh, "The Japanese Situation on the West Coast," Lash Papers, FDR Library; author's interview with Joseph L. Rauh, January 5, 1989, Washington, DC.
17. Rauh to Joan Z. Bernstein, May 21, 1982, Lash Papers, FDR Library.
18. Ibid.
19. BVC, SC and Joseph L. Rauh, "The Japanese Situation on the West Coast," Lash Papers, FDR Library.
20. Ibid.
21. Ibid.
22. Ibid.
23. Ibid.
24. Ibid.
25. TGC, quoted in Joseph P. Lash, *Dealers and Dreamers: A New Look at the New Deal* (New York: Doubleday, 1988), p. 6; Joseph L. Rauh, quoted in ibid., p. 465.
26. See, among several books and articles on the subject, Lucy S. Dawidowicz, *The War Against the Jews* (New York: Holt, Rinehart & Winston, 1975); Lucy S. Dawidowicz, *What Is the Use of Jewish History?* (Syracuse, N.Y.: Syracuse University Press, 1981); Henry L. Feingold, *Bearing Witness: How America and the Jews Responded to the Holocaust* (Syracuse, N.Y.: Syracuse University Press, 1995); Verne W. Newton, *FDR and the Holocaust* (New York: St. Martin's Press, 1996); William D. Rubenstein, *The Myth of Rescue: Why the Democracies Could Not Have Saved More Jews from the Nazis* (New York: Routledge, 1997); and David S. Wyman, *The Abandonment of the Jews* (New York: Garland Press, 1984).
27. Rubenstein, *The Myth of Rescue*, pp. 34–35, 61–62.
28. Quoted in Saul S. Friedman, *No Haven for the Oppressed: United States Policy toward Jewish Refugees, 1938–1945* (Detroit, Mich.: Wayne State University Press, 1973), pp. 227, 225.
29. *United States v. Carolene Products Co.*, 304 U.S. 144 (1938), at 152.
30. *Betts v. Brady*, 316 U.S. 455 (1942); Benjamin V. Cohen and Erwin N. Griswold, "Denial of Counsel to Indigent Defendant Questioned," *New York Times*, August 2, 1942, section IV, p. 6.
31. *Minersville v. Gobitis*, 310 U.S. 586 (1940); BVC to CCB, June 8, 1940, CCB Papers, Harvard Law School.
32. BVC to CCB, January 28, 1944, CCB Papers, Harvard Law School.
33. See Ruth B. Russell, *A History of the United Nations Charter: The Role of the United States 1940–1945* (Washington, D.C.: The Brookings Institution, 1958), p. 220n; Edward R. Stettinius, Jr., *Roosevelt and the Russians* (Garden City, N.Y.: Doubleday, 1949), p. 15.
34. Ickes Diary, September 9, 1944, p. 9204.
35. See generally Georg Schild, *Bretton Woods and Dumbarton Oaks* (New York: St. Martin's Press, 1995), pp. 142–67.
36. Ickes Diary, January 29, 1944, p. 8597.

37. BVC, "Memorandum Concerning a Fourth Term," Lash Papers, FDR Library, p. 1.
38. "The Barkley Incident," *Time*, March 6, 1944, p. 18.
39. "Memorandum Concerning a Fourth Term," Lash Papers, FDR Library.
40. Ibid.
41. Townsend Hoopes and Douglas Brinkley, for example, in *FDR and the Creation of the U.N.* (New Haven: Yale University Press, 1997), do not even mention Cohen in connection with Dumbaron Oaks.
42. It is perhaps not too speculative to suggest that Cohen's comment about the "Johnnies" on the Supreme Court was a veiled reference—conscious or otherwise—to Felix Frankfurter.
43. BVC to CCB, November 17, 1944, CCB Papers, Harvard Law School; Ickes Diary, September 9, 1944, p. 9204. Ickes, however, observed that Cohen "evidently thinks that he was very influential in the Dumbarton Oaks agreement" (Ickes Diary, November 26, 1944, p. 9361); Francis Biddle to FDR, November 14, 1944, Official File, FDR Library, X1N6.55; Francis Biddle and BVC to CCB, November 17, 1944, CCB Papers, Harvard Law School; CCB to BVC, November 22, 1944, CCB Papers, Harvard Law School; "Memorandum for the President," December 27, 1944, Official File, FDR Library, XN6.56; Ickes Diary, December 2, 1944, p. 9325.
44. BVC to CCB, November 17, 1944, CCB Papers, Harvard Law School; Ickes Diary, November 26, 1944, p. 9361; Edward F. Prichard to FF, January 5, 1945, FF Papers, LC, Reel 27/Box 45.
45. Edward F. Prichard, Jr., to FF, January 5, 1945, FF Papers, LC, Reel 27/Box 45; "FDR Blocks Job for Ben Cohen," *PM*, January 4, 1945.
46. Edward F. Prichard, Jr., to FF, January 5, 1945, FF Papers, LC, Reel 27/Box 45; "Cohen Stays on War Job after Session with FDR," *PM*, January 6, 1945.
47. Ickes Diary, January 7, 1945, p. 9465; January 13, 1945, p. 9476.
48. FDR to BVC, January 13, 1945, PSF, FDR Library, Box 14; Ickes Diary, January 21, 1945, p. 9502.
49. FDR to BVC, January 13, 1945, PSF, FDR Library.
50. FDR to BVC, January 13, 1945, PSF, FDR Library, Box 14; Raymond Moley, "The Virtue of Resignation," Oakland *Tribune*, January 9, 1945.
51. BVC to FDR, January 16, 1945, PSF, FDR Library, Box 127.
52. FDR to BVC, January 20, 1945, PSF, FDR Library, Box 127.

Chapter 15.
Diplomat

1. "Jimmy had always been on his own in the Senate and elsewhere," FDR had told Stettinius in explaining his decision not to appoint Byrnes. "I am not sure that he and I could act harmoniously as a team." Stettinius replied, "In other words, Jimmy might question who was boss," and Roosevelt agreed: "That's exactly it." David Robertson, *Sly and Able: A Political Biography of James F. Byrnes* (New York: Norton, 1994), p. 379.
2. James F. Byrnes, *All in One Lifetime* (New York: Harper and Brothers, 1958), pp. 252–55.
3. Robert Messer, *The End of an Alliance: James F. Byrnes, Roosevelt, Truman, and the Origins of the Cold War* (Chapel Hill: University of North Carolina Press, 1982), pp. 35–37.
4. Ibid., pp. 53–58.

5. Ernest K. Lindley, "Byrnes, the Persuasive Reporter," *Newsweek*, March 12, 1945, p. 42; Messer, *End of an Alliance*, pp. 62–64.

6. Walter Brown to James F. Byrnes, March 12, 1945, Byrnes Papers, Clemson University, file 1298.

7. Ibid.

8. Byrnes, *All in One Lifetime*, p. 288; Ickes Diary, July 8, 1945, p. 9682. Portions of the Ickes Diary were published as Harold L. Ickes, *The Secret Diary of Harold L. Ickes*, 3 vols. (New York: Simon and Schuster, 1953). Other portions remain unpublished and are located in the Ickes Papers, LC. In these notes, references to the published edition are given as "Ickes, *Secret Diary*"; references to the unpublished edition are referred to as "Ickes Diary."

9. John H. Crider, "Liaison Man for a 'Big Three' Team," *New York Times Magazine*, August 12, 1945, p. 16; Byrnes, *All in One Lifetime*, pp. 288–89.

10. Walter Brown Diary, Byrnes Papers, Clemson University, file 54 (1); BVC to FF, August 13, 1945, FF Papers, LC, Box 45; Charles L. Mee, Jr., *Meeting at Potsdam* (New York: M. Evans & Co., 1975), p. 11.

11. Ickes Diary, August 26, 1945, p. 9947.

12. Messer, *End of an Alliance*, pp. 137–55; Robertson, *Sly and Able*, pp. 440–52. Byrnes's own account appears in *All in One Lifetime*, pp. 351–45.

13. Robertson, *Sly and Able*, p. 452.

14. See Byrnes, *All in One Lifetime*, pp. 342–47; Messer, *End of an Alliance*, pp. 156–68; Robertson, *Sly and Able*, pp. 452–59.

15. The text of the Stuttgart Speech appears in Kendrick A. Clements, *James F. Byrnes and the Origins of the Cold War* (Durham, N.C.: Carolina Academic Press, 1982), pp. 113–23.

16. BVC to James F. Byrnes, March 21, 1958, Byrnes Papers, Clemson University, File 122 (2).

17. Ibid.

18. George F. Kennan, *Memoirs: 1925–1950* (Boston: Little, Brown, 1973), p. 547 (the full text of the "Long Telegram" is reproduced at pp. 547–59); Robertson, *Sly and Able*, p. 489.

19. Paul Mallon, "Cohen Scared the Treasury," August 1, 1947 (clipping in Harris Papers).

20. "Merry-Go-Round," Washington *Herald*, nd (clipping in Harris Papers).

21. Benjamin V. Cohen, "The Evolving Role of Congress in Foreign Affairs," *Proceedings of the American Philosophical Society* 92 (October 1948): 211–16.

22. Ibid, pp. 213–14.

23. Ibid., p. 215.

24. Israel announced its independence at 4:00 pm, May 14, 1948 (10:00 am in Washington). The American recognition came at 6:11 pm, May 14, 1948 (Washington time), which was 12:11 am, May 15, 1948, in Israel.

25. Michael J. Cohen, *Truman and Israel* (Berkeley: University of California Press, 1990), p. 91.

26. BVC to Robert Lovett, July 30, 1947, BVC Papers, LC, Box 12.

27. Cohen, *Truman and Israel*, pp. 77–82.

28. Ibid., pp. 188–89.

29. See FF to BVC [undated], returning BVC's March 1, 1948, speech draft of Palestine, BVC Papers, LC, Box 8; Cohen, *Truman and Israel*, p. 189.

30. Lowenthal Diary, May 12, 1948, June 3, 1948; Lowenthal Papers, University of Minnesota.
31. Lowenthal Diary, May 15, 1948, Lowenthal Papers, University of Minnesota; Cohen, *Truman and Israel*, p. 218.
32. Lowenthal Diary, July 22, 1948, Lowenthal Papers, University of Minnesota.
33. Lowenthal Diary, July 22, August 4, 1948, Lowenthal Papers, University of Minnesota; BVC to FF, November 6, 1948, FF Papers, LC, Reel 27.
34. Cohen, *Truman and Israel*, pp. 237–39; 254–55.
35. BVC to James F. Byrnes, November 5, 1948, Byrnes Papers, Clemson University, File 683(1).
36. BVC to FF, November 6, 1948, FF Papers, LC, Reel 27.
37. BVC to James F. Byrnes, October 1, 1948, Byrnes Papers, Clemson University, File 683 (1); BVC to Jane Harris, September 15, [1948], Harris Papers; BVC to Jane Harris, December 8, 1948, Harris Papers.
38. BVC to Jane Harris, December 8, 1948; December 15, 1948; Harris Papers.
39. BVC, "Disarmament," Chester Bowles Papers, Yale University Library, Box 126.
40. "Statement Presented to the United States Delegation to the General Assembly," September 19, 1954, Harris Papers.
41. "Disarmament," undated memorandum by BVC, enclosed with BVC to Chester Bowles, Yale University Library, Chester Bowles Papers, Box 126, Folder 134; "Statement Presented to the United States Delegation to the General Assembly," September 19, 1954, Harris Papers. See also BVC, "U.S. Efforts towards Disarmament," Department of State Publication 4902, January 12, 1953.
42. "Text of the Statement by the Honorable Benjamin V. Cohen, United States Delegate to the General Assembly, before the Ad Hoc Political Committee, on the Suppression of Human Rights in Hungary and Bulgaria," April 18, 1949, BVC Papers, LC, Box 16.
43. "Text of Statement by the Honorable Benjamin V. Cohen before the Plenary of the General Assembly, October 21, 1949, on the Question of the Observance of Human Rights and Fundamental Freedoms in Bulgaria, Hungary and Rumania," Harris Papers.
44. Ibid.
45. BVC to Jane Harris, January 21, 1952, Harris Papers.
46. Ibid.; Benjamin V. Cohen, "The United Nations in Its Twentieth Year," David Niles Memorial Lecture at the Hebrew University of Jerusalem, April 27, 1965, Harris Papers; BVC to Jane Harris, December 29, 1951, Harris Papers.

Chapter 16.
Elder Statesman

1. Julius C. C. Edelstein, "Reminiscences and Thoughts on Benjamin V. Cohen," April 1991, Harris Papers.
2. BVC to Jane Harris, January 25, 1953, Harris Papers.
3. Joseph P. Lash, *Dealers and Dreamers: A New Look at the New Deal* (New York: Doubleday, 1988), pp. 453–54.
4. Jane Harris to BVC, July 29, 1980, BVC Papers, LC, Box 22.
5. Townsend Hoopes, *The Devil and John Foster Dulles* (Boston: Little, Brown, 1973), pp. 85–88.

6. Joseph Alsop, "Matter of Fact: Sherm Again," New York *Herald Tribune* (clipping in Harris Papers), 1955.
7. BVC, "Draft Platform—Foreign Policy," Chester Bowles Papers, Yale University Library, Box 126.
8. Ibid.
9. "Disarmament," undated memorandum by BVC, Chester Bowles Papers, Yale University Library. Box 126.
10. Ibid.
11. Now The Century Foundation, Inc.
12. *Benjamin V. Cohen, 1894–1983* (New York: The Twentieth Century Fund, 1983), §§VIII, XXIX.
13. Ibid., §VIII.
14. "Exploration of Corporate and Governmental Plans for Dealing with Atomic Disaster," Twentieth Century Fund Archives, New York, nd.
15. Minutes, Executive Committee Meeting, November 13, 1958; Minutes, Special Meeting of Board of Trustees, The Twentieth Century Fund, November 14, 1958, Twentieth Century Fund Archives, New York.
16. *Benjamin V. Cohen, 1894–1983*, §XXIX.
17. Quoted in ibid., §XIV.
18. "Address by Benjamin V. Cohen at Meeting of Washington Area Chapter of the United World Federalists, August 11, 1967," *Congressional Record*, 90th Cong., 1st sess., August 22, 1967, p. 23563.
19. Benjamin V. Cohen, "The United Nations in Its Twentieth Year," David Niles Memorial Lecture at the Hebrew University of Jerusalem, April 27, 1965, BVC Papers, LC, pp. 8, 13.
20. "Address by Benjamin V. Cohen at Meeting of Washington Area Chapter of the United World Federalists," p. 4.
21. "The United Nations in Its Twentieth Year," p. 27.
22. Benjamin V. Cohen, "Speech upon Receiving the Isaiah Award," November 13, 1969, Harris Papers.
23. Quoted in Lash, *Dealers and Dreamers*, pp. 464, 463.
24. Emily Yoffe, "A Fork in the Road," *The New Republic*, September 17, 1977, p. 23.
25. Thomas G. Corcoran, "Introduction of Benjamin Cohen," *Congressional Record*, March 15, 1977, p. 7575.
26. Benjamin V. Cohen, "The New Deal Looks Forward," Congressional Record, March 15, 1977, p. 7576.
27. Tom Mathews and James Doyle, "The New Deal: Born Again," *Congressional Record*, March 15, 1977, p. 7578; Cohen "The New Deal Looks Forward," pp. 7577–78.
28. Stuart Eizenstat to BVC, December 27, 1979, BVC Papers, LC, Box 3.
29. Robert Stoner to Bernard Freund, August 20, 1983 (original in the possession of Bernard Freund).
30. Frederick B. Weiner to David Ginsburg, August 30, 1983 (in the possession of the author).
31. Robert A. Katzmann, "Remembering Benjamin V. Cohen" (in the possession of the author).
32. "Adviser to FDR Dies; Was Native of Muncie," *Muncie (Indiana) Star*, August 16, 1983; Denis G. Gulino, "Benjamin Cohen: 'Never Be Another Like Him,'" *Muncie (Indiana) Star*, August 21, 1983.

33. Benjamin V. Cohen Fellows Program publicity material (in the possession of the author).

Chapter 17.
Architect of the New Deal

1. Remarks of Arthur M. Schlesinger, Jr., in *Benjamin V. Cohen, 1894–1983* (New York: The Twentieth Century Fund, 1983), §III.
2. Jordan A. Schwarz, *The New Dealers: Power Politics in the Age of Roosevelt* (New York: Knopf, 1993), pp. 120–21.
3. Alan Brinkley, *The End of Reform: New Deal Liberalism in Recession and War* (New York: Vintage Books, 1995), p. 54.
4. Ibid., p. 56 (footnotes deleted).
5. Quoted in Katie Louchheim, *The Making of the New Deal: The Insiders Speak* (Cambridge: Harvard University Press, 1983), p. 111.
6. Quoted in Tom Mathews and James Doyle, "The New Deal: Born Again," *Congressional Record*, March 15, 1977, p. 7578.
7. Quoted in Brinkley, *End of Reform*, p. 57.
8. Quoted in Joseph P. Lash, *Dealers and Dreamers: A New Look at the New Deal* (New York: Doubleday, 1988), pp. 169, 165.
9. Schwarz, *The New Dealers*, p. 122.
10. LDB to Chaim Weizmann, January 13, 1918, quoted in Philippa Strum, *Louis D. Brandeis: Justice for the People* (Cambridge: Harvard University Press, 1984), p. 275.
11. Schwarz, *The New Dealers*, p. 122.
12. BVC to Robert E. Healy, November 23, 1934, NPPC/BVC, National Archives, Box 10.
13. *United States* v. *Schechter Poultry*, 295 U.S. 495 (1935).
14. Quoted in Arthur M. Schlesinger, Jr., *The Age of Roosevelt* (Boston: Houghton Mifflin, 1957): vol. 3, p. 280.
15. Strum, *Louis D. Brandeis*, p. 352.
16. For a discussion of the Brownlow committee, see John A. Rohr, *To Run a Constitution: The Legitimacy of the Administrative State* (Lawrence: University Press of Kansas, 1986), pp. 135–53.
17. President's Committee on Administrative Management, "Administrative Management in the Government of the United States," Washington, D.C.: Government Printing Office, Washington, D.C., 1937, p. 5.
18. United States Senate, "Reorganization of the Executive Departments: Message from the President of the United States Transmitting a Report on the Reorganization of the Executive Departments of the Government," Senate Document No. 8, 75th Cong., 1st sess., 1937, p. 19.
19. Arthur M. Schlesinger, Jr., *The Imperial Presidency* (Boston: Houghton Miffflin, 1973), pp. x, viii.
20. Benjamin V. Cohen, "Presidential Responsibility and American Democracy," in Benjamin V. Cohen et al., *The Prospect for Presidential-Congressional Government* (Berkeley, Calif.: Institute of Governmental Studies, 1977), pp. 17–23.
21. Ibid., pp. 19, 21.
22. Ibid., p. 22.
23. Ibid., pp. 26–28.

24. Ibid., pp. 31–32.
25. Ibid., p. 33.
26. *Benjamin V. Cohen, 1894–1983* (The Twentieth Century Fund, 1983), §XXIX; David Ginsburg to Bernard Cohen, March 26, 1991 (letter in the possession of the author).
27. Philip Dunne, "In Memory of the Brain behind the New Deal," *Los Angeles Examiner*, September 1983 (Harris Papers).
28. Denis G. Gulino, "Benjamin Cohen: 'Never Be Another Like Him,'" *Muncie Star*, August 21, 1983.
29. Alan Brinkley, *The End of Reform*, pp. 267, 269, 271.
30. "Remarks of Julius C. C. Edelstein to Dinner Meeting of the Benjamin V. Cohen Memorial Foundation," Ball State University, April 1, 1991 (in the possession of the author).

Index